The Civilian Tradition and Scots Law

Aberdeen Quincentenary Essays

Schriften zur Europäischen Rechts- und Verfassungsgeschichte

Herausgegeben von Prof. Dr. Reiner Schulze, Münster,
Prof. Dr. Elmar Wadle, Saarbrücken,
Prof. Dr. Reinhard Zimmermann, Regensburg

Band 20

The Civilian Tradition and Scots Law

Aberdeen Quincentenary Essays

Edited by

David L. Carey Miller
Reinhard Zimmermann

Duncker & Humblot · Berlin

Die Deutsche Bibliothek – CIP-Einheitsaufnahme

The **civilian tradition and Scots law** : Aberdeen quincentenary essays / ed. by David L. Carey Miller ; Reinhard Zimmermann. – Berlin : Duncker und Humblot, 1997
(Schriften zur europäischen Rechts- und Verfassungsgeschichte ; Bd. 20)
ISBN 3-428-09011-X

Fremddatenübernahme und Druck:
Berliner Buchdruckerei Union GmbH, Berlin
Printed in Germany

ISSN 0937-3365
ISBN 3-428-09011-X

Gedruckt auf alterungsbeständigem (säurefreiem) Papier
entsprechend ISO 9706 ♾

Preface

On 10 February 1995 the University of Aberdeen celebrated its quincentenary. On that day in 1495 Pope Alexander VI had issued to Bishop William Elphinstone the founding Bull giving authority for the teaching of theology, Canon and civil law, medicine and the liberal arts. In the case of law, it was decided to mark the quincentenary by holding a symposium which would reflect upon the nature and influence of the civilian tradition with special emphasis on its influence in Scotland.

This symposium was organized by David L. Carey Miller and it took place on 4 and 5 September 1995. Scholars from Scotland, England, the Netherlands, South Africa and Germany were asked to deliver papers on various aspects within the general theme. The present law teachers of the University of Aberdeen are very grateful for the enthusiastic response received. They also wish to record their sincere thanks to a number of sponsors who made the symposium possible: The Society of Advocates in Aberdeen; The Faculty of Advocates; The Law Society of Scotland; The Royal Society of Edinburgh; and the Aberdeen law firms of Campbell Connon, Mackinnons and Peterkins. The presence and support of the following persons was also much appreciated: the then Lord President and Lord Justice-General, Lord Hope of Craighead, now a Lord of Appeal in Ordinary; Senator of the College of Justice, Lord Cullen, now the Lord Justice Clerk; Sheriff Principal Douglas Risk Q.C.; the Dean of the Faculty of Advocates, Mr. Andrew Hardie Q.C.; and the Bishop of Aberdeen, the Rt. Rev. Mario Conti.

Very much younger than Aberdeen is the University of Regensburg. Regensburg and Aberdeen being twin cities, the Chancellor of the University of Aberdeen presented the Rector of the University of Regensburg with a ceremonial mace when that University was established. For more than eight years the law faculties of the two universities have maintained a lively student exchange under the Erasmus (now Socrates) scheme, established by Professors Geoffrey MacCormack and Reinhard Zimmermann. Thus, it appeared appropriate to prepare the Aberdeen papers for publication in Regensburg, within the series of "Schriften für Europäische Rechts- und Verfassungsgeschichte". Philip Simpson, a graduate of both the Aberdeen and Regensburg law faculties, assisted in the process of editing. We are very grateful to him as well as to Mrs. Gabriele Schmitt, secretary to the Chair of Civil Law at Regensburg, and to Mrs. Christine Gaue, Alford (Scotland), who prepared the indexes. We are equally grateful to the City Council of the City of Regensburg, to the Leibniz-programme of the German Federal Research Association, and to past Aberdeen Principal Maxwell Irvine for their contributions towards the printing costs.

Finally, we would like to extend our good wishes to our colleagues in the University of Edinburgh who will be celebrating the next Scottish law faculty quincentenary in 2056.

David L. Carey Miller
University of Aberdeen

Reinhard Zimmermann
University of Regensburg

Summary of Contents

Introduction

Table of Contents

Introduction

Looking Back: The Influence of Roman Law and Roman Legal Thinking in Europe

Abbreviations

Abdn Fasti	= *Fasti Aberdonenses: Selections from the Records of the University and King's College of Aberdeen* Spalding Club, Aberdeen, 1854
ABGB	= Allgemeines Bürgerliches Gesetzbuch
A.C.	= Appeal Cases (Law Reports)
AcP	= Archiv für die civilistische Praxis
All E.R.	= All England Law Reports
A.P.S.	= Acts of the Parliament of Scotland
Art.	= Article
BGB	= Bürgerliches Gesetzbuch
BW	= Burgerlijk Wetboek
C.	= Justinian's *Code*
C.A.	= Court of Appeal
C.L.J.	= Cambridge Law Journal
C.M.L.R.	= Common Market Law Reports
D	= Dunlop's Session Cases 1838-62
D.	= Justinian's *Digest*
D.L.R.	= Dominion Law Reports
E.C.R.	= European Court Reports
E.C.S.C.	= European Coal and Steel Community
E.D.C.	= Reports of the Eastern Districts Court of the Cape of Good Hope
E.L.R.	= European Law Review
E.R.P.L.	= European Review of Private Law
Harvard L.R.	= Harvard Law Review
H.C.G.	= Reports of the High Court of Griqualand
H.L.	= House of Lords
H.L.C.	= House of Lords Cases 1847-66
J.L.H.	= Journal of Legal History
J.R.	= Juridical Review
Lloyd's Rep.	= Lloyd's Law Reports
L.Q.R.	= Law Quarterly Review
L.R. Eq.	= Law Reports, Equity (England) 1865-75
Macq.	= Macqueen's House of Lords Reports 1851-65
Michigan L.R.	= Michigan Law Review
M.L.R.	= Modern Law Review
Mor.	= Morison's Dictionary of Decisions (Court of Session) 1540-1808
O.J.	= Official Journal of the European Communities

OR	=	Swiss Obligationenrecht
Oxford J.L.S.	=	Oxford Journal of Legal Studies
RabelsZ	=	Rabels Zeitschrift
RIDA	=	Révue Internationale des Droits de l'Antiquité
SA	=	South Africa, South African Law Reports
S.A.L.J.	=	South African Law Journal
S.A.R.	=	Reports of the High Court of the South African Republic
S.C.	=	Session Cases
S.C.L.R.	=	Scottish Civil Law Reports
S.L.T.	=	Scots Law Times
S.M.E.	=	The Laws of Scotland: The Stair Memorial Encyclopaedia
Stellenbosch L.R.	=	Stellenbosch Law Review
S.U.L.I.	=	Scottish Universities Law Institute
T.H.R.H.R.	=	Tydskrif vir Hedendaagse Romeins-Hollandse Reg
T.R.	=	Tijdschrift voor rechtsgeschiedenis
T.S.A.R.	=	Tydskrif vir die Suid-Afrikaanse Reg
Tulane L.R.	=	Tulane Law Review
W. & S.	=	Wilson & Shaw's House of Lords Cases 1825-34
W.L.R.	=	Weekly Law Reports
ZEuP	=	Zeitschrift für Europäisches Privatrecht
ZSS (GA)	=	Zeitschrift der Savigny-Stiftung für Rechtsgeschichte (Germanistische Abteilung)
ZSS (RA)	=	Zeitschrift der Savigny-Stiftung für Rechtsgeschichte (Romanistische Abteilung)

Introduction

A Scottish Celebration of the European Legal Tradition

By David L. Carey Miller

I. Introduction

This chapter is by way of introduction to the present volume. All the subsequent chapters are based on papers given at a conference under the title 'A Celebration of the European Legal Tradition' held to mark the Quincentenary of the University of Aberdeen in 1995. The now formally established Centre for the Study of the Civil Law Tradition at the University of Aberdeen existed in only *de facto* form when the idea of a Quincentenary law conference on this theme was conceived. It may be noted that this *de facto* form has existed around the holders of the Chair of Jurisprudence commencing with *David Daube* in 1951, continuing with *Peter Stein* (1956-1968) through *Michael Meston* (1968-1971) to *Geoffrey MacCormack* (1971-1996) and now residing in *Robin Evans-Jones*. Not to say that the *de facto* centre for Civil law has been a one-man operation because at various stages other Aberdeen legal scholars have done work relevant to its emerging shape. Since the 1970s *Geoffrey MacCormack*, *Robin Evans-Jones* and the present writer have contributed on pure Roman law, Roman-Dutch law and civilian aspects of Scots law. A consequence of the range and variety of work of the successive chairholders and the others involved is that the Aberdeen concept of the civilian tradition is a broad one. The present chapter will support the view that the nature of the relationship between Scots law and Roman law is consistent with a wide notion of the civilian tradition.

After a chapter on the development of the teaching of law at the University of Aberdeen by Professor *Hector MacQueen* this collection sets out to deal with three aspects of what will be referred to in the present chapter as the civilian tradition – the civil law, the Canon law and the subsequent *ius commune*. The first theme, involving chapters three to eight, is concerned with setting the scene – looking back and identifying the influence, across Europe, of the civilian tradition. The second theme, involving chapters nine to fourteen, aims to take stock and identify the significance of the influence of the tradition in the legal systems of England, Scotland and the continental European countries. The final theme, involving three chapters, looks to the future and, in particular, to the position of the civilian tradition in the future law of Europe with the emphasis upon Community law as developed by the European Court of Justice.

In the first two themes identified above – constituting some three-quarters of this volume – the primary emphasis is on the civilian factor in Scots law. In terms of essential thrust the scope of this collection may be seen as an examination of the nature and extent of the influence of civil law and Canon law and the associated legal thinking in Scotland with some comparison to the position of English law all in the wider context of Europe, past, present and future. Hence the title 'The Civilian Tradition and Scots Law'. The primary emphasis in this introductory chapter will accordingly be on Scotland. To this extent the chapter is not an introduction to this collection of essays but, rather, a contribution which simply seeks to add a perspective on the recurring theme of the civilian tradition of Scots law.

Through much of the second half of the present century Scots law has been concerned – within the normal process of the development of the law – with a definite reidentification and, indeed, assertion of its individual national character. It is no coincidence that this epoch coincides with the ascent into control over the administration of justice in Scotland, Scottish legal practice and Scottish academic law of the first generation trained full-time in the post-war law schools of the ancient Scottish Universities of Aberdeen, Edinburgh and Glasgow as well as the newer schools of Dundee and Strathclyde. Although, of course, the modern strengthening of the identity of Scots law has been a process to which many have contributed, the late Professor Sir *Thomas Smith* Q.C. can be particularly singled out[1]. Sir *Thomas*' leadership included vastly more than the mere putting of words on paper but two major publishing projects have been particularly significant to the reasserted identity of Scots law.

The Scottish Universities Law Institute (S.U.L.I.) was founded by Professor *T. B. Smith* (later Professor Sir *Thomas Smith*) in 1960 to promote the publication of works on Scots law. The significant body of modern literature which has appeared in the S.U.L.I. series ended a phase of relative inactivity in legal publishing which prevailed for much of the first half of the 20th century. Since the early 1980s a large constituency of Scots lawyers, led by a significant sector of the academic lawyers of Scottish universities, have been working on 'The Laws of Scotland: The Stair Memorial Encyclopaedia' – also a product of the vision and leadership of *T. B. Smith*. At the time of writing all but one volume of this major collaborative work – hereafter referred to as the 'Stair Memorial Encyclopaedia' (S.M.E.) – has been published; the final volume, concerned with obligations, is expected to appear in 1996. Although, of course, there is still room for further work, alternative views, and differences of opinion, the 'Stair Memorial Encyclopaedia' is almost certainly the most important single modern contribution to the literature of Scots

[1] For an account of the life of *T. B. Smith* up to 1981 see Lord *Hunter's* appreciation in 1982 J. R. 1. See also Professor *W. A. Wilson's* obituary in 1989 J. R. 1 and the tribute of Lord *President Hope* in his foreword in: D. L. Carey Miller and D.W. Meyers, edd., Comparative and Historical Essays in Scots Law: A Tribute to Professor Sir Thomas Smith Q. C., 1992, at p. xi.

law. As such and given the level of its coverage one may ask to what extent it reflects civilian influence.

The primary aim of the present chapter will accordingly be to give an account of the extent of civilian influence in the law on the basis of what is said in the 'Stair Memorial Encyclopaedia'. This will be done under the respective headings of 'Where the Civil Tradition Stands' and 'The Dynamic of Scots Law', the former being directed at the influence of the civilian tradition on the substantive law and the latter concerned with the extent to which the operating system of Scots law reflects that tradition. It should be made clear that this chapter seeks to do no more than report on the extent to which the Stair Memorial Encyclopaedia reflects the civilian tradition in Scots law, sometimes with a comment, but without any serious attempt to assess the correctness of what is said.

II. Where the Civilian Tradition Stands

Before commencing to look at the extent to which the most recent major statement of Scots law reflects the influence of the civil law an obvious point may be anticipated. Is not a system presented as an encyclopaedia the antithesis of 'civilian' in that the foundation structure of the civil law is replaced by an alphabetical order of subject matter? The answer is that in Scots law the vehicle of an encyclopaedia does not reflect an absence of structure but is no more than a convenient way of bringing together the separate contributions of many authors. But, in any event, the diversity and multi-faceted character of the modern law of Scotland is far removed from the simple divisions of *Justinian*'s 'Institutes'. This said, the fundamental divisions of property, succession and obligations are reflected in separate parts of the 'Stair Memorial Encyclopaedia' while what would properly be included in the law of persons is readily identifiable. This, of course, simply reflects the traditional approach of Scots law in which writers have "clearly been influenced by the structure of Justinian's Institutes"[2].

The wide and diverse nature of the influence of the civilian tradition upon Scots law very much emerges from the 'Stair Memorial Encyclopaedia' despite the fact that the influence is to a large extent buried in the history of the system. What is immediately striking is how much the acknowledgement of civilian influence reflects differing degrees of actual influence within a system which by tradition treats Roman law at least as a kindred legal culture[3]. The range is from what would appear to be a reference relevant solely on the basis of cultural identity to an influence so strong as to amount to an acknowledgement of the virtual reception of an area of law. The influence of matters of fundamental legal orientation or grammar

2 S.M.E., vol. 22, 1987, para. 554.

3 This point is made in my chapter in: R. Evans-Jones, ed., The Civil Law Tradition in Scotland, 1995, p. 154.

– for example, the Canon law principle that seriously intended promises are binding or the civil law distinction between real and personal rights – are probably as important as the instances of extensive particular influence within an area. Between these extremes there are at least two other forms under which the civil law comes in. First, there is the quite common phenomenon of the mere use of a particular civil law label or term – sometimes to reflect something not necessarily civilian in substantive content or meaning. Secondly, there is the reference to Roman or Canon law as something actually relevant to initial Scottish development even though the civilian factor has been largely lost in the course of subsequent development. Accordingly, the influence of the civilian tradition reflected in the 'Stair Memorial Encyclopaedia' will be considered under the sub-headings of 'Cultural Identity', 'Terminology, Labels and Maxims', 'Foundation Influence' and 'Substantial Reception'. But just as it is difficult to identify the overall civilian influence it is somewhat arbitrary to attempt to classify different forms and levels of influence. The basis of classification adopted here is no more than one of various possible ways of making the breakdown.

1. Cultural Identity

In *Stair's* 'Institutions of the Law of Scotland', the greatest work of Scottish legal literature, there is extensive reference to Roman law, an approach consistent with *Stair*'s statement in the preliminary part of his work concerning the affinity between the law of Scotland and the "civil law of the Roman commonwealth or empire" which, "though it be not acknowledged as a law binding for its authority, yet being, as a rule, followed for its equity"[4]. But reference to Roman law as a matter of cultural identity is a tradition in Scottish legal literature which pre-dates *Stair*. *T. David Fergus* and Professor *G. Maher* writing on the historical sources of Scots law in the 'Stair Memorial Encyclopaedia' title on sources of law note the existence of this intellectual tradition in respect of the very earliest Scottish law books:

> "The contents of *Regiam Majestatem* and the other medieval law books are primarily feudal and customary, and there is little in them to suggest that Roman law was, in any systematic way, beginning to affect the substantive law or the procedures of the lay courts. They do contain Roman terminology and the occasional extract from Roman or Romano-canonical sources, but these only illustrate that the Roman law of the *ius commune* was not considered as alien but part of an intellectual tradition with which Scotland was in touch"[5].

---

[4] *Viscount Stair*, Institutions of the Law of Scotland, 1681, 1, 1, 12. See *Alan Watson*, The Reception of Roman Law in Scotland, in: *idem*, Legal Transplants, 1974, p. 48. Professor *Watson* points out that on the usage of the time 'as a rule' would not have meant 'generally' but, rather, something like 'as a code of conduct'.

[5] S.M.E., vol. 22, 1987, para. 551.

In the 'Stair Memorial Encyclopaedia' a statement of the civil law position, on a given issue, merely as a point of reference or as a matter of cultural identity, is surprisingly common in the context of a work essentially concerned with the modern law and subject to obvious limits in terms of the scope for any substantive treatment of historical background.

An example of a reference to Roman law simply as a matter of cultural identity appears in the title dealing with cautionary obligations and representations as to credit – the area of personal security or 'suretyship' – in the 'Stair Memorial Encyclopaedia'. *Sandra M. Eden* notes that "on the whole, caution, in contrast to *adpromissio* in Roman law, has been relatively untroubled by legislative attempts at reform"[6] and "the absence of any perceived need for statutory intervention in modern times provides a contrast to the legislative activity of the Romans"[7].

Another example of a reference to Roman law as a matter of general kindred legal culture can be found in the title on advertising by *W.C.H. Ervine* of the University of Dundee. On the point that attitudes to advertising have attracted criticism throughout history the author notes as follows: "The Digest of Justinian contains indications that Roman merchants were prone to over-enthusiasm when extolling their wares"[8].

Even in an area as modern as company law one finds a broad reference to material of the civil law tradition. Commenting on Lord *Kames*' justification for an early form of limited liability *David A. Bennett* W.S. noted that *Kames*[9] "typically for a Scots lawyer, quoted the Roman-Dutch commentator Grotius, stating that any other view would deter investment in trading companies"[10].

A comment by Sheriff *Robin G. McEwan* Q.C., in his title on agency, questions the utility of a reference to Roman law of a type which probably falls into the 'cultural utility' category. On the problem of the undisclosed principal[11] Sheriff *McEwan* comments in a negative manner on a reference to Roman law by *John McLaren* (later Lord *McLaren*) in his edition of *Bell*'s 'Commentaries'[12]: "The author's reference to Roman law, while accurate, is of little value"[13].

---

6 S.M.E., vol. 3, 1994, para. 814.

7 S.M.E., vol. 3, 1994, para. 815.

8 S.M.E., vol. 1, 1987, para. 501. D. 21, 1, 18 is cited.

9 *Lord Kames*, Select Decisions of the Court of Session 1752-1768, Edinburgh, 1780, 135.

10 S.M.E., vol. 4, 1991, para. 302.

11 A development of English law? See *W.W. Buckland, Arnold D. McNair*, Roman Law and Common Law, 2nd ed. by F.H. Lawson, 1952, at pp. 217-218.

12 *G. J. Bell*, Commentaries on the Law of Scotland and the Principles of Mercantile Jurisprudence, 7th ed. by J. McLaren, Edinburgh, 1870, vol. 1, p. 540.

13 S.M.E., vol. 1, 1987, para. 657, n. 5.

2. *Terminology, Labels and Maxims*

Any attempt to make a comprehensive survey of the use of Romanist terms, labels and maxims in Scots law would involve a study of some magnitude; for present purposes no more will be attempted than to give some examples from the 'Stair Memorial Encyclopaedia'. The substantive content of maxims distinguishes them from terminology and labels but the common shorthand factor probably justifies treatment together.

Almost any venture into a range of Scottish legal literature will demonstrate the extent of the use of terminology which would be associated with the civilian tradition. The 'Stair Memorial Encyclopaedia' is no exception and a cursory examination of its volumes shows that only those areas which are of essentially modern development do not make use of Latin terms and labels.

Even in unlikely areas there are instances of the use of apparently civilian terminology as terms of art. These are often cases of convenient shorthand in which the term has come to have an established meaning within the system of Scots law. In the title on betting, gaming and lotteries by *Brian M. Hughes* the terms *sponsiones ludicrae* and *pacta illicita* are used. The term *sponsiones ludicrae* – frivolous agreements – conveys the notion that the courts should not demean themselves to adjudicate upon undertakings such as bets and wagers[14]. *Pacta illicita* is a convenient label referring to a contract "which is, by statute, common law or public policy, illegal and unenforceable"[15].

In a title on animals *Sheena M. Clifford* uses well-known terminology to deal with questions of ownership. Wild creatures are, in principle, open to acquisition by *occupatio*[16]; specifically in respect of pigeons: "Wild pigeons are *ferae naturae* and *res nullius*. Enclosed pigeons are *mansuetae naturae* and are private property"[17]. Without putting into question that the correct meaning in Scots law is the only matter in issue the use of terms of art in the title concerned tends to show the risk of true meaning and import becoming obscured in technical words. As an associated point it is interesting to note that the *ferae naturae/mansuetae naturae* dichotomy was used in the English common law tort of *scienter* with a stricter form of liability applying to damage caused by an animal *ferae naturae*. Used in this sense a wild animal reduced to captivity might remain *ferae naturae* but, of course, it would not be *res nullius* – a point which demonstrates the danger of confusion where terms of art or labels are used in distinct areas of the law without clarification of meaning in particular context[18].

---

14 S.M.E., vol. 2, 1988, para. 1502.

15 S.M.E., vol. 2, 1988, para. 1505.

16 S.M.E., vol. 2, 1988, para. 103.

17 S.M.E., vol. 2, 1988, para. 108.

18 Professor *Glanville Williams*, in his classic work Liability for Animals, 1939, at p. 294, does not regard the *ferae/mansuetae naturae* distinction as appropriate to the *scienter* action,

A distinct aspect of the widespread Latinity of Scots law is a high prevalence of maxims but, of course, this is also a feature of English law. Clearly enough the civilian ancestry of a given maxim must be established before it can be added to the civil law side of the scales of influence of Scots law. The maxim *de minimis non curat praetor* is referred to in the title concerned with interpretation of statutes, deeds and other instruments and *J. Fleming Wallace* Q.C., author of the relevant part[19], quotes the following dictum of Lord *Fraser*:

> "... it may be that the English doctrine, which I think is generally expressed as *de minimis non curat lex*, differs in its scope and application from the Scots doctrine, in which the final word is not *lex* but *praetor*"[20].

That a maxim is necessarily not civilian because it is known to English law must surely be open to question; on the other hand the fact of prevalence in English law probably means that derivation needs to be checked. *Niall R. Whitty* makes a statement relevant to this in his title on nuisance[21]. On the role of nuisance in Scots law the writer refers to a number of "prevalent misunderstandings" including one which he describes in the following terms:

> "The reception of the maxim *sic utere tuo ut alienum non laedas* is not, as so many Scots authorities have surmised, evidence of the Roman origins of the law of nuisance but is rather evidence of English legal influence. This example of seventeenth century English legal pedantry tells us nothing about the law".

There are, however, instances of maxims in which the sources establish civilian lineage beyond doubt. This must be so of *qui in utero est pro iam nato habetur* referred to by Professor *M.C. Meston* in the title on succession on the authority of the Digest[22], the same *nasciturus* text being referred to by *Elaine E. Sutherland* in an initial paragraph in the parent and child part of the title on family law[23].

The need for caution in any possible assumption of influence on the basis of Latin terminology is a lesson which may be taken from Professor *Alan Watson*'s use of the example of *furtum usus* to demonstrate the point that error as to derivation is not necessarily a handicap to healthy development.

> "The name, of course, is Latin, and most jurists concerned with the modern law believe that *furtum usus* was a Roman concept and term which they now either accept or reject. This is just not the case. The expression *furtum usus* does not appear in the Roman sources, and the Romans had no such concept but only the basic idea of *furtum*, theft"[24].

---

and makes the point that in any given context it is "desirable to avoid words that have become appropriated for other purposes".

19 S.M.E., vol. 12, 1992, para. 1170.

20 *Angus Assessor v. George Ogilvie (Montrose) Ltd.* 1968 S.L.T. 348, at p. 352.

21 S.M.E., vol. 14, 1988, para. 2017.

22 S.M.E., vol. 25, 1989, para. 660.

23 S.M.E., vol. 10, 1990, para. 1015.

24 See *Watson* (n. 4) 54.

A final example on the use of Latin maxims in a substantive role comes from the title on fraud by Professor *Joseph M. Thomson*. Referring to the assignment of a creditor's right Professor *Thomson* makes the point that the assignee is subject to whatever defences were available against the original creditor, a doctrine which:

> "can be summarised in the two Latin maxims, *resoluto jure dantis resolvitur jus accipientis* (where the cedent's right is annulled the transferee's right is also annulled) and *assignatus utitur jure auctoris* (the assignee can only assert as good a right as his cedent)"[25].

The above is a very small sample of the different forms of the widespread but somewhat inarticulate presence of terminology redolent of the Civil law in Scots law – one would not put it any stronger than that. As writers *Fergus* and *Maher*, already quoted, have pointed out on the historical sources of Scots law in the 'Stair Memorial Encyclopaedia': "The use of Roman terminology alone does not necessarily indicate the adoption of a Roman institution"[26]. By way of illustration *Fergus* and *Maher* note that

> "Scots law has adopted the provisions of the *Lex Rhodia* which are also found in the Roman sources, but this does not necessarily indicate direct borrowing; the provisions of the *Lex* were part of the general mercantile custom of Europe and would probably have come to Scotland even if Roman law had not"[27].

3. Foundation Influence

In certain areas of Scots law civilian influence occurred as a foundation factor but did not necessarily maintain any significant role in the development of the law. The nature and extent of the influence varies in individual areas and can only be established by particular research. The present exercise seeks to do no more than identify 'Stair Memorial Encyclopaedia' titles in which the authors concerned contend for some civilian factor in the foundation or development of the area.

There may, of course, be overlap between the imprecise classifications of 'terminology' and 'fundamental influence' in that the latter may have occured where the former is present. Thus, for example, in the title on game *Stanley Scott Robinson* and *G.W.S. Berry* demonstrate the fundamental importance of the concept of *res nullius*[28] in showing that despite early legislation[29] protecting game there was no departure from the common law right to acquire a *res nullius* by *occupatio*:

---

25 S.M.E., vol. 11, 1990, para. 766.

26 S.M.E., vol. 22, 1987, para. 556.

27 S.M.E., vol. 22, 1987, para. 556.

28 See above, text to nn. 16-18.

29 The Wild Birds Acts of 1427 and 1457 and the Game Act of 1600.

> "All game, being wild animals, are *res nullius* in accordance with the principles of Roman law which were adopted by the Scots institutional writers; as *res nullius* they can be appropriated by any person who can capture them"[30].

Modern Scots adjectival law would probably be thought of as belonging to the Anglo-American rather than the European legal tradition. Be this as it may there are strong elements of continental European influence in the development of both civil and criminal procedure in Scotland. In the title on the general and historical sources of law *James J. Robertson* – a leading expert on Canon law and a contributor to the present volume – notes the influence of the Canon law on the procedural law of Scotland[31].

Certainly, in criminal procedure Scots law remains distinctive in an Anglo-American context; as *T.B. Smith* noted "the divergence between Scottish and English law is probably more pronounced in the field of criminal procedure than in any other"[32].

In the area of civil procedure a Romano-Canonical form in which writing dominated gave way in the 19th century to a system which gave greater scope to oral argument[33]. Sheriff *I.D. Macphail* Q.C. acknowledges the Civilian orientation of the earlier Scots law of evidence in his 'Stair Memorial Encyclopaedia' title:

> "A full history of the law of evidence in Scotland has yet to be written. It appears, however, that the earlier law was much influenced by a distrust of oral testimony, which was typical of Roman law and found its way into the civilian tradition"[34].

It may be noted that in the critical matter of fact-finding in civil procedure Judge *David Edward* Q.C. – the author of a chapter in this volume on the civilian tradition in the work of the European Court – recognizes the distinctive tradition of Scots law but places the modern system in the common law rather than the civil law camp[35].

The modern law of bankruptcy is provided for in legislation but the development of the common law principles owe something to Roman law. Dr. *David C. Coull* in his 'Stair Memorial Encyclopaedia' title on bankruptcy refers to the adoption of the *cessio bonorum* procedure of the *lex Julia*:

---

30 S.M.E., vol. 11, 1990, para. 803.

31 S.M.E., vol. 22, 1987, para. 582.

32 A Short Commentary on the Law of Scotland, 1962, at p. 207. A summary of the distinctive features of Scots criminal procedure is given by *Elspeth Attwooll* in her chapter Scotland: A Multi-dimemsional Jigsaw, in: Esin Orucu, Elspeth Attwooll, Sean Coyle, edd., Studies in Legal Systems: Mixed and Mixing, 1996, p. 24.

33 See *T. B. Smith*, British Justice: The Scottish Contribution, Hamlyn Lectures, 1963, pp. 75-77.

34 S.M.E., vol. 10, 1990, para. 502.

35 See *David A. O. Edward*, Fact-finding: A British Perspective, in: D. L. Carey Miller and Paul R. Beaumont, edd., The Option of Litigating in Europe, United Kingdom Comparative Law Series, vol. 14, 1993, p. 43.

> "This remedy was, by adaption from its Roman origins, made available at common law in Scotland in order to mitigate the harsh provisions whereby a debtor who had failed to obtemper diligence was subject to imprisonment without limit of time and deprivation of all normal rights"[36].

The very considerable influence exercized by the Civilian tradition in the various stages of its European evolution over the development of the Scots law of obligations will be considered under the heading of 'Substantial Reception'. Under the present heading consideration will be given to the fundamental influence in respect of particular contracts.

In respect of the contract of carriage Professor *D.M. Walker* Q.C., notes that "carriage by land or '*locatio mercium vehendarum*' is a species of *locatio operis faciendi*"[37]. With regard to the sources of the law of carriage Professor *Walker* writes:

> "The principles of the Scottish law of carriage by land are drawn from the Roman law, but they have been substantially modified by modern legislation. In particular Scots law has adopted from Roman law the rule of strict liability of a carrier for the loss of or damage to goods carried"[38].

Regarding deposit *John A.K. Huntley* writes that the "real contract of deposit ... is firmly rooted in the Roman law contract of *depositum* or *commendatum*"[39]. In the following paragraph the writer makes another reference to Roman law:

> "The contract of deposit is based on the agreement of the parties. As a consequence, a recipient of property cannot become a depositary of that property without indicating his consent thereto. Roman law differentiated *depositum ex necessitate*, but even here the *depositorius* was under no obligation to take custody of the depositor's property"[40].

In the title on loan *Nigel M.P. Morrison* Q.C. gives an account of the development of the 'Roman origins' of the subject[41] and proceeds to note that in Scots law loan is no longer gratuitous and that in modern law the loan of money for interest is "practically the only modern form of *mutuum*"[42]. In a subsequent paragraph concerned with the essentials of *mutuum* the writer observes as follows:

> "Essentially, *mutuum* is a gratuitous contract; if it were onerous, the contract would be *locatio conductio rei* (hire). This was certainly so in Roman law. However, as will be

---

36 S.M.E., vol. 2, 1988, para. 1301.

37 S.M.E., vol. 3, 1994, para. 601.

38 S.M.E., vol. 3, 1994, para. 602, citing D. 4, 9, 1.

39 S.M.E., vol. 8, 1992, para. 1, citing D. 16, 3, 1.

40 S.M.E., vol. 8, 1992, para. 2. See also para. 3 where D. 16, 3, 8 is cited as authority for the proposition that "[i]f the depositary accepts remuneration or reward for custody, the contract between the parties is the consensual contract of *locatio custodiae*".

41 S.M.E., vol. 13, 1992, paras. 1702, 1703.

42 S.M.E., vol. 13, 1992, para. 1704. *Gai.* Inst. 3, 90 and *Justinian*'s Institutes 3, 14, 2 are cited.

seen later, in Scots law loan of money for interest has been treated or classified as *mutuum*. But for *mutuum* proper, the Roman law holds good in Scots law"[43].

Of donation Professor *William M. Gordon* – a distinguished author and contributor to the present volume – writes that "it is clear that (both in terminology and substance) the Scots law of donation owes a good deal to Roman law"[44]. Professor *Gordon* continues:

> "This is not to say that the Scots law has simply borrowed from Roman law; it has adapted as well as adopted Roman rules. Nevertheless some account of Roman law is desirable as a background to discussion of Scots law and its development"[45].

In the title on location *R. Bruce Wood* goes into some detail in explaining the significance of civilian sources in the development of the law regarding the leasing and hire of moveables:

> "Basic texts for reference in any contemporary examination of the essentials of the contract are not judgments in nineteenth century cases but rather the *Corpus iuris* itself, the institutional writers, and most especially *Pothier*, whose treatise on the 'Contrat de Louage' is cited copiously by all the institutional writers (apart, of course, from *Stair*, whom *Pothier* postdates) and also by several modern authors. Curiously, this lack of judicial precedent and the derivation of law from Roman texts is also true in England, although there, of course, the development has been different. The equivalent contract in England falls within the ambit of the law of bailment, a difficult concept unknown in Scots law"[46].

The displacement of the law of sale as developed in Scots law on the basis of civilian principles by the English-law based Sale of Goods Act 1893 (now 1979) is widely seen as a major low point in the evolution of the private law of Scotland. *T.B. Smith* in his 1961 Hamlyn lectures left his audience in no doubt as to the extent to which he saw the Sale of Goods Act as a negative development:

> "The Sale of Goods Act, 1893, has left a legacy of unsolved and virtually insoluble problems. Many of these are highly technical and I must pass them by. I can only pause to mention that sale is the only bilateral contract in Scots law, except compromise, which is not in theory governed by general principles of good faith; that property in sale passes by agreement (not as in pursuance of other contracts by delivery); and that the warranty of Roman law against latent defects rendering the thing unfit for ordinary use is no longer implied"[47].

---

43 S.M.E., vol. 13, 1992, para. 1706. In para. 1705, defining *mutuum*, *Gai.* Inst. 3, 90 and *Justinian*'s Institutes 3, 14, 2 are cited. In para. 1783 concerned with *commodatum* reference is made to to D. 13, 6 and Inst. 3, 1, 4.

44 S.M.E., vol. 8, 1992, para. 602. See also para. 603: "In the treatment of donation Scots law has broadly followed the lines of Roman law".

45 S.M.E., vol. 8, 1992, para. 602.

46 S.M.E., vol. 14, 1988, para. 1003.

47 See *Smith* (n. 33) pp. 178-179. See generally *D. L. Carey Miller*, Corporeal Moveables in Scots Law, 1991, para. 9.01, but see now Lord Rodger's article (n. 187).

William J. Stewart, author of the title on sale and exchange, refers to the civil law on the distinction between sale and exchange[48] and cites the contribution of *A.J. Mackenzie-Stuart*[49] (now Lord *Mackenzie-Stuart* – author of the final chapter in this volume) in the Stair Society's introduction to Scottish legal history[50]. What is said in respect of the contract of exchange demonstrates the civilian character of the Scots common law in respect of the passing of property and risk[51]:

> "Thus in a contract of exchange the maxim *traditionibus, non nudis pactis, dominia rerum transferuntur* applies ... This is the common law rule. The contract visits the parties with only a right to demand delivery. Delivery itself is necessary before ownership passes. Following the pre-1893 Scots law of sale, risk passes without delivery. Risk passes when the contract is complete[52]. The maxim is *periculum rei venditae nondum traditae est emptoris*"[53].

Of course it is one thing to acknowledge the role of the civil law as a fundamental factor in the development of a particular form of contract but another matter to urge for any continuing role of the ancient sources. Writing on partnership *Judith J.H. Pearson* draws attention to a note of caution sounded by *Bell*[54] as to the utility of Roman sources in respect of a legal concept which had come to be fundamentally different in its modern form:

> "The origins of the law of partnership in Scotland have been widely attributed to the Roman law of *societas*, as it was modified by Dutch and French influences. It was noted by Bell, however, that whilst the Roman law itself provided rules to govern matters between those contracting to combine for a common purpose, it did not contemplate the society dealing as an entity with outsiders, and he cautioned against acceptance of any definition of partnership borrowed or derived from the writings of the civilians"[55].

While what *Judith Pearson* has noted in relation to partnership illustrates a conscious avoiding of the full implications of a civil law concept a passage in Professor *Joseph M. Thomson*'s title on fraud draws attention to what may be the more common case of a resulting position following from a failure fully to grasp what might otherwise have been available through a development based on the civil law. Concerning fraud as a delict and with regard to contractual and delictual remedies Professor *Thomson* writes:

> "In a contract for the sale of goods, for example, if the innocent party elected to affirm the contract, the common law of Scotland did not allow him to recover the difference in

48 S.M.E., vol. 20, 1992, para. 801.

49 S.M.E., vol. 20, 1992, para. 802, n. 2.

50 An Introduction to Scottish Legal History, 1958, at pp. 255-260.

51 See *A. D. M. Forte*, A Civilian Approach to the Contract of Exchange in Modern Scots Law, (1984) 101 South African Law Journal 691.

52 See *Widermeyer v. Burn Stewart & Co. Ltd.* 1967 S.C. 85.

53 S.M.E., vol. 20, 1992, para. 900.

54 *Bell* (n. 12) vol. 2, pp. 499-500.

55 S.M.E., vol. 16, 1995, para. 1001.

price between the goods contracted for and the goods delivered: this was because the *actio quanti minoris* was unknown to Scots law[56] except in exceptional circumstances"[57].

The influence of the civilian tradition in Scotland occurred over much of the development of the system and although the influence is particularly strong in certain areas its mark appears in a wide range of areas. The above references to the 'Stair Memorial Encyclopaedia' titles show the intensity of the influence in respect of particular forms of contract. What follows, under the present heading, seeks to show the spread of influence over a wide range of areas.

Under the title 'Hotels and Tourism' *John J. Downes* refers to the edict *nautae, caupones, stabularii* as lying "at the root of the Scots law of reparation and of the liability of the hotelkeeper for the property of the guest brought to the hotel"[58]. The author of the title gives the Latin text and a translation of the edict from the Digest[59] and also refers to a late 19th century article in the Juridical Review by Edinburgh civil law Professor *James Mackintosh*[60]. On the basis of the same authority the point is made in a subsequent paragraph that "the liability arises without express intimation to, or acceptance by, the hotelkeeper or his agent"[61].

In respect of guardianship in an introductory paragraph on the protection of persons under legal incapacity *John D. Campbell* and Professor *J.W.G. Blackie* write as follows:

> "In Scots law, the offices of those who have the charge of the interests of, or have responsibility for the obligations of such persons, are known as tutory and curatory. The resemblance to these offices in Roman law is marked and significant"[62].

Passing reference has already been made to *Niall R. Whitty*'s title on nuisance[63]. This valuable treatment can now be looked at in greater detail from the point of view of fundamental influence. The author notes that it was only in the late 18th century that the Court of Session began to develop any law to protect the occupiers of land from interference with their "comfortable enjoyment". In so doing the Court had regard to various sources including the decisions of local courts and English authorities but also certain civilian-based sources.

According to *Whitty* one source of civilian influence was the doctrine of *aemulatio vicini* the origin of which "lies in a series of disparate texts in the *Corpus iuris*

---

56 See *R. Evans-Jones*, The History of the actio quanti minoris in Scotland, 1991 J.R. 190. See, also, Professor *Evans-Jones'* comments in The Civil Law Tradition in Scotland (n. 3) 6.

57 S.M.E., vol. 11, 1990, para. 721.

58 S.M.E., vol. 11, 1990, para. 1702.

59 D. 4, 9, 1.

60 James Mackintosh, The Edict Nautae Caupones Stabularii, (1891) 3 J.R. 306.

61 S.M.E., vol. 11, 1990, para. 1741.

62 S.M.E., vol. 11, 1990, para. 1202.

63 See n. 21.

civilis" and "[w]hether or not these texts or any of them disclose a general principle of emulous abuse of rights, medieval and later European jurists found such a principle in them"[64]. The second source of influence is taken to be the *immissio* principle provided for in the Digest[65] in respect of which *Whitty* notes that "in this text it is stated that an occupier can prohibit an *immissio* of smoke from a cheese factory (*taberno casiaria*) into his house, the reason being *'in suo enim alii hactenus facere licet quatenus nihil in alienum immittat'* "[66]. The third source of influence identified by *Whitty* is a rule distinguishing between direct and consequential damage derived by *Kames*[67] from Roman sources – "[t]he formal source of Kames' principle was the distinction in the Digest[68] between *damnum* and deprival of benefits enjoyed merely *de facto*"[69].

In succession *T.B. Smith* observed that "[p]erhaps Scottish practice has made a contribution to British justice by its constant repudiation of the doctrine of complete freedom of testation, and by its recognition of the legal rights of surviving spouse and children in the estate of the deceased"[70]. This, of course, does not necessarily imply a civilian factor. The 'Stair Memorial Encyclopaedia' title on succession under the principal authorship of Professor *M.C. Meston* does not make any general claim to civilian influence but one specific reference to the Digest has already been referred to[71]. Professor *Meston*'s title shows the strength of the individuality of Scots law in an area in which a very active case law – "the largest in our digests of cases"[72] – has long been a dominant feature.

Very much associated with succession is the law of trusts. In the title concerned with trusts (by various writers, co-ordinated by Lord Justice-Clerk *Ross*) the point is made that the absence of equity jurisdiction in the development of Scots law rules out any close affinity with the notable English law institution of trust[73]. In the Scottish development of trust civilian influence is seen to have been a factor:

> "Another root of trust in Scotland – although its growth was restricted – is *fideicommissum*, a Roman doctrine received in various forms by European civil law jurisdictions which had, like Scots law, adopted feudal systems of land tenure"[74].

---

64 S.M.E., vol. 14, 1988, para. 2008.

65 D. 8, 5, 8, 5-7.

66 S.M.E., vol. 14, 1988, para. 2009.

67 *Lord Kames*, Principles of Equity, 3rd ed., Edinburgh, 1778, vol. 1x, pp. 46-57 is cited.

68 D. 39, 2, 26.

69 S.M.E., vol. 14, 1988, para. 2010.

70 *Smith* (n. 33) 191.

71 See above (n. 22). *D. B. Walters'* "comparative and historical" contribution to the succession title (S.M.E., vol. 25, 1989, paras. 601-638) deals with English, French and German but not Scots law.

72 *Lord Cooper* in: M. C. Meston, W. D. H. Sellar and Lord Cooper, The Scottish Legal Tradition, 1991, p. 78.

73 S.M.E., vol. 24, 1989, para. 1.

74 S.M.E., vol. 24, 1989, para. 4.

It may be noted that Professor *David Johnston* – a contributor to this volume – has observed that: "[s]triking parallels exist between the Roman law of *fideicommissa* and the English law of trusts"[75].

The continuity of Scottish legal development means that there is still debate in Scots law about matters to do with Roman law – an indication of the extent of the perceived relevance and role of the Civil law tradition in the development of the law. Reference has already been made to Sheriff *McEwan's* title on agency[76]. In considering the specific question of the reception of a substantive aspect of the civil law the writer may be taken to demonstrate the need to examine the details of any particular instance of perceived influence:

> "Although the exercitorial action is probably part of Scots law, it is quite clear that shipping cases are regarded as ones involving disclosed principals ... It is by no means as certain that the *actio institoria* was accepted as part of Scots law ... but in any event it also was more akin to disclosed principal"[77].

4. Substantial Reception

In the areas of property and obligations it can probably be said that the cumulative effect of civilian influence amounted to a substantial reception. The difference between what has already been considered under fundamental influence and the idea of a substantial reception does not involve any identifiable difference in the manner or process by which the influence occured but, rather, is merely a matter of identifying the end result of a substantial total influence within a cognate area. The fact that the Faculty of Advocates requires intrants to have passed an examination in the Roman law of property and obligations is an indication of the recognition accorded to the practical importance of foundation aspects in these two areas of modern Scots law[78].

Part of the reason for the emphasis upon property and obligations is the critical relevance of the distinction between the two categories. Professor *Joseph M. Thomson*, in his title on fraud[79], refers to the distinction with regard to the right of rescission and its relevance to questions of property:

> "It is important at the outset to distinguish the respective spheres of the law of obligations and the law of property. Where, for example, a contract has been induced by a

---

75 *D. E. L. Johnston*, The Roman Law of Trusts, 1988, at p. 283.

76 See above, n. 13.

77 S.M.E., vol. 1, 1987, para. 657, n. 5 citing, for the final proposition, D. 14, 1, 7, 2 and *W. W. Buckland*, Roman Law of Slavery, 1908, p. 173.

78 See the Faculty of Advocates' Regulations as to Intrants, as amended 31st July 1996: regs. 3(1)(a), 9(1) and 9(2) read with appendix A(1).

79 See above, n. 25.

> fraudulent misrepresentation, the innocent party will generally have a right to rescind the contract and claim restitution. Rescission, however, is *res inter alios acta*. If the innocent party had intended to transfer the *dominium* of the property, a good title will have passed to the transferee provided the appropriate method for the transfer of rights in corporeal moveables has been followed"[80].

In property the significance of the distinction between real and personal rights, recently affirmed in Scots law[81], is of the order of importance of the requirement of agreement in contract; in property and obligations principle rules and in both the input of principle into Scots law is unmistakeably civilian. In an early paragraph in the treatment of the general law of property in the 'Stair Memorial Encyclopaedia' volume on property principal author and co-ordinator Professor *Kenneth G.C. Reid* makes the point that Roman law and feudal law were the sources of the development of the law of property but while feudal law "is likely to leave few traces behind ... [t]he position of Roman law is otherwise"[82]. Professor *Reid* goes on to explain the significance of Roman law:

> "The modern law of property in Scotland is laid on the foundations of the Roman law. Many of the general concepts of the modern law, such as *dominium* or real rights or *traditio* or possession or *accessio*, are Roman concepts, and indeed the Roman name is often retained. Much of the content of the law is also Roman in origin, although it may have been substantially altered and developed in matters of detail. The influence of Roman law is at its most direct in the law of corporeal moveables, but it is strongly felt in the law of heritable property also, both at the level of general principles and also in relation to specific doctrines, such as servitudes and liferents. Thus, so far as property law is concerned, modern Scots law may be classified along with the civilian legal systems of Western Europe, such as France and Germany, and with other 'mixed' legal systems such as Louisiana and the legal systems of southern Africa. Conversely, it has little in common with English law, and with other Anglo-American systems, except in relation to those few topics, such as easements (servitudes) and accession, where English law has drawn on Roman law"[83].

The close affinity of the Scots law of corporeal moveables to the counterpart civil law is borne out by Professor *William M. Gordon*'s treatment of the subject in the 'Stair Memorial Encyclopaedia'. Professor *Gordon* commences his introduction with a quotation from late 18th/early 19th century Edinburgh Professor *G.J. Bell*'s 'Principles'[84] to the effect that moveables, unaffected by the feudal law "remained under the rules of a jurisprudence immediately derived from the Civilians; in many of its doctrines modified, and in some respects improved, by the Canonists". Professor *Gordon* elaborates as follows:

---

80 S.M.E., vol. 11, 1990, para. 762.

81 See *Sharp v. Thomson* 1995 S.L.T. 837. See also 1994 S.L.T. 1068 and *Kenneth G. C. Reid*, Sharp v. Thomson: A Civilian Perspective, 1995 S.L.T. (News) 75.

82 S.M.E., vol. 18, 1993, para. 2.

83 S.M.E., vol. 18, 1993, para. 2.

84 *G. J. Bell*, Principles of the Laws of Scotland, 1st ed., Edinburgh, 1829, s. 1283.

"The influence of Roman law and, more particularly, of Roman legal terminology on the Scots law of corporeal moveable property is clear; in this respect, Scots law is little different from other systems which have been exposed to that influence. At the same time, it must be noted that Scots law, even in its Roman garb, is not necessarily identical to the law as found in Justinian's Corpus iuris civilis. As *Bell*'s reference to the Canonists indicates, the influence of Roman law is combined with other influences and even where Roman law itself is concerned, account must be taken not only of the texts of the *Corpus iuris civilis* but of the interpretation of these texts by later scholars"[85].

Without gainsaying the conclusion that the sub-area of corporeal moveable property is strongly Romanist, in certain matters of detail it still reflects the typical Scottish pattern of originality stemming from mixed influences. In respect of the transfer of ownership the statement in Professor *Gordon's* classic Aberdeen work that Scots law reflects "the more complete acceptance of the whole Roman and Romanistic doctrine of *traditio*"[86] still leaves room for small but important differences of detail[87]. But such differences do not detract from the overall effect of a Civilian system.

In respect of the creation and transfer of real rights the influence of civilian principles is no less evident in respect of land law – heritable property in Scottish terminology – than of moveable property. It has only recently been recognized that the late 18th century saw the commencement of a process of separation of the subject of the creation of real rights in land – conveyancing – from general property law. As Professor *Kenneth Reid* has demonstrated the result of this was that "the law of heritable property came to be severed from the law of moveable property; and, just as damagingly, the law of heritable property came to be seen as an appendix to the law of conveyancing, rather than, as might have been expected, the other way around"[88]. In the 'Stair Memorial Encyclopaedia's' separate title on conveyancing by *J. H. Sinclair* an account is given of the common law method of conveyance of land in Scotland prior to the enactment of the Titles to Land (Scotland) Act 1858 (c.76)[89]. What is described has a definite affinity to the Roman *mancipatio* ceremony[90].

Positive (or acquisitive) prescription had a distinctive role in the Roman law of property which has not been duplicated in the development of Scots property law.

---

85 S.M.E., vol. 18, 1993, para. 530.

86 *W. M. Gordon*, Studies in the Transfer of Property by Traditio, 1970, 210.

87 See *D. L. Carey Miller*, Systems of Property: Grotius and Stair, in: D. L. Carey Miller and D. W. Meyers, edd., Comparative and Historical Essays in Scots Law, 1992, p. 13; *idem*, Stair's Property: A Romanist System, 1995 J.R. 70 and Derivative Acquisition of Moveables, in: Evans-Jones (n. 3) 128.

88 S.M.E., vol. 18, 1992, para. 1.

89 S.M.E., vol. 6, 1988, para. 402.

90 *Wessels*, History of Roman-Dutch Law, 1908, notes the likely relationship between the *mancipatio* ceremony and the forms of conveyance of land which developed in medieval customary systems of law.

Stair acknowledges this[91] and describes a common law system which is quite distinct from the Roman law position[92]. An examination of the treatment of prescription in the 'Stair Memorial Encyclopaedia' shows that the modern law has developed on a basis removed from the civil law. *Fergus* and *Maher* in their treatment of the historical sources of Scots law note that "[b]y the fifteenth century there are signs that Roman law was beginning to have a direct, even if generalised, influence ..."; they give, as an example, the passing of the Prescription Act of 1469 with its "Roman pedigree"[93]. In the prescription part of the title on prescription and limitation Professor *J. A. M. Inglis* identifies the Act of 1469 as introducing long negative prescription[94] but, of course, in the Roman context positive prescription – *usucapio* – was more important than negative prescription which was a relative latecomer to the scene.

Scots law distinguishes the substantive effect of prescription (whether positive or negative) from the procedural device of limitation, the latter being the termination, by lapse of time, of a right of action[95]. The title on prescription and limitation does not allude to any civil law influence and, indeed, the only reference to external influence in *Dr. David C. Coull's* treatment of limitation of actions is to English law[96].

The most significant role of positive prescription in the Scottish property context is to make possession of land, held for ten years on the basis of an *ex facie* valid title, exempt from challenge. A notable feature of this form of prescription – and a major point of distinction from the civil law – is that it applies in the *a non domino* situation without any requirement of good faith[97].

Scots law has tended to reject or severely limit the possibility of the creation of a right of security in moveable property without giving possession of the subject concerned to the creditor[98]. In modern law the need for security without possession in the context of commercial transactions between companies led to the introduction, from English law, of the floating charge[99]. According to *Alexander James Sim*, author of the relevant part of the 'Stair Memorial Encyclopaedia' title on rights in security, the position of the Scots common law in fact reflects a general rejection, in later European development, of the relatively liberal position of Roman law in respect of security over moveable property:

---

91 See *Stair* (n. 4) 2, 12, 11.

92 See *Carey Miller*, Stair's Property: a Romanist System? (n. 87) 76-80.

93 S.M.E., vol. 22, 1987, para. 551.

94 S.M.E., vol. 16, 1995, para. 2102.

95 S.M.E., vol. 16, 1995, para. 2133.

96 S.M.E., vol. 16, 1995, para. 2134.

97 S.M.E., vol. 16, 1995, para. 2106.

98 See *Carey Miller* (n. 47) para. 11.03.

99 See the Companies (Floating Charges) (Scotland) Act 1961.

"The liberal recognition accorded by Roman law to the creation of hypothecs did not, it appears, find favour in the countries of western Europe, even where the influence of Roman law was strong. It was considered inimical to commercial stability and confidence that debtors should remain in possession of property over which their debts were secured. Accordingly, the Scottish common law rejected conventional hypothecs except to a very limited extent"[100].

The entrenched nature of the notion that nothing amounting to a security interest should be allowed unless the creditor is in possession has been demonstrated in the saga of the adoption by Scots law of the so-called 'Romalpa' reservation of title device. In the result a device adopted by English commercial law in 1976[101] – on one view an instance of the influence of a modern *ius mercatorum* – came to Scotland in 1990; moreover, what was accepted in English law in a Court of Appeal decision only eventually became law in Scotland by way of the House of Lords[102].

At the time of writing the volume covering obligations had not been published but *Margaret Cherry*, Edinburgh Manager of Butterworths, very kindly gave me access to the galley proofs in the Butterworths' Edinburgh offices. The 'Stair Memorial Encyclopaedia' treatment of obligations is on the basis of the following division: obligations imposed by force of law, obligations arising from a wrongful act, voluntary obligations and substitutory redress (damages).

In the introductory part of the section dealing with obligations arising by force of law by Professor *Robert Black* Q.C. the category is stated to include "those obligations which in Roman law were described as arising *quasi ex contractu* and *quasi ex delicto*"[103].

"In Roman law, obligations arising *quasi ex delicto* were those in which liability for harm which one party had sustained were imposed upon another as if the latter had been at fault when in fact there was no need for either *dolus* or *culpa* on his part to be proved. They were cases in which liability to make reparation were imposed by law irrespective of fault on the part of the defender, that is to say they were cases of strict liability. In Scotland and elsewhere in Europe the expression 'quasi-delict' came in time to be misused to refer to situations in which liability to make reparation was imposed upon proof of *culpa* or negligence, as distinct from delict proper where *dolus* or intention required to be established[104]. This perversion of terminology has now, it is thought, died out in Scotland where 'delict' is used to refer to situations in which liability is imposed for fault irrespective of whether the fault consists of intentional or negligent wrongdoing"[105].

---

100 S.M.E., vol. 20, 1992, para. 3.

101 *Aluminium Industrie Vaassen B. V. v. Romalpa Ltd.* [1976] 1 W.L.R. 676 (C.A.). See *T. B. Smith*, Property Problems in Sale, 1978, at pp. 126-140.

102 *Armour v. Thyssen Edelstahlwerke A.G.* 1990 S.L.T. 891 (H.L.). The main events in the Scots law Romalpa saga are referred to in *Carey Miller* (n. 47) Chapter 12.

103 S.M.E., vol. 15, in press, para. 2.

104 Citing *P. G. Stein*, The Actio de Effusis vel Dejectis and the Concept of Quasi-Delict in Scots Law, (1955) 4 I.C.L.Q. 356.

105 S.M.E., vol. 15, in press, para. 2.

W. David H. Sellar, a leading Scottish legal historian who has contributed to this collection, in his introduction to the subject of unjust enrichment ('unjust' rather than 'unjustified' is used) draws attention to the view that the existing taxonomy is unsatisfactory. *Sellar* goes on to note suggested bases for reform including the position urged by *Robin Evans-Jones* identified as being that "more attention should be paid to the Roman law foundation and tradition of the European *ius commune*"[106]. As regards the foundations of unjust enrichment *Sellar* writes as follows:

> "The credit for recognising and isolating this area of law belongs to the civil and canon lawyers of the middle ages at the start of the *ius commune*; but its roots go back to the Emperor Justinian, and beyond that to the jurist Pomponius, who coined the famous dictum: 'Nam hoc natura aequum est neminem cum alterius detrimento fieri locupletiorem'"[107].

In the same paragraph the writer notes that "*Stair*'s treatment is grounded in the medieval *ius commune*, and can be understood only against that background; yet he made of the subject something uniquely Scottish"[108].

The treatment of unjust enrichment both reflects significant civilian influence and acknowledges this influence in giving some prominence to modern civil law writings. An instance of the former is *Sellar's* comment on the 18th century case of *Stirling v. Earl of Lauderdale:*[109].

> "The pleadings in the case disclose that the decision was only arrived at after full consideration of the relevant arguments and authorities. Jurists cited, in addition to the Digest itself, included *Cujas* and *Donellus*, *Grotius* and *Vinnius*"[110].

Sellar's readiness to resort to modern civilian writings is reflected in quite extensive use of the internationally acclaimed work on obligations of Professor *Reinhard Zimmermann* – my co-editor and a contributor to the present volume. One example is the quotation of that writer's description of the *condictio indebiti* as "one of the cornerstones of our modern law of unjustified enrichment"[111]. In the same paragraph *Sellar* refers to "Pomponius' famous principle"[112] which "lies at the root of this entire area of law"[113]. The justification for an approach which acknowl-

106 S.M.E., vol. 15, in press, para. 10 citing *R. Evans-Jones*, Unjust Enrichment, Contract and the Third Reception of Roman Law in Scotland, (1993) 109 L.Q.R. 663, and *idem*, Roman Law in Britain (sic) Scotland, Rechtshistorisches Journal 13 (1994) 494.

107 S.M.E., vol. 15, in press, para. 11. Digest texts 12, 6, 14 and 50, 17, 206 are cited as well as a *Corpus iuris canonici* variant found in the *Liber Sextus* of 1288 (6, 5, 13, 48).

108 S.M.E., vol. 15, in press, para. 11.

109 *Stirling of Northwoodside v. Earl of Lauderdale* (1733) Mor. 2930.

110 S.M.E., vol. 15, in press, para. 18.

111 *Reinhard Zimmermann*, The Law of Obligations: Roman Foundations of the Civilian Tradition, 1990, at pp. 834-835.

112 D. 12, 6, 14.

113 S.M.E., vol. 15, in press, para. 16.

edges and considers the civilian roots of Scots law is borne out by the recent five judge decision in which it was held that the *condictio indebiti* was available irrespective of whether the mistake or error under which payment had been made was one of fact or one of law[114]. Of this decision *Sellar* writes[115]:

> "*Morgan Guaranty Trust* is remarkable among recent Scottish cases for the breadth of authority cited and considered. The history of the *condictio indebiti* and of the controversy concerning error of fact and error of law is traced back to *Justinian's Corpus iuris civilis*. Earlier Scottish authorities, including both case law and writings, are fully considered, as is the scope of the maxim *ignorantia juris neminem excusat*. Considered too is the history of the controversy within the civilian tradition generally, including the law of South Africa".

The rich history which the Scots law of unjust enrichment connects into is shown in a paragraph under the subtitle of "Medieval Law, the *ius commune* and *Grotius*":

> "This history of unjust enrichment in the medieval *ius commune* can be traced back to the revival of Roman law studies at Bologna under *Irnerius* in the eleventh century. *Martinus of Gosia*, among the immediate successors of *Irnerius*, was much influenced by considerations of equity, and came nearest to articulating a general rule against unjust enrichment based on the texts in the *Corpus iuris civilis*. His arguments were taken further by later glossators and commentators, by the canon lawyers, and, in the sixteenth century, by the Spanish scholastics. Existing remedies in Roman law, particularly *negotiorum gestio*, were built and developed with considerable ingenuity to cover many new situations. It has been claimed that *Grotius*, writing in Holland at the beginning of the seventeenth century, was the first to articulate clearly a general rule against unjustified enrichment justifiable at law, and that this rule was carried into practice in the High Courts of Holland and Zeeland"[116].

The author is not, of course, making a general statement about the relevance of the history of continental European legal development to Scotland. Indeed, it is worth noting that in many of his writings on Scottish legal history he has cautioned against any tendency to assume Romanist influence; for example in a recent contribution with Professor *Hector MacQueen*: "Large and unjustifiable claims have sometimes been made as to the extent to which Scots law is based on Roman law"[117].

---

114 *Morgan Guaranty Trust Company of New York v. Lothian Regional Council* 1995 S.C.L.R. 225.

115 S.M.E., vol. 15, in press, para. 26.

116 S.M.E., vol. 15, in press, para. 75; citing *Zimmermann* (n. 111) 871-887 and other works.

117 *H. L. MacQueen* and *W. David H. Sellar*, Unjust Enrichment in Scots Law, in: Eltjo J.H. Schrage, ed., Unjust Enrichment: The Comparative Legal History of the Law of Restitution, 1995, 289, at p. 289. Many other relevant contributions of *W. David H. Sellar* are referred to under the heading 'Historical Revisionism: Has it Downgraded the Importance of the *ius commune*?' in: *Niall R. Whitty*, The Civilian Tradition and Debates on Scots Law, 1996 T.S.A.R. 227.

The comprehensive treatment of *negotiorum gestio* by *Niall R. Whitty* reflects a very considerable Romanist influence as well as a readiness on the part of the writer to make maximum use of civilian sources. In a paragraph entitled "Roman Law as a Source" he quotes a *dictum* of Lord *Clyde* in the recent *Morgan Guaranty* case[118] to the effect that it is widely recognized that, "[t]he doctrine of *negotiorum gestio* has been borrowed by our law from the Roman law"[119].

But even the most esteemed writer on the *ius commune* is open to a 'better view' argument. Thus in distinguishing *negotiorum gestio* from salvage *Whitty* rejects *Grotius'*[120] suggested affinity and notes that "there are many differences between the two doctrines"[121]. A rationale of former law may no longer apply – that the original purpose of *negotiorum gestio* was to provide for intervention in litigation on behalf of an absent party is plainly irrelevant to modern law[122]. But there are far more examples of empathy than the contrary. In the case of common interest of *dominus* and gestor: "In Scots law, as in Roman law, an action on *negotiorum gestio* may be excluded"[123]; something which would appear to follow from the foundation requirement, recognized in both systems, that "the administration must be unauthorised by the *dominus*"[124].

Whitty, also, relies on *Zimmermann's* work which, as part of a modern *ius commune*, in a sense becomes a source of Scots law.

> "Professor *Zimmermann* tells us that both the subjective and the objective approaches have been read into the Roman sources and that they still compete in modern German law but that the subjective theory dominated in the *ius commune* from the glossators through the Roman-Dutch jurists to modern South African law"[125].

Strict liability is another form of obligation imposed by force of law. Edictal liability has already been mentioned[126]; its position in Scots law is dealt with in the obligations volume[127] where the affect of legislation upon the common law is noted[128].

118 *Morgan Guaranty Trust Company of New York v. Lothian Regional Council* 1995 S.C.L.R. 225, at p. 242.

119 S.M.E., vol. 15, in press, para. 88.

120 *Hugo Grotius*, Inleiding tot de Hollandsche Rechtsgeleertheyd, 3, 27, 6.

121 S.M.E., vol. 15, in press, para. 93 citing *A. D. M. Forte*, Salvage Operations, Salvage Contracts and Negotiorum Gestio, 1993 J.R. 247, and *J. P. van Niekerk*, Salvage Operations and Negotiorum Gestio, 1992 Acta Juridica 148.

122 S.M.E., vol. 15, in press, para. 101.

123 S.M.E., vol. 15, in press, para. 104.

124 S.M.E., vol. 15, in press, para. 105 citing D. 17, 1, 6, 1, C. 2, 18, 5 and *Stair* (n. 4) 1, 8, 3.

125 S.M.E., vol. 15, in press, para. 111, citing *Zimmermann* (n. 111) 440.

126 See above, n. 60.

127 S.M.E., vol. 15, in press, paras. 144-150.

128 For example, in relation to hotelkeepers by the Hotel Proprietors Act 1956 (c. 62).

Professor *Kenneth Miller*, writing the strict liability section, also notes that neither the *actio de effusis vel dejectis* nor the associated *actio de positis vel suspensis* have been recognized to be part of Scots law. In fact both actions have been specifically rejected in decisions of the Sheriff Court[129]. It is significant, however, for present purposes that in the 'Stair Memorial Encyclopaedia' three paragraphs consider two actions which are acknowledged probably not to be part of Scots law[130]. One might say that this treatment keeps the actions alive in a certain sense in Scots law, an approach which would have been approved of by the founder of the 'Stair Memorial Encyclopaedia', Professor Sir *Thomas Smith* – whose comments on the rejection of *de effusis vel dejectis* may be mentioned. Referring to an article on the subject by his then Aberdeen colleague Professor *Peter Stein*[131] – another very distinguished writer in the present volume – Professor *T.B. Smith* noted that although the "offensive and insanitary" facts of the case would not be likely to be repeated in modern circumstances,

> "[n]evertheless objects or fluids may again be cast or poured from buildings through carelessness or malice; and there may be cause to recall that the Athens of the North is juristically an heir of Rome"[132].

Delict, of course, is a major area of Civilian influence. This is acknowledged but put into perspective in the introduction to the section on obligations arising from a wrongful act by Professor *Kenneth McK. Norrie*:

> "As with much of the Scots law of obligations, there are many traces of Roman law in the modern law of delict, though the place of civilian influence today is much circumscribed. English law is far more significant as a source for the development of the law, particularly through the common appellate structure headed by the House of Lords. Roman law terms are still frequently used by Scottish writers and in the Scottish courts, but often they are used as means of describing ideas and concepts of the modern law which have little real connection to the Roman law[133]. Nevertheless the history of the Scots law of delict cannot be fully understood without paying some regard to Roman law. Scots law has never accepted the English approach of extending the law only by analogy with previous precedents; rather, it is the civilian approach of looking for general principles that motivates legal development"[134].

As regards the substance of the law of delict Professor *Kenneth McK. Norrie* notes of the *actio injuriarum* and the *actio legis Aquiliae* that the "former is the primary source of the modern Scots law of defamation, the latter is the source of much of the rest of the modern law of reparation"[135].

---

129 S.M.E., vol. 15, para. 153 citing *Gray v. Dunlop* 1954 S.L.T. (Sh. Ct.) 75 and *MacCall v. Hoo* 1983 S.L.T. (Sh. Ct.) 23.

130 S.M.E., vol. 15, in press, paras. 151, 152 and 153.

131 *Stein* (n. 104).

132 See *Smith* (n. 32) 638.

133 "So e.g. *culpa* is equiparated to 'breach of a duty of care' ".

134 S.M.E., vol. 15, in press, para. 213.

In the case of defamation, the *actio injuriarum* is referred to as a primary or foundation source in the general sense of the influence of the action in the development of the notion of the protection of reputation[136]. The abovementioned statement to this effect appears in the general "history and function of delict"; in the subsequent treatment of defamation Professor *Norrie* describes a focus on the specific protection of reputation:

> "Defamation is the typical form of attack on a person's character, honour and reputation, and because of the element of honour the action originally came within the jurisdiction of the church courts, which jurisdiction came to be exercised by the commissaries. Though the original purpose of the action was to restore the pursuer's reputation (achieved by means of palinode, that is a public retraction of the accusation), the church courts were wont to regard attacks on character and honour as ecclesiastical offences and they could therefore impose the penalty of a fine"[137].

It may be noted that the absence in Scots law of any general common law basis for the protection of privacy could be seen as a failure to develop the potential of the *actio injuriarum*, with the South African development being the obvious model[138]; but, of course, this is predicated on an assumption as to the motivation to develop the legal protection of interests of privacy. Scots law's development in the area of interests of personality appears not to reflect the potential open to a system drawing on the civil law tradition. The delict of 'verbal injury' is seen by Professor *Norrie*, in its classic form, "to cover all forms of actionable statements that attack character, honour and reputation" – an approach which is stated to have "Roman law antecedents"[139]. But it is significant that the 'Stair Memorial Encyclopaedia' breakdown of 'Injuries to Particular Interests' is restricted to interference with liberty, interference with honour and reputation, economic relationships and family relationships, apparently without any general protection commensurate with the notion of *dignitas* under the *actio injuriarum*.

In respect of the more important matter of a general delictual action it has already been noted that the *lex Aquilia* is recognized to be basic to Scots law although in the wide and open form "long latent in the *ius commune* that a wrongful act or omission created an obligation to repair the loss caused thereby"[140]. Thus Professor *Norrie* notes, in respect of fault and unintentional injury, that "[i]n relation to injury caused not intentionally but carelessly the element of fault is in the

---

135 S.M.E., vol. 15, in press, para. 214.

136 For more detailed comments on the ancestry question see *K. McK. Norrie*, Defamation and Related Actions in Scots Law, 1995, at pp. 1-2.

137 S.M.E., vol. 15, in press, para. 471.

138 See the Scottish Law Commission, Memorandum No. 40, 1977, Confidential Information, paras. 50-54, where a case is made for following the development of the protection of privacy on the basis of the *actio injuriarum* in South Africa; see also *D. L. Carey Miller*, Privacy: Interception of Communications, 1980 S.L.T. (News) 209, at pp. 211-214.

139 S.M.E., vol. 15, in press, para. 557 citing D. 47, 1.

140 *Smith* (n. 32) 650.

modern law equiparated with the notion of *culpa*"[141]. Professor *Norrie* goes on to state that the English law duty of care was introduced in Scots law as a means of limiting the scope of liablity based on fault[142] – given that much of the modern development has been concerned with scope one can see that this would be a factor in the affinity between English and Scots law alluded to in an earlier paragraph[143].

Voluntary obligations stand alongside obligations arising from a wrongful act not only in importance but also in showing the individuality of Scots law. The comments of Professor *Robert Black* Q.C. in respect of unilateral promises are an example of this distinctiveness on a fundamental matter:

> "At least since the time of *Stair* the law of Scotland, diverging in this respect from the laws of most other civil law systems of western Europe, has not required, before an obligation is recognized as coming into being, that the promisee accept the benefit of the promise made in his favour; it has consequently seen no need, as other systems have, to resort to the device of a presumed acceptance by the beneficiary in order to hold the promisor to his undertaking"[144].

It has been shown that there is a significant measure of reference to civil or Canon law influence in the 'Stair Memorial Encyclopaedia's' individual treatment of a number of specific contracts. In the general part on voluntary obligations there are also important examples of the influence although, of course, much of the modern development has necessarily reflected the motivation of policy considerations rather than the facts of historical foundation.

In respect of contractually stipulated remedies *J. D. L. Hope* notes the early influence of Canon law in his historical introduction:

"Before the Reformation, under the influence of Canon laws against usury, the courts generally refused to give effect to penal stipulations[145]. After the Reformation, however, penalties were generally enforced, although with the proviso that the courts could modify those which were exorbitant"[146].

In the treatment of title to sue Professor *Hector MacQueen* refers to the distinctive position of Scots law in giving scope to the intention of the parties to a contract "to confer enforceable rights on third parties"[147]. The writer comments as follows on the doctrine of *ius quaesitum tertio*:

---

141 S.M.E., vol. 15, in press, para. 254, citing, *inter alia, G. D. MacCormack*, Culpa in the Scots Law of Reparation, 1974 J.R. 13.

142 S.M.E., vol. 15, in press, para. 257.

143 See above, n. 133.

144 S.M.E., vol. 15, in press, para. 614 citing *T. B. Smith*, Studies Critical and Comparative, 1962, at pp. 171-173.

145 *Home v. Hepburn* (1549) Mor. 10033 is cited with the author's note that "in that particular case the court appears to have made an exception 'in odium anglorum' simply because the penalty was inflicted against an Englishman!".

146 S.M.E., vol. 15, in press, para. 783. The writer notes that reference was often made to the *Lex Unica de Sententiis* (C. 7, 47).

"Scots law may therefore be contrasted to some extent with both classical Roman law and English law, neither of which gave or give great scope to third party rights in contracts. In particular there is no equivalent to the Common Law doctrine of privity. The Civilian tradition of the middle ages and afterwards departed from the classical restrictions to recognize both direct third party rights and assignation, with the result that this is the law of most modern Civilian systems[148]. The development of Scots law in this area clearly owes a good deal to the Civilian tradition, although some characteristically Scottish features have been developed by the courts"[149].

In a subsequent paragraph the particular history of the doctrine is considered by Professor *MacQueen* in a valuable insight into a particular instance manifesting immediacy of connection between Scots law and the various facets of continental European development:

"Roman law did not recognize third party rights arising directly from contracts: *alteri stipulari nemo potest*. It was the medieval Canon lawyers who first offered a generalised challenge to this view, and it may be suspected that it was through this source that Scots law recognized a form of *jus quaesitum tertio* before the end of the sixteenth century[150]. The Spanish scholastics of this period were exceptional amongst Civilians of the time in arguing for the enforceability of third party contractual rights, basing themselves on the by then widespread rejection of the Roman view that 'ex nudo pacto non oritur actio' and the preference for the Canonist *pacta sunt servanda*. It is significant that when *Stair* came to give the first general statement of the Scots law of *jus quaesitum tertio* in the later seventeenth century, he drew on the writings of one of the Spanish school, *Molina*. *Stair*'s discussion of *jus quaesitum tertio* follows the passage in which he has explained that, contrary to the view of *Grotius*, unilateral promises are obligatory without the promisee's acceptance, 'the Canon law having taken off the exception of the Civil law, *de nudo pacto*' "[151].

There are deep civilian pockets in the law concerned with voluntary obligations. However, in respect of the general principles of contract it is significant that one seeks in vain in the Stair Memorial Encyclopaedia for any indication of a general concept of good faith or a general concept of fault – features which are very much identified with the civil law systems but are largely unknown in the common law world[152]. That one would not expect to find any mention of these concepts is borne out by what is said by *Niall Whitty* in his recent valuable contribution 'The Civilian Tradition and Debates on Scots Law':

---

147 S.M.E., para. 814.

148 Citing *Zimmermann* (n. 111) 34-67.

149 S.M.E., vol. 15, in press, para. 814.

150 Citing *Wood v. Moncur* (1591) Mor. 7719.

151 S.M.E., vol. 15, in press, para. 826 quoting, at the end, *Stair* (n. 4) 1, 10, 4. *MacQueen* also refers to *Smith* (n. 144) 184-185, *Zimmermann* (n. 111) 42, and *A. F. Rodger*, Molina, Stair and the Jus Quaesitum Tertio, 1969 J. R. 34, 128 (2 parts), at pp. 130-135.

152 Professor *R. M. Goode* raises the issue 'jus strictum or jus aequum?' in Twentieth Century Developments in Commercial Law, (1983) 3 Legal Studies 283, at p. 284.

> "Scots law based its system of consensual contracts on the *ius commune* but like South African law it has not accepted the civilian doctrine that the exercise of contractual rights is subject to the principles of good faith. The better view is that like English law it requires strict adherence to contracts"[153].

III. The Dynamic of Scots Law

While major areas of Scots substantive private law are civilian to one degree or another and much of substantive law in general is distinctively Scottish, in mode of operation the system's orientation is towards the Anglo-American world. This is broadly true of the adjectival law as well as the actual system of Scots law – the means and manner by which the law operates and develops. But within a general position which would be more familiar to an English or American lawyer than to one trained in a continental European system Scots law has strongly individualistic traits.

It may be observed at the outset that what has just been noted at the end of the previous section in relation to a general concept of good faith in contract is a matter of dynamics in the sense that its absence has controlling implications for a major area of law.

The form of the operative legal rule of Scots law is the judicial decision. More specifically, the form which encompasses the effective statement of the legal rule derives from a judicial opinion and, significantly, this is true not only in respect of matters of common law but also of areas of the law based upon legislation. Systems of the Anglo-American and civilian traditions may not be too far apart in modern practice on the determination of the critical balance between legislative and judicial statement but, this said, the respective positions of the two major western legal families on the concept of *règle juridique* remains distinctive. Sir *Thomas Smith*, aware, of course, of the significance of this factor, presents Scots law as a late and only partial convert to *stare decisis*:

> "Formerly, of course, Scots law like other Civilian systems did not recognize the strict doctrine of *stare decisis*, and even today it is probable that the only single decision which the Court of Session could not disregard is a precedent established by the House of Lords in a Scottish appeal"[154].

Be this as it may the significance of judicial precedent as a source in modern law is manifest, something borne out by the comprehensive 'Stair Memorial Encyclopaedia' treatment of the subject by Professor *G. Maher* and Sir *Thomas*[155]. In

---

153 *Whitty* (n. 117).

154 *Smith* (n. 33) 84. See also, generally, *T. B. Smith*, The Doctrines of Judicial Precedent in Scots Law, 1952.

155 S.M.E., vol. 22, 1987, paras. 247-354. The general editor notes at the commencement of the section that "credit ... is substantially due to Mr. Maher".

particular one may quote the description of the *ratio decidendi* as a proposition of law as illustrative of the accepted role of judicial precedent: "The *ratio decidendi* of a case is the element of principle which is binding in later cases and as such is a proposition of law which the decision in the case embodies or illustrates"[156].

At the same time there at least should be room for the foundation principles which are present in aspects of Scots law to influence the development of the law by precedent. The 'Stair Memorial Encyclopaedia' introductory paragraph on delict quoted above suggests that this is the case[157]. In the treatment of judicial precedent there are also statements concerning the development of the law of delict. In a paragraph on the "Application of 'General Principles'" Professor *G. Maher* writes as follows:

> "The law of Scotland for damage caused by *culpa* or fault is based on the developed *lex Aquilia* comprehending deliberate and negligent harm, whereas English law developed separate remedies for deliberate and negligent harm. Mistaken extension of English concepts to Scots law frustrated the logical development of the Scots law of reparation in such fields as liability for economic loss and delictual remedies complementing those available in contract. Although the *lex Aquilia* and the English tort of negligence flow from divergent sources, their solutions now merge in principles of liability for harm caused by negligence, but not if extrapolated to the context of wilful harm"[158].

While one would not suggest that the principles which are basic to certain areas of Scots law have been cut off from any future role by case law it would be misconceived to identify the system as one in which court decisions are only supplementary to established principles.

The modern Scots law position relating to the law making power of judges through judicial precedent may reflect English influence but the recognition of a very high level of judicial power is reflected in the potential but seldom resorted to capacity of the High Court of Justiciary to declare conduct not previously regarded as criminal to be criminal – the 'declaratory power'[159]. That this capacity represents a deviation from any general European position is recognized by Professor *D. Neil MacCormick* in his title on general legal concepts. Under the heading *nulla poena sine crimine, nullum crimen sine lege* Professor *MacCormick* writes as follows:

---

156 S.M.E, vol. 22, 1987, para. 336.

157 See above, n. 134.

158 S.M.E., vol. 22, 1987, para. 276.

159 See the treatment of *M. G. A. Christie*, S.M.E., vol. 7, 1995, paras. 6-15. In para. 13 reference is made to the celebrated glue-sniffing case (see nn. 72, 26) of *Khaliq v. H. M. Advocate* 1984 J.C. 23 which may be taken to represent a reconciliatory approach to the declaratory power. See generally *S. C. Styles*, Something to Declare: A Defence of the Declaratory Power of the High Court of Justiciary, in: R. F. Hunter, ed., Justice and Crime: Essays in Honour of the Right Honourable The Lord Emslie, 1993, 211.

"The commonly observed European principle of civil liberty that no person should be punished save for a breach of an expressly pre-announced and prospective rule of the criminal law does not hold in Scots law"[160].

M. G. A. Christie, principal author and co-ordinator of criminal law, in the introductory part of his title also concedes the vulnerability of Scots law to a charge of failure to conform to the principle represented by the aphorism *nullum crimen sine lege* – "perhaps more honoured in the breach than otherwise in Scotland"[161]. Mr. *Christie*'s general comments as to the position of Scots criminal law in respect of certainty and retroactivity are persuasive but identify the extent to which the system is distinct from the continental European tradition which adheres to *Justinian*'s invocation to judges[162] to "decide not by precedent but according to the *leges*"[163]:

"A jurisdiction which depends to a considerable extent on non-statutory (that is, common law) crimes cannot fully adhere to a 'non-retroactive' regime. From case to case, as the result of judicial decisions as to the reach of the law, the account of any particular common law crime may sharpen, extend or even contract – in ways unknown prior to the bringing of such cases by the prosecution"[164].

In volume 22 of the 'Stair Memorial Encyclopaedia' a treatment of *nobile officium* follows the part dealing with the declaratory power under the general heading of 'equity'. The *nobile officium* also crops up in the title on administrative law by Professor *A. W. Bradley* who defines it as follows:

"... the residual equitable power of the supreme court to order justice to be done in circumstances in which to rely on existing rules of law would not achieve this, may be exercised upon petition by a decision of the Inner House"[165].

Returning to equity as a formal source of law *R.B. Ferguson* explains the modern exercise of the *nobile officium*:

"While we may agree that the *nobile officium* is not necessarily incapable of novelty, it goes too far to characterise it as 'theoretically unlimited'[166]. It is no less true today than formerly that it is incompetent for the court to exercise the *nobile officium* 'in order to override the express provision of a statute'[167]. The *nobile officium* may be invoked to meet a *casus improvisus* in a statute, but not 'to alter the statutory provisions of an Act of Parliament or enable anything to be done which is expressly rendered ineffective by the Act' "[168].

160 S.M.E., vol. 11, 1990, para. 1012.

161 S.M.E., vol. 7, 1995, para. 4.

162 D. 50, 17, 1.

163 *Buckland* and *McNair* (n. 11) 9.

164 S.M.E., vol. 7, 1995, para. 5.

165 S.M.E., vol. 1, 1987, para. 332.

166 Quoting *Lord Wark*, Law of Nature, in: The Sources and Literature of Scots Law, 1936, 249, at p. 254.

167 *Per* Lord Justice-Clerk *Dickson* in *Adair v. David Colville & Sons Ltd.* 1922 S.C. 672, at p. 677.

The necessity that in general legislation should operate only so as to affect what is put in place subsequent to its passing was well understood in the civil law[169]. Scots law and English law, however, together recognize the sovereign omnicompetence of the United Kingdom Parliament without limitation in respect of retrospective legislation. The position is explained in the introduction of Lord *Fraser of Tullybelton* to his title on constitutional law. Having mentioned the express barring of retrospective legislation in the United States Constitution Lord *Fraser* writes:

> "The United Kingdom Parliament has no such disability, although the courts, while recognising the effectiveness of retrospective legislation if clearly expressed, will endeavour to construe an Act in such a way as not to have retrospective effect if it is possible to do so"[170].

This statement, made in the context of the limitation deriving from the European Communities Act 1972[171], reflects a position at least inconsistent with that of the continental European civil law jurisdictions, the clear position of the latter being reflected in the European Court's statement that the principle against penal retrospectivity was common "to all the legal orders of the Member States"[172].

An example of legislation of Scots law which, arguably, fails to conform to the civilian principle against retrospectivity is the Family Law (Scotland) Act 1985. As is noted by Professor *Joseph M. Thomson* and *William J. Stewart* in the Family Law title although a system of separate property is the normal consequence of marriage the 1985 Act in effect produces a deferred community system:

> "It has to be remembered that should the marriage terminate, for example on divorce, some of the principles governing financial provision resemble a division of the couple's property which is similar to the deferred community of matrimonial property in Continental civil law"[173].

What is significant, of course, is that the 1985 legislation altered the property regime, in the event of divorce, of existing marriages. It is noteworthy that "the terms of any agreement between the parties on the ownership or division of any of the matrimonial property"[174] are one of a number of possible "special circumstances" which the court may take account of in determining an appropriate sharing of matrimonial property in terms of the Act. The introduction of what amounts

168 S.M.E., vol. 22, 1987, para. 431, referring, in the final sentence quoted, to the *dictum* of Lord President *Clyde* in *McLaughlin* 1965 S.C. 243, at p. 245.

169 See *Peter G. Stein*, Regulae Iuris, 1966, at pp. 19-24.

170 S.M.E., vol. 5, 1987, para. 311.

171 S.M.E., vol. 5, 1987, para. 310. E.C. law does not allow penal provisions to have retroactive effect: see *Stephen Weatherill, Paul Beaumont*, E.C. Law, 2nd ed., 1995, at pp. 257, 262-263.

172 Case 63/83 [1984] E.C.R., quoted from in *Weatherill/Beaumont* (n. 171) 257.

173 S.M.E., vol. 10, 1990, para. 872.

174 Family Law (Scotland) Act 1985, s.10(6).

to a "deferred community system" in the event of divorce may be commendable; what is open to objection, from the point of view of retrospectivity, is the inclusion of existing marriages and the consequent departure from what was in place, in terms of law or contract.

IV. Conclusion

That part of the 'Stair Memorial Encyclopaedia' dealing with the historical sources of Scots law – by *T. David Fergus*, Professor *G. Maher* and *James J. Robertson* (Canon law) – is presented under the following heads: Roman law, Canon law, feudal law, English influence, French and Dutch influences, the law merchant and the law of the Bible[175]. For present purposes the obvious point is that in addition to the actual civil law factor there is a civilian aspect in the Canon law and law merchant sources of influence as well, of course, as the influences specifically identified as French and Dutch. It is difficult to quarrel with the according of a 'civilian' label to a system showing this degree of direct and indirect civilian influence. In this regard, it is interesting to note the affinity between what are identified as the historical sources of Scots law and the elements of the Canon law, the law merchant and Germanic customary law which Professor *Reinhard Zimmermann* has recently noted to be instances of the "other strands of legal tradition ... woven into European law" apart from what has been derived from Roman law[176].

But while the reporting on 'Stair Memorial Encyclopaedia' titles carried out in this essay shows the wide influence of the civilian tradition, and its great importance in fundamental matters of private law, it confirms the generally accepted conclusion that Scots law is not an out and out civilian system but a mixed one[177]. Excluding consideration of the obvious difference arising from codification the civilian factor is generally more emphatic in continental European legal development than it is in Scots law. This, of course, is reflected in a more consistent civilian factor in the end product of the great European codes than can be found in the more diffuse make up of Scots law. It is true that in certain particular areas the impact of the civilian tradition has been profound but it may be significant that even in moveable property – sometimes identified as the single area of greatest influence – there are native Scottish features[178].

---

175 S.M.E., vol. 22, 1987, paras. 548-614.

176 In his foreword to *Tony Weir*'s translation into English of *Franz Wieacker*, A History of Private Law in Europe, 1995, at p. viii.

177 See, e.g., *O. F. Robinson*, *T. D. Fergus*, *W. M. Gordon*, European Legal History, 2nd ed., 1994, para. 8, 1, 1 identifying Scots law, with South African law, as "a mixed system where the Common Law has tended, for political or constitutional reasons, to dominate the civilian inspiration".

178 See *Carey Miller*, Stair's Property: A Romanist System (n. 87).

It would probably be arbitrary to identify a particular period or epoch as reflecting the formative stage in the development of Scots law. In this respect the history of the development of the system is more akin to that of English law than to most continental European systems. The long continuous period of the development of Scots law reflects a number of important influences including factors unrelated to the civilian tradition. It is also the case that the contribution of that tradition was within the context of a developing Scottish common law. An exception to this general position of domestic control was the Canon law aspect which had a foundation impact. As *James J. Robertson* notes in the 'Stair Memorial Encyclopaedia' Canon law was "a direct source of law in Scotland prior to 1560"[179]. The outline of the history of the system in the 'Stair Memorial Encyclopaedia' title already referred to shows the importance of domestic factors in the development of Scots law[180]. *Elspeth Attwooll*, in a recent contribution, has noted that the ingredients in this development have largely come from outside Scotland:

> "All in all, there is a sense in which Scotland has not known indigenous law. Celtic and Udal law were brought in by settlement. Feudal law was copied from the England of the Anglo-Normans. Canon law was established through the Church. Roman law filtered in from the Continent of Europe. In more recent times, case law has been influenced by other jurisdictions, predominantly of the common law kind"[181].

Be this as it may the evolution of the system has been a domestic process although probably not one marked by any consistent domestic policy to legal development. But as the many valuable contributions of Dr. *John W. Cairns* – including one in this volume – show, a distinctively Scottish approach to law and legal development is well established[182].

The development of the most important foundation feature of a particular Scottish common law has been described and put into the general post-11th century European context by *W. David H. Sellar*:

> "Everywhere in Europe the new learned law interacted with older customary law. Scotland was no exception. In Scotland, however, as already noted, the customary base was partially Celtic, rather than purely Germanic. Although the Norman Conquest of 1066 did not extend to Scotland, the feudal law and institutions which found their way into Scotland were unmistakably Anglo-Norman. In Scotland, as in England – but unlike, for example, the situation in France and Germany – the rulers of the kingdom were able to shape a law which was largely national rather than local, co-terminous with the bounds of their kingdom, a common law"[183].

---

179 S.M.E., vol. 22, 1987, para. 580.

180 S.M.E., vol. 22, 1987, paras. 503-522.

181 *Attwooll* (n. 32) 25.

182 See, e.g., *J. W. Cairns*, Sir George Mackenzie, The Faculty of Advocates, and the Advocates' Library, in: J. W. Cairns and A. M. Cain, edd., G. Mackenzie, Oratio inauguralis in aperienda jurisconsultorum bibliotheca, 1989, 18.

183 See *Meston/Cooper/Sellar* (n. 72) 33-34.

The base of Scots law, which was in large measure an indigenous development, was not substantially displaced by any reception of Roman law *in complexu* but, this said, cumulatively the civil law has had a very considerable influence which has been spread over almost the entire history of the system. Professor *W.M. Gordon*, in a recent study, has observed this as a matter of contrast with the extent of civilian influence upon the English Common law – the outstanding example of continuous and largely consistent domestic development:

> "Scots law in the course of its history has had much closer contact with the European civilian tradition than has the English Common law but there have also been significant influences from the Common law"[184].

On this basis the placing as 'Schottisches Recht im Spannungsfeld von civil law und common law'[185] is plausible.

It should be noted that the characterization of Scottish legal development – in terms of both what went in and when it went in – is very much the subject of debate and is in some respects controversial[186]. That there have been misconceptions has been demonstrated – Lord *Rodger of Earlsferry*, also the author of a chapter in this book, has shown that certain views concerning the development of Scottish commercial law were misconceived[187]. Some of the debate has been generated by law reform agendas and, of course, in respect of particular subjects it may be valid to identify an aspect of historical influence as pointing to an appropriate source from which to borrow – provided that what is contemplated is consistent with modern needs[188]. But it is doubtful whether there could be any overall general evaluation – other than the indeterminate identification as 'mixed' – which could be demonstrated to be valid in anything approaching a scientific sense[189].

---

184 *W. M. Gordon*, Roman Law in Scotland, in: Evans-Jones (n. 3) 13.

185 *Reinhard Zimmermann, Johann A. Dieckmann*, Das schottische Privatrecht im Spiegel seiner Literatur, ZEuP 3 (1995) 898.

186 *Niall R. Whitty* (n. 117) includes a very valuable survey and analysis of the different perspectives presented in the literature. See, also, *Alan Rodger*, Thinking about Scots Law, (1996) 1 Edinburgh Law Review 3.

187 *A. F. Rodger*, The Codification of Commercial Law in Victorian Britain, (1992) 108 L.Q.R. 570. See also the controversial view of *A. D. M. Forte*, A Great Future Behind it? Scottish Commercial Law and the Millenium, 1994 Aberdeen University Review 225.

188 See above (n. 105) in respect of unjust enrichment.

189 I am grateful to R. Evans-Jones and W. David H. Sellar for their comments on this chapter but they bear no responsibility for its faults and failings.

The Foundation of Law Teaching at the University of Aberdeen

By Hector L. MacQueen[1]

The subject of this paper has been comprehensively treated by *Leslie Macfarlane* in his monumental biography of Bishop *William Elphinstone*, the founder of the University of Aberdeen (and much else besides)[2]. It would be presumptuous indeed for me to pretend that there is much which can be added to the material gathered together by *Macfarlane* over a lifetime of scholarship, and I am indeed heavily indebted to his work for much of what follows. Where perhaps something fresh may be added is in carrying the story of the Elphinstonian Foundation down to its effective demise in the 17th century (although here I must acknowledge a further debt to the work of another friend and sometime Aberdeen scholar, *David Stevenson*[3]); and in some further discussion of the contexts in which the foundation of law teaching at Aberdeen must be set, in particular the significance of the civil and canon laws in the Scottish legal system of the medieval and early modern periods.

I. The Elphinstonian Foundation

I begin with a basic chronology which is little more than a synopsis of the work of the others already mentioned. On 6 February 1495 Bishop *Elphinstone* conveyed to Pope *Alexander VI* the petition of King *James IV* for the foundation of a university of general study in Old Aberdeen like those of Paris and Bologna, in which amongst all the other lawful faculties Canon and civil law would be taught.

1 I would like to acknowledge with thanks the guidance and comments of Dr. *John Cairns*, Dr. *Leslie Macfarlane* and Mr. *David Sellar* on a first draft of this paper. Professor *William Gordon* also kindly gave me sight of his paper on Roman law in medieval Scotland (cited below) in advance of publication, and I benefited from discussion of certain points with Professor *Geoffrey Barrow*, Mrs. *Winifred MacQueen* and Professor *Robert Feenstra*. I alone am responsible for the contents and conclusions of the paper.

2 *L. J. Macfarlane*, William *Elphinstone* and the Kingdom of Scotland 1431-1514: The Struggle for Order, 2nd ed., Aberdeen, 1995.

3 *D. Stevenson*, King's College, Aberdeen, 1560-1641: From Protestant Reformation to Covenanting Revolution, Quincentennial studies in the history of the University of Aberdeen, Aberdeen, 1990.

It was envisaged that the students would be both ecclesiastics and lay people, and that the primary area which the university would serve would be the northern and north-eastern parts of Scotland. The petition stated that this would tend to the improvement of the condition of the people of the kingdom, since its northern places were cut off from the rest of the realm by arms of the sea and very high mountains and were over-distant from the places where universities flourished. As a result the region was inhabited by men "who are rude, ignorant of letters and almost barbarous ... nay, are so ignorant of these letters that suitable men cannot be found not only for preaching the word of God to the people of those parts, but even for administering the sacraments of the church". Since Old Aberdeen was a place "in which a temperate climate prevails and where are found abundance of victuals, convenience of dwellings and good store of the other things pertaining to the requirements of human life", it was a suitable location for the new university[4].

The petition was granted and the Foundation Bull, dated 10 February 1495, was issued to *Elphinstone* for return to Aberdeen, where it still remains in the University archives[5]. The Bull authorized reading and teaching in every lawful faculty, including both Canon and civil law. Since *Elphinstone* was judged by contemporaries to be 'more skilled in law' than any other of his time[6], it seems likely that he intended teaching of the subject to be central in his foundation. A reference in the Bull to students "who are *at this time* reading and studying therein"[7] suggests that teaching may have been already under way in 1495; this teaching may have included Canon and civil law[8]. A basis for the study of Canon law already existed in the Cathedral's library, which had been built up since the early 15th century, but its civil law content apart from the Digest and lectures on the Codex was relatively insignificant[9]. The collection may also have been supplemented by the Founder's

4 Vatican Archives, Reg. Suppl. 1000, fos 81v-82v. The petition is also embodied in the Foundation Bull, for which see n. 5 below. For the topography of medieval Old Aberdeen see the contribution of *G. G. Simpson* in: J. S. Smith, ed., Old Aberdeen: Bishops, Burghers and Buildings, Aberdeen, 1991, 1.

5 University of Aberdeen, OCC/43/1. The text is printed with a parallel translation by *Gordon Donaldson* in: F. C. Eeles, ed., King's College Chapel Aberdeen: Its Fittings, Ornaments and Ceremonial in the Sixteenth Century, Edinburgh and London, 1956, 136.

6 J. Moir, ed., Hectoris Boetii Murthlacensium et Aberdonensium Episcoporum Vitae, New Spalding Club, Aberdeen, 1894, at p. 101. *Hector Boece* was the first principal of the new university and his book on the bishops of Aberdeen, including *Elphinstone*, was first published in Paris in 1522. See also for a comparison of *Elphinstone* with *Cusa*, *J. Durkan* and *J. Kirk*, The University of Glasgow 1451-1577, Glasgow, 1977, at p. 135.

7 *Eeles*, King's College Chapel, at p. 144 (*ceteris ipsis inibi pro tempore legentibus et studentibus*).

8 *Macfarlane* (n.2) 319.

9 *See Registratum Episcopatus Aberdonensis*, Spalding and Maitland Clubs, 1845, ii, pp. 129-34 for a catalogue of 1436 and Aberdeen University Library MS 249 for another of 1460. For comment see *Macfarlane* (n. 2) 322, 378, 381; *P. G. Stein*, The Character and Influence of the Roman Civil Law: Historical Essays, 1988, p. 305.

own library, which likewise consisted mainly of Canon law material (in particular the commentaries of *Nicholas de Tudeschis*), but also contained his father's lecture notes on civil law (taken at Louvain in the 1430s) and *Valla's* 'Elegantiae latinae linguae'[10].

Between 1495 and 1505 *Elphinstone* gathered the resources to permit the creation of buildings to house the University and endowments to pay for its teachers and students[11]. There was royal support, not only in the grant of revenues, but in the form of an act of parliament in 1496 (the so-called 'Education Act'), which required the eldest sons of barons and freeholders to study for three years at the 'sculis of art and jure' to gain knowledge of the laws[12]. The endowments included revenues to pay for what a royal charter of 22 May 1497 described as one teacher in the faculty of decreets (i.e. Canon law) and another in the faculty of imperial and civil law[13]. In September of the same year *Elphinstone* annexed certain revenues to pay a salary of 20 pounds Scots to a doctor of decreets if he could be had, being a priest and a reader and regent (that is, a teacher[14]) in that faculty; otherwise a licentiate or bachelor would receive a salary of 25 merks (i.e. £16.13.4d Scots). The same revenues were also to pay for a doctor or clerk as a reader and regent in civil law after the manner of the University of Orleans. He was to receive 20 pounds Scots or, if a licentiate, 25 merks; or if a bachelor, 20 merks[15]. The bachelor was one who had typically spent two or three years in his studies, while the licentiate had passed examinations and graduated. A licentiate could teach but would be paid less than one who had taken a doctorate, as shown by the evidence just cited. By 1497 *David Guthrie*, doctor of both laws[16] and professor of the laws of the Caesars and the pontificals[17], was expounding the pontifical law in the new University[18]. In 1499 *Elphinstone* united the vicarage of Old Aberdeen to the University and ordained that henceforth its vicars should be graduates, and at least bachelors in Canon law, and that they should read in that faculty in the University[19].

---

10 *L. J. Macfarlane*, William *Elphinstone*'s library, (1958) 37 Aberdeen University Review 253 sqq.; *idem* (n. 2) 18, 32-5, 37, 73-5, 378, 380-1; *idem*, William *Elphinstone*'s library revisited, in: A. A. MacDonald *et al.*, edd., The Renaissance in Scotland: Studies in Literature, Religion, History and Culture offered to John Durkan, Leiden, 1994.

11 *Macfarlane* (n. 2) 309-18.

12 Acts of the Parliaments of Scotland [A.P.S.], ii, 238 (c.3).

13 *Fasti Aberdonenses*: Selections from the Records of the University and King's College of Aberdeen, Spalding Club, Aberdeen, 1854, henceforth *Abdn Fasti*, pp. 11-14.

14 See *J. Verger*, Teachers, in: H. de Ridder-Symoens, ed., A History of the University in Europe, vol. 1, Universities in the Middle Ages, Cambridge, 1992, p. 145, for 'regents'.

15 *Abdn Fasti*, no. IX.

16 For *Guthrie* as *utriusque juris doctorem* see *Abdn Fasti*, pp. 19, 21, 22. It is not known where he obtained his doctorates.

17 This is how *Guthrie* is described in Moir (n. 6) 89.

18 Moir (n. 6) 90.

19 *Abdn Fasti*, no. XVI.

This began a long connection between the teaching of Canon law in the University and the church of St. Mary of the Snows (also known as the Snow Kirk), which was at the same time erected as the parish church of Old Aberdeen and stood just across the road and to the south of the marshy site upon which *Elphinstone's* new college was slowly being erected.

The construction of King's College (at first known as St. Mary's College) commenced about 1497, and occupation of the still uncompleted buildings probably began in 1505, when *Elphinstone* issued a foundation charter for the college[20]. The name King's College probably springs as much from the evident involvement of *James IV* in the foundation as from the decision to top off the campanile with a closed imperial crown, reflecting the Scottish crown's claim to "ful jurisdictioune and fre Impire" within the kingdom of the Scots[21]. The college was laid out in the quadrangular form still apparent today, with the chapel on the north side, teaching rooms and the great dining hall to the east, and residential accommodation on the south and west. The foundation charter also refers to the walls or enclosure (*septa*) and the gates of the college[22], which helped define its seclusion from the rest of the world and its affairs[23].

The evidence suggests that initially there were more students of Canon than of civil law[24]. In 1500 King *James IV* made representations to Pope *Alexander VI* that very few in his kingdom pursued their studies beyond the rudiments of literature or gave attention to the imperial or civil law. The king's supplication that ecclesiastics be allowed to read and study civil law in Old Aberdeen and obtain degrees therein was duly granted in a Bull published in October 1501[25]. In 1522 *Hector Boece*, the first principal, drew a picture of various lawyers associated with the early University: as well as *David Guthrie*, there were *Thomas Strachan* and *Alexander Vaux*, both deeply skilled in Canon law; *James Ogilvy*, professor of the laws of the Caesars; *Arthur Boece*, the principal's brother who was a doctor in pontifical law, a licentiate in civil law and 'our professor of law'; *Alexander Galloway*, who was erudite in Canon law; and *John Lindsay* and *Alexander Lawson*, who were to be counted amongst the finest *jurisperiti*[26].

The foundation charter of 1505 provides us with a fuller picture of the law faculties at King's, although obviously we should keep in mind that there is usually a wide difference between a formal constitution and what actually happens in any

20 *Macfarlane* (n. 2) 326-7.

21 *Macfarlane* (n. 2) p. 330; and see also *L. J. Macfarlane*, A Visitor's Guide to King's College, Aberdeen, 1992, pp. 9-10. The crown in place today is not the original, which fell in 1633. For the reference to 'ful jurisdictioune and fre Impire', see A.P.S., ii, 95 (c.6).

22 *Eeles* (n. 7) 166.

23 For verbal and visual representations of the college see *Macfarlane* (n. 21) *passim*.

24 *Macfarlane* (n. 2) 320-2.

25 *Abdn Fasti*, pp. 36-8 (nos XX and XXI).

26 Moir (n. 6) 89-92.

institution[27]. There was to be a doctor of Canon law and a doctor of civil law, or licentiates "if doctors cannot conveniently be found". That there was a problem in finding doctors to teach in the University is suggested not only by this phraseology in the foundation charter, but also by a 1506 Bull of Pope *Julius II* granting the power to confer degrees upon the bishop of Aberdeen, this being explicitly to meet a problem of the paucity of doctors in the new University and the great expense of bringing doctors in from other universities[28]. Appointment of the doctors of Canon and civil law was to be by the chancellor of the University, who was the bishop of Aberdeen. Each of these would receive a salary of 30 merks (20 pounds Scots), payable from the fruits of the churches of Aberluthnot, Glenmuik, Abergerny and Slains. Unlike most of the other masters and students of the college, neither the canonist nor the legist (*legista*) was to live or teach within its new buildings; each was to have a manse outwith the college. A contemporary source tells us, however, that the houses being built for the professors of Canon and civil law were still not complete at the time of *Elphinstone's* death in 1514[29], so it appears that the early teaching of law took place in the Cathedral precincts of the Chanonry. It seems certain, however, that the Snow Kirk and its grounds had been linked to the teaching of Canon law since the annexation of the church to the University in 1499, and that the foundation charter simply expected this existing situation to continue and develop. Certainly in 1513 *Master Henry Spittal*, licentiate in the laws, received his collation to the office of burse in Canon law together with the prebend of St. Mary of the Snows and the manse thereof, while in 1516 *Alexander Lawson*, bachelor in Canon law, was collated to the same burse, prebend and manse[30]. Whatever the position may have been, the canonist, the legist and their students were presumably relatively unaffected by the rules in the 1505 charter on college hours, under which the gates closed at 8 p.m. in winter and 10 p.m. in summer, reopening at 5 a.m. in winter and 4 a.m. in summer. But the prohibition on keeping public concubines, and the requirement of continuous study with no vacations throughout the entire year, can be taken to have applied to the lawyers as much as to the inhabitants of the college buildings. *Elphinstone's* charter prescribed the mode of teaching:

> "The ... doctors in Canon law [and] civil law ... ought to read in the said faculties on every lecturing day, in their own copes as is fitting, namely the canonist according to the form and custom of the sacred canons of the faculty and of the first regent of Canon law in the [mother] university of Paris, the legist according to the form of the statutes and praiseworthy customs of the university of Orleans (and he to have guardianship and to rule, to teach and instruct his scholars therein in the laws, and to be obliged every day in the same faculty to read the legal institutions of *Justinian*)".

27 See further *L. J. Macfarlane*, King's College Aberdeen: the Creation of its Academic Community, 1495-1532, (1995) 56 Aberdeen University Review 211.

28 *Abdn Fasti*, no. XLVIII.

29 Moir (n. 6) 96.

30 *Abdn Fasti*, nos. LVI (*Spittal*), LVIII (*Lawson*).

The doctors would have followed the characteristic mode of medieval university teaching, that is, dictating a text to the students and adding comments as they proceeded. Paris and Orleans were where *Elphinstone* himself had studied Canon and civil law respectively[31], and we may infer from the reference to these universities the content of the courses at King's. The canonist's texts would have been from the Decretals and other canonist authorities, while the civilist would certainly have included material from the Digest, the Code, the *Novellae* and the *Libri Feudorum* along with *Justinian's* Institutes[32]. The reading method ensured that the students produced their own copies of the core legal texts and their teachers' comments upon them, but none of these manuscripts are known to survive. The readings, or ordinary lectures, would have taken place in the mornings; afternoons were probably spent in 'extra-ordinary' lectures given by the bachelors, or in disputations and other exercises[33]. There is no way of telling how many students attended these classes; probably the number was always in single figures, although it should be kept in mind that most of those who attended would not have proceeded to any degree, at least in Old Aberdeen[34].

Teaching was presumably in Latin. It is noteworthy that the Education Act of 1496 required the obtaining of 'perfite Latyne' at the grammar schools before entry into the schools of art and jure to study the laws[35]. In 1514 *Elphinstone* was to ordain that all conversation amongst the inhabitants of the college was to be in Latin or French, and not in the vernacular[36]; it is difficult to believe that this could ever have been rigidly enforced, but it is also unlikely that a less formal atmosphere was expected to prevail in teaching than in conversation.

Some practical experience may have been available in the Official's court at the nearby cathedral. In 1514 *Elphinstone* was to prohibit theology students from appearing in any court, spiritual or secular, as procurators or advocates[37]. The law students are not mentioned, and it is probably legitimate to interpret the silence as signifying that they could and did act in court. When a student in Glasgow, *Elphin-*

---

31 *Macfarlane* (n. 2) 29-47.

32 See *Macfarlane* (n. 2) 39-40; *R. Feenstra*, L'organisation et enseignement du droit civil à Orleans au moyen age, Bulletin de la Société Archéologique et Historique de l'Orléanais, nouvelle serie II, 15, Orleans, 1962; *idem*, L'école de droit d'Orleans au treizieme siecle et son rayonnement dans l'Europe medievale, Revue d'Histoire des Facultés de Droit et de la Science Juridique (1992) 13.

33 On the style of teaching see *Macfarlane* (n. 2) 378-9; *Verger* (n. 14) 148-9, 154-9; also *R. C. Schwinges*, Student Education, Student Life, in: H. de Ridder Symoens (n. 14) 232-4.

34 In discussion with me Professor *Gero Dolezalek* has suggested that the law teaching in Old Aberdeen may often have been no more than an introduction to the subject before the student progressed to further study at a continental university. An example may be *Elphinstone's* own study of some Canon law at Glasgow before continuing his studies at Paris and Orleans (see further below).

35 A.P.S., ii, 238 (c.3).

36 *Eeles* (n. 7) 244.

37 *Eeles* (n. 7) 244.

stone himself acted as an advocate, taking the causes of the poor, most probably in the Official's court at Glasgow[38]. Over a century later, law students at St. Andrews were shown the practical application of their subject in the local consistory court[39], and it seems probable that similar practices prevailed from the beginning in Old Aberdeen.

Another important point arising from the 1505 charter's reference to Paris and Orleans as models for law teaching in the new university is that in 1219 Pope *Honorius III* had abolished civil law teaching in the former under his bull *Super speculam*. Formally this was on the basis that civil law was a secular concern only, and so should not be a matter for ecclesiastics; in fact it seems to have been the result of conflict between the papal and the Holy Roman Empire's claims to universal jurisdiction, with support for the papacy from the French king who sought to resist the authority of the civil law within his realm in favour of its own customary law[40]. The ban on civil law teaching was to remain in force at Paris until the 17th century. It did not extend, however, to Orleans, where teaching of Roman law was expressly authorized by Pope *Gregory IX* in 1235. While therefore Paris remained the leading university north of the Alps for Canon law, those of its students who wished also to study civil law commonly went to Orleans, *Elphinstone* himself being, as already noted, a prime example of this phenomenon[41]. Paris was thus an incomplete model for the study of law. The perception of civil law as a secular subject unfit for study by intending priests is an important one which undoubtedly lies behind the lack of students for the subject at Aberdeen and the petition of King *James IV* in 1500 referred to earlier, in which papal authority was sought to allow ecclesiastics to teach and study it; we shall return to this matter at a later stage in this paper.

In 1514 *Elphinstone* prepared a reconstitution of his College. For some reason, possibly connected with the bishop's death at the age of 83 on 25 October 1514, this reconstitution was not formally documented until a process which took place in St. Machar's Cathedral before *Elphinstone*'s second successor as bishop of Aberdeen, *Gavin Dunbar*, on 18 December 1529[42]. This retained the two doctors

---

38 Moir (n. 6) 61; *Macfarlane* (n. 2) 28.

39 R. Pitcairn, ed., The Autobiography and Diary of Mr. James Melvill, Minister of Kilrenny, in Fife, and Professor of Theology in the University of St Andrews, Wodrow Society, 1842, at pp. 28-9.

40 On the bull *Super speculam* see *W. Ullmann*, Honorius III and the Prohibition of Legal Studies, in: G. Garnett, ed., Law and Jurisdiction in the Middle Ages, London, 1988, no. XIII; and *S. Kuttner*, Papst Honorius III. und das Studium des Zivilrechts, in: Festschrift für Martin Wolff, Tübingen, 1952, reprinted in: Gratian and the Schools of Law 1140-1234, London, 1983, no. X.

41 On civil law at Orleans see in addition to the references (n. 32) above, *J. Kirkpatrick*, The Scottish Nation in the University of Orleans 1336-1538, in Miscellany II, Scottish History Society, Edinburgh, 1904, pp. 48, 53-4.

42 *Eeles* (n. 7) 196-265.

of Canon and civil law but gave the canonist a salary of 40 merks (subject to various deductions), which was to be derived from the fruits of the Snow Kirk. The canonist's manse or dwelling place was expressly stated to be in the grounds of the Snow Kirk, and here he was "to read in Canon law ... on every lecturing day in doctoral habit appropriate to him, like the first regent of the same faculty in the University of Paris". The civilist, as he was now known, was to have a salary of 20 pounds Scots, with a manse on the opposite side of the road from the Snow Kirk. He was to read civil law at his manse on every lecturing day, "like the regents of the University of Orleans, with similar doctoral habit appropriate to him". But the two doctors of the laws were now to be nominated by a group consisting of the rector, the procurators of the four student nations, the principal, the sub-principal, the civilist or the canonist as appropriate, the mediciner and the grammarian, while the role of the chancellor was reduced to the admission of the nominee to the post.

The most significant development in the 1514 reconstitution was the provision of endowments for two bachelors of civil law and one of Canon law[43]. The first bachelor of civil law was to hold a chaplaincy and chambers within the manse of the civilist, while the second was to be chaplain of St. Mary Magdalene within the church of St. Nicholas in Aberdeen. The bachelor of Canon law was to hold the chaplaincy attached to the Snow Kirk. The students' obligations were described as follows:

> "Of those students the duty will be to be present at the lectures on both laws and to attend to them, to read publicly the civil institutions in the manner of bachelors; the student endowed for Canon law and one of those for civil law shall, in addition, celebrate masses for their founders in our cathedral church and be present at divine worship in the college ... while the other student in civil law shall carry this out, as he will answer to God, in the parish church of St. Nicholas of Aberdeen, whereto he is bound and obliged by his foundation".

Further no regent or student in Canon or civil law was to go forth in public without a long pointed hood.

II. Law Teaching in King's College 1514 - ca. 1700

We know very little of the law faculties in Old Aberdeen between the death of *Elphinstone* in 1514 and the Scottish Reformation in 1560. We have the names of some holders of the posts of canonist and civilist, but little more[44]. *David Stevenson* has commented that "the law and medical faculties were characterised more

---

43 *Macfarlane* (n. 2) 340.

44 For not wholly reliable lists of the known canonists and civilists see P.J. Anderson, ed., Officers and Graduates of University and King's College Aberdeen 1495-1860, New Spalding Club, Aberdeen, 1893, pp. 29-34. See also *M. C. Meston*, The Civilists of Aberdeen 1495-1995, 1995 J. R. 153.

by suspended animation than by active life in the years before and after 1560. Teaching of these subjects was at best intermittent"[45]. The lectures on the sacrament of marriage by *William Hay* in 1533, which contain considerable discussion of the Canon law on the subject and have been published by the Stair Society, were delivered in the faculty of theology; *Hay*, who succeeded *Hector Boece* as principal, taught there and not in the faculties of law[46]. At the Reformation there was both a canonist and a civilist, while in 1564 *John Kennedy*, clerk of the diocese of Aberdeen, took up the civil law bursary together with the chaplaincy of St. Mary Magdalene, both of which were vacant after the death of *Hector Myrton*, last holder thereof[47]. In 1561, the First Book of Discipline, the initial programme for the reform of the church, provided that only municipal and Roman law should be taught in the universities of St. Andrews, Glasgow and Aberdeen, so excluding Canon law from the curriculum[48]; but this never took effect. In 1569 King's was purged and reformed as a Protestant institution. The canonist and civilist at this time (*Alexander Cheyne* and *Nicholas Hay* respectively) remained in office, however, *Cheyne* conforming to the new faith in 1573[49]. It is possible that by then the intention may have been that he should teach both laws[50], although *Hay* continued as at least the nominal civilist until his death in the 1590s. *Cheyne* died in 1587[51] and had no immediate successor, but a document of 1590 refers to "sindrie professoris of the lawis erectit of auld in the principal universities of sanctandrois and abirdene and suffecient stependis appoyntit to that effect"[52]. There was no provision for law teaching in the Melvillian New Foundation of the University which won parliamentary approval in 1597[53]; this saw the University's primary concern as the training of parish ministers, and there followed what has been described as an interregnum in the law faculties[54].

The Elphinstonian Old Foundation was restored in 1619 and brought with it revival of the posts of the canonist and the civilist. *Thomas Nicolson* was appointed civilist and *William Anderson* canonist. There was however little if any teaching by these gentlemen, despite recovery in 1624 of the previously alienated civilist's

45 *Stevenson* (n. 3) 48.

46 See J.C. Barry, ed., William Hay's Lectures on Marriage, Edinburgh, 1967.

47 *Abdn Fasti*, nos. XC, XCI.

48 J. K. Cameron, ed., The First Book of Discipline, Edinburgh, 1972, pp. 138, 140, 143-4.

49 See *Stevenson* (n. 3) 17-18.

50 *Stevenson* (n. 3) 28.

51 For the deaths of *Hay* and *Cheyne* see *Stevenson* (n. 3) 49.

52 See *W. C. Dickinson*, The Advocates' Protest against the Institution of a Chair of Law in the University of Edinburgh, (1926) 23 Scottish Historical Review 209; discussed in *J. W. Cairns*, The Law, the Advocates and the Universities in Late Sixteenth-century Scotland, (1994) 73 Scottish Historical Review 172, at pp. 174-5, 178.

53 For the parliamentary approval see A.P.S., iv, 153; and for the texts and a translation of the New Foundation by *G. Patrick Edwards* see *Stevenson* (n. 3) Appendix II.

54 *Meston* (n. 44) 157.

croft and canonist's manse[55]. By 1634 the canonist and dean of law was *James Sandilands*; the amount of teaching carried out by him is obscure but the civilist, an Edinburgh advocate called *Roger Mowat*, was certainly an absentee sinecurist[56]. *Sandilands* was succeeded as canonist by his son, also *James*, in 1634[57]; and *James* the younger was to become embroiled in an interesting controversy about his post with the General Assembly of the Kirk. In April 1639 he

> "wes dischargit as canonist [by a commission of the General Assembly], bot he maid appellatioun to the nixt generall assemblie, and craftellie be moyan got his place to teiche the cannon lawis be limitatioun, viz to teiche de matrimonio, testamentis and teyndis, because all the rest of these lawis smellit of poperie, as thay alledgit"[58].

The nature of the authority of the Canon law in a post-Reformation and protestant world was of course the subject of current juristic debate[59], and it is interesting to observe how *Sandilands*' successful defence of his position reflects something of the approach of *Thomas Craig* in his then still-unpublished 'Jus Feudale': "In Scotland, notwithstanding that we have thrown off the papal yoke, the authority of the Canon law endures: so much so, that where it differs from the civil law ... we follow the Canon law ... provided always that the rule of the Canon law is consistent with the principles of sound religion"[60]. It is also fair to say that marriage, wills and teinds were among the most important areas in which pre-Reformation Canon law did indeed continue as Scots law[61].

The younger *Sandilands* also managed to combine the offices of canonist and civilist[62], although they were separated again after his time. In this position *Sandilands* drew the contemporary comment that it was "strange to sie ane man admittit

---

55 *Stevenson* (n. 3) 67-70.

56 *Stevenson* (n. 3) 75, 103-4. It is however possible that an absentee professor who was also an advocate was of more use to the College in Edinburgh than he would have been teaching in Old Aberdeen, a point I owe to Dr. *John Cairns*.

57 *Stevenson* (n. 3) 83.

58 *John Spalding*, Memorialls of the Trubles in Scotland and in England 1624-1648 by John Spalding, 2 vols., Spalding Club, Aberdeen, 1850-51, vol. 1, p. 166, quoted by Anderson (n. 44) 30, and discussed in *Stevenson* (n. 3) 116. Note also the challenge to the superstitious Canon law at Aberdeen in 1638 discussed in *Stevenson* (n. 3) 114.

59 See, in particular, R.H. Helmholz, ed., Canon Law in Protestant Lands, Comparative Studies in Continental and Anglo-American Legal History, Berlin, 1992, and my review touching on Scottish aspects in ZSS (KA) 80 (1994). Note also the statute of 1567 seeking to abrogate all laws "canone civile and municipale" inconsistent with the true reformed religion (A.P.S., ii, 548 (c.2)).

60 *Thomas Craig*, Jus Feudale, I, iii, 24, transl. Lord Clyde. 'Jus Feudale' did of course have wide circulation in Scotland before its first publication in 1655. On the dates for the composition of 'Jus Feudale' (c.1598-1608) see *J. W. Cairns*, The breve testatum and Craig's Jus Feudale, T.R. 56 (1988) 317.

61 See *J. J. Robertson*, Canon Law as a Source, in: D. M. Walker, ed., Stair Tercentenary Studies, 1981, at pp. 116-22.

62 *Stevenson* (n. 3) 117.

to teiche lawis who was never out of the countrie studdeing and lerning the lawis"[63]. The significance and, indeed, irony of the remark arise from the fact that most Scots who obtained knowledge of Canon and civil law did so in European rather than Scottish universities, mainly in France but after *Sandilands*' time increasingly in the Netherlands[64]. There is evidence that *Sandilands* failed to attract students[65]. By 1664 the position of canonist was unoccupied, nor was there "any necessitie for that profession"[66]. *Robert Forbes*, who died in 1687, was the last canonist of Aberdeen[67], and thenceforth there would only be the civilist, together with the ruins of both the civilist's manse and the Snow Kirk[68], to serve after a fashion as rather sad and litigation-ridden relics of the Elphinstonian foundation until the revival of law teaching and scholarship at Aberdeen in the 19th century[69]. That was too late to save the canonist's manse at the site of the Snow Kirk; it was finally pulled down and replaced about 1860[70].

III. The Background to Law Teaching in Aberdeen

We may now turn to the contexts both Scottish and European in which must be set the narrative of events just given[71].

Elphinstone's foundation at Old Aberdeen was the third such episcopal venture in Scotland during the 15th century, universities having been established at St. Andrews by Bishop *Henry Wardlaw* in 1411 and at Glasgow by Bishop *William Turn-*

---

63 *Spalding* (n. 58) vol. 1, p. 241.

64 See *R. Feenstra*, Scottish-Dutch Legal Relations in the Seventeenth and Eighteenth Centuries, in: T. C. Smout, ed., Scotland and Europe 1200-1850, Edinburgh, 1986; also in an extended version in: H. de Ridder-Symoens, J.M. Fletcher, edd., Academic Relations between the Low Countries and the British Isles 1450-1700, Ghent, 1989; and see further *P. Nève*, Disputations of Scots Students Attending Universities in the Northern Netherlands, in: W. M. Gordon, T. D. Fergus, edd., Legal History in the Making, London and Rio Grande, 1991.

65 *Stevenson* (n. 3) 103-4.

66 *Abdn Fasti*, 320.

67 Anderson (n. 44) 30.

68 As shown in *James Gordon*'s well-known map of Old Aberdeen in c. 1660, for which see *Stevenson* (n. 3) p. 11, or J.S. Smith (n. 4) 8.

69 See *J. W. Cairns*, Lawyers, Law Professors, and Localities: the Universities of Aberdeen, 1680-1750, (1995) 46 Northern Ireland Legal Quarterly 304; *Meston* (n. 44) 158-65; *Lord Hope*, The Universities of Aberdeen and the Court of Session, 1995 J.R. 5; *S. D. Girvin*, Professor John Dove Wilson of Aberdeen, 1992 J.R. 60.

70 *R. S. Rait*, The Universities of Aberdeen: A History, Aberdeen, 1895, pp. 247-8.

71 For a valuable general discussion see *J. M. Fletcher*, The Foundation of King's College, Aberdeen in its European Context, in: P. Dukes, ed., The Universities of Aberdeen and Europe, Quincentennial Studies in the History of the University of Aberdeen, Aberdeen, 1995, pp. 9-56.

bull in 1451. All three fit into a European later medieval pattern of the proliferation of universities, mostly resulting from essentially local initiatives and serving local needs[72], but formally modelled on the University of Paris and so fully equipped with all four faculties – arts, theology, medicine and law[73]. The first question which might be asked is, what led to these initiatives in Scotland?

Since the 12th century Scots had travelled to Europe to undertake study in the universities of Italy and, more commonly, France, not to mention England. A very substantial number of these students studied law at some stage of their academic careers[74]. Professor *Watt* has written of the period 1340-1410 (i.e. that immediately preceding the foundation of St. Andrews)[75]:

> "The great majority of the 400 known graduates went to France where at least 230 studied at Paris, 55 at Orleans ... Between one-half and three-quarters of these 400 students are known to have obtained qualifications in only one faculty. In the some 230 cases where the faculty can be identified, it is perhaps surprising that Law (Civil and Canon) was studied by rather larger a number (120) than Arts (110), for it is not always appreciated that at this period Law was in many universities a basic undergraduate degree and not always a 'higher' subject. Besides this majority of relatively unambitious students, at least rather more than one-quarter of the total number added a second degree to a basic Arts qualification – some 80 are known to have studied Law also ... That a total of at least 200 should have a degree in Law is a striking feature of these figures ..."

Each of the founders of the three 15th-century universities exemplify this sort of course of study. Bishop *Wardlaw* of St. Andrews was an arts graduate of Paris who went on to study civil law at Orleans and Canon law at Avignon[76]. Bishop *Turnbull* of Glasgow, a protegé of *Wardlaw*, studied Canon law at St. Andrews initially, but moved on to Louvain before taking his doctorate in Canon law at Pavia[77]. *Elphinstone* studied Canon law at Paris and civil law at Orleans, as already noted, having previously studied arts and some Canon law at Glasgow. We may also note an interesting connection inasmuch as *Elphinstone* studied at *Turnbull's* foundation, he in turn having been a student in *Wardlaw's*. In the 15th century, there was a notable influx of Scots students at the new universities of Cologne (founded 1388) and Louvain (founded 1425). According to Professor *Lyall*, "the earliest Scots to arrive at Cologne [in 1419] were apparently drawn by its faculties of law ... Cologne had by 1419 acquired a large and distinguished array of legists, including several with

---

72 By contrast with the universalism of the ancient universities.

73 See *Verger*, Patterns, in: H. de Ridder-Symoens (n. 14) 55-9.

74 See the following works of *D. E. R. Watt*: University Graduates in Scottish Benefices before 1410, (1964) 15 Records of the Scottish Church History Society; A Biographical Dictionary of Scottish Graduates to A.D. 1410, Oxford, 1977; Scottish University Men of the Thirteenth and Fourteenth Centuries, in: T. C. Smout (n. 64).

75 Watt (n. 74) 'University Graduates', pp. 78-9.

76 Watt (n. 74) Dictionary, pp. 564-9.

77 See *R.J. Mitchell*, Scottish Law Students in Italy in the Later Middle Ages, 1937 J.R. 23, and *J. Durkan*, William Turnbull Bishop of Glasgow, Glasgow, 1951, at pp. 11-16.

experience in the great Italian law schools, Bologna, Padua and Pavia"[78]. In Louvain, Canon law was the most significant of the higher faculties for Scottish students[79].

The experiences of the various founders of the Scottish universities and their fellow-scholars may have had some part to play in their desire to establish new institutions in their homeland when the opportunities arose to do so[80]. Students were funded from benefices in Scotland, draining resources from the kingdom and its dioceses, and perhaps having some damaging effects on the cure of souls and the spiritual state of the individual parishes used in this way. Further, in at least some cases such revenues may perhaps have provided insufficient support to cover adequately the expenses of a foreign education. Although in the 14th century "it was uncommon for Scottish students to be poor"[81], the records show that at least in 15th-century Louvain many Scots were found among the *pauperes* requiring some form of assistance to continue their studies[82]. Here perhaps is part of the explanation for the desire to establish universities and law teaching in Scotland, which would reduce the expense to the individuals concerned, and ensure that the resources currently consumed in this way were re-deployed to the direct benefit of the kingdom and the Scottish church.

Bishops *Wardlaw*, *Turnbull* and *Elphinstone* were all lawyers by training, and it is evident that law teaching was seen as central in each of their foundations. There were four canonists amongst the founding teachers at St. Andrews, and the faculty of Canon law continued to be active up to the Reformation[83]. A faculty of civil law was also authorized in the foundation bull of St. Andrews but there is less evidence of its activity. In 1432 Pope *Eugenius IV* responded to a petition of the rector, masters, doctors and scholars of the university by granting a dispensation enabling ecclesiastics to study and gain degrees in civil as well as Canon law[84]. This

78 *R. J. Lyall*, Scottish Students and Masters at the Universities of Cologne and Louvain in the Fifteenth Century, (1985) 36 Innes Review 55-6.

79 *Lyall* (n. 78) p. 65. For a list see *J. H. Baxter*, Scottish Students at Louvain University 1425-1484, (1928) 25 Scottish Historical Review 327-34.

80 See for a general picture *Schwinges* (n. 33) especially pp. 206-11 and 240-1 on the resources available and the ways in which finance was obtained.

81 *D. E. R. Watt*, Scottish Student Life Abroad in the Fourteenth Century, (1980) 59 Scottish Historical Review 19; and pp. 17-21 for discussion of student finances, noting the possibility of cash-flow problems.

82 *Lyall* (n. 78) 67. Dr. *Leslie Macfarlane* advises me that this was also true of 15th-century Paris.

83 See *A. I. Dunlop*, Acta Facultatis Artium Universitatis Sanctandree 1413-1588, 2 vols., Edinburgh, 1964, vol. 1, Introduction, pp. cxlix-lvii, and *R. G. Cant*, The University of St. Andrews: A Short History, 3rd ed., St. Andrews, 1992, pp. 13, 193-5.

84 A. I. Dunlop, I.B. Cowan, edd., Calendar of Scottish Supplications to Rome 1428-1432, Scottish History Society, 4th series, vol 7, Edinburgh, 1970, at pp. 210-11. In a lecture delivered to the Stair Society in November 1995 Dr. *John Durkan* suggested that the petition may have been a response to a royal attempt to establish a school of civil law at Perth.

both reflects the uncertain suitability of civil law as a subject of study for ecclesiastics and anticipates the similar dispensation which Pope *Alexander VI* would grant to King's College in 1500; it is likewise suggestive of a failure to attract students for civil law at St. Andrews. It has been argued convincingly that Bishop *Turnbull* had "an ambitious project for a school of law at Glasgow"[85]. But although "in canon law there were some signs of vigour"[86], civil law struggled. Master *William Lennox* began to "read the rubric of the civil law" in the chapter house of the Blackfriars on 29 July 1451[87]. But "a succession of possible teachers of civil law can be established only as far as 1472 ... [T]he teaching in civil law languished utterly after the death of Bishop Andrew de Durisdeer [in 1473]"[88].

The overall pattern thus appears to be, first, that promotion of legal study along with a reduction in its cost was an important reason for the foundation of the three Scottish universities of the 15th century. Second, neither in the laws nor any other faculty did the three foundations staunch the overseas flow of students and church and other revenues. Third, in all three institutions the teaching of Canon law met with some limited success while civil law experienced considerable difficulties.

The importance and relative success of Canon law is easy to understand. Students of the subject had a variety of careers open to them[89]. The Church itself provided many outlets for those with a legal training. *Watt* comments[90]:

> "On the legal side most dioceses are known to have had an official in charge of a court operating in the bishop's name from the early thirteenth century onwards, and often it was a Doctor or licentiate of Canon Law who was appointed, or at least a Bachelor ... The existence of church courts at deanery, archdeaconry, diocese and provincial council levels (not to mention the Roman court) gave university men with law degrees opportunities for professional practice as lawyers. Again it is from the early thirteenth century that we find some retained by monasteries or cathedral chapters, or by individuals, to act as their proctors in the church courts. Some also practised as notaries, offering services which today we associate with solicitors as general men of business".

The career of *Elphinstone* himself is illustrative: studies at Glasgow, Paris and Orleans were followed by appointments as Official, first of the diocese of Glasgow from 1471, and then second, of Lothian from 1478-1483[91]. This provided part of

---

85 *Durkan* and *Kirk* (n. 6) 13-15.

86 *Durkan* and *Kirk* (n. 6) 131.

87 *Durkan* and *Kirk* (n. 6) 13-14, 127.

88 *Durkan* and *Kirk* (n. 6) 131; see also *Macfarlane* (n. 2) 26-7.

89 See generally on graduate careers *P. Moraw*, Careers of Graduates, in: H. de Ridder-Symoens (n. 14) 244.

90 *Watt* (n. 74) 'University Men', pp. 8-9. See also *G. Donaldson*, Scottish Church History, Edinburgh, 1985, pp. 40-45; *S. D. Ollivant*, The Court of the Official in Scotland, Edinburgh, 1982; and *P. C. Ferguson*, Medieval Papal Representatives in Scotland: Legates, Nuncios and Judges-delegate, 1125-1286, Columbia Ph.D., 1987, at pp. 144-286.

91 *Macfarlane* (n. 2) 53-79.

the platform from which he was in due course promoted to the ranks of the episcopacy. As this example and many others show, the study and practice of ecclesiastical law led to ecclesiastical preferment.

What of civil law? It was of course tainted by the imperial and secular associations which it had held in the eyes of the church even before the abolition of its study at Paris in 1219. The condemnation of civil law endured throughout the Middle Ages. In 1254 Pope *Innocent IV* issued the bull *Dolentes* which prohibited the teaching of the imperial law in those lands where the affairs of the laity were governed by lay customs and those of the church by the canons of the holy fathers. Amongst the countries expressly named in the bull was Scotland[92]. The prohibition surely provides the context for what has been rightly described as the cautionary story of *Adam Urry*, clerk of Glasgow diocese. We know no more of him than that he was educated (*litteratus*) in the lay laws, ignoring God's command against the *praetorialia* of *Ulpian*, but repented of his unclerical devotion to statutes and pleading in court for money before his death in 1288[93]. Again, in 1317 Pope *John XXII* was greatly concerned by the practice of regents of law neglecting their lectures to practise in the courts[94], while in his 1514 foundation of King's College *Elphinstone* sternly prohibited bursars in theology from studying laws or practising therein or holding the office of procurator or advocate in any court, spiritual or secular[95]. The recent observation that "canon law faculties usually had more students than civil law faculties"[96] is of a fact which probably reflects the continuing force of the prohibition as well as the better career prospects for canonists. Professor *Watt's* statistics, quoted earlier, show many fewer Scots students at civilian Orleans than at canonist Paris[97], although it would need a far more detailed analysis to show how many of the Paris students actually studied Canon law there as opposed to arts or theology.

The influence of the prohibition is also evident in the petitions made on behalf of St. Andrews and Aberdeen in the 15th century to enable ecclesiastics to study and teach civil law[98]; yet these documents also reveal some of the paradoxes lying

---

92 The text of the bull is to be found in *Matthew Paris*, Chronica Majora, H. R. Luard, ed., Rolls Series, London, 1872-83, vol. 6, p. 295. Its authenticity, which has been disputed, seems to be accepted by modern commentators: see *Ullmann* (n. 40) 183, n. 22, and *Kuttner* (n. 40) 84

93 Chronicon de Lanercost, Bannatyne Club and Maitland Club, Edinburgh, 1839, at p. 124, discussed in *Stein* (n. 9) 292-3, and *W.M. Gordon*, Roman Law in Scotland, in: R. Evans-Jones, ed., The Civil Law Tradition in Scotland, Edinburgh, 1995, p. 16. It seems right to correct the *praecorialia* of the Bannatyne edition as suggested in the text, since *Ulpian's* most significant work was his *Ad edictum praetoris urbani* and he was himself praetorian prefect. Ulpianic texts make up over a third of the Digest. It may add further to the point of the tale that *Ulpian* saw jurists like himself as the priests of the law (D. 1, 1, 1, 1).

94 *Verger* (n. 14) 156.

95 *Eeles* (n. 5) 244-5.

96 *A. Garcia y Garcia*, The Faculties of Law, in: H. de Ridder-Symoens (n. 14) 401.

97 See above, text to n. 75.

at the heart of official attitudes to civil law. Canon law was unthinkable without civil law: ***legista sine canonibus parum valet, canonista sine legibus nihil*** (a legist without the canons is worth very little, a canonist without the civil laws nothing)[99]. Canon law specifically embodied civil law, and teaching of the one required reference to the other[100]. Successive popes were prepared to license ecclesiastical study of the civil law at Orleans and elsewhere, and it is evident that large numbers of students, including *William Elphinstone*, took full advantage of these permissions.

The St. Andrews petition to Pope *Eugenius IV* spoke of the ill effects of the inability to teach civil law: there were few experts (*jurisperiti*) in civil law by whom justice could be administered in civil matters and so sometimes miserable persons were oppressed contrary to justice, various scandals arose and the state of the realm was injured in many ways. If a faculty of civil law were to flourish the kingdom would abound in *jurisperiti* by whom justice would be administered and the state well ruled[101]. It was King *James IV* who petitioned for the teaching of civil law at Aberdeen in 1500, suggesting that royal policy saw utility in the availability of civilians[102]. The language of the 1432 petition is also recalled by the emphasis which King *James II* laid on the benefits which would flow to the people at large when he confirmed the erection of a *studium generale* in Glasgow in 1451: the people would be ruled by the rod of equity and justice, contentious complaints would be determined, and to each would be rendered what he was due[103]. In all this the king must have had law and legal practice firmly in view. Again, the 'Education Act' of 1496 required all barons and freeholders to send their eldest sons to "the sculis of art and jure sua that thai may have knawlege and understanding of the lawis throw the quhilkis justice may reigne universalie throw all the realme sua that thai that ar schireffis or jugeis ordinaris under the kingis hienes may have knawlage to do justice"[104]. The reference to 'lawis' in the Act probably means the civil laws (*leges*) and may also include the Canon law. What is clear is the relevance and utility which the laws taught at the schools of art and jure were seen to have not only in the ecclesiastical but also the secular courts; and it is probably legitimate to read this into the references in the other sources of the period to the utility of civil law in the administration of justice. It was the legal system as a

98 See above text to nn. 25, 84.

99 Decretum, C. 7, D. 10.

100 See *H. Rashdall*, The Universities of Europe in the Middle Ages, F. M. Powicke, A. B. Emden, eds., Oxford, 1936, p. 322, n. 3, for teaching of civil law in Paris; also generally *R. C. van Caenegem*, An Historical Introduction to Private Law, 1992, at pp. 58-67; *J. Brundage*, Medieval Canon Law, London, 1995, at pp. 96-7.

101 Calendar of Scottish Supplications to Rome 1428-1432, at pp. 210-11.

102 A point reinforced by the suggestion of Dr. *Durkan*, made in the lecture to the Stair Society in November 1995 referred to (n. 84) above, that there was a royal attempt to establish a school of civil law at Perth in the 1420s.

103 *Munimenta Alme Universitatis Glasguensis*, Maitland Club, 1854, vol. 1, no. 2 (p. 6).

104 A.P.S., ii, 238, c.3. For some efforts in St. Andrews to give effect to the act see *Dunlop* (n. 83) pp. xxxix-xl.

whole which would benefit from the availability of *jurisperiti* trained in civil law at the Scottish universities.

IV. The Civil Law Tradition in Medieval Scotland

The penetration of the medieval Scottish secular legal system by the civil law has been well demonstrated by a number of scholars[105]. Pleaders, conveyancers, the draftsmen of legislation and other royal advisers all drew on the language and substance of the civil law. Men who had studied the civil law sat as judges in the king's council, and followed a procedure which clearly drew on that masterpiece of applied medieval logic, the Romano-canonical model[106]. The feudal law which had been incorporated into the *Corpus iuris civilis* was deployed in the sheriff and baron courts[107]. At least one 14th-century landowner possessed *libri civiles*, which may have been books of the civil law[108]. The writings of the Scots common law were romanized by shaping them into four books on the model of *Justinian's* Institutes[109], while *David I*, the twelfth-century king who figured in Scottish legal tradition as the founder of the law, became a Justinianic figure[110] whose career embodied all the virtues of law: "Quha lykis to lyve honestly / And to greve na man wrangusly / And to gyve ilkane, that thairis suld be, / This kyngis lyffe he rede and se," wrote the chronicler, *Andrew Wyntoun*, around 1420, clearly drawing on the precepts of the law stated at the outset of the Digest and Institutes[111]. The example of *Justinian* may even lurk behind the several 15th-century projects for the gathering together of the laws in a single authoritative volume for clarification and amendment where necessary[112].

So far as I am aware, Scottish medieval sources do not yield up any explicit statement of theory as to the place of civil or, indeed, Canon law in the secular courts. There were certainly areas of law where the Canon law and the church courts were recognized as having a competence which excluded secular jurisdiction and rules[113]. The 15th century saw legislative attempts to deny effect to 'the

---

105 *Stein* (n. 9) 269-333; *H. L. MacQueen*, Common Law and Feudal Society in Medieval Scotland, Edinburgh, 1993, at pp. 53, 77-9; *Gordon* (n. 93) 15-23.

106 For discussion see *H. L. MacQueen*, Pleadable Brieves, Pleading and the Development of Scots Law, (1986) 4 Law and History Review 403; and for an example of reference to civilian and canonist sources in debate before the king's council in 1503, see *A. B. Calderwood*, Acts of the Lords of Council 1501-1503, Edinburgh, 1993, p. 310.

107 *MacQueen* (n. 105) 53.

108 *Registrum Honoris de Morton*, Bannatyne Club, 1853, vol. 2, nos. 193 and 196.

109 *MacQueen* (n. 105) 93.

110 *MacQueen* (n. 105) 87-8.

111 Chron Wyntoun (Laing), vol. 2, 192; Institutes, I, 1; D. 1, 1, 10.

112 For these see *MacQueen* (n. 105) 91.

113 The subject needs further study, but see meantime *Donaldson* (n. 90) 40-1, and *Ollivant* (n. 90) 133-8.

lawis of other countreis [and] realmis' and to assert the exclusive authority of the king's common laws and statutes[114]. If this can be linked to the royal claims of 'ful jurisdictioune and fre impire' mentioned earlier, then these statutes may well have been attempts, at least in part, to restrict the use of the civil law, with its associations with imperial power in Europe. But such an interpretation seems inconsistent with all the contemporaneous efforts to establish civil law teaching at St. Andrews, Glasgow and Aberdeen for the benefit of the kingdom and its people. Yet the inconsistency may be more apparent than real. Sometime in the 1460s *David Reid*, a layman not known to have graduated from any university, was pleading before the justiciary court on behalf of Robert Lord Fleming. His pleadings drew on what he called 'the law of Scotland' and 'the law canon or civile', and included a specific reference to the Codex of *Justinian*[115]. If this means that the Canon and civil law were distinct from the law of Scotland, nonetheless the law of Scotland was not necessarily complete or the only possible resource for the lawyer. Reference to such external sources might be justified despite the statutory restrictions to the king's laws, for there might be matters on which his statutes and common law had nothing to say. Parliament spoke in 1473 of "the daily materis ... that as yit thare is na law for the decisioune of thame"[116]. Almost unavoidable in such circumstances, it is suggested, was the doctrine of the Commentators: that of the civil law as a subsidiary source to which, because it had force as the embodiment of natural law and reason, recourse might be had when native sources were silent[117]. This certainly became the clear doctrine in the next century in Scotland, as stated by writers such as *Sir John Skene* and *Thomas Craig*[118]. The extent to which civil law was actually used as the result of such doctrine was, of course, not necessarily the same at all times and in all places; by the end of the 16th century, it had plainly become one of the dominant characteristics of the Scottish legal system, whereas in the earlier period it is simply a feature of what is still essentially a customary system.

How far were the Scottish universities, and in particular King's College, Aberdeen, active agencies in this gradual transformation of medieval Scots law into the Romanist system which so worried English lawyers at the time of the Union of the Crowns in 1603[119]? Tactful though it might be on this occasion to suggest other-

114 A.P.S., ii, 9 (c.3) and 252 (c.24).

115 National Library of Scotland, Fleming of Wigtown papers, Ch. 16, 632.

116 A.P.S., ii, 105, c. 14.

117 See *O. F. Robinson, T. D. Fergus* and *W. M. Gordon*, European Legal History, 2nd ed., London, 1994, pp. 68-9; *van Caenegem* (n. 100) 53.

118 *J. W. Cairns, T. D. Fergus* and *H. L. MacQueen*, Legal Humanism and the History of Scots Law: John Skene and Thomas Craig, in: J. MacQueen, ed., Humanism in Renaissance Scotland, Edinburgh, 1990, pp. 60-6; see also *A.L. Murray*, Sinclair's Practicks, in: A. Harding, ed., Law-Making and Law-Makers in British History, London, 1980, pp. 101-3.

119 See *B. P. Levack*, The Formation of the British State: England, Scotland, and the Union 1603-1707, Oxford, 1987, at pp. 88-91.

wise, it cannot really be said on the evidence surveyed in this paper that the teaching of the Canon and civil laws at St. Andrews, Glasgow and Old Aberdeen was an important factor, or indeed played any role in the Reception in Scotland, even though it was an Aberdonian canonist of the 1550s, *John Lesley* bishop of Ross, who ca. 1570 first expressly stated the doctrine that Roman law was cited in matters where native law was wanting[120]. The teaching of the laws in Scotland touched only a few, and was probably intermittent and undistinguished at best where it did not fail altogether[121]. The keys to understanding an intensifying Romanism probably lie rather in the widening jurisdiction and increasing business of the Lords of Council and Session in Edinburgh; the rise of a professional bar pleading before the Lords, the members of which were educated not in Scottish but in European (mainly French) law faculties and in both laws[122]; and the destruction of papal jurisdiction (although not of the authority of the Canon law) following the Reformation[123]. But before we dismiss the Scottish faculties out of hand as irrelevant to general legal development in the later medieval and early modern periods, we should bear in mind the extent to which the ambitions of *Wardlaw*, *Turnbull* and *Elphinstone* may have been frustrated by a kind of vicious circle for the Scottish universities. A difficulty was always likely to be the attraction to Scotland of law teachers of a calibre equivalent to that to be found at the European universities. The best students would seek the best professors, and were unlikely to return to teach in Scotland if posts could be obtained at their continental universities, or more lucrative and influential careers pursued in ecclesiastical and royal government. There were resource problems, human as well as financial, of a type all too recognizable and familiar in the Britain of the late 20th century. The medieval law faculties were brave and ambitious projects for their time, and the courage underlying the attempts deserves recognition and salute today. Not until the 18th century would the vision of active, continuous and successful law teaching in Scotland become a reality. In a sense the comparative failure of the later medieval and early modern law faculties is necessary background to a proper understanding of the nature and scale of the later achievement. In considering the Civil Law Tradition and its influence in Scotland, it is very meet, right and the bounden duty of Scots lawyers to do so standing once again in King's College, the foundation of and magnificent monument to Bishop *William Elphinstone* and his vision.

---

120 *John Lesley*, History of Scotland from ... the Year 1436 to the Year 1561, vol. 1, at p. 120. For *Lesley* as the canonist in the 1550s see Anderson (n. 44) 29.

121 An exception to this generalization may be provided by St. Andrews in the later 16th century, when *William Skene* and *William Welwood* were the professors of the laws: see *Cairns* (n. 52) 178-85, and *idem*, Academic Feud, Bloodfeud, and William Welwood: Legal Education in St. Andrews, 1560-1611, forthcoming.

122 See *J. Durkan*, The French Connection in the Sixteenth and Early Seventeenth Centuries, in: T. C. Smout (n. 64) 25-7.

123 Note too the Protestant reference in 1558 to the 'godly approved laws of Justinian the Emperor'; *John Knox*, in: W. C. Dickinson, ed., History of the Reformation in Scotland, Edinburgh, 1949, vol. 1, p. 151.

Looking Back: The Influence of Roman Law and Roman Legal Thinking in Europe

The Medieval Rediscovery of the Roman Civil Law

By Peter G. Stein

I. Introduction

When we talk about the rediscovery of the Roman civil law, we should first remind ourselves of what was rediscovered.

The study of the civil law in western Europe since the 12th century has been essentially the study of the texts of a collection of material, made at the orders of the Byzantine Emperor *Justinian* in the 6th century, which came to be known as the *Corpus iuris civilis*[1]. It has three main components. The largest is the Digest, or Pandects, an anthology of extracts from the writings of jurists from the 'classical period' of Roman law, which ended in the second quarter of the 3rd century. It is larger than the Bible and *Justinian* plausibly claims that it represents about one-twentieth of the whole body of juristic writing with which its compilers were faced. It is divided into fifty books, and most books are sub-divided into titles, each title being devoted to a particular topic. The extracts collected within each title, sometimes eighty or more, are arranged in no obvious order.

The next largest component of the *Corpus iuris* is the Code, a collection of imperial constitutions, i.e., legislation in the name of the emperors. These were typically not the enactment of general rules, but rather rescripts, or answers to questions put to the emperor on the legal issue raised by a specific set of facts, each answer being drafted by jurists in the imperial civil service. The Code is in twelve books, with subdivision into titles, and the constitutions are arranged within each title in chronological order. The third part of the *Corpus*, in only four books, arranged in titles, is the Institutes, a student's textbook, intended to provide an introduction to the study of the law, but curiously given by *Justinian* the same legislative authority as the Digest and Code. *Justinian* continued to legislate after the completion of his compilation and a much abridged collection of some of these so-called novels (*novellae constitutiones*), known as the *Epitome Juliani*, was made in *Justinian*'s reign and intended for use in Italy.

1 For details, see *H. F. Jolowicz* and *B. Nicholas*, Historical Introduction to the Study of Roman law, 3rd ed., Cambridge, 1972, at pp. 478 sqq.

II. Roman Law in the Early Middle Ages

For over five hundred years after its publication *Justinian*'s compilation was hardly studied at all anywhere. Being written almost entirely in Latin, it was unintelligible to most lawyers in the Greek-speaking Eastern Empire, although around 900 A.D. a Greek version of the whole work, known as the *Basilica*, was published for use there. Very few manuscripts of the original reached Western Europe and those that did were generally beyond the capacity of such lawyers as there were to comprehend, because of the complexity of the contents. This was particularly true of the Digest, whose vast bulk and lack of systematic arrangement made it just too difficult to use.

During the early Middle Ages, as a result of the Byzantine connection with Southern Italy, some manuscripts of the Institutes and of the first nine books of the Code (the last three dealt with Byzantine administrative law and were separated from the rest) were known in Italy. In most of what had been the Western Empire, however, familiarity with Roman law was based neither on the original classical law nor on the law of *Justinian* but on the so-called vulgar law of the 4th and 5th centuries. The barbarian successor states to the Western Empire followed the personal principle in law and made no attempt to impose their own laws on their Romanized subjects. Instead the Visigothic and Burgundian kings, at the beginning of the 6th century, i.e., before *Justinian*, ordered collections of the existing Roman law to be made for them[2], and it was these pre-*Justinian* compilations which were the main source of knowledge of Roman law in the West in the subsequent centuries. The Visigothic Roman law figures prominently in 9th century Carolingian manuscripts. Even the existence of *Justinian*'s compilation seems to have been unknown in the west. In his encyclopedic *Etymologiae*, written in the 620s, *St. Isidore of Seville* mentions *Justinian*'s religious activities but fails to list him among the great legislators in Book V.

Interest in the Institutes and Code was shown mainly by churchmen, who used Roman materials to weld together the disparate materials, from church councils, patristic writing and papal legislation, into an embryonic canon law. The Germanic laws recognized that the personal law of the Church, as an institution, was the Roman law. In the words of the law of the Ripuarian Franks (61 (58) 1), "the Church lives by the Roman law"[3]. Notaries (*tabelliones*) continued to prepare legal documents, according to precedents contained in Latin formularies, with a Roman flavour, which they did not necessarily comprehend. Furthermore a few Roman legal texts were familiar as examples cited in the courses on rhetoric in the monastic and cathedral schools[4].

---

2 *Jolowicz* and *Nicholas* (n. 1) 466 sqq.

3 *T. J. Rivers*, Laws of the Salian and Ripuarian Franks, New York, 1966, p. 195.

4 *J. F. Winkler*, Roman Law in Anglo-Saxon England, (1992) 13 J.L.H. 101.

Justinian's law did not become generally known in the West until the end of the 11th century. There is some evidence of a school of Roman law at Ravenna, which had earlier been the seat of the Byzantine exarch, and of another school at Pavia, the former capital of the Lombard kingdom of Italy[5]. In the latter the exponents of Lombard law divided themselves into two groups in their attitude to Roman law. The *antiqui* concentrated their studies on Lombard law, which was contained in a collection of edicts and capitularies known as the *Liber Papiensis*, and drew contrasts between Lombard law and Roman law. The *moderni*, on the other hand, were characterized by their readiness to refer to Roman law as general subsidiary law to supplement and interpret Lombard law. Their work culminated about 1070 in the *Expositio* to the *Liber Papiensis*, which tries to reconcile Lombard law with Roman law. The *Expositio* refers to the Roman law sources which had been known for some time, Institutes, Code and *Epitome Juliani*, but it also contains nine extracts from the Digest.

There is no doubt that the standard of legal practice at Pavia was high. The aim of the law school was to maintain that standard, and ensure that Lombard judges should gain a sense of the science of law. The Lombard laws were written in Latin and when a dispute arose as to the precise meaning of a technical legal term, it was natural to turn for help to the main respository of authoritative legal discussion in Latin. Yet essentially the school of Pavia was a professional training school for lawyers intending to practise in the Lombard courts. Its primary interest was in Lombard law, and it is not inconsistent with that priority that the *moderni* wanted to establish that Lombard law could hold its own with Roman law. It is, however, an exaggeration to press the claim, which has recently been made[6], that it is to Pavia, rather than Bologna, that we must look for the origins of the scientific study of the Roman civil law.

III. The Recovery of the Digest

1. The Discovery of the Digest

Any study of Roman law is incomplete if it does not include the Digest. As *F.W. Maitland* vividly expressed it in a recently discovered letter to the historian of universities, *Hastings Rashdall*:

> "The Digest was the *only* book in which medieval students could obtain a knowledge of Roman law *at its best*. The Institutes are a slight text book. The Code is made up of detached ordinances. The Novels are not merely detached ordinances but are penned in a pompous, verbose style, likely to do as much harm as good ... but for the Digest Roman law could never have conquered the world. It was only in the Digest that the Geist

---

5 *F. Calasso*, Medio Evo del Diritto I, Milano, 1954, at pp. 281 sq. and 305 sqq.

6 *C. Radding*, The Origins of Medieval Jurisprudence, Pavia and Bologna 850-1150, New Haven, 1988; cf. the review by *A. Gouron*, T.R. 57 (1989) 178.

> des römischen Rechts could be found. Men would never have become *enthusiastic* students of other books ... the man who first teaches the Digest is the man who first teaches what the modern world has meant by Roman law ... it was only in the Digest that men could get any notion of keen and exact legal argument, precise definition etc."[7].

The impetus for the quite sudden revival of civil law studies, at the beginning of the 12th century, was the re-discovery of the complete text of the Digest. The main textual source was, and still is, a 6th century manuscript, then held at Pisa and taken in 1406 to Florence, where it is the jewel of the collection in the Laurentian Library. It has always been kept difficult of access. The text used in the 12th century schools at Bologna was the *vulgata* or *litera bononiensis*, which was derived from the 'Florentine', not directly but through a lost archetype, known today as *Secundus*, which was copied in the late 11th century.

The Digest came to the notice of scholars in the last quarter of the 11th century. As we have noted, the masters of Pavia made a few references to the Digest in their *Expositio* around 1070. An Italian collection of canon law dating from about 1080, and known confusingly as the *Collectio Britannica* since there is but a single manuscript and that in the British Library, has ninety-three extracts from the Digest. Where these texts were found is not clear but the manuscripts may have been in archives in Rome or in the great Benedictine monastery of Monte Cassino.

The texts of the Digest did not all become generally available at the same time. The *litera bononiensis* of the Digest was divided into three parts, known as *Digestum Vetus*, *Infortiatum* and *Novum*. The origin of this division is unclear, but it seems to reflect the order in which the parts were discovered and certainly *Vetus* was known before the other two parts. In the middle of the 12th century the last three books of the Code (the *Tres Libri*) were discovered and also a much better Latin version of the Novels (many of which were originally in Greek) than the *Epitome Juliani*. This was known as the *Authenticum* and was grouped in nine *Collationes* in imitation of the Code.

The whole *Corpus iuris* was now complete in five volumes, i.e., the three volumes of the Digest, the nine books of the (traditional) Code and finally the *Volumen Parvum*, a compendium consisting of the Institutes, the *Tres Libri*, the *Authenticum* and various other pieces that it was hoped to pass off as imperial legislation. These included constitutions of 12th century emperors and the *Libri Feudorum*, a collection of rules on feudal law, compiled by a Milanese judge early in the 12th century, and now presented as a tenth *Collatio*. The *Libri* were important in practice. The Glossators were occasionally consulted about actual cases and could not ignore feudal law; in particular, they did not want its exposition to be cornered by their rivals, the Canonists.

---

7 P. N. R. Zutshi, ed., The Letters of Frederic William Maitland, vol. II, Selden Society, 1995, p. 37.

2. *The Teaching of the Digest*

The first known named teacher of Roman law at Bologna was a shadowy figure called *Pepo*, who was a *causidicus*, or consultant judge[8]. He cited a Digest text in a case in 1076, but his teaching appears to have been confined to the Code and the Institutes. The master who is credited with the first systematic study of the Digest is *Irnerius*, a teacher of the liberal arts at Bologna[9]. His main technique was the gloss, or short explanation between the lines or in the margin of the text. Glosses had already been used by the masters at Pavia but they now became identified with the method of studying the texts of *Justinian* at Bologna. The school founded there by *Irnerius*, and known as the Glossators, invested the new-found texts with the authority of Holy Scripture, and had an appropriately grand vision of the all-embracing scope of the material contained in the texts and of their own function as its expositors. Jurists, as the opening text of the Digest text says, are the priests of the law, but when the 13th century Glossator *Accursius* asked himself: "Should a jurist then study theology?" his answer was "no, for everything is found in the *Corpus Iuris*" (*omnia in corpore iuris inveniuntur*, gl. *notitia* ad D. 1, 1, 1, 1).

The law contained in these texts was not actually the law applied in any court in any country at the time. In this respect civil law was in marked contrast with canon law, which was applied in the ecclesiastical courts in all countries. In the early 12th century, however, there was no authoritative collection of the texts of canon law. Various informal collections were in circulation, offering a heterogeneous body of decisions of church councils, opinions of church fathers, papal decretals and bits of Scripture and civil law, but what was law and what was opinion was unclear, and there were many opportunities for argument about whether an alleged rule really was part of canon law or not. The subject can be said to have become a discipline only after the publication of *Gratian*'s *Decretum* about 1140.

By contrast, it was accepted by all that the civil law was a discipline, based on a body of recognized texts, comparable to the study of the Bible. True, no one could argue that he needed civil law to practise it. Rather it came to be seen that wherever one wanted to practise, and whatever the actual system of law in force there, one was a better and more effective lawyer for having studied the texts of *Justinian*. New problems, arising out of the rise of commerce and urban life generally, and the administrative needs of both secular princes and ecclesiastical rulers, were demanding lawyers' attention, and the various regional customary laws provided no answers to the unprecedented questions they raised. *Justinian*'s law did not al-

---

8 *B. Paradisi*, Il giudizio di Martiri: alle origini del pensiero giuridico bolognese, in: Rendiconti dell'Accademia dei Lincei (Scienze Morali), Series 9, vol. 5, 1994.

9 For what follows, *S. Kuttner*, The Revival of Jurisprudence, in: R.L. Benson and G. Constable, edd., Renaissance and Renewal in the Twelfth Century, Oxford, 1982, p. 301; *P. Stein*, Introduction to: The Teaching of Roman Law in England around 1200, Selden Society, 1990; *E. Cortese*, Il rinascimento giuridico medievale, Roma, 1992.

ways provide direct answers to these questions; but they provided sophisticated legal arguments that could lead to the answers.

The early part of the 12th century saw a general recognition of the inadequacies of the local customary laws and of the fact that the only accessible source to supplement them was the *Corpus iuris*. It was the supermarket in which the lawyer could find whatever he wanted, whether it be a rule to fill a gap, a technique of interpretation or an argument for or against a particular proposition, and there was no question of its general authority. Within the bounds of the Holy Roman Empire this authority could be attributed to its imperial origins but even elsewhere its scientific superiority over any other set of laws was unquestioned.

This treasure house did not give up its secrets readily. What *Irnerius* and his successors at Bologna offered was an entree into the texts as a whole. Earlier jurists had known a few select passages but now a competent lawyer needed a mastery of all the texts. *Justinian* had assured his readers that his collection contained no antinomies or contradictions which could not be resolved by one who sought with a subtle mind the reasons for the differences (*subtili animo diversitatis rationes excutiet*, *Constitutio Tanta*, 15). There were, however, several texts that seemed to state quite contrary propositions and the sheer bulk of the texts presented great problems of analysis.

The earlier Glossators at Bologna, *Irnerius* and his immediate successors, the Four Doctors, concentrated on providing explanatory glosses to every text and cross-references to other texts dealing with the same point. In this way they provided a precise technical vocabulary, which was only dimly discernible in the vulgar law of the early Middle Ages, and a universal legal grammar, in which legal disputes of any kind could be discussed in a professional way.

All over Europe bishops and kings wanted to be able to exploit this new expertise by hiring those who had learned it and ambitious young men sought the new learning as a means of acquiring wealth and influence in high places. By the middle of the century, anyone who had a basic grounding in the arts and wanted to learn the civil law, felt that he had to go to Bologna as the one place where the original sources were studied in detail. Canon law was also studied there and many students obtained a grounding in civil law before moving to canon law. Its strategic situation at the junction of the main roads in Northern Italy made Bologna relatively easy of access. Thousands flocked there and its position as the legal centre of Europe was unrivalled throughout the 12th century: *Bononia mater legum*.

IV. The Law School Becomes a University

The law schools of Bologna were at first private secular institutions. The University of Bologna was not founded by a deliberate act; it grew up, around the middle of the 12th century, out of the need felt by the students of civil law to organize themselves, in order to ensure that they received the most effective teaching and to obtain a recognized qualification which they could take with them to obtain employment. Bologna thus became the model of a university governed by students, who employed the professors to teach them, in contrast to the type of university governed by masters, such as Paris or Oxford. The students elected the rector of the university and student leaders became a force with which the authorities of the *comune* had to deal. They were courted by both the emperor and the pope[10]. In the constitution *Habita*, which *Frederick I Barbarossa* caused to be inserted in the *Authenticum*, their independence of the *comune* was recognized. Later, at the beginning of the 13th century, Pope *Honorius III* interceded with the *comune* on behalf of the students and gave the power to confer the right of teaching everywhere to the ecclesiastical authorities of Bologna. It was understood that both the reputation and the economic well-being of the city were bound up with the attraction of the university as a place where one could obtain the passport to professional advancement.

Although other higher subjects, such as theology and medicine, were also taught at Bologna, it was the civil law and canon law that were dominant there. As part of a wider *universitas studiorum*, the study of the civil law was altered. The effect on the civil law of the change from informal professional school to university faculty was significant.

First, since only a subject which could be studied anywhere was worthy of study in a university, the status of the Roman civil law as having universal validity, superior to purely local law, was reinforced. Local law was never taught in universities in any country until the 17th century. Even when it was a common law for the whole country, as in England, it lacked the universality essential for a place in a university. Oxford and Cambridge taught only civil law (and canon law before the Reformation) until the 18th century. Secondly, as it became the subject of organized teaching, the subject became more scientific. We have no evidence of public teaching by *Irnerius* himself but his pupils, the Four Doctors, certainly lectured to large classes[11]. Copies of lecture notes could be bought and the glosses to individual texts were brought together to form *Summae* on particular parts of the *Corpus iuris* or on particular topics. Thirdly, the form of teaching acquired an adversarial element in that the students were consistently encouraged to argue about the problems raised by the texts through moots and debates, often under the supervision of their teachers.

---

10 *A. Garcia y Garcia*, The Faculties of Law, in: H. De Ridder-Symoens, ed., A History of the University in Europe, volume 1, Cambridge, 1992, chapter 12.

11 *Bulgarus*, being widowed, married a young woman whom he alone believed to be a virgin. The following day, when he came to lecture, the first text was C. 3, 1, 14, beginning, *rem nec novam nec inusitatem aggredimur*. The announcement that he "came to something neither new nor unused," provoked pandemonium among the students: *M. Bellomo*, Saggio sull' Universita nell'eta del diritto comune, Catania, 1979, p. 49.

V. The Effect of the Glossators on Roman Law

1. The Structure of Teaching at Bologna

The Bolognese Glossators did not show any interest in exploiting the new-found texts as sources of knowledge about antiquity in general, or in using lay literature to elucidate the legal texts. The legal texts contained within themselves all that was necessary for their exposition and they had to be mastered completely. The teaching of the Glossators has been characterized as "distinguished by refreshing clarity of thought, severe scholarship, exact references to the sources, attention to minute detail, linguistic and dogmatic exegesis, excision of all non-jurisprudential material or considerations"[12].

The requirements of teaching to an agreed curriculum, which was the product of negotiation between students and teachers, over a lengthy period, eventually fixed at five years for the first degree, meant that some form of order had to be imposed on the jungle of texts and that the method of expounding them had to be made uniform. Civil law inevitably became more scientific.

One of the main problems in expounding the civil law was that it was presented in a different order in the Digest, Code and Institutes. The latter provided a basic introduction to the categories of the law. The Institutes divided all law into persons, things and actions and subdivided things into individual physical things, inheritances and obligations. To supplement these categories, the Glossators constructed series of *distinctiones*. These were classifications, in which different fact-situations or legal institutions were divided and sub-divided into groups, sometimes with the aid of diagrammatic tables as an aid to memory. The underlying aim was to establish connections between what at first sight seemed to be disparate material and eventually to extrapolate from them an underlying structure which could be regarded as implicit in the texts.

Once the students were past the introductory stage, they had to deal with the Digest and Code, which were not arranged in any perceptible order. The Glossators' respect for *Justinian* was such that they did not feel free to separate the content of the individual texts from the form in which they were transmitted to them. That task was left to humanist initiatives in the second half of the 16th century.

With a view to making the intractable material more of a discipline, the Glossators put great emphasis on *regulae*, general principles which were thought to apply throughout the whole law and not to be limited in application to a particular part. Fortunately the last title of the Digest, 50, 17, was devoted exclusively to *regulae* and contained over two hundred of them[13]. This title attracted much attention, but

---

12 *W. Ullmann*, Law and Politics in the Middle Ages, London, 1975, p. 99.

13 *P. Stein*, Regulae iuris: from Juristic Rules to Legal Maxims, Edinburgh, 1966, at pp. 114 sqq.

the Glossators sought to extract *regulae* of general application from other texts as well.

They conceived of a *regula* as a generalization from a number of recurring instances. *Bulgarus*, the most influential of the Four Doctors, wrote a commentary, explaining how such rules worked[14]. The Digest text D. 50, 17, 1 says that if a *regula* is vitiated in any particular, it loses its *officium*. *Bulgarus* observes that the *officium* of a *regula* is to comprehend *singula*. Thus a *regula* cannot have any exceptions, since what is excepted is not comprehended. *Bulgarus* likens a *regula* to a genus containing a number of species. For example, there is a general rule that what belongs to no-one becomes the property of the first taker. This is the genus; the species are wild beasts, fish and birds, which all become the property of the first person to take them. Although a general rule should not have exceptions, it does not have unlimited application and *Bulgarus* explains how the scope of each proposition has to be reconciled with that of other propositions so that every rule has to be fitted into a comprehensive structure.

The Doctors differed strenuously among themselves and collections were made of the *dissensiones dominorum*. They encouraged the same habit of argument among their students, who could teach themselves by organizing *quaestiones disputatae*, a kind of moot court debates, in which each side presented an argument with supporting authorities, after which the master gave his *solutio*.

2. *Explaining the Texts*

Despite their enthusiasm for general propositions, the Glossators always stressed that the kernel of civil law study was the exposition of the individual text, or *lex*. *Johannes Bassianus*, a pupil of *Bulgarus* and himself the dominant figure in civil law teaching at Bologna in the third quarter of the century, describes his method of explaining a difficult text as having four stages[15]. First, there should be a a statement of the problem, the *casus*, without any frills. Secondly, texts giving a contrary rule should be cited and suggested reconciliations mentioned. Thirdly, the matter should be projected on a wider plane by adducing general principles relevant to the problem, "popularly called brocards". Finally, in the light of the foregoing, there should be a general discussion of the problem, either immediately in class or, in a case of real difficulty, postponed until the evening when there was more time available.

The method preferred by the Doctors was clearly one that started from the individual text and broadened outwards by relating it to other particular texts and to the structure of the legal system as a whole. One of the characteristic features of

14 Stein (n. 13) 134 sqq.

15 *Materia pandectarum*, quoted by *P. Weimar*, Die legistische Literatur und die Methode des Rechtsunterrichts der Glossatorenzeit, Ius Commune 2 (1969) 47.

the glossatorial method was the use of what *Johannes* referred to by the slang expression, brocards. These were collections of propositions with strings of texts supporting and denying them. Sometimes they were in the form of rule and counter-rule, sometimes in the form of an assertion, with texts in favour and against; sometimes there is a *solutio*, sometimes not; they have no set form. Their common function is to provide pegs on which arguments either way may be based, with authorities to be cited in support of those arguments. The name is a mystery. One suggestion is that it is a corruption of the name of the canonist *Burchard of Worms*, another that it is a corruption of *pro* and *contra*. The most attractive is that it derives from *broccus*, a protruding tooth, thus stressing their fiercely argumentative character, enabling the advocate to bite into his opponent's case[16]. Collections of brocards were widely used in practice, often by lawyers with only a superficial knowledge of the textual exegesis on which they were based. Thus analytical techniques devised to improve teaching could be abused as short-cuts and became ways of avoiding some of the drudgery associated with learning a complex subject.

The student was expected to familiarize himself with the texts by private study and to equip himself with a personal set of the most important texts. In Bologna *stationarii exempla tenentes* were booksellers who held authorized copies of the texts, which they hired out to students for them to make their own copies[17]. Then, when the time came for them to leave the university, they would have a set of basic material to take with them. Thus, even if they did not themselves become teachers, former students were able to disseminate a knowledge of the civil law throughout Europe by bringing the texts, usually accompanied by a basic set of glosses, to their home countries.

The Glossators' primary aim was to elucidate the content of *Justinian*'s texts, and not adapt them for practice, but in one case they made a significant contribution to the legal needs of the time. This was in their works on the nature of legal procedure, a topic that was not dealt with systematically by *Justinian*[18]. Just as they explained the nature of legal rules, so the early Glossators explained the nature of the legal process and the existence of certain principles, such as the need to give both sides a hearing and to decide according to the pleadings, which became part of the Romano-canonical procedure. The later development of this procedure was left to the canonists but it was the civil law Glossators who fixed its basic structure.

16 *P. Weimar*, Argumenta Brocardica, in: Studia Gratiana 14, Collectanea S. Kuttner IV, Bologna, 1967, p. 89.

17 *Bellomo* (n. 11) 113 sq.

18 *L. Fowler-Magerl*, Ordo iudiciorum vel ordo iudiciarius, Ius Commune, Sonderheft 19, Frankfurt am Main, 1984.

VI. Post-Glossatorial Developments

1. The Influence of Bologna

The form of teaching developed at Bologna was the model for the teaching of civil law in other *studia* that were established in Northern Italy in the later 12th century and also in southern France. Indeed, there is evidence of a flourishing school of Roman law in the Rhone valley already in the first half of the century, which shows Bolognese influence[19]. By the second half of the 12th century there was an active school of civil law in the Anglo-Norman kingdom, founded by Master *Vacarius*[20]. He was recruited at Bologna by Archbishop *Theobald* in the 1140s and remained in England until the end of the century. He produced an anthology of texts, called the *Liber Pauperum*, for poor students who could not afford the full range of Digest and Code texts. The glosses to the *Liber Pauperum* show a familiarity with current ideas at Bologna. In the 1190s those who used it, known as *pauperistae*, were notorious for their arrogance.

In view of the ferment of their debates, the Glossators tended to divide themselves into separate groups, founded by *Bulgarus* and another of the Four Doctors, *Martinus*. Since it was *Bulgarus* and his followers who attained dominance at Bologna, it is not surprising that the civil lawyers of the *diaspora* were those who tended to favour the ideas of *Martinus*. There was, however, little disagreement between these groups about technique and the new law schools assumed that the Bolognese methods were the best.

The work of the Glossators was synthesized around 1240, when the Bolognese master *Accursius* completed his *Glossa Ordinaria* to all five *volumina* of the *Corpus iuris*. This Great Gloss contained nearly 100,000 individual glosses, immediately superseded all earlier work and was henceforth always copied together with the original texts and from the 15th century printed with them. Since the legal significance of the texts was hardly intelligible without the comments and cross-references provided by the Gloss, the latter came to be regarded as having as much authority as the text itself. Thus the principle, still characteristic of the civil law, was established, that authoritative academic commentary on legislative texts is itself an authentic source of law.

2. The Commentators

By the second half of the 13th century, the school of Bologna had lost some of its vitality. The focus of civil law study became Orleans, where the civil law re-

---

19 *A. Gouron*, La science juridique francaise aux XIe et XIIe siecles, Ius Romanum Medii Aevi I.4.d, Milano, 1978, p. 33.

20 *P. G. Stein*, The Vacarian School, (1992) 13 J.L.H. 23.

ceived a boost from the papal prohibition of its study in Paris. Instead of the ingenious citation of opposing texts, the Orleans masters looked for the rationale behind them and extended reasoning by analogy beyond what the Bolognese would have considered the limits. Their techniques were brought to Italy by *Cinus of Pistoia* and were exploited by his pupil *Bartolus of Sassoferrato*, the leading jurist of the first half of the 14th century and by *Bartolus*'s own pupil *Baldus*, the leading jurist of the second half of the century.

These so-called Commentators continued to expound *Justinian*'s texts but their aim was now to find in those texts rules which would be appropriate for late medieval society but would still carry the authority of imperial law. *Bartolus* justified the existence of local custom but limited its scope by insisting that local law be interpreted according to the civil law. He developed a set of rules of conflict of laws by taking specific cases in the Digest and Code and generalizing their rulings[21]. The product was a set of convenient rules which were not expressly stated anywhere in the *Corpus iuris* but which could nevertheless claim to be immanent in it and so be authoritative.

Unlike the Glossators, the Commentators had to come to terms with the existence of canon law and where they came into conflict to reconcile them. The result was a blend of civil and canon law, which became a *ius commune* for the whole of Europe, based on the same texts and expounded in the same language, Latin[22]. The *ius commune* provided not only a basic legal grammar, adaptable to any set of local laws, but also a subsidiary law, which could be called on to fill gaps in other laws wherever they occurred. Its doctrinal antecedents, rooted in the academic tradition established at Bologna, were unchallenged.

---

21 *P. G. Stein*, Bartolus, the Conflict of Laws and the Roman law, in: P. Feuerstein and C. Parry, edd., Multum non Multa: Festschrift für Kurt Lipstein, Heidelberg, 1980, p. 251 (= *P. G. Stein*, The Character and Influence of the Roman Civil Law: Historical Essays, London, 1988, p. 83).

22 *M. Bellomo*, L'Europa del diritto comune, 5th ed., Roma, 1991.

The General Influence of Roman Institutions of State and Public Law

By David Johnston

I. Introduction

The influence on posterity of Roman public law seems an obvious and promising topic, at least at first glance: prominently displayed in the first fragment of the Digest is *Ulpian*'s celebrated remark that there are two branches of the study of law, public and private[1]. The significance of this division in the civil law tradition is almost impossible to exaggerate. The leading 16th-century legist *Charles Dumoulin*, for example, described it as "the prime and supreme division of jurisprudence"[2], and it remains absolutely fundamental to many civilian systems of law today. The Roman jurist *Ulpian* can claim to have been the first to postulate this fundamental divide. These are encouraging beginnings.

Yet this same topic might instead seem fraught with lack of promise and interest, for it is a commonplace that the Roman jurists were most uninterested in public law[3]. No extended discussions survive of constitutional checks and balances or means for keeping a magistrate or other authority within the proper bounds of his jurisdiction. Nothing of significance survives of the few jurists who are said to have been experts in public law. So there may be just a hint that, when in that celebrated text *Ulpian* distinguishes public from private law, he does so in order to clear it out of the way, together with *ius naturale* and *ius gentium*, and to leave the stage clear for the entry of the proper business of law, private law. It was perhaps considerations of this sort that led *Savigny* to take the view that Roman public law had not been received into modern legal systems. *Koschaker*, although less extreme, still thought Roman public law too much bound up with its own time to have formed the basis for modern public law[4].

More recently, however, attitudes have come to be somewhat more positive. *Coing* has urged that it is mistaken to suppose that the medieval jurist rigorously dis-

---

1 *Ulp.* D. 1, 1, 1, 2.

2 Omnia quae extant opera, vol. I, Paris, 1681, at p. 738.

3 *F. Schulz*, History of Roman Legal Science, 1946, at pp. 81, 138.

4 *F. C. von Savigny*, System des heutigen römischen Rechts, vol. 1, Berlin, 1840, Bk. 1, Chap. 1.3; *P. Koschaker*, Europa und das römische Recht, 4th ed., 1966, at p. 270.

tinguished between private and public law and determined that only private law was appropriate for reception. What was received was the whole of Roman law, public and private, every text being fair game for the elucidation of any point or principle[5]. Once that is accepted, it becomes clear that Roman public law can be expected to have had its influence; although, since Roman writings on private law are much greater in volume and sophistication, their impact must be expected to be greater. This paper, however, is concerned only with the influence of public law.

A difficulty in any study of the influence of ideas or institutions is where to draw the finishing line. A further difficulty, where space is not unlimited, is at which staging posts to stop on the way. No doubt any choice would seem arbitrary. This essay surges through centuries of jurisprudence at alarming speed, halting only to glance at the case of the Glossators and Commentators and then at that of *Jean Bodin*. Why precisely there? The medieval lawyers display extreme fidelity to the Roman texts; *Bodin* exhibits a critical and comparative attitude informed by humanism. If the balance on the question of Roman influence is to be weighed judiciously, both of these very different approaches have to be considered.

The next section discusses what the Romans understood by public law and the historical significance of the divide between public and private law. Section III considers specific cases of Roman influence at a constitutional or institutional level. Some of these have been closely examined in histories of political thought; they are dealt with briefly. Less well-worked is the stratum of what would now be called administrative law, so closer attention is paid here to the Digest texts touching on the notion of an office; the powers accorded to the holder of that office; what happens when the office holder exceeds those powers; and the concepts of power (*imperium*) and jurisdiction themselves. Section IV sets out some general conclusions.

II. *Ius publicum*

1. Classical Roman Law

"Public law is concerned with the Roman state (*status rei Romanae*), while private law is concerned with the interests of individuals, for some matters are of public and others of private interest. Public law comprises religion, priesthoods, and magistracies"[6]. This is *Ulpian*'s definition of *ius publicum*, and the only Roman one which survives. As noted at the outset, the divide which it postulated between public and private law was of the greatest significance, for it contained the germ of an idea that there was a sphere of law whose special concern was the state and its

---

5 *H. Coing*, Die Anwendung des Corpus iuris in den Consilien des Bartolus, in: L'Europa e il diritto romano: Studi in memoria di Paul Koschaker, vol. 1, 1954, at pp. 71-93.

6 D. 1, 1, 1, 2.

administration. When we come to the question of the content or distinguishing features of public law, however, it has to be admitted that the Roman sources were less far-reaching and less helpful. *Ulpian* lists three elements of public law: religion, priesthoods and magistracies, and the list seems to be intended to be exhaustive. Only the last of these elements looks much like public law to modern eyes, but this single word does not provide much guidance.

Moreover, the boundary between private and public law is scarcely explored in the Roman sources[7]. To take an obvious difficulty, the Roman jurists were ambivalent on the question whether a town (*civitas*) was to be treated according to private or public law. The purist view appears in the Digest: according to *Gaius*, the term 'public' applied to the Roman people, while towns were in the same position as private individuals[8]; similarly, *Ulpian* thought that the property of towns could be described as 'public' only by an abuse of language[9]. But these clear statements neither accorded fully with views expressed in other contexts by the same jurists[10] nor did they fully reflect Roman practice: for there were special legal rules and remedies which dealt with municipal property; they may not have been the same as those available to the Roman people, but neither were they the same as those open to private individuals.

Worse, the Roman jurists used the expression *ius publicum* in various senses: sometimes to denote the whole legal order of Rome, sometimes to refer to rules of law which were inderogable, and then sometimes in contexts clearly of private law: so, for example, institutions such as marriage, dowry, and tutors are said to belong to public law, but by this what appears to be meant is that they serve the public good: they are particularly important for the maintenance of civil society. Whatever else the Roman jurists suggested, it was rarely that *ius publicum* was conceived as a separate branch of the law concerned with the state or its constitution. A common theme which does, however, emerge in the jurists' references to *ius publicum*, at least from the reign of *Hadrian*, is its connexion with the common good or public interest, *utilitas publica*[11]. That association appears in *Ulpian*'s definition itself.

2. *The Later Development of* ius publicum

Ulpian's tripartite definition of *ius publicum* was seized upon by *St. Isidore of Seville* and by that route surfaced in the *Decretum* of *Gratian*, but curiously enough

7 There is only one other text in which the terms *ius privatum* and *ius publicum* appear together, and that is simply to the effect that the jurist *Tubero* was a great expert in both: *Pomp.* D. 1, 2, 2, 46.

8 D. 50, 16, 16.

9 D. 50, 16, 15.

10 *Gai.* D. 1, 8, 1 *pr.* (ambiguous) and D. 41, 3, 9; *Ulp.* D. 43, 24, 5, 4 and D. 50, 16, 17 *pr.*

in neither work is there any reference to the divide between *ius privatum* and *ius publicum*. Most of the Decretists and Decretalists make no reference at all to *ius privatum*, and it seems that canon law simply did not employ any distinction between the spheres of public and private law[12]. On the secular side, the notion of *ius publicum* surfaces from time to time; *Accursius* grandly pronounces that it exists to preserve the state[13]. There are reminiscences too of *Ulpian*'s remarks about public utility; *Bartolus* asserted that *merum imperium* was exercised essentially in the interests of public utility; *mixtum imperium* in those of private utility. But these remarks are made essentially in passing, and the recognition of public law as a special sphere of law was slow to come. Only from about 1600 did it begin to establish itself as an independent discipline in the universities in Germany. This in itself perhaps owed something to Roman law, namely to the aridity of *Ulpian*'s definition[14].

But this of course did not mean that no thought was given to questions of a public nature. Discussion proceeded in the absence of the concept: there is much, for example, in *Bartolus* about questions of political legitimacy[15]. There was authority in the texts, as we have seen, for confining the term 'public' and the noun *res publica* to the state itself, but there was also authority for taking 'public' to refer to municipalities as well[16]. Advantage could be, and was, taken of this uncertainty since, from the assertion that city and municipality were like the state itself within the public sphere, it was a swift step to the conclusion that they too enjoyed political powers, *imperium* and *iurisdictio*[17]. There will be more to say about this later.

3. Summary

The Digest therefore contained only the bare bones of the idea that there might be such a thing as an independent sphere of law embracing public matters. The unhelpfulness of the definition found there, and the exiguous treatment meted out to public law in general by the Roman jurists, do something to explain why the development of the area was slow and tentative.

---

11 *M. Kaser*, Ius publicum und ius privatum, ZSS (RA) 103 (1986) 1.

12 *H. Müllejans*, Publicus und privatus im römischen Recht und im älteren kanonischen Recht, 1961.

13 Gl. *publicum* on D. 1, 1, 1, 2: "ad statum conservandum ne pereat".

14 *M. Stolleis*, Geschichte des öffentlichen Rechts in Deutschland, vol. 1, 1988, at pp. 58, 75.

15 Cf. *Stolleis* (n. 14) 65.

16 Gl. on Auth. 1, 1. The debate continued among the Commentators: see *J. Canning*, The Political Thought of Baldus de Ubaldis, 1987, at p. 123.

17 *J. Gaudemet*, La contribution des romanistes et des canonistes médiévaux à la théorie moderne de l'état, in: Diritto e potere nella storia europea: Atti in onore di Bruno Paradisi, 1982, 1, at pp. 28-9.

III. Institutional and Constitutional Questions

In the surviving Roman texts two strands of public and constitutional thinking can be separated, and it is proper to treat them separately here. The first consists of occasional assertions about sovereignty and power. These are found in both Digest and Code and are mostly absolutist in character and Justinianic in date. The second strand is made up of the conceptions of *imperium* and *iurisdictio* which emerge from the discussions of the classical jurists. They are preserved in a few excerpts in the Digest.

1. Sovereignty and the Power of the Emperor

The position of the emperor is proclaimed in several texts, not all consistent. On the one hand, he is said not to be bound by statute (*princeps legibus solutus est*)[18]; it is well known that this sentence, lifted from *Ulpian*, came originally from the limited context of a commentary on the *lex Iulia et Papia*, and may have meant no more than that that composite law did not apply to the emperor. Be that as it may, in the Digest it signals unrestricted freedom from statutes. The same conception lies behind *Justinian*'s assertion that God had sent among men the emperor as a "living statute", to whom statutes themselves were subject[19]. Earlier, *Justinian* had proclaimed that the emperor alone had power to make statutes and to interpret them[20]. In the Code, on the other hand, a constitution of *Theodosius* and *Valentinian* stated that it was worthy of the emperor to profess himself to be bound by statutes[21].

On sovereignty, virtually the only text which raised the question of constitutional relations between emperor and people stated: "What the *princeps* decides has the force of statute, as the people, by the *lex regia* which was passed regarding his power, confers on him all its own power and authority"[22]. This can be read as democratic legitimation of the emperor by the people: by *lex* the people parts with its own *imperium* and *potestas* in favour of the emperor. The term *imperium* is being used loosely, since *imperium* in the narrow sense in which the jurists regularly use it was the preserve of the higher magistrates and pro-magistrates, and the people did not itself possess it. It may be thought that this text is no more than *ex post facto* rationalization by *Ulpian* of powers which in his day the emperor un-

18 D. 1, 3, 31.

19 Nov. 105, 2, 4 (536): "[imperator], cui et ipsas deus leges subiecit, legem animatam eum mittens hominibus".

20 C. 1, 14, 12, 3-5 (529): "explosis itaque huiusmodi ridiculosis ambiguitatibus tam conditor quam interpres legum solus imperator iuste existimabitur".

21 C. 1, 14, 4 (429): "digna vox maiestate regnantis legibus alligatum se principem profiteri".

22 *Ulp.* D. 1, 4, 1 *pr.*; cf. *Gai.* 1, 5.

doubtedly did have. But it is also possible that he is referring to the *lex de imperio* passed at the accession of the emperor and which invested him with power[23]. Whatever the truth of the matter for Roman times, there is no doubt that in subsequent political discourse this text was of the greatest importance.

2. General Theories of imperium *and* iurisdictio *in Classical Roman Law*

The Roman jurists provide no general account of the key notions of public law. Although the 2nd and 3rd centuries saw a fashion for writing books about the office of one magistrate or another (*libri de officio*), the most notable example of which is *Ulpian*'s ten books *de officio proconsulis*, the surviving material is disappointingly thin. There is no extended discussion of *imperium* or *potestas*, the rudiments of state power. Of the small number of texts on questions of what we would call constitutional law, few come from a *liber de officio*; and many more come from the ordinary run of commentaries on the edict or civil law. The most substantial contribution is made by discussions of the municipal provisions in the edict. That is an observation of some interest. It might be said that the jurists, having in their practice and study of private law no need or opportunity for exposition of the nature and extent of the powers and jurisdiction of state magistracies, determined to exploit the opportunity to do this in connexion with municipal magistrates instead. There was room for the development of similar theory, but there was the added attraction that the material to be expounded had a connexion with the traditional material of private-law debate: the edict.

From a few texts, however, it is possible to piece together a general account of *imperium* and of *iurisdictio*; it was from these same texts, used selectively rather than systematically, that medieval and later jurists constructed their own arguments about sovereignty and power. The questions at issue for them were of constitutional significance; it is difficult to maintain that the stakes were so high in the discussions in the Roman sources.

(a) *Imperium*

The central concept in Roman public law is *imperium*[24]. The concept of *iurisdictio* is also important. The following are perhaps the most significant of the various points which the jurists make about these two concepts. First, *imperium*. There were degrees of *imperium*, so that a consul had greater *imperium* than a praetor,

23 *P.A. Brunt*, Lex de imperio Vespasiani, Journal of Roman Studies 67 (1977) 95, at pp. 110-13.

24 See esp. *Th. Mommsen*, Römisches Staatsrecht, vol. 1, Leipzig, 1887, *passim*.

and the emperor had *imperium* greater than that of any magistrate. Accordingly, a magistrate had no *imperium* over a magistrate of the same or higher degree but could exercise it only over one of a lower degree[25]. *Imperium* could be exercised, at least by pro-magistrates, only within their provinces and for the period during which they had charge of them[26]. *Imperium* could be 'undiluted' (*merum*) and so include *iurisdictio* as well as 'the power of the sword' (*ius gladii* or *potestas*), a capital jurisdiction in criminal matters, or it could be 'mixed' (*mixtum*) and include *iurisdictio* only[27].

(b) *Iurisdictio*

Second, *iurisdictio*. Here it is necessary first to deal with the possible objection that it has nothing to do with public law. There is no doubt that the granting of a civil legal remedy (*iudicium dare*) is the original meaning of the word[28]. But there is equally no doubt that, already among the late classical jurists, the term was applied in relation to criminal and administrative matters[29]. Nor is the reason for this less technical usage far to seek: with the rise of the *cognitio* system of procedure, the difference between a private procedure conducted by an official, and any other kind of procedure conducted by the same official, was far from clear. *Iurisdictio* could therefore be used beyond the narrow realms of private law, to denote the powers of a magistrate in what would now be regarded as public law.

Iurisdictio embraced the general powers which a magistrate had to administer justice[30]. In the narrow sense, it did not include the power to make certain, mostly interlocutory, orders concerned with the administration of justice, because they properly belonged to *imperium*[31]. A magistrate had *iurisdictio* only over persons who had the appropriate domicile (which itself was a question for him to decide)[32]. His *iurisdictio* might be subject to territorial and financial limits[33], but could be prorogated by those otherwise not subject to it[34]. *Iurisdictio* could be exercised only personally, unless statute or convention allowed it to be delegated[35]. It could

---

25 *Ulp.* D. 36, 1, 13, 4; D. 4, 8, 3, 3; *Paul* D. 4, 8, 4.

26 D. 1, 18, 3; D. 1, 17, 1 and D. 1, 18, 17.

27 D. 2, 1, 3.

28 *M. Lauria*, Iurisdictio, in: Studi Bonfante II, Milan, 1920, 481, at p. 492; *M. Kaser*, Das römische Zivilprozeßrecht, 1966, at pp. 132 sqq.

29 *Lauria* (n. 28) 493-508.

30 In civil litigation it also has the narrower sense of the power to determine the issue to go to trial, and to make various interlocutory orders.

31 D. 2, 1, 4 and D. 50, 1, 26.

32 D. 2, 5, 2 *pr.*; D. 5, 1, 2, 6 and 5; C. 8, 1, 2 (260).

33 D. 2, 1, 20; D. 50, 16, 239, 8.

34 D. 2, 1, 15; D. 5, 1, 2 *pr.*; cf. D. 1, 16, 2 *pr.* and 16.

35 D. 1, 21, 1.

be exercised only by a properly appointed magistrate[36]. If the magistrate had no *iurisdictio*, an order pronounced purportedly in pursuance of it was null and void[37].

(c) Conclusions

With an eye to the future role of Roman law, two points can usefully be drawn from these brief outlines. The first is that in these texts we find the jurists adumbrating the concept of an office which must be exercised according to law, and which confers on its holder powers which are defined and delimited by law. Some of the powers are taken to be inherent in the nature of the office; others are expressly conferred by legislation of one sort or another. But the magistrate must act within those powers, and acts which go beyond them are void; for example, a magistrate who purports to act officially outside his own province acts to no effect: as *Paul* notes, he is treated as a private individual[38]. Equally, owing to the hierarchy of magistrates' *imperium*, the acts of magistrates lower in the pyramid can be controlled by those above. As *Ulpian* says, "a praetor has no *imperium* over a praetor nor has a consul over a consul"[39], and the solution, where there is an impasse owing to equality of powers, is to seek assistance from the emperor. These considerations about the legitimate exercise of power are manifestations of a rule-of-law rather than an absolutist model of the state and they are developed particularly in connexion with *iurisdictio*[40]. This is perhaps no more than we should expect: while *iurisdictio* itself is not a matter of private law, the concept does provide the very foundation of private-law (and other) procedure in the courts; it therefore falls within the sphere the jurists generally regard as their own.

Second, it is remarkable, considering the central role of the concept *merum imperium* in later political thought, how slight a part it plays in the writings of the jurists. It appears only three times in the Digest. The first sighting is in the well-known text from *Ulpian*'s book on the office of *quaestor* which explains that there are two types of *imperium*, *merum* and *mixtum*[41]. Unfortunately the context is unclear, since the text is one of only two which survive from that book, and it remains mysterious why it should have been necessary to discuss *imperium* in a work devoted to the *quaestor*, a magistrate who did not possess it. The remaining two appearances of *merum imperium* are in the context of delegation of jurisdiction. Both authors, *Papinian* and *Paul*, say that it is possible to delegate jurisdiction and that that will carry with it such *imperium* as is necessary for the exercise of jurisdiction,

---

36 D. 1, 14, 3.

37 D. 2, 2, 1, 2; D. 49, 1, 23, 1; C. 3, 3, 1 (242); C. 3, 4, 1 (440).

38 D. 1, 18, 3.

39 D. 36, 1, 13, 4.

40 C. 7, 48 collects a number of 3rd to 5th century rescripts raising similar points about judges in *cognitio* exceeding their authority.

41 D. 2, 1, 3.

but that *merum imperium* cannot be delegated. *Papinian* also draws a distinction between powers which are inherent in a particular office and powers which are attributed by special legal grant: only powers in the first category are delegable; *merum imperium* belongs in the second[42]. These three fragments might be thought a slight base on which to build elaborate theories in later law. But their generality left that same later law encouragingly untrammelled by constricting and unhelpful rules and details.

3. The Later Development of Public Law Concepts – Use of the Roman Texts and Terms

For several centuries after the rediscovery of the Digest, it was to be these Roman public-law concepts which supplied the basic vocabulary of debate about sovereignty, the powers of emperor and of city, the relations between emperor and magistrate. Their potency lay in an abstraction which permitted ready transfer to modern institutions; little or no hesitation was felt about such transfers. Many texts were put to new uses: for example, the question arose whether the emperor was bound by his predecessors' acts or legislation. *Accursius* held that he was not, since an equal did not have *imperium* over an equal. The Roman jurists had not employed that rule in that way[43]. The Roman jurists had also been sparing in defining concepts; it was open to their successors, when they took over Roman terms, to reshape them for their own purposes. Thus *Azo* defined *iurisdictio* as "a power publicly introduced with the necessity of stating the law and establishing equity"[44]. Romans would hardly have put it so broadly.

Roman terms, and the texts in which they appeared, were simply taken over – sometimes of course transformed in meaning – and applied to medieval institutions. At a mundane level, the medieval town could be described as *municipium* and the financial imposts on its citizens as *munera*[45]. Not surprisingly, it was the law of the later empire, known from the *Corpus iuris civilis*, which was taken over, with its decurions and *defensores civitatum*[46]. The titles and offices attested in the various rubrics of the first book of the Digest were laboriously translated to apply to contemporary hierarchies of office[47]. The medieval 'podestà' was compared to the Roman *praeses* or governor: both were temporary officials from outside the locality who, with their assessors, were responsible for the administration of justice. The 'podestà' was regularly assisted by assessors or represented by a judge-

42 *Pap.* D. 1, 21, 1, 1; *Paul.* D. 1, 18, 5.

43 Gl. on D. 1, 3, 31, citing D. 4, 8, 4 on this point.

44 *Azo*, Summa super codicem, ed. Viora, Turin, 1966, on C. 3, 13.

45 *Coing* (n. 5) 80.

46 *Gaudemet* (n. 17) 31.

47 *Stolleis* (n. 14) 66.

delegate, just as the governor had been in the later Roman empire[48]. Nor was the influence of the Roman model of administering justice confined to communities which adopted the 'podestà' constitution: it can also be seen in Sicily and Naples[49]. Furthermore, the powers of individual officials were sometimes supported by argument from Roman law[50]; and the extent of a community's jurisdiction might be supported in the same way[51]. Once allowances are made for changed political circumstances, it is clear that Roman institutions were received in later law, some transformed in the process until virtually unrecognizable[52]. It was not a purely Italian phenomenon: for example, the 14th century jurist *Philip of Leiden* regularly employed Roman terms in his 'De cura reipublicae et sorte principantis'[53].

Apart from this, however, the Roman texts provided the basis for constitutional doctrine; the development of the idea of the absolute state; the concept of sovereignty; the claim of the emperor to be the sole source, and sole interpreter, of statute. All these owed a debt to the absolutist position of the *princeps* asserted, or sometimes just assumed, in the *Corpus iuris civilis*. But the texts were sufficiently various and sufficiently malleable to be used not just in support of absolutist positions but also for republican ends. The earliest glossators, applying the statement that the emperor was *dominus mundi*, Lord of the World[54], to the position of the Italian city-states, reached the conclusion that, as a matter of law, those states must be entirely subject to the power of the emperor, and the emperor must be the sole bearer of *imperium*. A literal reading of the *lex regia* from *Ulpian*'s text supported that view, since by that statute the people had transferred its sovereignty and invested the emperor with it[55]. But this did not mean power without legal limit, since the medieval lawyers invariably followed, not the view expressed in the Digest that the emperor is not bound by the laws, but the rival assertion in the Code that it is worthy of a ruler to profess himself to be bound by them[56]. From this was derived the premise that there are legal limits on the exercise of public power[57].

---

48 *W. Engelmann*, Die Wiedergeburt der Rechtskultur in Italien, Leipzig, 1938, at p. 58.

49 *Engelmann* (n. 48) 61.

50 See, e.g., *Coing* (n. 5) 91 on Bart. Cons. 136, deriving the penal powers of the papal *capitaneus patrimonii* from D. 2, 3, 1 *pr.*

51 E.g. according to *Bartolus*, a *civitas* had the limited jurisdiction of a *defensor civitatis* (C. 1, 55, 1); villages had none: *Coing* (n. 5) 91. Cf. *Stolleis* (n. 14) 66, n. 46.

52 *F. Wieacker*, Privatrechtsgeschichte der Neuzeit, 2nd ed., 1967, p. 135.

53 *B. Hermesdorf*, Ius romanum medii aevi V 5 a, 1968, at pp. 93 sqq.; *R. Feenstra*, Philip of Leyden and his Treatise De cura rei publicae et sorte principantis, in: *idem*, Le droit savant au moyen âge at sa vulgarisation, London, 1986.

54 D. 14, 2, 9.

55 The Latin has *conferat*, 'conferred'; it is notable that the gloss on that word states *et transtulit*.

56 C. 1, 14, 4.

57 *Coing* (n. 5) 92.

By the end of the 12th century the republican potential of other texts in the *Corpus* was already being exploited. In his *Lectura super codicem*, treating the people of the city-state as a *universitas*, *Azo* was able to argue that the individuals who made up a people had transferred the exercise of *iurisdictio* to their ruler, but the *universitas* itself had not; it followed that the people as an *universitas* had never lost this power, and the transfer to the ruler was revocable[58]. Glossing the terms *iurisdictio* and *merum imperium*, *Azo* also argued that, since the higher magistrates of city-states had the power to establish new laws, they too must be bearers of *merum imperium*[59]. Here the Roman sources were used to legitimate a doctrine of popular sovereignty; and with the 12th century decretist *Huguccio of Pisa* began a similar line of argument about the relations between the pope and the *universitas* of the church. Indeed it is important to bear in mind the contribution made to these questions by the canonists. By singling out religion and priesthoods as two of the three elements of public law, *Ulpian* had given a clear signal to canonists to interest themselves in questions of public law. Just as *Azo* in his *Quaestiones* had maintained that every ruler had the same power in his territory as the emperor[60], so too, as early as 1202, had *Innocent III* acknowledged that the king of France, *Philip Augustus*, was an emperor in his own kingdom[61]. And, just as the civilians came to interpret their texts in support of civic autonomy, so too did the canonists[62].

4. Bartolus

With *Bartolus*, such arguments were further refined. He elaborated a complex hierarchical scheme of powers based on the Roman term *iurisdictio*[63]. It was taken as a genus which was divided into two species, *imperium* and *iurisdictio* in the narrow sense, which he called *iurisdictio simplex*. *Imperium* itself was further divided into *merum imperium* and *imperium mixtum*. For each of these three concepts *Bartolus* constructed a hierarchy in six degrees (*maximum, maius, magnum, parvum, minus, minimum*), so arriving at eighteen degrees of power in all. For example, the *maximum merum imperium* was held only by *princeps*, senate and praetorian prefect, while the *minimum* was simply the right to impose a small fine, and was much more widely held. Many editions of the Digest include this scheme represented in the pictorial form of the tree of jurisdictions[64]. The motivation for developing this

58 *Azo*, Lectura, reprint of ed. Pavia, 1506, Turin, 1966, 1, 14, 11.

59 *Azo*, Summa, reprint of ed. Pavia, 1506, Turin, 1966, gl. on C. 3, 13. There is here the basis of a hierarchy of powers such as was later developed in detail by *Bartolus* (see below); cf. also gl. *mixtum* on D. 2, 1, 3.

60 *Azo*, Quaestiones, ed. Landsberg, Freiburg, 1888, at pp. 86-7.

61 Decretal 4, 17, 13, Per venerabilem.

62 *S. Mochi Onory*, Fonti canonistiche dell'idea moderna dello stato, Milan, 1951.

63 See, e.g., In primam Digesti Veteris partem commentaria, in: Opera omnia, Basel, 1588, vol. 1, on D. 1, 21.

scheme was the attempt to bring the Roman texts into line with the realities of contemporary society. *Merum imperium* was not in reality exercised solely by the emperor; the cities could claim also to have wielded it for a very long time. This was tantamount to a claim that the cities were governed by free peoples, who wielded their own *imperium*. Each, in *Bartolus*' famous phrase, could be said to be a *princeps* to itself (*civitas sibi princeps*)[65]. By this means *Bartolus* extended the notion of the ruler who recognized no superior to the *civitas* itself[66]. None the less, the *merum imperium* which cities possessed was manifestly not the same as that of the emperor. The hierarchy of degrees of *imperium* was the solution to the problem.

Bartolus' scheme went far beyond anything the Roman jurists had ever imagined. The central role given to *iurisdictio* shows the persistence of Roman influence. It is of course true that the Bartolist conception of the word is remote from the Romans' own. The words *ius dicere*, which had been used by the Roman jurists to denote the granting of a remedy in civil litigation, in *Bartolus* come to mean simply the exercise of the magistrate's authority. But the very construction of *Bartolus*' hierarchy depended on understanding the powers of magistrates as defined and limited, a message clearly conveyed by the Roman texts. Equally, the Roman texts strongly supported the understanding of *iurisdictio* as a power within territorial limits; this may explain some of the appeal of the concept, since the Bartolist scheme was designed precisely to accommodate the powers of cities and regions[67]. In details too this scheme owed much to Roman law and to two texts in particular: *Ulpian*'s distinction between *imperium merum* and *mixtum*, and *Papinian*'s distinction between powers inherent in an office and powers specially attributed to its holder. Applying *Papinian*'s distinction, *Bartolus* found the lowest two degrees of power in his hierarchy to be delegable[68], and the remaining four non-delegable.

Although Roman in inspiration, this was in no sense a historical picture of Roman practice. In Roman terms *iurisdictio* was not the archetype of power itself, but a concept subordinate to *imperium*. As *Cujas* pointed out, for the Romans there was no such thing as *iurisdictio simplex*: since there could be no *iurisdictio* without some degree of *imperium*, it followed that *imperium mixtum* and *iurisdictio simplex* were the same thing[69]. But such objections miss the point. In his use of these

---

64 *M. P. Gilmore*, Argument from Roman law in Political Thought 1200-1600, Cambridge, Mass., 1941, pp. 36-44.

65 *Q. Skinner*, The Foundations of Modern Political Thought, vol. 1, 1978, at pp. 9-12.

66 *Bartolus* (n. 63) on D. 4, 4, 3.

67 *Bartolus* (n. 63) on D. 2, 1, 1, n. 15. For further discussion, see *D. Willoweit*, Rechtsgrundlagen der Territorialgewalt, 1975, e.g. on *Baldus*, at pp. 26 sqq. There is a parallel development in the canonists in relation to the territorial limits of the authority of bishop and priest: *Mochi Onory* (n. 62) 261.

68 To some extent the hierarchy of powers and the indelegability of the higher powers had already been worked out in the Gloss: gl. *mixtum* on D. 2, 1, 3.

69 *J. Cujas*, Observationes et emendationes 21, 30; the objection is in fact anticipated in gl. *mixtum* on D. 2, 1, 3.

concepts *Bartolus* can be seen shaping the malleable conceptions of Roman public law to serve new ends. The essence was to explain and to justify a plurality of jurisdictions such as a feudally organized society presented. The model of delegated and territorial powers put forward in the Roman sources turned out to be remarkably apt for this[70]. *Bartolus*' complex scheme married Roman concept and social fact in a way scarcely to be repeated[71].

The whole medieval debate on public powers is therefore informed by the spirit of Rome. This does not, of course, mean that there is close adherence to the doctrine of Roman law. What it does mean is that Roman terms are used to describe modern institutions; Roman terms are defined or redefined to answer modern demands; Roman texts are applied, distinguished or combined to produce arguments to meet modern needs. In short, the whole debate about the state and the powers of the sovereign is carried on in Roman terms. That is the extent of the influence of Roman public law.

5. *Jean Bodin*

To jump from *Bartolus* to *Bodin*, though undisturbing alphabetically, may seem unwarranted. Excuses have been pleaded already. This is a jump from the medieval to the modern concept of authority. And *Bodin* offers an opportunity to assess the continuing influence of Roman law at a time when it had already faced the critical challenge of humanism. *Bodin*'s views about the merits of the medieval Commentators were scathing, and he professed the view that the first accomplishment of the jurisprudence of his day had been to purge medieval errors and restore the "pristine dignity" of Roman law[72]. He also expressed doubts about the value of continuing to study Roman law, asserting that there were *Papinians* and *Labeos* enough, if only they would break with the authority of Roman law and create a system of their own[73]. The question arises how far in his own work *Bodin* did break free.

Not far, it seems, in his early work of 1566, the *Methodus ad facilem historiarum cognitionem*. There *Bodin* divided the authority of a magistrate into two parts, one granted to him by law and the other held by virtue of his magistracy; the latter power alone was delegable[74]. This division was based on *Papinian*'s distinction

70 Cf. *Willoweit* (n. 67) 32.

71 Others simplified his scheme without challenging its essence: *Baldus* found three rather than six degrees of *imperium* to suffice; *Jason de Mayno* settled for four of *imperium merum* and three of the others: *Gilmore* (n. 64) 43. For comprehensive discussion of *Baldus*, see *Canning* (n. 16).

72 *J. Franklin*, Jean Bodin and the Sixteenth Century Revolution in the Methodology of Law and History, 1963, at p. 65, citing *Bodin*'s Methodus in: P. Mesnard, ed., Oeuvres philosophiques 107, at p. 108A.

73 *Franklin* (n. 72) 107B.

74 *Gilmore* (n. 64) 103.

between powers inherent in an office and powers specially attributed. *Bodin* held that from society to society the answer to the questions whether magistrates had *merum imperium* and what the content of that *imperium* was might differ[75]. For *Bodin*, as for *Bartolus*, there were degrees of *merum imperium*.

Ten years later, in his 'Les six livres de la republique' of 1576, *Bodin*'s concern was essentially to identify the nature of sovereignty, and he did this by looking not only at the French or Roman position but at a great variety of other states besides. This universality was new. Can it be said that here at last we reach the end of the influence of Roman law? The answer to this question must again be 'no'. While *Bodin*'s approach was neither uncritically nor exclusively centred on Rome, the questions he asked could hardly be considered in isolation from all that had gone before. His very concern to identify the marks of sovereignty might even be seen as a reformulation of an old question: which 'political' powers were unique to the king or sovereign and which were also to be found in lesser authorities? In essence *Bodin* put this question in another way: which powers could the sovereign cede to other authorities without ceasing to be sovereign?

When *Bodin* came to discuss the marks of sovereignty, the first one he identified was the power of the sovereign "to give law to all in general and to each in particular". This power carried with it the power to repeal, to correct, and to interpret the laws as appropriate[76]. Lurking barely concealed behind this mark of sovereignty is *Justinian*'s claim as emperor to be the sole source and sole interpreter of law[77]. Roman conceptions also surface in connexion with those holders of power who are not sovereign. A magistrate who exceeds his jurisdiction is to be regarded as a private individual[78]. The same applies to a governor or regent, but not to the sovereign himself, since the people has transferred all power and authority to him[79]. Here, in one and the same chapter, we find the absolutist doctrine of the *lex regia* combined with republican doctrine about the restraints on the use of *imperium*. Roman law had left its mark.

IV. Conclusions

In the late medieval period the influence of Roman public law on contemporary public law had been almost total: Romanization of modern terminology had been carried on as a matter of course, and the term *iurisdictio* had been taken over from

75 *Gilmore* (n. 64) 101-4.

76 *J. Bodin*, Six livres de la république, Paris, 1583; repr. Aalen, 1961, I.10, at pp. 221-3.

77 C. 1, 14, 12, 3-5 (529).

78 *Bodin* (n.76) III.5, p. 445; III.6, p. 464.

79 *Bodin* (n. 76) I.8, p. 127.

Roman law to organize the varying degrees of power possessed by emperor, cities and territories. In the 16th century the direct influence of Roman law became more subdued but, even when the focus of attention shifted with *Bodin* to sovereignty, there was no clean break with the Roman heritage. The Roman texts on *iurisdictio* and the *lex regia* continued to inspire a debate about sovereignty and territorial power which persisted through the earlier years of the 17th century[80]. During the 16th and 17th centuries, new positive public laws played a part of increasing importance and the space left for Roman law as the source of law of last resort steadily shrank.

Yet, rooted in the discipline of public law which now went on to develop independently, were concepts and structures of Roman creation[81]. Firmly entrenched too was the methodology of Roman legal argument, although that was the legacy essentially of private law. And there persisted concepts so well established that their Roman origin was no longer observed: the claim of the sovereign to a monopoly on the passing and the interpretation of legislation; the concept of the public office exercisable only within defined limits and powers. There is an element of paradox here. On the one hand, the Roman sources provided a model of the most unrestrained absolutism, apt for the elaboration of theories of sovereignty and unfettered power. But on the other hand, less prominent but unmistakably present in the Roman sources was a theory of control of powers worked out by the jurists in relation to magistrates. These two very different models do much to account for the continuing appeal of Roman law under the most various regimes. The Digest contained a selection of absolutist and republican texts to suit all tastes.

---

80 *Stolleis* (n. 14) 62.

81 *Stolleis* (n. 14) 63.

The Development of European Private Law: A Romanist Watershed?

By Robert Feenstra

I. Introduction

In addressing a most distinguished company of jurists at the Quincentenary of Aberdeen University I would like to begin with a personal recollection. Thirty-six years ago I was invited by this University to deliver some lectures; it was my first visit to Scotland. One of my lectures was entitled 'The Reception of Roman Law in the Netherlands'. It was a topic I had dealt with in my inaugural lecture at Utrecht University in 1950. My approach to it had been much inspired by a fundamental German book, published shortly after the end of World War II: *Paul Koschaker*'s 'Europa und das römische Recht'[1]. Receiving the invitation to speak at the present conference on the role of Roman law in the development of European private law I was reminded not only of my earlier Aberdeen paper and its origins but also of the reaction of one of my then audience, Dr. *Leslie Macfarlane*, who drew my attention to a very special link between this University and my subject: the presence in Aberdeen University Library of three manuscripts which had come from the father of the founder of the University, *William Elphinstone* senior, and which include civil law lecture notes taken at the University of Louvain in the first decade of its existence (around 1430), a crucial period in the reception of Roman law in the Netherlands. I received microfilms of these manuscripts and examined them thoroughly but, although I returned to Aberdeen to deliver a special lecture on the provisional results of my research, I never ventured to publish my final conclusions. For a moment I was tempted to do so in the form of my present contribution to the Quincentenary celebrations but I soon realized that this would be a much too limited subject for my audience on this occasion[2].

In dealing with the much broader subject announced on the programme of this conference I may first recall some developments in the bibliography on 'Europe

---

1 1st ed., München and Berlin, 1947; 4th ed., München, 1966.

2 I have started the publication of my research in this field with an article on Henricus Brunonis de Piro (+ 1473) in T.R. 64 (1996) 3 sqq.; this article will soon be followed by a study on the other Louvain professors represented in the Aberdeen manuscripts.

and the Roman law' since the publication of *Koschaker*'s book. This work would indeed appear to us nowadays as the starting point for a trend among modern German speaking Romanists to emphasize the role of Roman law in the history of private law in Europe. *Koschaker*'s book was followed in 1952 by the first edition of *Franz Wieacker*'s 'Privatrechtsgeschichte der Neuzeit'[3], and although it does not refer to 'Europe' in its title, this book is so completely devoted to the European background of its subject that it seemed necessary to add the subtitle 'unter besonderer Berücksichtigung der deutschen Entwicklung'. In 1954 the first edition was published of *G. Wesenberg*'s 'Neuere deutsche Privatrechtsgeschichte im Rahmen der europäischen Rechtsentwicklung', of which three further editions appeared, prepared with much care and most valuable additions by *G. Wesener*[4]. The founding in 1964 of a Max-Planck-Institut für europäische Rechtsgeschichte in Frankfurt am Main led to the publication in 1973-1988 of a number of volumes under the title 'Handbuch der Quellen und Literatur der neueren europäischen Privatrechtsgeschichte', edited by *Helmut Coing*[5], who finally wrote himself a manual devoted to the private law institutions under the title 'Europäisches Privatrecht' (1985-1989)[6].

It is in particular *Coing*'s manual which in recent times has provoked reactions from the side of non-Romanists. I may refer to[7] an article by *Wilhelm Brauneder*, entitled 'Europäisches Privatrecht – aber was ist es? Anmerkungen zu Coing und Zimmermann'[8] (reference is made to the latter's fundamental work on the law of obligations[9]), and to an article by *Pio Caroni*, 'Der Schiffbruch der Geschichtlich-

3 Göttingen 1952; 2nd ed., 1967. An English translation by Tony Weir was published at Oxford, 1995.

4 4th ed., Köln and Graz, 1985.

5 München, 1973 onwards. Unfortunately the series is not completed: the gaps are particularly regrettable for the period 1500-1800, for which even the volumes that have appeared bear no indexes. Still more a torso is the series Ius romanum medii aevi, Mediolani, 1961 onwards (38 fascicula, published in arbitrary order without indexes); it includes, however, some useful monographs on the reception of Roman law.

6 Vol. 1: Älteres gemeines Recht (1500-1800), München, 1985; vol. 2: 19. Jahrhundert, München, 1989.

7 Besides the two articles mentioned in the text reference should be made to *Reiner Schulze*, Vom Ius commune bis zum Gemeinschaftsrecht – das Forschungsfeld der Europäischen Rechtsgeschichte, in: *R. Schulze*, ed., Europäische Rechts- und Verfassungsgeschichte, Ergebnisse und Perspektiven der Forschung, Berlin, 1991, 3 sqq.; less polemical than *Brauneder* and *Caroni*, *Schulze*'s contribution gives some broader starting points than *Coing*'s book. For further orientation cf. also *T. Giaro*, Europäische Privatrechtsgeschichte: Werkzeug der Rechtsvereinheitlichung und Produkt der Kategorienvermengung, Ius Commune 21 (1994) 1 sqq. A recent well-balanced study is *P. L. Nève*, Ius commune oftewel 'gemeen recht': Traduttore traditore?, in: Tertium datur, Drie opstellen aangeboden aan Prof. Mr. J. A. Ankum, Tilburg, 1995, 3 sqq.

8 Zeitschrift für neuere Rechtsgeschichte 15 (1993) 225 sqq.

9 *Reinhard Zimmermann*, The Law of Obligations: Roman Foundations of the Civilian Tradition, 1990 (reprint 1993).

keit: Anmerkungen zum Neo-Pandektismus'[10], which is in the first place directed against articles by *Zimmermann* but indirectly also against *Coing*'s manual.

One of the objections is that *Coing* and *Zimmermann* neglect those elements in the development of the private law in European countries which do not belong to the *ius commune* in the sense of a law based on the Roman law of Antiquity. As examples of such 'non – *ius commune* elements' are mentioned[11] feudal law, *ius mercatorum*, the law of the medieval German *Rechtsbücher* (especially the 'mirrors of the law' such as the *Sachsenspiegel*) and the *Stadtrechtsfamilien* ('families of urban law', i.e. law that groups of towns had in common as a result of adopting statutes from each other).

Coing's reply to this objection would be that the rules of these other 'systems' of law were given their place, *eingeordnet*, in the *ius commune*; in his view it was precisely one of the characteristic properties of the *ius commune* to do this. This is what *Coing* states in another context[12], a remark which *Brauneder* criticizes by stating, with irony, that in this way it is easy to construct a 'European private law'[13].

In my opinion it should always be borne in mind that, in a description of historical processes, 'European private law' can be nothing else than an anachronistic term used for reasons of convenience. Strictly speaking we should say: "the law that was applied in different territories which are now considered as parts of Europe", adding that we will only be concerned with "rules which we now call private law". This at least is the way the term should be interpreted in the title of the present contribution.

Where this title mentions 'a Romanist watershed', reference is made to the 'revival' of the Roman law since the 12th century. This was a revival of jurisprudence, closely linked to the full accessibility of the *Corpus iuris civilis*. I do not see it as my task at this meeting to describe once more this process[14]; the paper of *Peter Stein* mainly deals with this subject. The revival was at the origin of a legal science that could be called European because, after its birth at Bologna, it rapidly spread over the different parts of Europe. This European legal science certainly was mainly a science of private law (in anachronistic terminology again). In the final section of this contribution I will say something on the development of this science of private law in itself. But I see it as my principal task to discuss the influence it had on the private law rules as they appear in statutes and records of cus-

---

10 Zeitschrift für neuere Rechtsgeschichte 16 (1994) 85 sqq.

11 *Caroni* (n. 10) p. 91; besides the examples given in the text he mentions 'das adelige Standesrecht'.

12 *Coing* (n. 6) vol. 1, pp. 32-33.

13 *Brauneder* (n. 8) 228.

14 I have done this recently in my contribution to R. Jenkins, ed., The Legacy of Rome, A New Appraisal, Oxford, 1992, 399 sqq., in particular at pp. 403 sqq.

tomary law. Could one really also speak of a 'Romanist watershed' as far as this 'European private law' is concerned?

There is a long tradition, particularly in Germany, to deal with 'European private law' in terms of a conflict between Roman law and Germanic law. I will not deny that for a certain number of institutions this may have been the case, but in my opinion the contrast has been generalized too easily. I would like to show what I mean by discussing an example.

II. The *bona fide* Buyer of Moveable Property

My example will be a more or less central problem of private law (as we see it today): the protection of the *bona fide* purchaser of moveables not belonging to the seller. It is a subject that has fascinated me since I wrote my thesis on the right of the unpaid seller to reclaim the object of the sale ('recht van reclame')[15] and to which I have returned[16] recently[17]. It has a special flavour of topicality this summer, because in the August issue of the Zeitschrift für Europäisches Privatrecht an article was published by *Werner Hinz* on the development of *bona fide* acquisition of moveables in European legal history[18].

Werner Hinz is the author of a book on *bona fide* acquisition of moveables in the period of the *usus modernus Pandectarum* and Natural Law (16th, 17th and 18th centuries)[19]. In his article he gives priority to the history of the law in the German speaking countries and in France but deals also with developments in England, the

---

15 Reclame en revindicatie, Onderzoekingen omtrent de rol in de ontwikkelingsgeschiedenis van het recht van reclame gespeeld door den Romeinschrechtelijken regel omtrent eigendomsverkrijging en prijsbetaling bij koop (Inst. 2, 1, 41), Haarlem, 1949; cf. later revisions of my opinions in T.H.R.H.R. 50 (1987) 123 sqq. and in T.R. 58 (1990) 133 sqq. These 'revisions' go in the same direction as what I argue below on the protection of the *bona fide* purchaser: one should not too easily admit a 'Romanist watershed' in the development of some institutions of private law.

16 'Revisiting' an article published in 1955: Zum Ursprung des Lösungsrechts beim Kauf gestohlener Sachen auf dem Markte, besonders nach einigen spanischen und südfranzösischen Quellen, in: Festschrift Guido Kisch, Stuttgart, 1955, 237 sqq., reprinted in: *R. Feenstra*, Fata iuris romani: Etudes d'histoire du droit, Leyden, 1974, 73 sqq.

17 Revendication de meubles et "Lösungsrecht" de tiers acquéreurs (droit romain, droit wisigothique, droit coutumier médiéval en Espagne et dans le Midi de la France), in: Collatio iuris romani, Etudes dédiées à Hans Ankum, Amsterdam, 1995, 87 sqq.; cf. also Vindikation von Mobilien und Lösungsrecht in den nördlichen Niederlanden im 17. Jahrhundert, T.R. 63 (1995) 355 sqq. (on two recent publications; one of them is that of *Hinz*, mentioned below (n. 19)).

18 *W. Hinz*, Die Entwicklung des gutgläubigen Fahrniserwerbs in der europäischen Rechtsgeschichte, ZEuP 3 (1995) 398 sqq.

19 *W. Hinz*, Die Entwicklung des gutgläubigen Fahrniserwerbs in der Epoche des usus modernus und des Naturrechts [Hamburger Rechtsstudien, 80], Berlin, 1991; cf. my review article in T.R. (n. 17).

Netherlands and the Scandinavian countries. The choice is understandable, although it would have been preferable to add at least Spain, for which many interesting sources and good surveys are available. The article shows otherwise some of the difficulties with which all research in European legal history has to cope: for countries outside his own the author has not always used the most recent and authoritative studies.

1. Early Germanic Law

Hinz's approach is rather traditional[20]. The Roman law of Antiquity is opposed to early Germanic law. In the former there was an 'absolute concept of ownership' and the original owner could demand the restitution of his property from every person in whose possession it had come, not only when it had been stolen but also when the owner had lost it in another way; the only protection was given in the form of short terms of acquisitive prescription. In early Germanic law the situation was different. No developed ownership of moveables existed. Legal consequences were attached only to a form of qualified possession, the so-called 'Gewere'. If this 'Gewere' of a person was offended, he could – with an action called 'Anefang' – reclaim it from everybody into whose hands it had come. If there had been no theft but the property had been entrusted to someone else who abused the original possessor's confidence, the latter could only demand satisfaction from the unreliable bailee; a third party who had acquired the property could keep it. This solution is characterized as the Germanic principle 'Hand wahre Hand'.

I have called this way of opposing Roman law and Germanic law principles traditional. I should perhaps say: traditional for German legal historians. The idea that the 'Hand wahre Hand' principle existed already in the earliest Germanic law has been criticized by several recent German authors and it has even been questioned whether it can still be called the current opinion in Germany. For a survey of the developments in a European context it should have been avoided as a starting point.

2. The Later Middle Ages

For the period of the later Middle Ages – 13th, 14th and 15th centuries – *Hinz* states that the 'Hand wahre Hand' principle occurs in many European legal sources, directly or indirectly. He first mentions German sources such as the *Sachsenspiegel* and the urban law of Lübeck; the latter, which applied the principle with

20 A less traditional approach is found in *D. Olzen*, Zur Geschichte des gutgläubigen Erwerbs, Juristische Ausbildung 1990, 505 sqq., and in *A. Völkl*, Das Lösungsrecht von Lübeck und München: Ein Beitrag zur Geschichte der Fahrnisverfolgung [Forschungen zur neueren Privatrechtsgeschichte, 28], Wien, Köln, and Weimar, 1991.

some restrictions, influenced the law in certain regions and towns around the Baltic. *Hinz* then turns to France, stating that numerous texts, in particular from Northern France, would permit the conclusion that the 'Hand wahre Hand' principle applied. The implication seems to be that this might go back to Germanic roots of the customary law of this part of the country. I have doubts on this way of interpreting the French sources.

As a variant of the said principle – a variant occurring particularly in France – *Hinz* discusses the so-called 'Lösungsrecht': this term is commonly used[21] to indicate a right of the *bona fide* third party to say that he is only bound to return the goods if the original owner is willing to refund the price that had been paid for them. *Hinz* specifies that this rule applies mostly to purchasers who had bought goods on a market. He does not go into the question whether this variant also is of Germanic origin. In any case it has not been inspired by Roman law: it is rejected very clearly by a text in the Justinianic Code (C. 6, 2, 2), originally dating from the beginning of the 3rd century. It would have been worthwhile to mention that the 'Lösungsrecht' is not completely unknown to sources, usually considered as early 'Germanic' law[22]: apart from a statute of *Hlothaere* and *Eadric* (7th century), giving a 'Lösungsrecht' to a man from Kent who had bought moveable property in London that appeared to belong to somebody other than the seller, such a right occurs – be it only for half of the price – in the *Lex Visigothorum* (also 7th century) and already in the *Codex Euricianus* (end of the 5th century), which very probably is also a piece of Visigothic legislation[23]. Germanic law? Probably not: more likely a sort of compromise decision of the Visigothic king or his councillors.

The rule of the *Lex Visigothorum* – which continued to exercise much influence in Spain under the name 'Fuero Juzgo' – was maintained in the fueros of some parts of Spain, in particular in Aragón. A 'Lösungsrecht' for the full price occurs as early as the end of the 11th century in privileges given by the Castilian king to two towns in the Upper Ebro region: Logroño and Miranda; from there it was extended to parts of Castile. It concerned purchases made in a market or on 'the road of the king' (*via de rege*), which was the road taken by pilgrims to Santiago de Compostella. Nothing typically Germanic about that rule. In a wider sense it could be seen as an example of *lex mercatoria*, which was easily extended to other parts of Europe. It is tempting to suppose that the frequent occurrence of a 'Lösungsrecht' for purchases in markets in France was influenced by these developments in Spain. The 'Lösungsrecht' appears rather early in France: in the 'pays de droit écrit' as well as in the 'pays de droit coutumier' there are texts from the second half of the 12th century which mention it[24].

---

21 See *R. Feenstra*, Zum Ursprung (n. 16) 238 [74] n.8.

22 For occurrence in sources of the law in Antiquity (Babylonian law, Hellenistic law, Jewish law) see *W. Felgentraeger*, Antikes Lösungsrecht [Romanistische Beiträge zur Rechtsgeschichte, 6], Berlin and Leipzig 1933; cf. *R. Feenstra*, Revendication (n. 17) 89 sqq.

23 For details see *R. Feenstra*, Zum Ursprung (n. 16) 243 [79] sqq., and *R. Feenstra*, Revendication (n. 17) 90 sqq.

Hinz mentions the 'Lösungsrecht' also as typical for the Netherlands[25]. He seems to think of the Northern Netherlands in particular, but it also occurs in the Southern Netherlands, at least in Flanders[26].

In Germany the 'Lösungsrecht' was not very common. The most clear texts are found in the urban law of Schleswig, where in an early version a 'Lösungsrecht' for half the price appears and in a later version one for the full price[27]. In the urban laws of Lübeck and Munich there are also questions of 'Lösung', but probably not of a 'Lösungsrecht' as it occurs in the texts from Spain, France and the Netherlands.

From a historical point of view it should be emphasized that nowhere can the 'Lösungsrecht' rule be considered as a successor to the Germanic 'Hand wahre Hand' principle, as a sort of mitigation of that principle under the influence of the rule *ubi rem meam invenio ibi vindico*, founded in the Roman law. This statement applies not only to the Visigothic legislation but also to the later medieval developments in Spain, France and the Netherlands. The 'Lösungsrecht' rule should rather be seen as an exception to the rule that an original owner whose property is stolen can always reclaim it, a rule that was common to Roman and Germanic law[28].

For medieval English law *Hinz* sees limitations of the claiming back of moveables both by the 'Hand wahre Hand' principle and by the 'Lösungsrecht' rule. I do not feel competent to give a wellfounded opinion in this matter but it would seem to me that in any case there is little evidence of the application of the 'Hand wahre Hand' rule. The only clear limitations seem to lie in the protection – in particular for merchants – of the possession of goods bought in markets and fairs (or in the shops of the city of London, being a 'market overt'). This protection could either be that the purchaser was allowed to keep the goods or was only bound to return them if the original owner was willing to refund the price ('Lösungsrecht'). However this may be, in the English situation there could not have occurred a change in these matters by any factor that could be qualified as a form of reception of Roman law.

Such a change as an effect of the so called reception of Roman law[29] is postulated by *Hinz* for continental Europe. If we keep to statutory provisions and judi-

---

24 See *R. Feenstra*, Revendication (n. 17) 99 sqq.

25 For applications of the 'Hand wahre Hand' rule in the Netherlands see below (at n. 33 sqq.).

26 See *R. Feenstra*, Zum Ursprung (n. 16) 251 [87] n. 69, and cf. *R. Feenstra*, Revendication (n. 17) 103 and n. 117.

27 The earlier mention of the 'Lösungsrecht' seems to go back to the oldest nucleus of the urban law, dating from the second half of the 12th century: see *R. Feenstra*, Zum Ursprung (n. 16) 247 [83] n. 50, and cf. *R. Feenstra*, Revendication (n. 17) 94 and n. 48; the later version dates from about 1400.

28 This does not exclude the application of the 'Lösungsrecht' rule also to cases in which the property was not stolen but had been entrusted to somebody who had abused the original possessor's confidence.

cial decisions – and exclude the opinions of authors who could be seen as exponents of the European science of private law – the changes are, however, not spectacular.

For Germany *Hinz* mentions in particular, apart from nuances in the – Roman law influenced – statutes of Hamburg and Lübeck, judicial decisions in Saxony, which have more or less eliminated the rule of the 'Sachsenspiegel' that formed the prototype of the 'Hand wahre Hand' principle. These decisions would indeed seem to have a certain importance.

For France the examples taken by *Hinz* from the officially codified 'coutumes' are not very convincing, unless one starts from the idea that the 'Hand wahre Hand' principle originally applied, in particular in Northern France[30]. Although not stating it explicitly[31] *Hinz* suggests that the original situation was described by the rule 'meubles n'ont pas de suite' – considered as more or less equivalent to 'Hand wahre Hand' – and that, as a result of the reception of Roman law, this rule would have been limited to mortgage: 'meubles n'ont pas de suite par hypothèque'. This supposed development is, in my opinion, erroneous. Probably 'meubles n'ont pas de suite' originally meant only than an unpaid creditor, to whom the debtor had 'generally obligated' ('obligation générale') his goods for purposes of execution, could not exercise his rights on moveables[32]. Only after the fusing of the Roman *hypotheca* with the 'obligation générale' could this be interpreted in terms of a limitation of the creditor's *ius in rem*: influence of Roman law indeed, but without fundamental effect on the law.

As far as the Netherlands are concerned, *Hinz* mentions the application of the rule *mobilia non habent sequelam* only in the case of mortgage; he could have added that this rule had probably been taken over from France. *Hinz* says nothing about the 'Hand wahre Hand' principle being put aside in the Netherlands by Roman law influence. In my opinion the situation was not much different from that in Germany and in France. In a period in which in general little influence from Roman law is to be supposed, in the Northern as well as in the Southern Netherlands, there are texts in which one can see application of the 'Hand wahre Hand' principle (if that principle indeed existed at that time). There is even one text, the urban law of Deventer from about 1450, in which 'hand sal hand waren' is explicitly mentioned[33]. In the 16th and 17th centuries there are no texts which, as in Ger-

29 On this concept see my remarks in The Legacy of Rome (n. 14) 408 sq.

30 Cf. above, before note 21.

31 Explicit statements are found in traditional works like that of *E. Jobbé-Duval*, Étude historique sur la revendication des meubles en droit français, Paris, 1881; cf. *R. Feenstra*, Vindikation (n. 17) 372, n.100.

32 See *A. G. Pos*, Meubles n'ont pas de suite: le sens originaire de cette règle en droit français, T.R. 41 (1973) 45 sqq.

33 It remains to be questioned whether this formula always implies that one could never claim from a *bona fide* purchaser: it is sometimes used in contexts where this implication would not seem to be meant. In Deventer, however, the implication seems to exist.

many, would more or less eliminate existing forms of application of the principle. In the 17th century the majority of the texts seem to imply that moveables could be claimed from third parties, even if they were not stolen. Apart from the specific exceptions for purchase in a market (whether or not with a 'Lösungsrecht') there are only a few other exceptions. One of them is the rule that appears in the urban law of Antwerp from 1582 and which was 'received' in the urban law of Amsterdam: no claim from third parties when merchandise had been trusted to agents who sold it in contravention of their instructions[34]. There has been much misunderstanding about this specific Antwerp-Amsterdam rule: already in the 17th century some authors interpreted it as if it were the general *mobilia non habent sequelam* rule[35]. These interpretations might have been encouraged by a black and white attitude of people accustomed to the rules of Roman law – but this is a problem of the influence of the European legal science.

III. The European Science of Private Law

In expounding the problem chosen as an example of a possible conflict between Roman law and Germanic law I have already made some incidental comments on the question whether we could speak here of a 'Romanist watershed'. My conclusion would be that this is not the case. The changes in the law – as far as we can trace them – mainly concern issues that do not seem connected with the 'reception' of Roman law. This does not exclude, of course, the possibility that other examples could be found where the answer would be different. My purpose has been to give a warning: such examples should be examined very thoroughly before formulating conclusions.

I now return to the development of the European science of private law in itself, as opposed to the private law appearing in statutes and records of customary law. There can be no doubt that the revival of the Roman law in the school of the Glossators was a starting point for a European science of private law. Two questions, however, remain to be asked: (1) Was it the only starting point?; (2) Have there been, since the beginning of the 12th century, fundamental changes in the development of this European science of private law that could be styled as watersheds?

1. Starting Points of the European Science of Private Law

As to the first question something has to be said on Canon law. Could the school of the Glossators have been the starting point for a European science of private law

34 This is the main case; next to it the lending of household effects to people who then sold them is mentioned.

35 See *R. Feenstra*, Vindikation (n. 17) 367 sqq.

without the help of the Canonists? *Coing* has stated[36] that the Roman Catholic Church was the first great organization which called in lawyers and that it was the first stronghold of the new legal profession in Europe; by 'lawyers' and 'the new legal profession' *Coing* means people who had studied at universities, in Bologna or other Italian cities and later also in France. From the second half of the 12th century the Church, which for our purposes of today can be seen as the first European organization, had begun to reorganize its judicial system. Rules of procedure could be found in many parts of the *Corpus iuris civilis* but the Romans had never gathered them systematically or studied procedure as an autonomous subject. This was done in the *ordines judiciarii* (short guides to procedure) of the 12th and in the voluminous treatises of the 13th century; "they did what the Romans had never done explicitly, they created a doctrine of procedure"[37]. Now procedure is usually not seen as part of the private law; Roman law was, however, not only introduced into the procedure but also into the substantive rules applied in the ecclesiastical courts, whose jurisdiction was by no means restricted to purely ecclesiastical affairs (in the modern sense of the word): it covered, for instance, matters of marriage and divorce, questions of wills and many cases of contracts. In modern terminology we would call them important parts of the private law. There certainly were other parts of this law where the doctrines of the Glossators – and later those of the Postglossators – exercised influence without the mediation of the Canonists but this influence was probably more incidental and with more variations depending on the regions of Europe where it occurred. As for the first steps in the development of a 'European science of private law' the help of the Canonists may have been essential for the 'Romanists'.

2. Other Watersheds

This brings us to the second question just mentioned: have there been watersheds in the development of the European science of private law since the foundation period of the Romanists and Canonists in the 12th and 13th centuries?

My answer would be that the existence of two such watersheds could be discussed: the rise of a systematical tendency in the works of some of the legal Humanists and the penetration of the doctrines of the School of Natural Law. Both started in the course of the 16th century.

---

36 *H. Coing*, The Roman law as ius commune on the Continent, (1973) 89 L.Q.R. 505 sqq., at p. 511.

37 *R. C. van Caenegem*, The "Reception" of Roman Law: a Meeting of Northern and Mediterranean Traditions, in: The Late Middle Ages and the Dawn of Humanism outside Italy [Mediaevalia Lovaniensia, Series I, Studia 1], Leuven and The Hague, 1972, 195 sqq., at p. 200.

(a) Legal Humanism

As to the legal Humanists, their achievements did not only consist in a critical study of the original texts, modelled on the techniques of philology (with which they eliminated all medieval elements of interpretation that could not stand up to this criterion). There also was a tendency – in any case in the works of some French humanists – to rearrange the materials of the *Corpus iuris civilis* in a more coherent and systematic form. *Justinian's* Institutes, the only part of the *Corpus iuris civilis* which shows a system with a relatively simple structure, became the object of special attention. Some Humanists, however, went farther and built up a system of their own; they argued, as *Stein*[38] puts it, that the subject of a legal system is the Latin *ius* or French 'droit', not in the sense of objectives rules, but in the sense of subjective rights attaching to individual powers which they could assert through the legal system. The main representative of this approach was *Donellus* (*Hugues Doneau*, 1527-1591) who as a Huguenot had to leave Bourges and France during the Massacre of St. Bartholomew in 1572 and subsequently taught *inter alia* at the newly founded University of Leyden in Holland.

Stein has recently shown[39] *Donellus*' role in developing the modern concept of private law. In his 'Commentarii iuris civilis' *Donellus* makes for the first time a clear distinction between *nostrum ius* and *iuris nostri persecutio*, i.e. our (subjective) right and the procedural enforcement of our right[40]. In treating the subjective rights as a whole and in the order of *Justinian's* Institutes he creates a system of private law that brings important new concepts, such as that of *iura in re aliena*, a concept that has had much success in the School of the Pandectists[41]. Stein rightly concludes, however, that *Donellus*' contribution to the formulation of the modern civil law has not been given the credit it merits[42]. His influence in the 17th and 18th centuries has been overshadowed by the School of Natural Law, one of whose main representatives, *Hugo Grotius*, owes much to him.

38 *P. Stein*, Judge and Jurist in the Civil Law: A Historical Interpretation, (1985) 46 Louisiana Law Review 241 sqq. (reprinted in *P. Stein*, The Character and Influence of the Roman Civil Law: Historical Essays, London and Ronceverte, 1988, 131 sqq.), at p. 249 [139].

39 *P. Stein*, Donellus and the origins of the modern civil law, in: Mélanges Felix Wubbe, Fribourg/Suisse, 1993, 439 sqq.

40 *Stein* (n. 39) 449.

41 See *R. Feenstra*, Dominium and ius in re aliena: The Origins of a Civil Law Distinction, in: New Perspectives in the Roman Law of Property: Essays for Barry Nicholas, Oxford, 1989, 111 sqq. (reprinted in *R. Feenstra*, Legal Scholarship and Doctrines of Private Law, 13th-18th Centuries, Aldershot, 1996, as Nr. III).

42 *Stein* (n. 39) 452.

(b) Natural Law

I have mentioned the penetration of the doctrines of the School of Natural Law as a second possible watershed in the history of the European science of private law. The role of this school certainly has been more generally acknowledged by legal historians than the role of the systematic branch of the legal humanists. In 1947 *Hans Thieme* published a lecture, given at Bâle under the title 'Das Naturrecht und die europäische Privatrechtsgeschichte'[43]; a rather provoking title at that time when there existed no such things as a European Community or a European Union. After invoking the necessary provisos in regard to the concept 'history of European private law' and speaking of the 'isolation' of the different European peoples as to their laws, *Thieme* states that the development of Natural law was one of the three grandiose efforts that were made to overcome this isolation[44]. In 1953 *Thieme* published an innovative article[45] in which he specified that the starting point of this Natural law should be sought in the works of the so-called Spanish or Late Scholastic School, consisting of a number of mainly Spanish 16th century theologians, writing commentaries on the *Summa theologica* of *Thomas of Aquino*. In the Middle Ages moral theology and jurisprudence had been strictly separate domains, but in the 16th century some humanist authors propagated the idea that Roman law and Natural law belonged together. This link between the Humanist School and the Natural Law School, emphasized by *Thieme*, has unfortunately not yet been sufficiently worked out.

However this may be, the Natural lawyers brought many new elements and concepts into legal science; they continued, though, to draw a good deal from Roman law, which was used for most of the examples given to illustrate these new elements and concepts. This applies in any case to *Hugo Grotius*, who is not only to be seen as a pioneer of public international law but also had much importance for the development of the European science of private law. Though *Grotius*' main work, 'De iure belli ac pacis' (1625), contains much more in the field of private law than its title would suggest, the essential work is his 'Inleidinge tot de Hollandsche rechtsgeleerdheid' ('Introduction to the Jurisprudence of Holland') which he wrote in 1620, when he was in prison as a result of political troubles. It gives a synthesis of Natural law, Roman law and Dutch local customs in a way that certainly was instrumental in making Roman law accepted in practice. It was only in the 18th century that Natural law doctrines were sometimes used to resist the influence of Roman law. In general, however, it can be said that the Natural Law School, which propagated the idea of a universal unchangeable law, common to all

---

[43] Basel, 1947, 2nd ed. 1954, reprinted in: *Hans Thieme*, Ideengeschichte und Rechtsgeschichte: Gesammelte Schriften, Köln and Wien, 1986, 822 sqq.

[44] The two other efforts being the development of (medieval) Roman Law and Canon Law.

[45] *H. Thieme*, Natürliches Privatrecht und Spätscholastik, ZSS (GA) 70 (1953), 230 sqq., reprinted in *Hans Thieme* (n. 43) 871 sqq.

times and all peoples, found much useful material in the Roman law and, by a process of adaptation, helped to make it keep its central place in the European legal science, in particular in the science of private law.

The European science of private law did not abruptly cease to exist with the death of the most influential members of the School of Natural Law in the 18th century. However, the movement towards codification in many European countries in the second half of that century – a movement for which, to a great extent, this school has been responsible – inevitably led to a nationalization of legal science in those countries which eventually obtained national codes of law. It is true that in Germany – where only regional codes had come into being (Bavaria, Prussia and Austria) – there was no national codification until the end of the 19th century[46]; accordingly a more or less general science of private law could continue to exist. But the form it took under the influence of the School of the Pandectists deprived it soon of a European character. The simple fact that their books were not written in Latin any more, but in German, was of course an important factor.

IV. Conclusions

Our conclusion can be that 'reception of the Roman law' was mainly effectuated by the impact of a European legal science. This science was created by the Glossators – and their successors, the Postglossators – and propagated with the help of the medieval Canonists. The Legal Humanists and the School of Natural Law brought important innovations but these cannot be seen as bringing watersheds. The revival of jurisprudence in the 12th century certainly was a watershed in the development of European civilisation, but strictly speaking it was not a watershed in European legal science because it was the very beginning of such a science. As far as European private law is concerned – in the sense of rules that appear in statutes and records of customary law in different European countries – the changes we can see in it as a result of the revival of jurisprudence are certainly important, but there are so many variations in this process, depending on the kind of legal institution and the country or region examined, that the term 'watershed' should be used with all possible reservation.

46 England and Scotland had no codification either. I do not consider it as my task here to sketch the developments in the private law of these countries. The influence of the European science of private law has lasted until the present day in Scotland, just as in South Africa. These developments have been discussed in various other lectures at the conference.

The Canon Law Vehicle of Civilian Influence with Particular Reference to Scotland

By J. J. Robertson

I. Introduction

A vehicle is a means of conveyance. If Canon law is to be regarded as a vehicle, certain questions can be asked. Where is the beginning of the journey, where is the ultimate destination, and, in particular, what is being carried? The vehicle may have begun the journey relatively unladen but becoming much more laden as the journey progressed. A vehicle can also be seen as a medium of exchange, transmuting one thing into another thing.

The Canon law of the Roman church may be defined as the *corpus* of legislation given either by God or the competent ecclesiastical authority for the regulation and administration of the members of the Roman church. Although the origins of the Roman Canon law may be traced to the late 1st century, the impetus for the development of the law was given by the Edict of Milan, whereby *Constantine* and *Licinius* in 312 promoted religious toleration throughout the empire. Thereafter throughout the 4th and 5th centuries there was the growing competence of the bishops of the Roman church – especially of the bishop of Rome – in developing the scope and practice of the Canon law. It must be stressed that the administration of the early Roman church was firmly embedded in the administrative techniques of the late Roman empire. In particular, disputes within the ecclesiastical community could be resolved by adopting and adapting the legal procedural machinery of Roman law. *The Codex Theodosianus*, promulgated in 438, referring to a decree of *Valentinian II* given in 376, states that "whatever is customary in the conduct of civil suits shall likewise be observed in ecclesiastical litigation ..."[1].

By the 4th century the conduct of civil suits was by the investigative process of the *cognitio*. The adjudication of a civil action was now from beginning to end before an imperial magistrate. In outline, the procedure of a *cognitio* commenced with the pursuer lodging with the magistrate a written claim in a *libellus conventionis* which was intimated to the defender by the magistrate. If there was to be a defence, the trial would commence with both parties taking the oath *de calumnia* that the action was genuine. Thereafter there was *litis contestatio* followed by the par-

1 *Codex Theodosianus* 16, 2, 23, C. Pharr, ed., Princeton, 1952.

ties through advocates presenting or defending their positions, the hearing of witnesses or the considering of written evidence, culminating in the magistrate's *sententia* and the execution thereof. Procedure by *cognitio* also introduced a system of appeals.

The elements of the procedure before the church courts originate in the procedure of the *cognitio*[2]. It is this procedure, based on Roman law, which is from the 12th century developed and perfected by canonists for the adjudication of causes in the European hierarchy of church courts. In the field of procedure, the Canon law can clearly be seen as a vehicle transporting to new destinations elements of Roman law.

II. The Scottish Dimension

It is trite to say that Roman law is a source of Scots law. It can, however, be maintained that the Canon law was not the main vehicle for importing elements of Roman law into Scotland. There was no wholesale reception of Roman law. It can be argued that the greater part of any reception of Roman elements was mainly a post-reformation happening influenced by the recourse from the late 16th century of Scots law students to the protestant universities of the Netherlands where Roman-Dutch law was being taught and developed. Nevertheless, it is proposed to demonstrate that through the administration within pre-reformation Scotland by Scottish churchmen of the supra-national Canon law one influential element of Roman law was introduced into Scotland. It has been generally acknowledged that in the 15th and early 16th centuries "the only corps of professionally trained judges in the country were the church lawyers. ... they filled a vacuum left by the secular courts, offering justice where it could not be obtained elsewhere. In dealing with such cases they naturally used the Romano-canonical procedure"[3]. There must now be considered the emergence and practice in Scotland of this Romano-canonical procedure which can be regarded as the main element of Roman law which has been conveyed by the Canon law into later Scottish civil procedure.

III. Canonical Procedure in Scotland

The diocesan structure of the Roman church in Scotland was established in the 12th and 13th centuries. The office of the bishop's official in 9 of the 13 dioceses had been created by the middle of the 13th century. The officials of Caithness, Orkney and Ross were created no later than the middle of the 15th century and that of

2 For a fuller discussion see Dictionnaire de Droit Canonique, R. Naz, ed., Paris, 1935-65, vol. 7, col. 285 sqq.

3 *P. Stein*, The Procedural Models of the 16th Century, 1982 J.R. 195.

the Isles no later than 1510[4]. The duty of the official was to exercise judicial functions delegated to him by the bishop. He adjudicated in causes raised in the diocesan courts. The procedure in these courts was the *cognitio* as adapted and refined by the 12th and 13th century European canonists. This is reflected in the compilation of the Decretals by *Gregory IX* in 1234. In Book II the pattern of the *cognitio* can be seen in the titles, particularly in the following which are derived from the elements of the Roman *cognitio*:

Title 1 *De judiciis.*

2 *De foro competenti.*

Title 3 *De libelli oblatione.*

5 *De litis contestatione.*

7 *De juramento calumniae.*

8 *De dilationibus.*

10 *De ordine cognitionum.*

14 *De dolo et contumacia.*

19 *De probationibus.*

20 *De testibus et attestationibus.*

22 *De fide instrumentorum.*

25 *De exceptionibus.*

27 *De sententia et re judicata.*

28 *De appellationibus.*

The steps or process of a cause which is to be judicially settled are to be found in these titles. There are three stages in the process. These are the preparatory acts, the suit and the concluding acts. There are five parts to the preparatory acts. The first is the petition containing the libel. The second is the citation and certification of service. The third is the appointment of procurators and the lodging of the libel in court. The fourth and fifth parts are the reception from the defender or *reus* of dilatory exceptions and the fixing of the term dilatory to deliberate these exceptions which are preliminary pleas by the defender which must be considered before the matter becomes a suit.

The second stage is the suit or the instance of the cause which is in three parts. Firstly, there is contestation or joining of issue with the acts following being termed the suit. Secondly, there is the lodging by the defender of peremptory exceptions which may defeat or perempt the suit and to be decisive cannot be propounded until the cause has become a suit. The oath of calumny is then taken.

---

4 *D. E. R. Watt*, Fasti Ecclesiae Scoticanae Medii Aevi ad annum 1638, St. Andrews, 1969, under the title Official in the entry for each diocese.

Thereafter, written interrogatories are put to the defender where he has to answer upon oath certain positions extracted from the libel. Thirdly, there follows the proof where the pursuer or *actor* attempts to prove the libel and the defender to prove his exceptions within a term *ad probandum* assigned by the judge. Evidence may be from fact, confession, witnesses or written instruments.

The final stage of the process comprehends the sentence, the execution of the sentence and, if made, the appeal from the sentence.

All of these steps of process are clearly seen in *Stair's* Institutions. In Book IV of the 1693 edition, *Stair* outlines the main elements in Scottish civil procedure. These elements closely follow the elements of canonical procedure which are themselves based on Roman procedure. The procedure as found in *Stair* has continued in modified form to the present day[5].

The reason for the prominence of canonical procedure in Scots civil law lies in the late emergence of a supreme civil court. Prior to 1532, when the Court of Session was established, the dispensation of centralized royal justice with a developed indigenous procedure had not been perfected, as it had been in England since the 12th century, by a body of professional royal judges. The only professional judges in Scotland were the canonists in the officials' courts. The movement from the 15th century towards the establishment of a supreme civil court was much influenced by Scottish canonists. Of the 15 members of the Court of Session on its original creation, the first president, *Alexander Myln*, Abbot of Cambuskenneth and 7 others were churchmen. It would seem, therefore, to be inevitable that the procedure of the court would reflect canonical procedure since there was no refined secular procedure to follow.

Lord Cooper brought to the attention of modern scholarship the importance of the extent to which resort was being made in Scotland to church courts to resolve legal controversies. He points out that "the immense debt which Scots Law owes to Canon Law and Practice has never been sufficiently acknowledged"[6]. *Cooper* futher states, notwithstanding the incompleteness of surviving records, "that until the later years of the 13th century important civil controversies ... were usually left to the decision of the skilled and ubiquitous ecclesiastical lawyers, who in Scotland found ample scope for their activities owing to the absence of a fully organized judicial system and a legal profession to work it"[7]. In referring to the canonist tradition in procedure *Cooper* demonstrated "that the old Canonist practice calls to mind many features of modern procedure"[8].

---

5 For a fuller discussion of the comparison between canonical and Scottish procedure see *J. J. Robertson*, Canon law as a source, in: Stair Tercentenary Studies, D. M. Walker, ed., Edinburgh, 1981, at pp. 119-20; for a summary of canonical civil procedure see *James A. Brundage*, Medieval Canon Law, London, 1995, at pp. 129-34.

6 *T. M. Cooper*, Select Scottish Cases of the 13th Century, Edinburgh, 1944, p. xxii.

7 *Cooper* (n. 6) xxiv.

8 *Cooper* (n. 6) xxxv-vi.

Cooper writes in general terms. Surviving sources indicate that there was an extensive knowledge and practice of canonical procedure in late mediaeval Scotland. Such evidence is to be found in the St. Andrews Formulary, which is a collection of 615 styles, many dealing with canonical procedure, compiled by Master *John Lauder* between 1521 and 1546. *Lauder* was a notary apostolic and secretary to Archbishop *Forman* of St. Andrews and to Cardinal *David Beaton*. The significance of the Formulary to the legal historian is that the "... legal procedure which it illustrates ... belongs to a period when the civil judicature ... was shaping its practice under the influence of churchmen expert in Canon law ... the *Formulare* specimens of summons and inhibition and the instruments narrating the execution of these writs ..., the appeals and refutation of appeals, the commissions to examine witnesses ... and the narratives of processes ... must be viewed as part of the body of legal knowledge and experience which was carried by the clergy to the judicial committees of Parliament and Council and so to the Court of Session"[9].

The surviving records of the Scottish officials' courts are minimal and come from the archdiocese of St. Andrews between 1541 and 1553. These records show that the canonical procedure in these courts was reflected in the procedure of the Court of Session. *Ollivant* in his study of the officials' court[10] suggests that "the close ties" between the officials' court and the Court of Session "may help to explain this community of practice". As has been shown, the immediate cause of this community of practice lies in the dominant influence of ecclesiastical lawyers in mediaeval Scotland. Where is the source of this influence? *Ollivant* suggests an answer. In a picturesque summary he states that "[e]cclesiastical procedure acquired both definition and uniformity at an early stage, and it was a uniformity shared by the developments at the very heart of the church's legal machine – at Rome. If we turn again to consider the *Rota*, we find in its procedure one illustration of the hub of that wheel whose spokes eventually reached into the court of the sheriff of Fife". Indeed, the spokes penetrated every diocese in Scotland. The influence of the *Rota* on Scottish procedure must now be considered.

IV. Scotland and the *Sacra Romana Rota*

In a prophetic statement based on no apparent evidence, *Mackay* in 1877 considered that the Court of Session "resembled the *Rota Romana*, the supreme Court at Rome ..."[11]. The *Rota*, as one of the supreme tribunals of the Roman church has

9 St. Andrews Formulary, 1514 - 1546, G. Donaldson and C. Macrae, edd., Edinburgh, 1941 and 1944, vol. 1, at p. ix.

10 For an illuminating discussion on Canon law and Scots law, see *S. Ollivant*, The Court of the Official in Pre-Reformation Scotland, Edinburgh, 1982, at pp. 130-33. The extracts from *Ollivant* are in these pages.

11 *A. J. G. Mackay*, The Practice of the Court of Session, Edinburgh, 1877, vol. 1, at p. 22.

existed from the 14th century to the present day. *Mackay* could have been aware of the general structure of the *Rota* but he could not have known of the Scottish material or of the significance of that material which has been recovered from the archives of the *Rota* now held in the Vatican Archive.

To understand the significance of the material an outline must be given of the structure of the *Rota* in the 15th and 16th centuries[12]. In 1418 *Martin V* erected the *Rota* into a collegiate court of 30 auditors or judges, this number being reduced to 12 by *Sixtus IV* in 1472. Although the *Rota* was a collegiate body each auditor had his own court. To these courts cases at first instance or on appeal poured in from all of western Christendom. The volume of litigation in the *Rota* was immense. Apart from research which has been carried out on the Scottish cases it is impossible to quantify the number of cases heard by the *Rota* since no systematic examination has yet been made of the entire archive.

To administer and record cases, each auditor had a notary principal who had three notaries-substitute to assist him. It was the duty of the notary to record in a *manuale* the steps of procedure in every action. The entries in the *manuale* record daily the cases heard by the auditor. Each entry is headed with the name of the diocese whence the case originated and the subject matter of the case. As the case progresses each step of procedure is recorded, often in great detail. It is therefore possible to follow a case in detail from the lodging of the initial complaint to the final sentence. Depending on the nature of the case there may be only a few entries covering 2 or 3 months. On the other hand a case may continue for 2 or 3 years with an abundance of entries in several *manualia*.

The surviving *manualia* commence in 1464[13]. From that date to 1560 when papal jurisdiction was abolished in Scotland, there are 309 volumes of *manualia*; at least 362 Scottish cases have been found in 212 of these volumes. The number of English cases for the same period is approximately 20. It should be noted that many *manualia* have been lost. *Manualia* appear to have been in existence from the end of the 14th century. It has been estimated that only about 1/6th of the 15th and early 16th century *manualia* survive[14]. In examining the Scottish cases, there are many incomplete records which indicate that the missing entries must have been recorded in *manualia*, or parts of *manualia*, which are now lost. Other evidence shows that Scottish litigation which is known to have taken place in the *Rota*

---

12 For a fuller account of the history and procedure of the *Rota* and the related tribunals of the *Signatura Iustitiae* and the *Penitentiaria* see *J. J. Robertson*, Scottish Legal Research in the Vatican Archives: A Preliminary Report, (1988) 2 Renaissance Studies, at pp. 340-44.

13 Archivio Vaticano (A.V.), Indice 1057, Manualia Actorum et Citationum (Man.).

14 Until the present Scottish research, *Hilling* is the only scholar who has systematically examined the *manualia* for entries relating to the diocese of Hildesheim. Based on the number of known notaries who were preparing *manualia* he argues persuasively that only 1/6th to 1/7th of the *manualia* have survived: *N. Hilling*, Die römische Rota und das Bistum Hildesheim am Ausgang des Mittelalters (1464-1513), in: Reformationgeschichtliche Studien und Texte, Part 6, Münster, 1908, at pp. 17-18.

has not been recorded in any surviving *manuale*. There are references in letters of *James V* of 9th April and 18th May, 1538 to cases concerning the Priory of Ardchattan and the vicarage of Panbride for which there are now no surviving records[15].

From the evidence now available from the *manualia* it can be shown that the elegant rotal procedure refined out of the Roman *cognitio* was well known to the many Scottish litigants who proceeded to Rome. The cases were initially prepared in Scotland. Scottish procurators were much involved in presenting the cases before the *Rota*. Documentary evidence to conform with rotal practice was prepared in Scotland by Scottish notaries. Scottish witnesses were frequently and numerously present in Rome. Between 1464 and 1560 there was no year in Rome without Scottish litigation. It may be of interest that two Scots who became presidents of the Court of Session were involved in Roman litigation. *Alexander Myln*, Abbot of Cambuskenneth, raised a protracted case against *Robert Wemys* on the right to the teinds of salmon which commenced on 5th June, 1534, and was still before the *Rota* on 29th October, 1543[16]. *Robert Reid*, Abbot of Kinloss, appeared as a witness on 28th June, 1529 in a case on the right to teinds and the usurpation of fruits[17].

Scottish procurators, in preparing their cases, could have been assisted by various printed handbooks and formularies on rotal practice which were circulating in Rome and in Europe from the end of the 15th century. Three of these are in Glasgow University Library although they are not of Scottish provenance. These are the *Formularium Instrumentorum ad usum Curie Romanae*[18], the *Termini causarum in romana Curia servari solita in causa beneficiali*[19] and the *Formulare Advocatorum et Procuratorum Romane Curie et Regii Perlamenti*[20]. In Aberdeen University Library there is the *Formularius procuratorum curiae Romanae*[21] which is of Scottish provenance. It is undated but can be ascribed to the late 15th century. It is inscribed *Libellus magistri Thome Pyot etc Vicarie de Cluny etc*[22]. A Thomas Pyot, "clerk of St. Andrews", appeared as a witness on 3rd July, 1472 in a case before the *Rota* concerning a vicarage[23]. The formularies not only give the steps of

15 *R. K. Hannay*, The Letters of James V, 1513-1542, D. Hay, ed., Edinburgh, 1954, at pp. 346-47. There are also letters of January 18th, 1539, at pp. 363-64 and January 1st, 1540, at p. 386 which illuminate the records of cases on the prebend of Strabrok and the rectorship of Kinnoul in Man. 221ff. 89 – 141 and Man. 187ff. 935v – 1053 continued in Man. 217ff. 21 – 30v. This latter case involves *restitutio in integrum*.

16 Man. 173ff. 46 -375v and Man. 203ff. 95v – 628.

17 Man. 156ff. 9 – 24v.

18 Shelf-mark Mu 27-e.5, compiled by *Stephen Plank* and dated 7th September 1487.

19 Shelf-mark Mu 16-f.29 printed by *Schofer* in Mainz, 1490.

20 Shelf-mark Mu 14-f.20 printed in Germany, c. 1507.

21 Shelf-mark Inc 26.

22 f. H 9 v.

23 Man. 6f. 85.

procedure which are to be followed in a variety of actions but also give detailed formulae for instruments which are to be lodged in process, whereas the *Termini causarum* is a short procedural guide of only 13 folios, a procurator's *vademecum*, which could easily be slipped into a pocket. It outlines the 15 consecutive stages or terms in the progress of a case. They are as follows:

1. *Ad dicendum contra commissionem.*
2. *Ad libellandum.*
3. *Ad iurandum de calumnia.*
4. *Ad articulandum.*
5. *Ad dicendum contra articulos.*
6. *Ad producendum omnia.*
7. *Ad dicendum contra producta.*
8. *Ad declarandum seu declarari videndum positiones et articulos.*
9. *Ad respondendum.*
10. *Ad audiendum voluntatem dominorum Auditorum super admissione et repulsione articulorum sive positionum.*
11. *Ad videndum iurare testes.*
12. *Quando articuli probantur per instrumentum, litteras et alia iura.*
13. *Ad publicandum et ad videndum et audiendum omnia et singula dicta sive attestationes testium.*
14. *Ad concludendum.*
15. *Ad audiendum sententiam definitivam in scriptis ferri vel promulgari servatur.*

The 15 terms are the practical consequences of the procedure, based on the *cognitio*, as defined in the Decretals. It is this procedure which *Stair* adapts in the Institutions.

It is appioprate in this Quincentenary celebration to illustrate for the first time from the surviving cases from the diocese of Aberdeen the extent of the participation of Scottish procurators before the *Rota*[24]. In the 25 cases, 15 of the 30 procurators are almost certainly Scots. They are *William Marshall*, *Richard* (no surname), *Thomas Brown*, *Robert Dallache*, *Nicholas Greenlaw*, *William Cupar*, *John Fern*, *Thomas Crag*, *Adam Simpson*, *James Brown*, *John Lauder*, *James Salmon*, *David Methven*, *David Bonard* and *John Spens*. It should be noted that *James Salmon* appears in 5 of these cases. The same distribution appears in the cases from the other Scottish dioceses; approximately half of the procurators are Scots, either acting alone or along with foreign procurators.

---

24 See Appendix 1 for a list of the cases.

An insight should also be given of the essential detailed progress of a case before the *Rota*. Again it seems appropriate to illustrate this by giving summaries of the first four Aberdeen cases[25]. These are typical examples of the diverse nature of the actions. They also show something of the professionalism and skill of the participating procurators. It must also be stressed that the cases in the *Rota*, apart from their value to legal history, also throw much new light on the ecclesiastical and general history of Scotland.

V. Conclusion

At the beginning of this contribution it was suggested that a vehicle can be seen as a medium of exchange transmuting one thing into another thing. The practice of the Canon law in pre-reformation Scotland should be considered as a potent vehicle in transmuting the classical Roman *cognitio* into the civil procedure of post-reformation Scotland. Perhaps the practice of the Canon law in Scotland was also the medium for the introduction of a more intangible civilian influence into Scots law. The Scottish procurators and litigants who went to Rome were entering the heart of the romano-canonical scheme of things. The legal atmosphere was romano-canonical. Scottish procurators, waiting to appear before the auditors of the *Rota*, were literally rubbing shoulders with procurators from Italy, Spain, Germany and France. This legal cameraderie must have engendered debate and discussion imbued with the concepts of the romano-canonical tradition. English procurators were noticeably absent. This is not to say that canonists were not active in England. There was much litigation in the English diocesan courts but there is little evidence of extensive resort to the *Rota*[26]. By the 13th century the English royal courts had established their own procedure leaving little scope for romano-canonical influence. As has been shown, the situation in Scotland was very different. From the 12th century there was the growing pervading influence of the ecclesiastical lawyers in the Scottish legal scheme of things. It can be argued that this influence was at its greatest when the Court of Session was founded. It was therefore inevitable that romano-canonical procedure and ways of thought would dominate and for long continue to influence the practice of the civil law in Scotland. Perhaps this is symbolized in a case before the *Rota* concerning the monastery of Kilwinning where on 27th October, 1518, a Scottish witness is referred to as "solicitor, notary and *negotiorum gestor*"[27].

---

25 See Appendix 2 for Summaries.

26 See *Brundage* (n. 5) 134-38.

27 Man. 109ff. 15-48.

Appendix 1

Aberdeen – Cases recorded in the *Manualia* of the *Rota*

No.	References	Dates	Entries	Titles	Litigants	Procurators
1	8A. 39^{v} – 110	23. 3. 1474 2. 9. 1474	22	Archidiaconatus	Not recorded but probably Alexander Rate against Robert Stewart, see Watt, Fasti p. 19.	1. Johannis Gerona 2. Antonius de Eugubio
2	13. 172^{v} - 175^{v}	28. 5. 1483 30. 5. 1483	2	Cancellarie	1. George Brown 2. Not recorded	1. Petrus Altissen 2. Not recorded
3	14. 1^{v} - 124	30. 9. 1484 27. 1. 1486	34	Archidiaconatus	1. James Lindsay 2. Gavin Vaiche	1. Paulus de Ceretanis, Nicolaus, Richardus, (no surname) Petrus de Bertis. 2. Thomas Brun, Johanis Gerona, Johanis Fabri, Robert Dallache, Nicolas Greenlaw, Gasperus de Regno, Jacobus de Bonaretis, Hugo de Spina.
4	16. 80	20. 5. 1487 21. 5. 1487	2	Impositionis Nove Pensionis	1. Alexander Giffird	1. Leonardus de Senis
5	28. 326 - 491^{v}	2. 12. 1495 9. 1. 14973	2	Vicarie de Petracult	1. Michael Ker 2. William Rolland	1. Jeremias de Vulteris 2. William Cuper
6	38.1. - 209^{v}	26. 4. 1497 13. 6. 1498	36	Illegitimitatis	1. Christina 2. William (no surnames)	1. Laurentius Algas 2. Antonius de Poldo
7	56.139 - 143	5. 4. 1503 13. 4. 1503	3	Vicarie Parochialis de Loge-durno	Not recorded	Not recorded

8	84.177^{v} - 179	14. 7. 1512 25. 7. 1512	2	Vicarie De Lesly	1. Walter Mortimar	Not recorded
9	86.1^{v} - 20	21. 10. 1535 23. 11. 1535	9	Canonicatus Et de Monymusk Prebende	1. Henry Forsithe 2. John Duncanson	1. John Fern 2. Thomas Crag
10	102.449	4. 1. 1518 5. 1. 1518	2	Vicarie de Colsamond	1. Thomas Nudre	Not recorded.
11	105.52^{v}	16. 5. 1517	1	Parrochialis de Saline	1. John Shawe 2. James Cirandi (?)	Not recorded
12	105. 340-358	20. 7. 1518 28. 9. 1518	3	Canonicatus et Pre-bende	1. Robert Forman 2. Alexander Galloway	1. Simon Rosa 2. Adam Sanson (Simpson?).
13	124.1 This entry is on a folio which prefaces the Manualia entries and is a frag-ment of a book of commissions which were dis-tributed amongst the rotal notaries	27. 11. 1511	1	Canonicatus et Preben-da de Philorth et Perpe-tua Vicaria Parrochialis de Peterugy (Peterhead)	1. John Duncanson 2. Richard Richardson	Not recorded.
14	134.5^{v} - 260^{v}	28. 2. 1522 6. 7. 1523	15	Canonicatus et Pre-bende in Kinkel	1. Alexander Galloway 2. Robert Forman	1. Adam Synson. 2. James Brown.
15	142.90	9. 9. 1525	1	Canonicatus et Pre-bende	Not recorded	John Lauder, Clericus, St. Andrews.
16	173.152^{v}, 153	24. 11. 1534	1	Capellanie de Ileyn (?)	1. John Elphinston	1. James Salmon.

No.	References	Dates	Entries	Titles	Litigants	Procurators
17	175.91	7. 7. 1534	1	Canonicatus et Prebende de Rofery (?)	1. Franciscus Frescobaldi	1. Not recorded.
18	178.253^{v}	16. 10. 1535	1	Canonicatus et Prebende	1. William Barclaye 2. Thomas Gadier (?)	1. Not recorded. 2. James Salmon.
19	183.142 - 179^{v} 180.16 (Book of Commissions)	14. 10. 1535 10. 12. 1535 14. 10. 1535	6 1	Canonicatus et de Farchen Nuncupta Prebenda Ecclesie Aberdonensis (from 180.16)	1. Alexander Lokert 2. Alexander Dunbar	1. Bonavistus de Catellanis, mercator Florentinus. 2. James Salmond.
20	220 (no foliation due to poor condition of volume) 180.57^{v} (Book of Commissions.	25. 11. 1544 12. 6. 1545 25. 3. 15458	1	Parochialis Vicarie de Eycht	1. John Stracherin (?) 2. Henry Scincler	1. David Methven. 2. James Salmond.
21	228.73^{v} - 94	18. 12. 1547 10. 8. 1547	3	Pensionis	1. Robert Kecht	1. David Bonard.
22	236.47 - 541	5. 6. 1546 5. 5. 1550	82	Cancellarie	1. James Salmon 2. George Marschell	1. Not recorded but acting for himself (?). 2. John Spens, Rector of Crichis.
23	263.119^{v}	19. 6. 1551	1	Vicarie de Eyck	1. Henry Sincler	1. James Salmond.
24	270.368 - 458	12. 10. 1553 4. 7. 1554	2	Vicarie de Colsamond	1. William Salmond	1. James Salmond, Clericus, Glasgow.
25	294.271	3. 12. 1559	1	Canonicatus et Prebende	1. William Creyton	1. Not recorded.

Appendix 2

Aberdeen – Summary of the first 4 cases recorded in the *Manualia of the Rota*

1. Archidiaconatus

Manuale 8A, ff. 39v – 110; 22.3 – 2. 9. 1474; 22 entries; Auditor, Matheus de Porta.

Litigants Names not recorded of *actor* or *reus* but probably Alexander Rate against Robert Stewart (1).

Procurators of *actor*: Johannes Gerona and *reus*: Master Antonius de Eugubio, Guillermus Marschall, master Alexander de Saxoferrata.

Witnesses for *actor*: Thomas Brunning, layman, St. Andrews, Ghisbertus Iuvenis (Young), cleric, Glasgow.

Synopsis.

22. 3. 1474	New commission presented for Gerona to the auditor, Matheus de Porta.
23.3.	Eugubio "... because of an injustice committed by the auditor ... sought ... an appeal for his party ...".
30.3.	Eugubio to be excommunicated "... unless within one day the outstanding fee for the notary for the prior instance should have been paid ...".
22.4.	"Master Nicolaus Cruzenack, notary of the prior instance of the same cause before Johannes Franciscus, Lord Auditor, procured that the register in the present cause held before his said own auditor ... should be transported and assigned to me, the notary in the present cause ...".
9.5.	Eugubio "produced ... letters excommunicatory at the instance of ... Nicolaus de Allegritis (2) merchant of the Roman Curia against certain things described in those letters ... by Jacobus de Micharellis, Auditor of the ... Apostolic Camera ... and subscribed by Werispolonius de Pistia, notary ...".
23.5.	"Gerona ... to see to the swearing of witnesses".
25.5.	Eugubio to be excommunicated unless he paid the notary of the cause his outstanding fee.
27.5.	"Gerona ... in presence of Eugubio ... moved the auditor to pronounce judgement ... the auditor having recalled the dilatory exceptions ... and the letters refutatory ... regarding the appeal ... pronounced judgement in terms of the schedule ... which he read out according to its terms ...".
27.6.	"Gerona ... appeared again and a schedule of expenses having been lodged by him ... obtained from the auditor the taxation of expenses in the sum of [blank in text] gold ducats of the Camera, a sworn statement having been received from ... Gerona ... as to how much necessary expenses had been incurred in prosecuting the litigation ... and obtained ... letters executorial ...".
2.9.	"Saxoferrata, substitute ... of Eugubio ... moved and obtained from the auditor that the written depositions produced ... on behalf of his party should be ordered to be restored to him".

Commentary.

This case illustrates the continuation of a cause, the first instance before the auditor Johannes Franciscus, being appealed by Eugubio. Financial matters concerning payments to the Apostolic Camera appear to have been an issue in the first instance. Gerona's actions for the award of the archdeanery to his client follow normal procedure with the lodging of the libel, articles, production of the register of the prior instance, oath of calumny, interrogatories for witnesses, taking of exceptions and sentence in his favour. Eugubio resorts to delaying tactics which are impeded by censures of excommunication for non-payment of notaries' fees (3). Eugubio's successful request for the return of his client's depositions suggests that a further appeal was being contemplated.

(1) *D.E.R. Watt*, Fasti Ecclesiae Scoticanae Medii Aevi ad annum 1638, St. Andrews, 1969, at pp. 19, 20.

(2) Allegritis acted as agent in earlier Scottish financial transactions in the Camera: see *A.I. Cameron*, The Apostolic Camera and Scottish Benefices 1418-1483, London, 1934, at pp. 61, 63.

(3) For further comment on censures see *O.J.A. Reichel*, A Complete Manual of Canon Law, London, 1896, vol. 2, at pp. 143, 320, 321.

2. Cancellariae

Manuale 13, ff. 172v – 175v; 28.5 – 30. 5. 1483; 2 entries; Auditor, Johannes de Ceritanis.

Litigants George Pron (Brown) *actor*; *reus* not recorded but probably Andrew Young (1).

Procurator of *actor*: Master Petrus Altissen.

Witnesses for *actor*: Robert Fernonder, cleric, St. Andrews, Alan Meldron, commissary, St. Andrews.

Synopsis.

28. 5. 1483	"Altissen ... lodged a bull of provision, articles and George Brown's supplication ... witnesses swear to the articles seeking a penal monitory ...".
30.5.	Auditor granted monitory to Altissen.

Commentary.

The record of this case is incomplete. It appears to be an unopposed petition by Brown establishing his claim to the benefice and warning others not to intrude. Brown became bishop of Dunkeld in October, 1483.

(1) *Watt*, Fasti, p. 13; *Cameron*, The Apostolic Camera, p. 206.

3. Archidiaconatus

Manuale 14, ff. lv – 124; 30. 9. 1484 – 27. 1. 1486; 34 entries; Auditor, Hieronimus de Porcariis.

Litigants James Lindisay *actor*; Gavin Vach *reus*.

Procurators of *actor*: Master Paulus de Ceretanis, Master N. "substitute of ... Ceretanis," Master Richard, Master Petrus de Bertis and *reus*: Masters Thomas Brun (1), Michaelis Boneti, Johannes Gerona, Johannes Fabri, Robert Dallache, Nicholas Grenlau, Gasperus de Regio, Jacobus de Bonaretis, Hugo de Spina.

Witnesses for *actor*: David Seton, John Eguerdi (Edwardson) provost of Dunglass, St. Andrews, William Turnbul, archdeacon of Shetland, David Spens, canon, Glasgow, Robert Daloqui, canon, Moray and for *reus*: Alexander Abercromi, vicar of Tervis, Aberdeen, Lucanus Catinas, vicar of Telling, Dunkeld, Benedictus Gundeti, cleric, Lugdunensis, Robert Foreceder, canon, Caithness, Thomas Andersone, presbyter, St. Andrews, Masters Symon Volstia and Matheus Bertoris, procurators of causes in the Roman curia, Master Conradus Millies, notary of the palace, Johannes Ysore, cleric, Velucicensis, Petrus Corghueti, cleric, Tornacensis, Paulus Ceottis, cleric, Cremonensis, James Lindisay, cleric, Candida Casa, Nicholas Grynlaw, cleric, St. Andrews, Robert Nicolai, presbyter.

Synopsis.

19. 2. 1485	"Ceritanis ... on the contumacy of the opposing party not swearing the oath of calumny ... swore the oath ... and lodged articles ...".
5.3.	"Eguerdi ... witness for Lindsay ... showed ... a process of resignation to have the seal ... of Petrus Bogart, doctor of decreets, protonotary apostolic, judge and executor in the process and recognised ... the signet of Johannes Merck ... apostolic and imperial notary in the process ... and the signet ... of Robert Leys, presbyter, Aberdeen, imperial and royal notary, on two instruments of execution of citation ... later, Turnbul examined as witness ...".
21.3.	"Master Richard [no surname] procurator ... of Lindsay ... shows his mandate of procuration in hand of ... David Hugonis, M.A., presbyter, Glasgow, apostolic and imperial notary ...".
8.4.	"David Spens recognized the signet ... of Hugonis ... and on being shown an instrument of execution of citation, David Seton and Robert Daloqui recognised the signet ... of Leys ... and Robert and David Spens recognized the signet ... of John Willelmi ... [Williamson], presbyter, St. Andrews, imperial and royal notary, on an instrument of diligence of execution ...".
13.4.	"Brun ... lodges articles ...".
22.4.	"Boneti ... produced three witnesses ... Abercromi ... Catinas ... and Gundeti ... interrogatories to be ... given ...".
2.5.	Brun compelled "Johannes Cantus, cleric, Macloviensis, ... to produce a closed transumpt sealed with the signet of the register ...".
16.12.	Bertis cited to recognize the signet on the transumpt and thereafter to its opening but did not appear. Signet recognized by "masters Conradus Millies and Nicolaus Gleneris ... notaries of the palace ... before ... the auditor ... as the signet of the register of supplications ...". Transumpt then opened.
23.12.	Brun compelled "Johannes Vockynck, cleric, monasteriensis, being present ... to ... produce ... a manuale ... of Godfredus de Grollis ... notary ... in which ... notes are written of a fulmination of a process by ... Robert Blackeder concerning two canonries and prebends in the cathedrals of Glasgow and Aberdeeen by ... Peter, bishop, Tirasonensis, judge and exe-

cutor of the fulmination ... and he produced two witnesses ... Volstia and Bertoris ... who, on being shown the manuale, recognised Grollis' hand ... Volstia produced a transumpt from the register of bulls ... with the seal and signet ... of the secretary of Pope Innocent VIII along with an instrument of acceptance and provision ... of Blackader of the said archdiaconate by Patrick Makcllech, M.A., presbyter, Candida Casa, notary apostolic and an instrument of requisition and insinuation of the said acceptance and provision by the same Patrick Makculloch."

9. 1. 1486 Brun "produced three witnesses ... Millies, Ysore and Corghueti ... to recognise the transumpt of the register ... of Pope Sixtus IV ... later ... Pancratius Rotunda, *sollicitator* of apostolic letters ... produced ... an instrument of possession ... of Blackeder formerly protonotary apostolic ... subscribed by Mathew Patok, cleric, St. Andrews, imperial and royal notary ... again Brun produced three witnesses, Ysore, Corghueti and Ceottis who, when shown the protocol of fulmination of the process of Blackeder's expectative grace, recognised it to have been written and subscribed by Gerardus Dresis, apostolic and imperial notary ... and further produced four witnesses ... James Lindisay, Nicholas Grynlaw, Alexander Abercromi and Robert Foreceder who, when shown Blackeder's instruments of acceptance and provision, Nicholas, Robert and James recognised the signet ... of Patrick Makculloch ... and when shown Blackeder's instrument of possession ... Robert and Alexander recognised the signet ... of Mathew Patok ...".

11.1. "Bertis cited by Brun to lodge interrogatories ... Bertis protested verbally against the witnesses and what they had said".

Commentary.

This case illustrates the reliance of litigants on documentary evidence to substantiate their claims and the high standard of proof required for establishing the authenticity of the evidence and of procurators' mandates. The reference to the *manuale* indicates that Blackadder had already litigated in the Rota. There is no surviving evidence in the archive of this earlier case. Robert Dallache (Daloqui) appears as a witness for Lindsay and as a procurator for Vach. Nicholas Greenlaw appears as a procurator and witness for Vach. Lindsay's claim is based on a resignation by an unspecified person. Vach is relying on Blackadder's claim which may have been assigned to him. The record is incomplete with no decision being recorded. Although Lindsay had been appointed to the archdiaconate on Rait's death in 1479, considerable litigation ensued before his appointment was secure (2).

(1) On 5th February, 1485 Brun (Brown) paid annates on behalf of Vach for the deanery of Aberdeen, see *Cameron*, The Apostolic Camera, at p. 213.

(2) *Watt*, Fasti, at p. 20; *L.J. Macfarlane*, William Elphinstone and the Kingdom of Scotland, Aberdeen, 1985, at p. 209.

4. Impositionis Novae Pensionis.

Manuale 16, ff.80; 20 -21. 5. 1487; 2 entries; Auditor, Johannes de Ceritanis.

Litigants Alexander Giffard *actor*; *reus* not recorded.

Procurator of *actor*: Leonardus de Senis.

Synopsis.

20. 5. 1487	Commission on the dependence presented to the auditor at his house.
21.5.	"Senis ... obtains authority to cite, with power to inhibit, the parties to the suit to appear, under censure, within 60 days...".

Commentary.

Giffard is either the principal *actor* or has intimated his interest in current or pending litigation. To safeguard his claim he has cited his opponents to appear and has inhibited them from intromitting with the subject of the claim pending a final decision. There is no further record of this case which may have been raised as a tactical move to obtain extra-judicial settlement.

A Comparison of the Influence of Roman Law in England and Scotland

By William M. Gordon

I. Introduction

The title of this essay carries certain implications, in particular that there is something which can be identified as Roman law and that Roman law did exercise influence both in England and in Scotland. It is implied, furthermore, that it is worthwhile to make a comparison between these two countries and jurisdictions in this respect. The question of what is meant by Roman law is somewhat more complicated than might at first appear and more is said on this below. So far as comparison is concerned, on a simplistic view it might seem that there is little or no scope for that process. England is the mother country of the common law and English lawyers are proud of that remarkable system and have been unwilling to concede that it has owed anything to outside influence, least of all to the civil law. Scotland, on the other hand, has participated in the civilian tradition and Scots lawyers, we are told, are equally proud of belonging to that tradition and not anxious to see Scots law affected or further affected by an influence from the common law which has at times been baneful. English law and Scots law are, therefore, in different families or camps – and 'camps', with its military connotations, might seem the better metaphor considering the vigour with which the debate on the respective merits of the common law and the civil law has often been conducted. This would lead to contrast rather than comparison.

But such a simplistic view needs to be modified. English lawyers, while remaining proud of their traditions and convinced that the common law has much to teach others, are no longer so ready to hold that the common law holds the only acceptable answers to legal problems. The European Union has been a factor there as well as the disappearance of the British Empire which has deprived English law of its claims to be the predominant law of a world-wide empire and not merely the national law of part of one small country. There is a greater readiness to admit, as common lawyers from the United States have been more ready to admit, that the common law may have owed something to the civil law. It can even be contended, although it must be said that the contention has not been advanced by a common lawyer, that English law has shared in the tradition of the *ius commune*[1]. From a

[1] *R. Zimmermann*, Der europäische Charakter des englischen Rechts, ZEuP 1 (1993) 4; see also the American scholar *R.H. Helmholz*, Continental Law and Common Law: Histori-

different standpoint, comparative lawyers point out that the civil law countries do not simply apply the civil law; French law is not the civil law translated into French nor German law the civil law translated into German. *Réné David* in his introduction to the study of comparative law preferred the descriptive term 'Romano-Germanic' to make this clear. Comparative lawyers also recognize 'mixed' legal systems where there has been cross-breeding between civil and common law, producing hybrid vigour or monstrosities according to one's point of view. Scots law is one of those systems. Again, in relation to Scots law, Scottish legal historians increasingly refer to the common roots of the English and Scottish legal systems in the Middle Ages[2].

All this points to the possibility of fruitful comparison between the English and Scottish experiences in relation to Roman law but before going further it is as well to start by considering what is meant by Roman law in the context of its influence on other systems.

II. Roman Law

1. Roman Law and Civil Law

When talking about the influence of Roman law on other legal systems there is merit in making a terminological distinction between Roman law and civil law. 'Roman law' can then be used to refer to the law of ancient Rome, including that law as applied in the new Rome of Constantinople up to the 6th century. Roman law in this sense was captured by *Justinian* and his compilers in the Institutes, Digest and Code and this compilation, added to by the mainly Justinianic Novels, forms what modern Roman lawyers treat as the *Corpus iuris civilis*. Roman law in this sense has sometimes been called half-jokingly 'Roman Roman law'. 'Civil law', on the other hand, can be used to refer to the law expounded and created, on the basis of a *Corpus iuris civilis* somewhat differently constituted (including, for example, the Books of the Feus) by Roman lawyers of various schools from the Glossators of the 12th century through to the Historical School and the Pandectists of the 19th. These Roman lawyers constructed for themselves what they conceived the Roman law to have been, largely on the basis of their interpretation of the texts of the *Corpus iuris*, with a view to its application in practice or at least with a view to its possible application in practice. What they conceived the law to have been does not necessarily coincide with what a modern Romanist would think it was but it was their views which could exert influence.

---

cal Strangers or Companions, 1990 Duke Law Journal 1207, concluding that they have been companions.

2 E.g. *H. L. MacQueen*, Common Law and Feudal Society in Medieval Scotland, Edinburgh, 1993.

It is to Roman law in the former sense that most scholarly endeavour has been directed by Roman lawyers for the last hundred years or so. Even where scholars have looked beyond the law of ancient Rome to the later development of that system they have in general been more concerned to elucidate that development in its historical context than to consider how far the later development was and still is of relevance to the current law and how the current law might be influenced through knowledge both of Roman law and the civilian tradition. So far as continuing influence is concerned, therefore, Roman law as studied by modern Romanists might sometimes seem of more concern to classicists and medievalists than to modern lawyers and therefore to have less claim to inclusion in the curriculum of a degree in law. Modern Romanists have been seen, however unjustly, as reinforcing this appearance by concentrating their attention on the law up to *Justinian*, particularly on the classical law of the first two and a half centuries A.D. Again, by emphasizing that Roman law was not a fixed body of rules but a legal system in evolution they have made recourse to it for guidance on issues arising in modern law more problematic in two main ways. On the one hand, by increasing the complexity of the task of discovering what Roman law was and how it might be used they have made it more difficult to use it; access to Roman law scholarship has become even more difficult for the non-specialist than it is for the specialist Roman lawyer. On the other hand, looking at Roman law as a system in evolution tends to deprive it of the authority it might claim derived from its provision of what seem to be timeless solutions to legal problems.

It may be remarked in passing that it is somewhat ironical that many modern Romanists, and certainly all those familiar with the common law tradition, would see the classical jurists who largely made Roman law and whose work was excerpted to form the Digest, the very core of the *Corpus iuris*, as the soul-mates of the common lawyers rather than of the Roman lawyers who were responsible for putting together that same *Corpus iuris* which, with its variations, is the foundation of the civilian tradition. But in turn it may be asked whether those who worked on the *Corpus iuris* were always so different from the common lawyers because, as will be noted below, some of the characteristics of modern civilian jurisdictions seem to derive at least as much from the rational Natural law as the civil law.

2. The Civilian Tradition

The danger of not making the distinction between Roman law and civil law clear when Roman and civil law have exercised influence and are still resorted to and the merit of trying to clarify the distinction by a distinction of terminology comes out in Scottish cases in which use has been made of Roman or civil law in recent times. I think particularly of *Glasgow Corporation v. Lord Advocate*[3] and *Sloans Dairies Ltd. v. Glasgow Corporation*[4] in which reference was made to modern Ro-

3 *Glasgow Corporation v. Lord Advocate* 1959 S.C. 203.

manists and to civilian writers without any apparent awareness that it might be necessary to approach differently what they said, or were thought to have said. In the former case it was decided that a payment made in error by reason of what was held to be a wrong interpretation of a statute could not be recovered, as the payment had been made under an error of law relating to the general law. Modern authorities, such as *Buckland's* Manual and Textbook of Roman Law were cited to the effect that in Justinianic law such an error of law did not found the *condictio indebiti* because the error was to be regarded as inexcusable and this view of what Roman law had been was clearly a factor in the decision. In the latter case it was held that in a sale of heritable property the risk passed to the purchaser as soon as the missives of sale had been concluded; a range of authorities from *Voet* through to *Mackintosh*, *Moyle* and *de Zulueta* was cited and they were discussed as if all were on a par. It may or may not be significant that the former decision has been departed from[5] and that the latter is normally got round by contractual provisions delaying the date from which risk passes to a purchaser. The point which matters is that the civil law tradition could also provide support for different conclusions from those reached by the court in the relevant cases and a proper distinction between Roman law and civil law was not drawn[6]. The distinction is no less important in looking for Roman or civilian influence. The search cannot be confined to the Roman texts and their modern interpretation.

It is also worth noting that from the 17th century onwards the civil law was competing with the rational Natural law as a source of persuasive authority. Indeed, at least one of the features commonly seen as characteristic of civilian jurisdictions, that the law is normally to be found in a code or codes, is more a consequence of Natural law influence than a normal or necessary step in the evolution of civilian jurisdictions. Although the *Corpus iuris civilis* might be regarded as a sort of codification and has often been referred to as such it has not the systematic structure which one would expect of a modern codification (except for the Institutes which are a very small part of the whole). To a degree at least the medieval *ius commune* formed from the civil and the canon law might be described as a case-law system and the rules or practices developed to deal with ascertainment of the *communis opinio* of the learned as a source of authority in the *ius commune* are not dissimilar to the rules or practices on the handling of precedent in the common law[7]. It is true that the Humanist interest in orderly treatment of the law was a factor in the more systematic presentation of the law and there is a civilian input to the ideas of the Natural lawyers but the decisive push towards codification came from the Natural lawyers (in association with rulers prepared to give effect to their ideas).

---

4 *Sloans Dairies Ltd. v. Glasgow Corporation* 1977 S.C. 223.

5 *Morgan Guaranty Trust Co. v. Lothian Regional Council* 1995 S.L.T. 299.

6 See further on this point, *R. Evans-Jones*, Unjust Enrichment, Contract and the Third Reception of Roman Law in Scotland, (1993) 109 L.Q.R. 663.

7 *L. Lombardi*, Saggio sul diritto giurisprudenziale, Milan, 1967, at pp. 164 sqq.

III. Scotland

1. Early Scots Law

Although England appears first in the title of this essay there is much to be said for starting the comparison with Scotland because it seems to me that Scotland in most respects fits into a general pattern of the development of civilian jurisdictions. The ways in which England differs, in so far as it does differ, may then appear more clearly. Without going into details, for which I may refer to a fuller account which I have given elsewhere[8], it can be said that the earliest evidence of the use of Roman law in Scotland indicates that knowledge of Roman law first came to Scots lawyers through the Canon law. Typical is the use of the *Summa decretalium* of *Goffredus de Trano* in *Regiam Majestatem*[9]. This feature of the early reception of Roman law is something neither unique to Scotland nor surprising. Roman law was a subsidiary source of Canon law and the *Corpus iuris civilis* can be used effectively only by sophisticated lawyers, which Canon lawyers were.

Once introduced through Canon law Roman law was used in Scotland increasingly in the secular courts from the 14th century onwards. The evidence of such use becomes even clearer in the 15th century and there is no reason to doubt the statement made in the 16th century by *John Lesley*, one of the judges of the Session, Scotland's central court which developed out of the king's council and was reorganised by the College of Justice Acts of 1532 and 1540, that that court turned to Roman law whenever it was faced with a difficult case on which there was no native authority. The evidence is there in the records and there is negative evidence in the complaint of *Skene*, in this respect as in others a not untypical 16th-century Humanist[10], that Scots lawyers spent too much time on the civil law to the neglect of the sources of their own system. He had, it is true, an interest in making this claim as he was seeking to provide his countrymen with convenient editions of the early native sources but it does seem to be the case that any systematic study of the law undertaken by Scots lawyers at the time would have been based on the civil law rather than Scottish sources. This was particularly true of those whose systematic legal education was obtained at a continental university as for so many it was until the later 18th century.

---

8 *W. M. Gordon*, Roman Law in Scotland, in: R. Evans-Jones, ed., The Civil Law Tradition in Scotland, 1995, 13.

9 *P. G. Stein*, The Source of the Romano-canonical Part of Regiam Majestatem, (1969) 48 Scottish Historical Review 107.

10 *J. W. Cairns*, *T.D. Fergus* and *H. L. MacQueen*, Legal Humanism in Renaissance Scotland, (1990) 11 J.L.H. 40, at pp. 44-48.

2. The Institutional Period

The onward march of the civil law in Scotland continues in the 17th and 18th centuries and is most easily observed in the works of the institutional writers, *Craig*, *Stair*, *Mackenzie*, *Forbes*, *Erskine* and *Bankton* – I use 'institutional' to cover both introductory works, such as *Mackenzie's* slim volume of Institutions, and those more massive works, such as the Institutions of *Stair* and the Institutes of *Erskine*, which Scottish courts treat as authoritative sources. The extent to which and the way in which the civil law is used varies among these authors but it is clear that in their systematic treatments of Scots law the civil law provides in large measure a legal terminology, it influences, even where it does not actually provide, the structure of the treatment and it often sets the agenda for the discussion of problems such as the transfer of risk in sale where native authority was limited or non-existent. The works of the institutional writers also show the considerable extent to which rules derived from the civil law had been or were being adopted. The records have not been fully explored but the reports conveniently collected in *Morison*'s Dictionary confirm the picture which emerges from reading the institutional writers. At the same time the contribution of the rational Natural law is also visible in the institutional works and it is stated by all writers and confirmed by the case-law that the civil law is of persuasive authority only.

3. The Effect of the Union with England

Whether Scots law would in due course have been codified had it remained wholly within the civilian tradition is a matter of speculation. What is not a matter of speculation is that the Union of 1707, which created a new state of Great Britain in place of the former states of England and Scotland, brought Scots law into closer contact with the common law than it had been since the Middle Ages. The Treaty and the Act of Union did preserve the Scottish legal system, subject to the possibility of an unrestricted assimilation of the public law of the two countries and to the possibility that the private law might be altered but only 'for evident utility of the subjects within Scotland'. The fact was that Scotland no longer had its own legislature but shared with England a legislature which even historians who should know better seem to regard as the parliament of England in unbroken succession and that appeal to the, essentially English, House of Lords in civil matters was soon admitted in default of any specific provision on the matter in the Treaty or the Act which followed on it.

Those who have sought, or even fought, to revive and defend Scots law's civilian heritage have seen the House of Lords as a Trojan horse or worse, introducing the alien and unwanted common law into Scots law through the practice of the courts. There have certainly been unfortunate decisions by the House of Lords. Against this it must in fairness be said that litigants and their advisers in the 18th century were ready enough to make use of the opportunity of appeal – litigants, and other users of a legal system, are probably more concerned with achieving a result favourable to them than with preserving the integrity of the system which they use. Contemporary interest in English law is also very clear from other sources such as the observations on the law of England inserted systematically in *Bankton's* Institute.

In the wake of the loss of Scotland's own legislature there has also been a great deal of unsatisfactory legislation for Scotland by the British parliament, particularly where Scottish provisions have been tacked on to English legislation or Scottish legislation has followed too closely an English model. But Scots lawyers and the Scottish business community have often been quite happy to follow English models and to see legislation for an assimilation of Scots and English law which, for political reasons, has almost inevitably meant the application of English law to Scotland[11]. I do not propose to discuss these issues now. I am concerned only with the fact that Scots law for whatever reasons has in many ways and particularly since the 19th century departed from the civil law tradition and been brought within the common law tradition through the Union.

This is not to say that the civil law tradition died out in the 19th century. Contact certainly continued, with interest shown in the work of the Historical School and the Pandectists and in German legal education. Moreover, in so far as the common law, as we shall see, made contact with the civil law in the 19th century in such areas as mercantile law and the theory of contractual obligation, Scots lawyers and common lawyers were drawing on common sources. *Pothier*, for example, plays a prominent role in both jurisdictions. Roman law remained a compulsory part of the curriculum of legal studies in the 19th century but it was forming a declining proportion of the curriculum as new subjects were added in consequence of reforms of university education. It may be suspected also that it formed a declining proportion of the intellectual baggage of the practising lawyer and that partly because once civilian ideas had been incorporated into Scots law they could be developed on the basis of the Scottish authorities without necessarily referring back to their origins. The civilian heritage was coming under threat and it required a conscious effort by those anxious to preserve the separate identity of Scots law as a civilian jurisdiction to arrest a tendency towards too ready reliance on the common law in the 20th century. But the occasions on which Roman law and the civil law come into play in the courts are relatively few. The erosion of the place of Roman law in the curriculum even at the universities which teach it has continued. The Law Society of Scotland has dropped its requirement; the Faculty of Advocates has, wisely, so far retained a requirement that intrants should have some knowledge of the Roman system, but this does not apply to solicitor advocates.

---

11 *A. F. Rodger*, The Future of the Legal Profession in Scotland. Marching to an Alien Tune?, 1991 J.R. 1; The Codification of Commercial Law in Victorian Britain, (1992) 108 L.Q.R. 570.

4. The European Union

How far the tendency of the common law to take over will be altered by the entry of the United Kingdom into the European Union remains to be seen. Judge *Edward* has expressed a sceptical view of the supposed advantages which Scots lawyers might have over English lawyers in dealing with European law through their closer connection with the civilian tradition[12]. The teaching of Roman law in European universities has declined and as the teaching of Roman law in Scotland has also declined, partly through the increased demands by other subjects on the limited time available within the law curriculum, this common element in education which might lead to increased common understanding is less often to be found in lawyers from the different jurisdictions in the European Union. It would certainly seem sensible to try to repair this part of the foundations of the civilian tradition if there is to be hope of a common European private law but that is another story.

IV. England

1. English Law in Splendid Isolation?

The place of Roman law, or of the civil law, in England is a question on which views have been very much influenced by political considerations of one kind and another. The predominant view over the centuries has undoubtedly been that English law has owed little to the civil law and that this has been a good thing too. The famous remarks of *Heinrich Brunner*[13] to the effect that English law was inoculated against destructive infection by an early dose of the learning of the Glossators and the slightly less jaundiced, but scarcely less negative, verdict of *Holdsworth*[14], that Roman law was received at various times in small homoeopathic doses so that it acted as a tonic and not as a drug or a poison, give the flavour. At the same time it is interesting that *Scrutton* in his Yorke Prize essay on the question of the influence of Roman law[15], devotes the whole of the first part of his work to a refutation of arguments that Roman law had exercised a significant influence on English law before the revival of its study by the Glossators. Not everyone in the past has sought to minimize the role of the civil law in England and there is undoubtedly nowadays a greater readiness to acknowledge both the possibility of influence and the existence of some influence in the course of the centuries.

---

12 *D. A. O. Edward*, Scots Law and Six Heresies, (1994) 39 Journal of the Law Society of Scotland 159.

13 See *H. Brunner*, The Sources of English Law, in: Committee of the Association of American Law Schools, ed., Select Essays in Anglo-American Legal History, 3 volumes, Boston and Cambridge, 1907-9, vol. 2, p. 7, at p. 42.

14 *W. S. Holdsworth*, History of English Law, vol. 4, 1924, p. 293.

15 *T. E. Scrutton*, The Influence of the Roman Law on the Law of England, Yorke Prize Essay 1884, Cambridge, 1885.

2. The Use of Civil Law in England

That said, it appears to me that the issue of the extent of civilian influence on English law has been somewhat obscured by a tendency to equate 'English law' with the common law as developed by the common law courts, ignoring or marginalizing those parts of English law which were administered elsewhere, in particular in Chancery, in the ecclesiastical courts, in the courts of admiralty and in the conciliar courts. In fact, while I have some reservations on Professor *Zimmermann's* thesis that English law has actually shared in the tradition of the *ius commune*, it is more than doubtful whether a minimalist interpretation is the correct one. In my view it is only possible to maintain the judgment that the influence of the civil law was insignificant in England by confining attention to the common law in the narrower sense. Even there there is some room for argument but as soon as one looks beyond the common law in this sense it is evident that English law did undergo civilian influence, along with the influence of the Canon law and, looking at the whole picture, it might reasonably be said that the only question is how extensive that influence was in comparison with so-called civilian jurisdictions. There does remain the big difference that English common lawyers have not in general perceived themselves as having significant links with the civil law and English lawyers have overwhelmingly perceived English law as being the common law in a narrow sense so that the civil law, if used, has to be more or less smuggled in or referred to as a comparator rather than a source. Where the civil law comes into play it simply happens that civil law reaches the same conclusion as the common law and it is an interesting phenomenon that two so different systems agree on a solution; acknowledging this poses no such threat to the common law as might seem to arise from acknowledging that they agree on the solution because the civil law has inspired it.

I do not propose to deal in any great detail with the use of Roman law in England. There are limits of time, space and my own knowledge. I rather confine myself to a couple of general observations and a sketch of the contacts made with the Roman and the civil law. The first of these general observations is that in one respect England conforms to the pattern of civilian influence described for Scotland, namely, early contact with the civil law comes through the Canon law, and this is only to be expected. England was within the jurisdiction of the universal church, whatever peculiarities there may have been in the relationship between England and Rome, and the Channel could not cut off all contact with mainland Europe, particularly when the English crown held extensive lands in France. The author of *Glanvill*, the major source of Scotland's *Regiam Majestatem*, clearly was familiar with Roman law although it does not appear that much was taken from it either in organisation or content; the probability is that his knowledge of Roman law came primarily through Canon law[16]. Much the same may be said of *Bracton* where the

---

16 See *R. V. Turner*, Who was the Author of Glanvill? Reflections on the Education of Henry II's Common Lawyers, (1990) 8 Law and History Review 97 (cf. also Judges,

borrowing is more extensive and there is evidence of direct use of *Azo*. But this initial use of Roman law did not lead to increasing resort to the civil law by the central secular courts to assist in the solution of new problems as happened in Scotland and elsewhere.

As a second general observation, at this point two features which distinguish English law from other systems may be noted. The first of these is that if there is one characteristic which does clearly distinguish English law from systems which have undergone more obvious influence from the civil law it is its legal terminology which is based substantially on Norman French. One mark of a civilian system obviously is the use of civilian terminology which sometimes conceals a failure to adopt civilian ideas or the substance of particular civilian rules. Native ideas or rules are simply translated into their nearest civilian equivalent. English law offers, it seems to me, an example of the converse phenomenon in which the use of what was or became a native terminology – Norman French was, after all, an import – may give the impression that the system itself is wholly of native growth and may conceal the adoption of civilian rules or ideas which are translated into Norman French or English.

3. Legal Education and Interest in Civilian Ideas

The other feature which makes a major distinction between England and civilian jurisdictions has been the form of legal education, particularly education in the common law in the narrower sense. English law has been predominantly a remedy-based system, the judges have been drawn from the practitioners in the courts and legal education has been based largely on how to operate the system of remedies available. Legal education in the Inns of Court, which have been described as the third university of England, that is, the third alongside Cambridge and Oxford[17], does show in moots and readings the influence of contemporary university education and more specifically contemporary education in law; but little of the substance of the law taught in the universities of the Middle Ages, the civil and the Canon law, seems to have been taken over with the form[18]. The English common law based on its native remedies did not have a body of ready-made native law comparable to the bodies of civil and Canon law to turn to for ideas but the common lawyers who were educated in the use of the writs which initiated actions in the common law courts did not apparently turn to the civil and the Canon law for ideas to expand the scope of the common law, at least to a major extent. It was rather left to the chancellors to turn to the civil and the Canon law to help in build-

Administrators and the Common Law in Angevin England, London and Rio Grande, 1994, 71).

17 See *J. H. Baker*, The Third University of England: The Inns of Court and the Common-law Tradition, Selden Society Lecture, London, 1990.

18 Observations by *J. H. Baker* at P. Chiene Seminar, Edinburgh, 28 April 1995.

ing up that alternative system of law called 'equity' which provided remedies lacking in the common law. Where other jurisdictions, such as Scotland, looked to the civil and Canon law to help build unified legal systems enriched from these sources England, it seems, chose to build parallel systems applied by parallel court systems. The result is peculiar but the course of development may not be as different as might at first sight appear. The civil law may have contributed relatively little to the common law but English law still benefited from contact with the learned laws in other ways. Apart from Chancery, the church courts and other jurisdictions, such as admiralty, which used the civil and the Canon law and had their own specialized bar centred on Doctors' Commons until the 19th century should not be forgotten.

The 16th century sees an ambivalent relationship with the civil law. Regius chairs were created in Cambridge and Oxford by *Henry VIII* and there have been suggestions that the common law was threatened by a civilian take-over. It is not entirely clear, looking back, that there was a real threat to the dominance of the common law tradition in the first half of the century[19] but there was some cause for concern. At the beginning of the following century the common lawyers were certainly concerned that *James VI and I's* abortive plans to have one law for the two kingdoms over which he ruled after the Union of the Crowns of 1603 would mean the introduction of the civil law and were strong opponents of his plans for that reason among others[20]. The civil law also was associated with absolutism and the common law with the parliamentarians' challenge to royal power which led to civil war later in the century. The fact that the civil law could provide not only texts favouring absolutism – the ruler's pleasure has the force of law (D. 1, 4, 1 *pr.*) or the ruler is not bound by the laws (D. 1, 3, 31) – but also texts favouring popular sovereignty – what affects everyone must be approved by everyone (C. 5, 59, 5, 2) – did not save it from vituperation. Opposition to the civil law by common lawyers (and *vice versa*) has not always, if ever, been based on an objective assessment of the respective merits of the civil and the common law. An objective assessment might, after all, lead to the less exciting conclusion that there is value in both.

If in Scotland in the 18th century there are signs of a rapprochement with the English common law there is in England evidence of rapprochement with the continental tradition. For example, interest in the civil law is evidenced by *Wood*'s Institute and interest in the rational Natural law is evidenced by *Strahan*'s translation of *Domat*. A link with the tradition of institutional literature appears belatedly in the shape of *Blackstone*'s Commentaries but *Blackstone*'s teaching in Oxford and the later foundation of the Downing chair in Cambridge did not lead to a civilian

19 See *D. Jenkins*, English Law and the Renaissance, Eighty Years on: In Defence of Maitland, (1981) 2 J.L.H. 107; *C. P. Rodgers*, Humanism, History and the Common Law, (1985) 6 J.L.H. 129.

20 See The Jacobean Union. Six tracts of 1604, B. R. Galloway and B.P. Levack, edd., Scottish History Society, 4th series, 21, Edinburgh, 1985.

style of legal education in the universities. Law teaching did not gain a firm foothold in English universities until the later 19th century. Even then a law degree did not provide the normal route into the legal profession nor did the teaching of law in the universities mean that the universities were seen as the place in which law should be taught for the profession in the sense that passes in university examinations in law automatically exempted candidates from the final professional examinations.

England therefore remained distinctive in respect of legal education throughout the 18th century. The law and procedure of the common law courts were also distinctive and these courts were tending to extend their jurisdiction; the conciliar courts had been victims of the Civil War. Equity was hardening as a parallel system of law. In spite of all this there was indeed some contact with the civil law and with the civil and rational Natural law, which were partners as well as rivals. *Pothier* was well known. *Lord Mansfield* in particular tried to use the civil law to bring English commercial law administered by the common law courts into the mainstream of European development but he was only partially successful, failing in particular in his attempts to persuade his colleagues that the doctrine of consideration in contract could be dropped.

In the 19th century, following on from the contacts found in the 18th, there is evidence of interest both in *Pothier* and in the work of the Pandectists, part of whose intellectual heritage is to be found in the rational Natural law – the idea, that is, that the law should be a logical construct from basic principles. For those who did attend university as part of their legal education Roman law was a required subject in Cambridge, London and Oxford and it was even required for the bar examinations when legal education was reformed in the latter part of the century. Another strand of influence can be traced in jurisprudence or legal theory. In so far as that has dealt with the analysis of legal concepts Roman law in various guises made and for a long time continued to make a significant contribution; how far that has influenced the law is less clear and probably the analysis of legal concepts now features less prominently in jurisprudence syllabuses than it did where jurisprudence is taught[21].

Yet another strand of influence can be traced in the production of treatises which draw on the civil and Natural law to help in the organization and theoretical construction of branches of the law, such as contract[22]. What was taken was not Roman law as the Romans knew it but it is all part of the civilian tradition and gave

---

21 See *H. Barnett*, The Province of Jurisprudence Determined – Again!, (1995) 15 Legal Studies 88.

22 *A. W. B. Simpson*, Innovation in Nineteenth Century Contract Law, (1975) 91 L.Q.R. 247; and *idem*, The Rise and Fall of the Legal Treatise: Legal Principles and the Forms of Legal Literature, (1981) University of Chicago L.R. 632, both reprinted in: *idem*, Legal Theory and Legal History. Essays on the Common Law, London and Ronceverte, 1987, 171 and 273 respectively; *S.A. Riesenfeld*, The Impact of Roman Law on the Common Law System (1985) 1 Lesotho Law Journal 267.

the common law a limited connection with that tradition. But there were reversals too. Doctors' Commons disappeared in the middle of the century with the transfer of matrimonial jurisdiction from the church courts and the common law expanded its scope. It may be suspected that the creation of the Supreme Court of Judicature with Queen's Bench as the first named of the divisions of the High Court and now able to grant equitable remedies gave the common lawyers a feeling of superiority. Certainly English lawyers saw English law as the proper law of a world-wide empire with something to teach the legal world. The Privy Council was an Imperial court usually administering the common law although it had also to deal with appeals from civilian or mixed jurisdictions such as South Africa.

In the 20th century Roman law studies in England have come under similar pressures to those which have affected Roman law in Scotland but there has, of course, been less to lose as Roman law was less well entrenched outside Cambridge, London and Oxford. Knowledge of Roman law is no longer required for entry to the bar. Reference to Roman or civil law in the courts is probably even less common than in Scotland. How far contact with Europe will change the situation is, as for Scotland, an open question although European contact certainly appears to have helped to break down belief in an innate superiority of the common law and English notaries, who still require a knowledge of Roman law, have found Europe a useful source of business. It is not yet clear, in particular, that English lawyers perceive themselves as part of a European tradition or are persuaded that common law methods are not the best even where civilians may have some good ideas, as in the law of restitution.

V. Conclusion

Scotland in the general lines of its legal development followed the civilian tradition until it was brought into close contact with England as a result of the union of 1707. Contact with the common law has turned it into a mixed jurisdiction and in legal method there is not a great deal to distinguish Scots law from its larger neighbour although differences in style remain. England has in some respects gone its own way in legal development. English lawyers speak their own language. Practising lawyers have never really accepted as natural that legal education should take place in the university and that the universities can be trusted to give would-be practitioners a sound legal education although it has become fairly normal for practitioners to start with a law degree. Law and equity are still separated in the minds of English lawyers although the English courts of law and equity were fused more than a century ago. English lawyers think in terms of precedents and specific remedies, the Mareva injunction for instance[23]. Codification is a rather dangerous

23 An injunction granted to prevent the removal of assets out of the jurisdiction by a party to a litigation, from the case *Mareva Compania Naviera S. S. v. International Bulk Carriers* [1957] 2 Lloyd's Rep. 509 in which such an injunction was first granted.

idea. In most of these respects England represents at least a partial contrast with Scotland and Scotland is nearer to the civilian tradition. But in part the differences seem to stem more from a determination to appear different than from the existence of wholly independent legal traditions. English law seen as a whole owes more to the civilian tradition than might appear. Scots law was not the civil law in tartan even before Scotland and Scots law were brought again into a close relationship with England and the English common law after 1707. Both systems have the opportunity to find a place in what may become a new common law drawing on all that the Western legal tradition has to offer but the Roman and the civil law are not wholly assured of the continuing contribution which they could make to that law.

The Resilience of the Scottish Common Law

By W. D. H. Sellar

One of the outstanding features of the history of Scots law has been the continuity of legal development; a continuity which stretches back, without serious interruption or political dislocation, to a very remote past, to a time indeed before our earliest legal records begin[1]. One of the guiding threads which, in my view, helps to explain this continuity of development – perhaps the most important guiding thread – is the concept of a Scottish "common law". This paper considers the rise of the common law of Scotland and its relations with the feudal law, the Canon law and the civil law[2]. It seeks to demonstrate the resilience and adaptability of the common law in the face of the incoming tide of the civil law and, in particular, as regards the "Reception" of Roman law; and to suggest some reasons for this resilience[3].

I. The Emergence of a Scottish Common Law

The idea of a specifically Scottish common law is first articulated about the middle of the 13th century. The emergence of such a concept at such a time can be explained by the combination of two crucial factors. The first was the extension of

1 As argued in *W. D. H. Sellar*, A Historical Perspective, in: M. C. Meston, W. D. H. Sellar, and Lord Cooper, ed. S. C. Styles, The Scottish Legal Tradition, Edinburgh, 1991, p. 29. For a contrary view, see Lord President *Cooper* in his original Scottish Legal Tradition, Edinburgh, 1949; reprinted in 1991 as above. See also *W. D. H. Sellar*, The Common Law of Scotland and the Common Law of England, in: R. R. Davies, ed., The British Isles 1100-1500: Comparisons, Contrasts and Connections, Edinburgh, 1988, p. 82.

2 For the rise of the Scottish common law, see *W. D. H. Sellar*, The Common Law of Scotland and the Common Law of England (n. 1), and Custom as a Source of Law, in: The Laws of Scotland. The Stair Memorial Encyclopaedia, vol. 22, Edinburgh, 1987, 355-393; and *H. L. MacQueen*, Common Law and Feudal Society in Medieval Scotland, Edinburgh, 1993.

3 For many years the main contributions on the influence of the civil law on Scots law were *Peter Stein*'s The Influence of Roman Law on the Law of Scotland, 1963 J.R. 205, reprinted in *P. G. Stein*, The Character and Influence of the Roman Civil Law: Historical Essays, London and Ronceverte, 1988, p. 319; and *P.G. Stein*, Ius Romanum Medii Aevi, pars V, 13b, Milan, 1968, reprinted as Roman Law in Medieval Scotland, in: P. G. Stein, The Character and Influence of the Roman Civil Law: Historical Essays (as above), p. 269. Now see also the contributions to R. Evans-Jones, ed., The Civil Law Tradition in Scotland, Edinburgh, 1995, and the papers in the present volume.

the terms 'Scots' (*Scoti* or *Scotti*) and 'Scottish' to cover all the peoples within the territory of the king of Scots; and of the term 'Scotland' or *Scotia* to describe that territory. These terms as applied to land and people alike originally had a purely Irish frame of reference, but by the beginning of the 11th century had become as apt to attach to the longstanding colony of the Gaels in Britain as to the Gaels of Ireland[4]. At the end of that century, in 1094, in the earliest surviving Scottish charter, the style used by King *Duncan II*, son of *Malcolm Canmore*, is *rex Scotiae*[5]. The regular style of his brother Edgar (and of his successors for centuries to come) was *rex Scottorum*[6]. At first, however, the Scots were only one of several peoples addressed by the kings of Scots in their charters, and not usually the people addressed first at that. Thus, a typical charter of King *David I* (1124-53), or of his grandson *Malcolm IV* (1153-64), would address the king's subjects *Franci*, *Angli*, and *Scotti* alike. Sometimes the address might include other peoples also: *Walenses* in the territory of the old kingdom of Strathclyde; and *Galwalenses* (Galwegians) in the far south-west. The pecking order is reasonably clear: French first, English second, and Scots a poorish third. In the south-east of the kingdom, indeed, the Scots might not be mentioned at all[7]. Thus when King *William I* (1165-1214) granted a toft of land in Berwick to the Abbey of Kelso, the address is restricted to *Franci* and *Angli*[8]. The term *Scotia* had at first a similarly restricted meaning. In King *David*'s time it denoted the country north of the Forth and Clyde. Earlier still it may have excluded land north of the Spey. By the middle of the 13th century, however, this terminology was rapidly changing. The farsighted policy of King *David* and his royal successors was succeeding in melding the various peoples in their kingdom into a single nation, the nation of the Scots: and the growing perception was that of one people, the Scots, under one king, within the kingdom of *Scotia*.

The second factor which helps to explain the emergence of the concept of a Scottish common law at this time requires little further elaboration, especially in this company: the rise of the English common law. There can be no doubt that the terminology of a 'common law' as it came to be used in Scotland (*communis lex* or *ius commune* in Latin; *la commune lei* in French) was borrowed direct from Eng-

---

4 On this see now *Dauvit Broun*, The Origin of Scottish Identity, in: Claus Bjørn, Alexander Grant, K. J. Stringer, edd., Nations, Nationalism and Patriotism in the European Past, Copenhagen, 1994, p. 35; see also *E. J. Cowan*, Myth and Identity in Early Medieval Scotland, 1984 Scottish Historical Review 111.

5 *Lawrie*, Earliest Scottish Charters, Glasgow, 1905, no. XII. The authenticity of this charter has been disputed on a number of occasions, but now appears to be generally accepted.

6 *Lawrie* (n. 5) nos. XVIII-XXII.

7 *G. W. S. Barrow*, Regesta Regum Scottorum: The Acts of Malcolm IV King of Scots 1153-1165, Edinburgh, 1960, pp. 73 sq. and *passim*; and *G. W. S. Barrow*, Witnesses and the Attestaion of Formal Documents in Scotland, 12th – 13th Centuries, (1995) 16 J.L.H. 1, at p. 6.

8 Cosmo Innes, ed., Liber Sancte Marie de Calchou (Cartulary of Kelso Abbey), Bannatyne Club, Edinburgh, 1846, no. 32.

land[9]. To these two factors a third should be added, a corollary of the first: the fact that the kings of Scots, like the kings of England, had been remarkably successful in bringing their various subjects under a single body of law common to all the kingdom, declared in the king's courts. In this Scotland and England were unlike, for example, France and Germany, where there was one king, but not for many centuries a single body of law.

II. The Symbolism of the Crown

The concept of the common law of Scotland has had a continuous history from the 13th century until the present day. I have tried to chart its progress elsewhere, and *Hector MacQueen* has studied the early centuries of the common law in his 'Common Law and Feudal Society in Medieval Scotland'[10]. The earliest reference to the Scots common law so far observed occurs in 1264, in a royal brieve (*jus commune*)[11]. In the course of the judicial competition for the Crown of Scotland in 1291-2, known as 'The Great Cause', there are frequent references to 'la commune lei e les usages de Escoce e du reaume de Engleterre', or similar, and at least one reference to 'la commune lei expresse de Escoce'[12]. There are references also, incidentally, to that other long-lived *ius commune*, which denoted a blending of the civil and Canon learned law: the 'Paris Lawyers' consulted by *Edward I* in the form of a *quaestio* for their opinion on the Scottish succession, refer to *leges communes scilicet imperiales*, and to *leges communes imperiales tam juri canonico quam civili*[13]. In *Robert the Bruce*'s legislation of 1318, passed after his victory at Bannockburn, the phrase *communis lex et communis iusticia* describes the law of the realm[14]. In 1399, as is well known, the Scots Parliament was concerned about 'the mysgouvernance of the Reaulme and the defaut of the kepyng of the common law'[15]. Later the Scots Parliament passed Acts in 1426 and 1504 which stress that the laws in use in the realm of Scotland should be the king's own statutes and the common law of the realm, and no 'particular' laws, nor the laws of other countries or realms[16].

What other laws are struck at by these ordinances of 1426 and 1504? Without doubt, any laws in particular parts of the kingdom, such as the Western Isles, which

---

9 See below (nn. 11-16).

10 For the main sources drawn on here, see above (n. 2).

11 Innes (n. 8) i, no. 309.

12 *E. L. G. Stones* and *Grant G. Simpson*, Edward I and the Throne of Scotland, Oxford, 1978, vol. 2, pp. 336 and 326.

13 *Stones* and *Simpson* (n. 12) vol. 2, pp. 359 and 363. See also *G. J. Hand*, The Opinions of Paris Lawyers upon the Scottish Succession c. 1292, (1970) 5 The Irish Jurist 141.

14 Acts of the Parliament of Scotland ('A.P.S.'), i, 467.

15 A.P.S., i, 572.

16 A.P.S., ii, 9 (1426); A.P.S., ii, 244 (1504).

might be in conflict with the king's common law, for these are mentioned specifically. But laws external to the kingdom are intended also. For, and this is highly relevant to the story of Scots law in its relations with the civil law, the kings of Scots were determined to be masters in their own house, or as it was sometimes expressed, emperors in their own kingdom. It is well known that the French attitude towards the authority of Roman law as a source was partly conditioned by the determination of the kings of France to demonstrate their independence of the Holy Roman Emperor; and that what was true of *Philip the Fair* of France was true also of *Edward I* of England. In Scotland too, it can be argued, that the desire of the Scottish kings to be seen to be independent of the Empire, coupled with the existence of a Scottish common law, prevented an uncritical adoption of Roman law in the late medieval period, when it had, in *Maitland's* famous phrase, "gone halfway to meet the medieval facts"[17].

In the first half of the 15th century a cohort of Scotsmen can be found studying the law, Canon and civil, at the University of Leuven (Louvain)[18]. One of them was *William Elphinstone* senior, father of the *William Elphinstone* the Quincentenary of whose foundation of Aberdeen we celebrate. In fact, *William Elphinstone* senior's lecture notes are the earliest to survive from the University of Leuven[19]. Many of these law students rose later to prominent position in Scotland, none more so than *Archibald Whitelaw*, royal secretary from 1462 to 1493, first to King *James III*, and then to his son *James IV*. Yet it was in the reign of *James III* (1460-88) in particular, that the fact that the Scottish kingdom was an empire in itself came to be emphasized.

In 1469 the Scots Parliament enacted in striking language that notaries licensed by imperial authority would no longer be recognized in Scotland unless licensed by the king of Scots:

> "Item It Is thocht expedient that sen Oure Soverane lord hes ful Jurisdictioune & fre Impire within his Realme that his hienes may mak notaris & tabellionis quhais Instrumentis sal have ful faith in all contractis Civile within the Realme And in tyme cumyn that na notaris maid nor to be maid be the Imperouris Autorite have faith in contractis Civile within the Realme les than he be examinyt be the ordinare & approvit be the kingis hienes"[20].

James III also used the symbolism of empire in his coinage. The groats and halfgroats of *James*'s last issue of c.1484-88 display one of the most striking portraits

---

17 *F. Pollock* and *F. W. Maitland*, The History of English Law Before the Time of Edward I, 2nd ed., London, 1898, reprinted with an introduction by *S. F. C. Milsom*, London, 1968, vol. 1, at p. 223: "Roman law must come sooner or later; the later it comes the stronger it will be for it will have gone half way to meet the Medieval facts".

18 *R. J. Lyall*, Scottish Students and Masters at the Universities of Cologne and Louvain in the Fifteenth Century, (1985) 36 Innes Review 55.

19 *Leslie Macfarlane*, William Elphinstone and the Kingdom of Scotland 1431-1514: The Struggle for Order, Aberdeen, 1985, at p. 18.

20 A.P.S., ii, 95.

in the whole range of the Scottish coinage. The king is shown three-quarter face – a fine Renaissance portrait, and one of the few successful three-quarter portraits in numismatic history – and wearing, in token of the independent status of his kingdom, a closed or 'imperial' crown[21]. A few years later, in the reign of *James IV*, the same symbolism was used in the building of the new University of Aberdeen; for the tower of Bishop Elphinstone's foundation of King's College was surmounted by an imperial crown. As *David McRoberts* has suggested, "[i]f, as seems probable, the imperial crown over King's College was gilded, then Bishop Elphinstone's assertion of the independent sovereignty of King James IV would have looked even more spectacular than it does at the present day"[22]. It is this crown in stone, renewed in 1633, which the University has taken as the symbol of its Quincentenary. A few hundred yards away the same symbolism recurs in the heraldic ceiling of St. Machar's Cathedral, which dates from early in the reign of *James V*, for there again the king of Scots is given an imperial crown[23].

III. Scottish Common Law and English Common Law

The common law of Scotland which emerged in the 13th century was not only named in imitation of the English common law, then in its own early years, but derived much of its content from that source also. As Lord *Cooper* wrote, "[f]or roughly 200 years after the accession of David I, the legal statesmen of Scotland were actively engaged in the construction of a legal system founded upon Anglo-Norman law"[24]. I differ from Lord *Cooper*, however, in his belief that this period was marked by "a false start and a rejected experiment". On the contrary, I see the period as crucial in the formation of a specifically Scottish common law[25]. It is true, of course, that after the 13th century, and especially after the Wars of Inde-

21 *I. H. Stewart*, The Scottish Coinage, 2nd ed., London, 1967, at p. 67. The groat is displayed on the dust jacket of *Norman Macdougall*, James III: A Political Study, Edinburgh, 1982. *David McRoberts*, The Heraldic Ceiling of St. Machar's Cathedral Aberdeen, Friends of St. Machar's Cathedral Occasional Papers no. 2, Aberdeen, 1981, discusses the use of the closed or imperial crown by *James III* and *James IV* at p. 12, noting its adoption by *Charles VIII* of France in 1495, and *Henry VII* of England in 1485. *Macfarlane* (n. 19) 330 also discusses the matter, and notes that *Hector Boece* specifically describes the crown on King's College as imperial, rather than royal. See also *William Ferguson*, Imperial Crowns: A Neglected Facet of the Background to the Treaty of Union of 1707, 1974 Scottish Historical Review 22. I am most grateful to Dr. Ferguson for discussing the symbolism of the imperial crown with me. See also below (n. 53).

22 *McRoberts* (n. 21) 12.

23 *McRoberts* (n. 21) 12.

24 Lord President *Cooper*, From David I to Bruce, 1124-1329: The Scoto-Norman Law, in: G. Campbell H. Paton, ed., An Introduction to Scottish Legal History, Edinburgh, 1958, 3, at p. 3.

25 *Sellar*, The Commmon Law of Scotland and the Common Law of England (n. 1).

pendence, English law ceased to exercise such a direct influence on the development of Scots law; although its influence in the later Middle Ages was never entirely negligible. But the foundations had been solidly laid. At the very core of the later common law of Scotland lies what Lord *Cooper* called the 'Scoto-Norman' law, based to a considerable extent on the Anglo-Norman law of England. I do not think that it is misleading to talk of a 'Reception' of the Anglo-Norman law, so complete was its influence on substantive law, legal administration and procedure. Indeed, this earlier Reception had a sharper chronological focus, and was in many ways more dramatic and transparent, than the later Reception of Roman law.

The Anglo-Norman law which came from England was, of course, a variant of the feudal law of western Europe, which found its most influential expression in the *Libri Feudorum*, 'The Books of the Feus', of the Lombard jurist *Obertus de Orto*, compiled in the mid-12th century. The feudal law was in a very real sense the common law of post-Carolingian Europe, and the *Libri Feudorum*, which incorporated the Constitutions of several of *Charlemagne*'s imperial successors, were often regarded as an appendix to the civil law of the Emperor *Justinian* himself[26]. The English common law in its infancy, it should not be forgotten, was very much in tune with contemporary European legal culture. It was its precocious development which set it apart. As *Michael Clanchy* has written:

> "The distinctive style of English common law derived from many sources and traditions: Anglo-Saxon, Norman, ecclesiastical, Roman and scholastic. The system took the form it did because it developed in the period of the twelfth century Renaissance and it retained that form for centuries thereafter because bureaucracy perpetuated it. Hence later lawyers praised as peculiarly English something that was really peculiarly 12th century and cosmopolitan ... Its distinctive form was therefore a product of England's close contacts with the continent at the time and not in opposition to them"[27].

As will be noted below, one early Scottish jurist at least, *Thomas Craig*, was well aware of the historical background to the English common law.

The strength and lasting effect of the influence of the Anglo-Norman law on the common law of Scotland can nowhere be better observed than in *Stair*'s treatment of custom as a source of Scots law in his 'Institutions of the Law of Scotland'[28]. For *Stair* custom is the best and purest source of law, superior to statute. In an elegant and memorable passage he concludes:

> "Yea, and the nations are more happy, whose laws have entered by long custom, wrung out from their debates upon particular cases, until it come to a consistence of a fixed and known custom. For thereby the conveniences and inconveniences thereof through a tract of time are experimentally seen; so that which is found in some cases convenient, if in

26 For the Libri Feudorum see, for example, *O. F. Robinson, T. D. Fergus, W. M. Gordon*, Eurpoean Legal History, 2nd ed., London, Dublin, Edinburgh, 1994, at pp. 37 sq.

27 *M. T. Clanchy*, England and its Rulers 1066-1272, London, 1983, at pp. 158 sq.

28 See *W. D. H. Sellar*, English Law as a Source [in *Stair*'s Institutions], in: D. M. Walker, ed., Stair Tercentenary Studies, Edinburgh, 1981, p. 140.

other cases afterwards it be found inconvenient, it proves abortive in the womb of time, before it attain the maturity of a law"[29].

Stair distinguishes between "our ancient and immemorial customs, which may be called our common law", and recent custom, by which he meant the gathering body of judicial decisions emanating from the Session. The ancient customs to which *Stair* referred were so well established that they needed no proof. *Stair* instances "our primogeniture, and all degrees of succession, our legitim portion of children, communion of goods between man and wife, and the division thereof at their death, the succession of the nearest agnates, the terces of relicts, the liferent of husbands by the courtesy, which are anterior to any statute, and not comprehended in any, as being more solemn and sure than they are"[30]. Each of these customs particularly mentioned by *Stair* can be found in *Regiam Majestatem*, which draws on these matters virtually word for word from *Glanvill's De Legibus et Consuetudinibus Angliae*[31]. And so we are faced with the apparent paradox that the core of our common law, as understood by our greatest legal writer, is to be found in the leading text on Anglo-Norman law.

Several of the imports from the Anglo-Norman law were long to outlast *Stair*'s time. The law of deathbed, for example, survived, much embroidered, until 1861[32]. The law of conquest – the law which governed succession to acquired as opposed to inherited land – survived until 1874, some 600 years after it had ceased to apply in England[33]. The division between heritable and moveable succession continued until 1964; and the six rules identified by *Maitland* as most characteristic of succession to land in England at the close of the reign of *Henry III* in 1272, remained true of heritable succession in Scotland until 1964 also[34]. The legal right of courtesy, with its peculiar rules which puzzled English lawyers already in *Edward I*'s reign, and also that of terce, again survived until 1964; while the legal rights of *ius relictae* and legitim in favour of widows and children which, despite their Romanistic names, came to Scots law from the Anglo-Norman law by way of *Glanvill* and *Regiam Majestatem*, are with us still[35].

---

29 *James Dalrymple, Viscount Stair*, Institutions of the Laws of Scotland, Edinburgh, 1681, 1, 1, 15.

30 *Stair* (n. 29) 1, 1, 16.

31 *Sellar* (n. 29) 145 sq.

32 The law of deathbed was abolished by the Law of Deathbed Abolition (Scotland) Act 1861.

33 The special rules relating to conquest were abolished by the Conveyancing (Scotland) Act 1874, s. 37.

34 *Pollock* and *Maitland* (n. 17) vol. II, at 260; *Sellar*, The Common Law of Scotland and the Common Law of England (n. 1) 89.

35 On courtesy see *Sellar*, The Common Law of Scotland and the Common Law of England (n. 1) 90.

All these examples concern 'succession to defuncts', considered by *Stair* to be "the most important title in law"[36]. But survivals from the Reception of Anglo-Norman law can be found elsewhere: for example, in the office of sheriff and that of Justiciar, later Lord Justice General[37]. In criminal matters, our solemn procedure of trial by jury following on indictment can also be traced back to the Anglo-Norman law[38].

IV. Scottish Common Law and Celtic Customary Law

However, if the feudal law in Anglo-Norman guise was at the heart of the common law of Scotland, that law did not entirely supersede the older customary law, much of it Celtic in origin, but containing also elements of Anglo-Saxon and Scandinavian (or Anglo-Danish) law. This customary law too, often remodelled or reinterpreted, had its influence on the later common law of Scotland. This is in no way surprising. All over Europe, feudal law merged with customary law; and in Scotland, unlike England, there had been no Norman Conquest to mark a break with the past. Indeed, there can be few if any parts of Europe where there has been such longstanding political continuity as in Scotland. In Scotland north of Forth and Clyde, there has been no clean break with the past for over a thousand years – since the time of *Kenneth* the son of *Alpin* (843-58)– and arguably for longer still.

The influence of Celtic law, in particular, can be found in the mainstream of later Scots common law[39]. This influence is not always easy to recognize or trace, but three instances of the tenacious survival of a technical term of Celtic law down to modern times may be noticed in passing. The term 'culrath', meaning literally a back security, is found in regular use in connection with the procedure of repledging an accused from one jurisdiction to another, until repledging itself came to an end in the mid-18th century. 'Letters of Slains', from 'slán' meaning 'indemnity', indicating full and formal remission of rancour by the kin of the victim, were in constant use in connection with actions for assythment until the same century[40]. A style of these letters is given as an appendix to Lord *Kames*' 'Historical Law Tracts'[41]. The phrase last surfaced judicially (although its Celtic origins were not

---

36 *Stair* (n. 29) 3, 4.

37 For the Justiciar see *G. W. S. Barrow*, The Justiciar in the 12th and 13th Centuries, 1971 J.R. 97, reprinted in: *G. W. S. Barrow*, The Kingdom of the Scots, London, 1973, 83.

38 *Sellar*, The Common Law of Scotland and the Common Law of England (n. 1) 88 sq.

39 For a discussion and examples see *W. D. H. Sellar*, Celtic Law and Scots Law: Survival and Integration, (1989) 29 Scottish Studies 1.

40 *Robert Black*, A Historical Survey of Delictual Liability in Scotland for Personal Injuries and Death, Part One, 1975 Comparative and International Law Journal of Southern Africa 46. For the use of the term slán in Celtic Ireland, see *Kenneth Nicholls*, Gaelic and Gaelicised Ireland, Dublin, 1972, at p. 187; and *Fergus Kelly*, A Guide to Early Irish Law, Dublin, 1988, at p. 321.

41 *Henry Hume, Lord Kames*, Historical Law Tracts, 1st ed., Edinburgh, 1758.

recognized) only twenty-five years ago, when the action of assythment was revived, albeit without success, in the case of *McKendrick v. Sinclair*[42]. The third term is 'cain', a payment made to a lord in token of his authority, comfortably traceable in a legal context until the 19th century, and last noticed occurring in accounts drawn up annually in an Edinburgh legal office in the 1960s[43].

V. The Influence of Canon Law and Civil Law

If the 13th century marked the emergence of the Scottish common law, it also marked an important stage in the consolidation of the medieval Canon law, with the promulgation in 1234 of the Decretals, compiled for Pope *Gregory IX* through the genius of *St. Raymond of Peñafort*; and the appearance later in the century of the standard manual on Romano-Canonical procedure, the *Speculum Judiciale* of *William Durantis*. Together with the civil law, Canon law became the *ius commune* of Western Christendom: the learned law, known and influential everywhere. Where did the emerging common law of Scotland stand in relation to the *ius commune*?

Unlike civil law, the Canon law, as *Walter Ullmann* always emphasized, was a living law, the living law of Western Christendom[44]. The Church had its own courts and its own procedures, governed by Canon law. In Scotland, as elsewhere, these courts of the Church existed side by side with the lay courts, and were possessed of a wide jurisdiction, which included the constitution and dissolution of marriage, contracts entered into under oath, and, at least in Scotland and England, executry matters and moveable succession[45]. This jurisdiction continued, exclusive to the Church and no part of the common law of Scotland, until the Scottish Reformation in 1559-60. After the Reformation, however, jurisdiction in these matters, still heavily influenced by the Canon law, became the concern of the secular courts, and merged gradually into the common law, the Court of Session being described by Act of Parliament in 1609 as "his majesteis great consistorie"[46].

However, the Canon law had influenced the development of the common law of Scotland long before this merger of jurisdictions. For example, as is well known, the Canon law doctrine of legitimation *per subsequens matrimonium* was accepted early into the Scots common law, and applied to succession to heritage, in marked contrast to the position in England[47]. Another clear borrowing is the rule enshrined

---

42 *McKendrick v. Sinclair* 1972 S.C. (H.L.) 25.

43 *Sellar* (n. 39) 19.

44 See, for example, *Walter Ullmann*, Law and Politics in the Middle Ages, Cambridge, 1975, chapters 4 and 5, The Canon Law and The Scholarship of Canon Law.

45 *Gordon Donaldson*, The Church Courts, in: G. Campbell H. Paton (n. 24) 363.

46 A.P.S., iv, 430.

47 *A. E. Anton*, Parent and Child, in: G. Campbell H. Paton (n. 24) 116, at pp. 117 sq.

in the Terce Act of 1503, by which a widow claiming her terce (that is, her right to a liferent over one third of her deceased husband's heritable estate) was allowed, if her marital status was challenged, to point to the fact that she and her alleged husband had been generally held and reputed spouses ('that the woman askand this terce beand repute & haldin as his lauchfull wife in his life tyme') as *prima facie* evidence of her status, pending determination of the question, if required, in the Church courts[48]. In later centuries, as memory of the Canon law background grew dim, the Act of 1503 was mistakenly believed to have introduced the doctrine of marriage by cohabitation with habit and repute into Scots law[49]. Other significant pre-Reformation imports from the Canon law, or rather from the *ius commune* – for these drew partly on the Civil law as well – were rules on arbitration which appear already in *Regiam Majestatem*; and the Romano-Canonical procedure, increasingly in use in the central judicial bodies in the 15th century, and adopted by the Session from 1532, and the Sheriff Courts from 1540[50].

There were imports from the civil law also. These are considered by others in this volume, as is also the question as to whether and at what time such imports into Scots law should be regarded as constituting a Reception[51]. The point to emphasize here is that the common law of Scotland, as it developed from the 13th century onwards, remained open to the influence of the learned laws, both Canon and civil, in a way not equally true of the common law of England. One channel of this influence, undoubtedly, was provided by those who sat in a judicial capacity. Many of those who served on the central judicial bodies before 1532 were churchmen with a formal training in Canon law, and who had cut their teeth as Bishop's Official. The prime example is, of course, *William Elphinstone*, whose service to the Crown as a Lord of Council and Lord Auditor of Causes and Complaints between 1478 and 1514 was second to none. He studied Canon law at Paris, and also civil law at Orleans, and was from 1471 to 1478 Official of Glasgow, and from 1478 to 1483 Official of Lothian[52]. After 1532, half the judges on the newly constituted Session, now established as the College of Justice, as also the Lord President of the Court, were by statute churchmen.

---

48 A.P.S., ii, 252.

49 *W. D. H. Sellar*, Marriage by Cohabitation with Habit and Repute: Review and Requiem?, in: D. L. Carey Miller and D. W. Meyers, edd., Comparative and Historical Essays in Scots Law: A Tribute to Professor Sir Thomas Smith Q.C., Edinburgh, 1992, 117.

50 On arbitration, see *Regiam Majestatem* II.1.10 (Stair Society edition; A.P.S., ii, 1-7). For Romano-canonical influence in *Regiam Majestatem* generally, and the debt to the Canonist *Goffredus de Trano* (d. 1245), see *P. G. Stein*, The Sources of the Romano-Canonical Part of Regiam Majestatem, 1969 Scottish Historical Review 107.

51 See also, for example, *W. M. Gordon*, Roman Law in Scotland, in: Evans-Jones (n. 3) 13; and, generally, the references above (n. 3).

52 For Elphinstone's judicial career see *Macfarlane* (n. 19); also *A. L. Brown*, The Scottish 'Establishment' in the Later 15th Century, 1978 J.R. 89.

VI. Sir John Skene's Views on the Scottish Common Law

I should like to conclude by examining what two of the principal writers on Scots law at the turn of the 16th and 17th centuries, Sir *John Skene* and *Thomas Craig*, had to say about the relationship between the common law of Scotland and the other laws we have had under consideration – the Canon law, the civil law, the feudal law and Anglo-Norman law. How did they perceive the historical relationship between these laws? How did they rate them as formal sources of law? And how far were they conscious of Scots law as a system in itself?

As a young man *Skene*, as he informs us himself in the elegant dedication to *James VI* in his Latin edition of *Regiam Majestatem* published in 1609, had spent seven years abroad, and had studied civil law at the University of Wittenberg[53]. *Skene* makes a clear distinction between Scots law (*jurisprudentia Scotica*) and civil law (*jus Civilis Romanorum*). He was interested, he says, in exploring the similarities and differences between these laws – *quae varia est, et multiplex* – and in combining the foreign and the municipal (*peregrina cum domesticis*)[54]. In an oft quoted passage *Skene* complains that all too often aspiring Scots jurists had studied the Civil law, but neglected their own Scots law, because, in *Peter Stein*'s translation, "[they] found the old Scottish laws obscure and their language distasteful (*stylo horrido et aspero scriptas*)"[55].

The dedication flatters King *James* in fulsome terms, paying tribute to the singular erudition of this pupil of *George Buchanan*. *Skene* notes that *James* had long wished to see the laws of his ancestors (*tuorumque majorum leges*) clarified and expounded for the greater utility of his subjects in the kingdom of Scotland. *Skene* adds that these laws of the king's ancestors agreed for the most part with the laws of the kingdom of England, to which *James* had just succeeded. *Skene*'s edition includes not only the text of *Regiam Majestatem*, but other legal texts also, such as *Quoniam Attachiamenta*, and statutes ascribed to various Scottish kings before the reign of *James I* (1406-37); collected, as he says, from the public records and from old books and manuscripts. In the same year *Skene* also published a separate Scots edition of the same texts, "translated out of the Latine into the Scottish language, to the *use and knawledge of all the subjects within this Realme*"[56]. Of *Skene's* commitment to Scots law as a separate and independent system there can be no doubt.

---

53 *Sir John Skene*, Regiam Majestatem Scotiae Veteres Leges et Constitutiones, Edinburgh, 1609. An engraving of an imperial crown figures prominently in this edition, appearing, for example, on the title page and at the beginning of *Skene*'s dedication to the King. For *Skene*'s career and writings see *John W. Cairns, T. David Fergus, Hector L. MacQueen*, Legal Humanism in Renaissance Scotland, (1990) 11 J.L.H. 40, at pp. 44-48.

54 *"Juris-prudentiam Scoticam perscrutari, ejusque cognitionem, cum juris Civilis Romanorum scientia conferre, et utriusque communionem et differentiam (quae varia est, et multiplex) annotare, et ad meam utilitatem, peregrina cum domesticis conjungere decrevi."*

55 *Stein*, The Influence of Roman Law on the Law of Scotland (n. 3) 217.

56 *Skene*'s italics: *Sir John Skene*, Regiam Majestatem The Auld Lawes and Constitutions of Scotland, Edinburgh, 1609.

In the preface to his Latin edition of *Regiam Majestatem*, *Skene* explains he had tried to establish the best text from the many variant readings in the manuscript sources by making comparisons with relevant passages from the civil law, the Canon law, the Norman law (*jus Nortmannicus*) – for this is how *Skene* refers to the feudal law – and from English law (*jus Anglicus*). He notes that civil law, Canon law, Norman law and English law were the sources from which nearly all the older Scots law had been drawn, or with which it agreed. He adds that the debt to English law (*leges Regni Angliae*) was such that anyone able to understand English law would understand a great part of Scots law also[57]. *Skene*, therefore, while recognizing civil law, Canon law and feudal law as historical sources of the Scottish common law, particularly stresses the value of the study of English law, which he expressly distinguishes from Norman or feudal law, as an aid to understanding the older Scottish laws.

VII. Thomas Craig and His Views on the Scottish Common Law

1. Scottish Common Law and English Common Law

In his insistence that there was substantial common ground between Scots law and English law, *Skene* was at one with his contemporary *Thomas Craig*[58]. In both his celebrated Jus Feudale and the less well known *De Unione Regnorum Britanniae Craig* made much of points of comparison between Scots and English law[59]. In *Jus Feudale* he wrote of a "fundamental identity between the principles underlying the legal systems of both countries", and of "the closest affinity of method [between the two systems] in legal argument, expression, and analysis"[60].

57 *"Fontes ipsos unde singulae fere leges desumtae sunt, aut cum quibus consentiunt, annotavi, ex Jure Civili, Canonico, Nortmannico. Et ex legibus Regni Angliae, cum quibus nostrae magna ex parte concordant, adeo ut qui has intellexerit, illas quoque magna ex parte, intellegere possit."* Note, however, that despite his recognition of the debt owed by the Scottish common law to English law, *Skene* continued to maintain that *Glanvill's De Legibus* was copied from *Regiam Majestatem* rather than the other way round; on which see, most recently, *H. L. MacQueen*, Glanvill Resarcinate: Sir John Skene and Regiam Majestatem, in: Alasdair A. MacDonald, Michael Lynch, I. B. Cowan, edd., The Renaissance in Scotland: Studies in Literary, Religious, Historical and Cultural History Offered to John Durkan, Leiden, 1994, p. 385.

58 *Sellar*, The Common Law of Scotland and the Common Law of England (n. 1); and see *Cairns/Fergus/MacQueen* (n. 53) especially pp. 48-60.

59 *Thomas Craig*, Jus Feudale, Edinburgh, 1655; 3rd ed., J. Baillie, ed., Edinburgh, 1732, translated in two volumes by James Avon Clyde, Edinburgh and London, 1934; *Thomas Craig*, De Unione Regnorum Britannie Tractatus, C. Sanford Terry, ed. and trans., Scottish History Society, 1909. I have followed Sanford Terry's translation of *De Unione*; but have not always adhered to Lord President *Clyde*'s rather free translation of *Jus Feudale*. Latin quotations from *Jus Feudale* are from the third edition. I am grateful to Dr. *John Durkan* for pointing out to me that there appears to be no contemporary evidence for the title 'Sir' generally accorded to *Craig*.

In the *De Unione* he asserted "that at the present day there are no two nations whose laws and institutes more closely correspond than England and Scotland"[61]. In *Jus Feudale Craig* cites up to eighteen 'axioms', as he terms them, or adages, taken from English law which "find a close reflection in our Scottish jurisprudence"[62]. Most of these examples are taken from land law or succession: thus, "the eldest son succeeds to the whole heritage, daughters succeed to the heritage per capita"; "Moveable goods belong not to the heirs but to the executors appointed by the last will of the deceased"; and, "the feudal rights of ward and marriage, and also of relief, belong to the lord". In the *De Unione Craig* ranges through English law, public and private, in order to demonstrate the similarities between Scots and English law[63]. Again he concentrates on land law and succession, but he also points, for example, to the use of the jury in criminal proceedings in both countries, and towards a similarity of approach towards sources of law.

Some of *Craig*'s examples, there can be little doubt, are somewhat strained. His views are those of an apologist for closer union between the kingdoms of Scotland and England, and, therefore, to an extent, partisan. Such views were not universally held by his contemporaries, as *Craig* freely acknowledges. There were jurists, he notes, who held that England followed her own municipal law while Scots law was founded on civil law[64]. However, *Craig*'s reflections on the similarities between Scots and English law need to be set in a wider context. It was the breadth of *Craig's* vision and the depth of his historical understanding that enabled him to make comparisons where others saw none[65].

2. Feudal Law and Civil Law

If *Craig* thought that there was a fundamental identity between Scots law and English law, it was partly because he saw both systems within the wider context of the feudal law and the civil law. *Craig* reckoned the feudal law to be part of the native law, the *jus proprium*, of Scotland, broadly defined: *hoc jus proprium huius regni dici potest (si latius juris proprii nomen extendamus)* – 'we may call this the

60 Clyde (n. 59) Epistle Dedicatory, p. 9.

61 Terry (n. 59) p. 304. *Craig* continues: "On fundamental principles of jurisprudence they agree perfectly, though in procedure they differ, a fact which by no means obscures the general resemblance between their systems of law. Though I am not deeply versed in English law ... I should say, from such study as I have given to the subject, that there is not that diversity between the two systems of law as is popularly supposed to exist".

62 *Craig*, Jus Feudale (n. 59) 1, 7, 13-14.

63 Terry (n. 59) pp. 305-327.

64 Terry (n. 59) p. 326. Plus ça change, plus c'est la même chose!

65 *J. G. A. Pocock*'s The Ancient Constitution and the Feudal Law, Cambridge, 1957, reissue with a retrospect by the author, Cambridge, 1987, restored *Craig* to his rightful place in European legal historiography; see also *Cairns/Fergus/MacQueen* (n. 53).

jus proprium of this kingdom, if we take a broad view of the definition of *jus proprium*'[66]. "For feudalism", continued *Craig*, "is the source and origin from which most of the law in daily use in our courts, and all our legal usages and practice are derived." English law too owed much to the feudal law, even if English lawyers were reluctant to acknowledge this fact. One reason, says *Craig*, why he gave so many examples of similarities between the 'axioms' of English law and Scots law, was to "shew that the law of England owes much to the Feudal law, little as the debt may be openly acknowledged in a system which rather professes to be independent of all others"[67]. In the *De Unione* he writes to the same effect, "Our English neighbours are therefore far out in their reckoning in their belief that their legal system is indigenous and unlike those of other countries"[68].

If English law, like Scots, was grounded in the feudal law, it also, in *Craig*'s estimation, owed much to the civil law. *Craig*'s views on this subject are worth quoting at some length. In the *De Unione* he writes:

> "The Civil law, so the English imagine, has but little vogue among them. Indeed though you will find in every branch of study very learned men in England, there are very few who have made the study of Civil law their main pursuit. They are content to merely salute it from the threshold, and in its room to give consideration to the institutes and customs of their native law. It has indeed been held by some jurists that England follows her own municipal law, whereas Scotland's system is rooted in Civil law. But in fact the Civil law has never been so exiled from English practice as to prevent its principles and decisions from flashing light on every point and illuminating every controversy. But this illumination they prefer to ascribe to their own jurists rather than to the ancient jurisconsults. And yet, however little Civil law may be professed among them, it none the less shines so clearly amid all their legal controversies that any one skilled in it will very readily discover that all of them are easily capable of solution by the Civil law and the responses of the jurisconsults or rescripts of the Caesars, as is frequently noticeable in the cases reported by Plowden and Dyer"[69].

It is against the wider background, therefore, of a common European legal tradition, that *Craig*'s comparison of Scots law with English law must be understood.

3. The Hierarchy of Sources

Craig also considered the ranking of the formal sources of Scots law, the earliest of our Institutional writers to do so[70]. His treatment of these sources is consistent

---

66 *Craig*, Jus Feudale (n. 59) 1, 8, 16. The translation of this passage is my own.

67 Terry (n. 59) 311.

68 Terry (n. 59) 311.

69 Terry (n. 59) 326 sq. There is a passage in *Jus Feudale* (1.7.22) to the same effect. See also *Gordon* (n. 51). For a telling re-assessment of the debt of English common law to the *ius commune*, which supports *Craig's* view, see *David J. Seipp*, The Reception of Canon Law and Civil Law in the Common Law Courts before 1600, (1993) 13 Oxford J.L.S. 388.

with his understanding as to the historical origins of the law. When controversy arises, says *Craig*, the first question to ask is whether the matter is covered by the *ius scriptum* of Scotland – effectively the Acts of the Scots Parliament. Failing this, the next source is Scottish customary law, a settled course of judicial decisions or practice: *judicatarum consuetudo observatur, quam nos 'praxin' vocamus.* If neither the written nor the customary law of Scotland can provide the answer, the next place of resort is the written feudal law: *post consuetudinem tertium locum juri Feudali scripto tribuemus.* This is to be preferred to the civil or Canon law. Failing feudal law, says *Craig*, we must have recourse to the civil law, but he adds that the civil law must give way to Canon law where they differ. This is in keeping with his account of the Canon law earlier in *Jus Feudale*, where he says that even although Scotland has "thrown off the papal yoke, the authority of the Canon Law endures: so much so that where it differs from the Civil Law" – and *Craig* says that this is often the case, and that much has been written about the differences – "we follow the Canon law" (*jus Canonicum praeferamus*)[71]. The civil law, therefore, as an independent system of law, rates surprisingly low in *Craig*'s hierarchy of sources.

The same approach towards sources of law is to be discerned in *Craig*'s *De Unione*. At the close of his discussion on Scots and English law, *Craig* considers how they might best be harmonized. "Should the attempt be made", he says, "it would be necessary to revert to the sources of feudal law, that is ... to the Norman law (*Ius Normannicum*), in whose idiom the laws of England were and still are written". If that did not provide an answer, it would then be necessary to go back beyond the Norman law, "to the feudal law (*Ius Feudale*) from which that of Normandy was derived". If common ground could not be found even there, then, says *Craig*, it would be necessary to have recourse to the civil law, "whose principles are so equitable and of such widespread acceptance that it deservedly merits the appellation, common law (*Ius commune*)". This view of the relationship between civil law and Scots law, namely that the civil law was followed for its equity rather than any inherent authority, appears also in *Jus Feudale*, where *Craig* states that in Scotland Roman law is accepted in so far as it accords with nature and right reason (*quatenus legibus naturae & rectae rationi congruunt*)[72]. *Craig*'s assessment in turn is in full agreement with *Stair's* later and better known statement that Roman law was not acknowledged in Scotland as a law binding for its authority, but was followed rather for its equity[73].

At the heart of *Craig*'s ever widening circles of generality lies the native law of Scotland, and to this, despite his arguments in favour of harmonization, he, like

---

70 *Craig*, Jus Feudale (n. 59) 1, 8.

71 *Craig*, Jus Feudale (n. 59) 1, 8.

72 *Craig*, Jus Feudale (n. 59) 1, 2, 14.

73 *Stair* (n. 29) 1, 1, 12. Neither *Craig* nor *Stair* quote the well known tag *non ratione imperii sed imperio rationis*, but such was undoubtedly their view.

Skene, was strongly attached: "Our Scottish forms of legal process and judicial procedure are, no doubt, different from those in use in England," he wrote in the 'Epistle Dedicatory' to his *Jus Feudale*, "but, with all respect to our neighbours, I make bold to say, and to say advisedly, that the forms we use in Scotland are better than those used in any other country I know of"[74]. Again, this puts us in mind of *Stair*, who wrote that, "[t]he law of Scotland in its nearness to equity, plainness and facility in its customs, tenors, and forms, and in its celerity and dispatch in the administration and execution of justice, may be well paralleled with the best law in Christendom"[75].

Lord President *Dundas*' remark, made towards the end of the 18th century, has often been quoted: "I respect the Civil law; but I will not haul it in to destroy our own institutions"[76]. Whatever view one takes of the Reception of Roman law in Scotland, can one doubt that the same sentiment could have been expressed by *Stair* at the end of the 17th century or *Thomas Craig* at the end of the 16th? This is not, of course, to deny the importance of the civilian tradition in the shaping of Scots law. On the contrary: in some areas of Scots law, for example, unjustified enrichment, an appreciation of the civilian background is the beginning of understanding. But the story of the Reception of Roman law in Scotland is a complex one which can only be properly understood against the background of a strong and resilient native tradition.

---

74 Clyde (n. 59) Epistle Dedicatory, p. 9.

75 *Stair* (n. 29) 1, 1, 16.

76 Hailes Decisions, ii, 987.

Taking Stock: The Significance of the Civilian Tradition in England, Scotland, and Continental Europe

More Logic and Less Experience: The Difference between Scots Law and English Law

By Peter B. H. Birks

I. Instability and Indifference to Classification

"The life of the law has not been logic, it has been experience"[1]. *Holmes*'s seductive observation should never be repeated without a counterweight: "Fallacy and contradiction are enemies of justice". *Holmes*'s *dictum* reminds us of the need for flexibility and adaptability, in short for constant change in the pursuit of justice. It is important to remember that we do live in a legal world where continual and rapid change is an inescapable reality. It is that reality which provides the background of Lord *Goff*'s very important Maccabaean Lecture[2]. However, the counterweight is a warning against intellectual disorder, against change which outstrips the intellect and loses touch with the demands of justice for stability and consistency. *Blackstone* described law as the highest branch of the study of ethics[3]. It is true that law has additional burdens. A principal difference between law and moral philosophy is that, while philosophers can debate and disagree, law must make up its mind. For law supposes judges deciding cases day by day, deeply affecting the lives of ordinary citizens. If it is to promote peace in society rather than stir up more unrest, that process of continual adjudication in turn requires consistency and stability. Like cases must be treated alike. Where the law is muddled, courts find it virtually impossible to do that. The aspiration of serious lawyers must therefore be law which is muddle-free.

That is a goal which is none the less important for being imperfectly attainable. Muddle turns out to be an enemy with remarkable powers of recovery. The question is whether the common law is well enough armed for the battle. The answer is that it is not. The common law is a great and glorious achievement. But in the course of its long development it has been protected against instability and inconsistency by a variety of mechanisms which history has now largely disabled or withdrawn. There is no crisis, only a cloud on the horizon. The shape and nature of

---

1 *Oliver Wendell Holmes*, The Common Law, Boston, 1881, at p. 1.

2 *Robert Goff* (*Lord Goff of Chieveley*), In Search of Principle, (1983) 69 Proceedings of the British Academy 169.

3 *W. Blackstone*, On the Study of the Law, in: Commentaries on the Law of England, vol. 1, at p. 27. Used as the preface to the Commentaries this was *Blackstone's* inaugural lecture as first Vinerian Professor, given on 25th October 1758.

the cloud can just be detected. If the common law cannot install new mechanisms against intellectual disorder, it will come under increasing criticism and it will not be able to resist the next wave of enthusiasm for codification. More attention must be paid to the rational strength of the law. The search for principle must be conducted more vigorously[4]. That means more logic and less experience, more system and less empiricism.

A certain kind of rational weakness is endemic. Long dependence on the alphabet has encouraged the survival of disorderly and conflicting categories. The common law has never streamlined the categories of its thought. That is what is meant by the absence of system. This kind of weakness makes trouble at every level. At the highest level, the level of the whole law, common lawyers have no shared vision, just lists of more or less familiar topics. At the lowest levels, where individual liabilities are determined, contradictory angles of approach not infrequently co-exist. At this introductory stage, a few examples will have to suffice.

The House of Lords recently decided *Spring v. Guardian Assurance*[5]. An employer wrote a reference which made incorrect assertions of fact about a former employee and thus caused that employee pure economic loss. Was the employer liable in negligence? The answer was 'yes'. This is somewhat surprising. The reference was a communication which was subject to qualified privilege as being written as a matter of duty to a person with an interest to receive it. In defamation the employer could not therefore have been liable without proof of malice. One commentator asks whether, if the case had been argued in defamation, the House of Lords would have changed the law applicable to that tort[6]. Since the law seemingly was that such a defendant could not be liable except for malice and since the law now is that he can be liable for negligence, one might equally put the question differently. Has the decision in negligence changed the law of defamation?

This is a conundrum of disorderly categories. It is a species of problem which disfigures the law. It is discreditably elementary. Two categories intersect. Defamation is a wrong, like inducing breach of contract or interference with chattels, which is manifestly named by reference to the interest infringed. Defamation is the infringement of the interest in reputation. Negligence is a wrong named by reference to a kind of fault. It follows that the two categories must often intersect. In other words infringement of the interest in reputation will often be negligent. Is there one wrong or two? My canary is yellow and eats seeds. If all birds are seed-eaters, yellow, or others, my canary counts twice. Are there two birds or one? The double vision is due to the bent classification. There is only one bird.

The question about negligence and defamation is slightly more difficult than the question about yellow birds and seed-eaters. There is at least an argument that the

---

4 *Lord Goff*'s message (n. 2) more than a decade ago.

5 [1994] 3 W.L.R. 354 (H.L.).

6 *T. Allen*, Liability for References: The House of Lords and *Spring v. Guardian Assurance*, (1995) 58 M.L.R. 553, at p. 560.

two categories might be so constructed, or reconstructed, as not to intersect. We need not pursue it. It is enough that we see the makings of an intellectual disaster. The whole law of tort is bedevilled by the same essentially trivial problem. The law cannot tolerate, or should not be able to tolerate, torts named so as to intersect. It is symptomatic of the common law's worrying indifference to system that academic literature has not eliminated this kind of intellectual trap.

The same general area of law provides another example, again a taxonomic shortcoming. The question has begun to be mooted whether by pleading a case in breach of fiduciary duty a plaintiff may be able to sidestep restrictive rules in the law of tort, as for instance the requirement of foreseeability, rules relating to remoteness of damage and rules prescribing periods of limitation[7]. These are startling ideas, since the restrictive rules in question are not archaic or hyper-technical irritations but well-considered limits designed to ensure that liabilities are not imposed except where, in the view of the law, it is just and reasonable that they should be imposed. Be those matters as they may, the essential question to ask first is whether the fact that breach of fiduciary duty is not encountered in books on tort means that it is not a tort. Young children's books generally suppress the nature of whales. Pictures of whales follow pictures of sharks. In the end we put away childish things. The discovery that a whale is a mammal is exciting.

The ancient duality between common law and equity means that a breach of duty may be equitable or legal. But these labels have no necessary analytical weight, no more than fish-like adaptations indicate fish. 'Equitable' and 'legal' in this context classify only according to jurisdictional history. Before the law accepts or begins to exaggerate important remedial differentiations, it ought to resolve the question whether, analytically, there is any material difference between the historically distinct sets of wrongs. If there is not, an equitable pedigree should not allow a wrong, fortuitously, to outflank restrictions on tortious liability. Experience has no part to play in these matters, which pose essentially logical problems. Observation is of course an essential preliminary. The data must be correctly gathered. But in the law taxonomic problems are in the end logical problems.

The next two examples must be very brief. Trusts are classified, and the classification has statutory blessing in section 53 of the Law of Property Act, 1925, as express, implied, resulting or constructive. It is reasonably evident that this series is based on their creation and, more particularly, on the role of intent. At one end of the spectrum express trusts arise from declared intent, at the other constructive trusts come into existence by operation of law, irrespective of intent. But there is a cuckoo in the nest. A resulting trust, according to the somewhat elusive meaning

7 This development is reviewed by *The Hon. Sir Anthony Mason*, The Place of Equity and Equitable Remedies in the Contemporary Common Law World, (1994) 110 L.Q.R. 238, esp. at p. 243. In the same issue, Professor Sir *John Smith* draws attention to curious consequences of the not unrelated excursion in proprietary responses to equitable 'torts': *Lister v. Stubbs* and the Criminal Law, (1994) 110 L.Q.R. 180; cf. *Birks*, 1994 University of Western Australia Law Review 8.

of that latinate word, is one which jumps back (*resalire* = to jump back): a trust in which the beneficial interest jumps back to the settlor. The quality of jumping back does not align with modes of creation. If I convey my land to you on trust for me, the interest jumps back and the trust is express. But there is only one trust. It might have been arguable once that the term 'resulting' was tied to trusts arising by presumed intent and in this series meant just that. But that is now highly controversial[8], and with the controversy is realized the risk which was taken when this bent taxonomy was set in statutory stone. If, which is not certain, there is no way of saying that the things which we want to call resulting trusts all arise in the same way, they really must recur under every head. The problem is then no more complex than that of the canary which is both yellow and eats seeds, but its simplicity is less easy to spot. Generations of law students, not to mention their elders and betters, are needlessly foxed.

The final example is unkind, in the sense that it concentrates on the title of a rather good article and one which is concerned with the need for good taxonomy. The background is the indifference of modern English law to the classification of obligations. Many young graduates emerge from law school with both contract and tort under their belt but wholly unaware that they relate together as major parts of something larger called the law of obligations. They are then accused of having a 'stovepipe mentality', a new metaphor evidently for tunnel vision. They cannot move, it is said, from one pipe full of knowledge to another. The imbecile suggestion is then advanced that the categories should be abandoned altogether, as though the human mind could function better on raw data. What is needed is not dissolution of categories but more attention to the exercise of classification, which includes the relation of one category to another. Not stoves, but organs: the lawyer should see that, properly assembled, the pipes add up to a single and extraordinarily versatile instrument. We have a long way to go. When Professor *Burrows* wrote his well-known article on the classification of obligations, he was encouraging common lawyers to go down that path, to think how their categories fitted together, but his title nonetheless exemplified, if he will forgive me for saying so, the characteristic English indifference to the dangers of poor taxonomy. His title was 'Contract, Tort and Restitution – A Satisfactory Division or Not?'[9]. The division is manifestly unsatisfactory on its face. 'Restitution' cannot align with 'Contract' and 'Tort', since restitution is a legal response to events (like compensation and punishment) and they are events to which the law responds. The common law has chosen to call its law of unjust enrichment 'restitution', thus requiring us to read the response as denoting the event responded to. It is a risky strategy. And then, who would dare to say that contract, tort and unjust enrichment (*alias* restitution) exhaust the whole law of obligations? Of course they do not. A defendant must pay the damages awarded against him by a court, a citizen with an income

---

8 Since *Re Vandervell's Trusts (No.2)* [1973] 3 W.L.R. 744 (elaborating *Vandervell v. I.R.C.* [1967] 2 A.C. 291) reversed, without touching this point, [1974] Ch. 269.

9 (1983) 99 L.Q.R. 217.

must pay income tax, a parent must maintain children, and so on. The second taxonomic indifference in this title (chosen by an author far from indifferent to taxonomy) is the omission of a residual miscellany. Had he forced himself to add 'Other Causes' or 'Other Events', the selection of the noun might have alerted him to the potentially bent nature of a series in which the word 'Restitution' was expected to identify the event to which it was, in its natural meaning, the response.

Indifference to classification, which is the same as indifference to system, is a cross borne by the common law. It creates traps for the unwary. Fortunately judges are not on the whole unwary. They are too learned and intelligent not to recognize the nature of these not very profound but often awkwardly concealed difficulties. They may nevertheless be tempted to exploit them: the life of the law has not been logic. If, say, a bent classification creates room for a seemingly satisfactory solution to a difficult case, why not use it? In other words, why not use muddle for a good purpose, to facilitate change? Such instrumentalism is contrary to basic tenets and expectations. It makes a mockery of the rule of law. And it denies the very nature of law as beyond, even if imperfectly beyond, the prejudices of the court.

Holmes and the Realists who followed him have much to answer for in this respect. Legal science decays if logic, under whose aegis taxonomy belongs, yields too much ground to empirical serendipity, and the law then becomes the thinnest of veils for the exercise of naked power. Immediately after the war Professor *A.H. Campbell* recorded a memorable *dictum* of *Heydrich*, the chief of the Gestapo: "For the fulfilment of my task I do fundamentally that for which I can answer to my conscience ... I am completely indifferent whether others gabble about breaking the law"[10]. The *forum internum* is too evidently fallible, and at all times and places.

II. The Scottish Institutional Tradition

There are different ways of reducing the incidence of confusion in the law. The best is to take a lesson from the natural scientists and to pay attention, as they do, to taxonomy. *Darwin* would have achieved nothing if he had neglected taxonomy. In the same way poor classification disfigures the law and delays the progress of legal science. Scots law has enjoyed an advantage in this respect over English law. Ever since the 17th century the way in which the law of Scotland has most obviously differed from the law of England has been in its strong tradition of overview literature. *Mackenzie*, *Stair*, *Bankton* and *Erskine* all wrote successful and influential books on the whole law[11]. They did not simply throw the law together in

10 *A. H. Campbell*, Fascism and Legality, (1946) 62 L.Q.R. 141, at p. 147.

11 *Sir George Mackenzie*, Institutions of the Laws of Scotland, Edinburgh, 1684; *James Dalrymple, Viscount Stair*, Institutions of the Law of Scotland, Edinburgh, 1681/1693; *Andrew McDouall, Lord Bankton*, An Institute of the Laws of Scotland in Civil Rights: with Observations upon the Agreement or Diversity between them and the Laws of England,

any order that came to hand. They wrote according to a system which rationally related together all the parts of the law, much as a grammar relates together the diverse elements of a language. The system which they used derived from Roman law and, in particular, from *Justinian*'s 'Institutes', perhaps the most important book, the Bible apart, in the history of European civilization[12].

The institutional scheme was invented by *Gaius* in the 2nd century A.D. and overhauled by *Justinian*'s Commissioners in the 6th century. Very briefly, in *Justinian*'s version it first affirms that all the law is either public or private. Public law is only very slightly represented in the text, in the first few pages on law-making institutions and in the last on crime. The book's main business is private law, which is divided according as it is concerned with persons who make claims, things claimed or the actions by which they are claimed; of these three categories, the law relating to things (or, as we might prefer, assets) is largest and sub-divides according as things are either corporeal or incorporeal; then, among things incorporeal are obligations, and, on the next level, obligations arise from contract or from wrongs or *quasi* from contracts or *quasi* from wrongs. Modern reinterpretation of the content of the law of things tends to draw a firmer line between obligations and the rest or, in other words, to move the main subdivision from the line between corporeal and incorporeal things to the line between property (rights *in rem*) and obligations (rights *in personam*). This is an incomplete account, but it gives some idea of the taxonomy of law which the Romans handed down[13].

It is reasonable to assert that the scheme of classification and exposition derived from the 'Institutes' was Scots law's single most important legacy from Roman law. As in many other civilian jurisdictions, the 'Institutes' became the vehicle for the exposition of national law[14]. The great Scots writers adapted the systematic of the 'Institutes' and used the resulting categories to provide the structure within which to expound the law of Scotland. Jurists engaged on this exercise modified the institutional scheme in different degrees. *Stair* was one who attempted a fairly radical revision[15]. Although his book showed a high level of intellect and intellec-

---

Edinburgh, 1751-3; *John Erskine*, The Institutes of the Law of Scotland, Edinburgh, 1773 – published posthumously. The principal vehicle of *Erskine*'s influence was his shorter work, Principles of the Law of Scotland in the order of *Sir George Mackenzie*'s Institutions of that Law, Edinburgh, 1754 which in successive editions was the way into Scots law for nearly two centuries.

12 Further: *P. Birks* and *G. McLeod*, Justinian's Institutes, London, 1987, at pp. 12 sqq.

13 More detail in *Birks* and *McLeod* (n. 12) pp. 13-15; *P.G. Stein*, Legal Institutions: The Development of Dispute Settlement, London, 1984, at pp. 125 sqq.

14 This movement is discussed by *K. Luig*, The Institutes of National Law in the 17th and 18th Centuries, 1972 J.R. 193; also *A. Watson*, Justinian's Institutes and some English Counterparts, in: P. G. Stein and A. D. E. Lewis, edd., Studies in Justinian's Institutes, London, 1983, p. 181.

15 *Stair*'s revisionist position involved eliminating the law of persons (as to this see text immediately below) and moving the law of obligations to the beginning, after the introductory section. He also fundamentally reorganized the sub-divisions of the law of obligations.

tual independence, his modifications of the Roman structure did not on the whole prove successful. *Erskine*'s more conservative adaptations proved more attractive and more enduring[16].

Despite the failure of his main modifications, *Stair*'s intellectual spirit is what we chiefly need to encourage. It is difficult to capture its character in a short space. But it is worth trying to exemplify. He thought that a law of persons was superfluous, since the object of legal science should always be rights and, if one concentrated on the incidence of rights, one would necessarily take in the differences between persons. The vigour and precision of his intellect can to some extent be appreciated from the following quotation from his discussion of this point:

> "The Roman law taketh up, for its object, persons, things and actions, and according to these, orders itself; but these are only the extrinsic object and matter, about which law and right are versant. But the proper object is the right itself, whether it concerns persons, things or actions, and according to the several rights and their natural order, ought to be the order of jurisprudence, which may be taken up in a threefold consideration; first, in the constitution and nature of rights; secondly, in their conveyance or translation from one person to another, whether it be among the living, or from the dead; thirdly, in their cognition, which comprehends the trial, decision and execution of every right by the legal remedies"[17].

In nearly all the other jurisdictions of the civilian tradition the structural overview is no longer to be found in juristic literature but rather in their codes. Codification has interrupted and fragmented the tradition. But the codes also reflect the institutional scheme, some following *Justinian's* Institutes very closely and others, like the German, revising and modernizing it, in the intellectual tradition of *Stair*. There is much to be said for the structure developed and sustained by juristic literature, and not rigidified in the form of a code. Codification impedes subsequent criticism and innovation. Natural scientists know that taxonomy is never complete. New discoveries and insights require new classifications, and new classifications in turn generate new understandings. A systematic which rests on overview literature remains, in contrast to one which is set firm in the form of a code, constantly open to discussion and review. It provides stability and a foundation for analysis and reflection without inhibiting improvement. Scots law might therefore have congratulated itself on a notable, and notably valuable, asset.

However, this asset is arguably being frittered away. Although the institutional systematic is still very evident in *T. B. Smith*'s 'Short Commentary'[18], there are

---

16 Successive editions of *Erskine*'s Principles dominated the scene until well into the present century. The last was the 21st, by Sir *John Rankine* in 1911. The classificatory power of the work had by that time declined (as witness the inclusion of the delict of negligence, unimportant when the book was first written and almost passed over, as an *addendum* to the law of persons, lamely excused on the ground that it was a 'personal wrong': 1,7A).

17 *Viscount Stair* (n. 11) 1, 1, 23.

18 *T.B. Smith* (*Sir Thomas Smith*), A Short Commentary on the Law of Scotland, Edinburgh, 1962.

various forces at work to weaken the advantage which the long overview tradition conferred on Scots law. The universities, which are willing enough to pay lip homage to the civilian history of Scots law, are not any longer paying real attention to it. Few lawyers in Scotland leave law school with any greater sense of structure than their equivalents south of the border, and, as in the natural course of things university lawyers retire and are replaced, that means in turn that still fewer university lawyers care to keep alive, much less keep under critical review, the knowledge of that structure and its continuity through centuries of legal thought. The last link with the systematic which is or was the characteristic feature of Scots law is the ordinary course in Roman law, based on the 'Institutes', offered in the first year. But that course hangs by a thread which the Faculty of Advocates could cut at any time. If the Faculty were to drop the requirement of Roman law, the number of people studying the Institutes would fall away to a tiny trickle.

Outside the Roman law course, very little attention is paid to the classification of the law. *Gloag* and *Henderson*[19] does not dwell on its own organizing principles, and no reader who was not expressly looking for it would now recognize in its sequence of chapters the vestiges of the traditional institutional scheme. Another fragmenting influence is the fact that in the university law schools a higher degree of specialization among teachers means that each is concerned with a smaller and smaller area. This affects both teaching and writing. Teaching or writing, a lawyer who specializes in delict and thus considers himself to be a delict lawyer is unlikely to spend time relating delict to other areas of the law of obligations and obligations to other parts of the law of things. Finally, the 'Stair Memorial Encyclopaedia'[20], ambitious project as it is, is arranged alphabetically. It will dominate the work of practitioners, and it will make the Scots law seem more and more like the English law. *Halsbury*'s Laws of England[21] is likewise based on the alphabet.

Scots law is thus becoming more English. Some Scots lawyers take the view that the identity of Scots law consists in the content of particular rules, and they are willing to spend energy salvaging the Scots content from English contamination. Their energies are misdirected. The true difference consisted in the commitment to the institutional scheme or, in other words, to a more systematic approach. Scots law might have claimed a higher rationality, because concern to arrange the law intelligibly is the clearest manifestation of a determined rationality.

---

19 *W. M. Gloag, R.C. Henderson*, Introduction to the Law of Scotland, 9th ed., A.B. Wilkinson and W.A. Wilson, edd., Edinburgh, 1987. It is said that the 10th edition, now in the press, will do something to reverse the abandonment of the institutional systematic.

20 The Laws of Scotland: Stair Memorial Encyclopedia, Law Society of Scotland, continuing. It is true, of course, that Professor Sir *Thomas Smith* and Professor *Robert Black*, successive superintendents of this huge project, have divided the alphabetical task into blocks some of which do reflect the institutional scheme, as for example by devoting one whole volume to the law of obligations.

21 *Halsbury*'s Laws of England, 4th ed., Lord Hailsham of St. Marylebone, ed., London, continuing.

III. Lists of Actions

There are other mechanisms for promoting stability. Both Roman and English law show in their history that it is possible for the law to reach a considerable degree of sophistication without any systematic overview. Both inherited from their more or less intuitive beginnings an effective provision for stability, albeit one with an inherently limited potential. They took their structure from the forms of action. With hindsight we can see that a structure of that kind will inevitably have to be demolished at a certain point of maturity. The crucial question is what then follows. What provision for stability and consistency is put in place when the forms of action are abandoned? That is the question which the common law has never managed to answer satisfactorily. We must first look back to the earlier period.

The earlier principle of organization was the list of all claims claimable. That is what we mean when we speak of the forms of action. Every 'form of action' was a claim claimable or, in other words, a proposition which a plaintiff was permitted to advance and which, if he could substantiate it, would win him his case. In short an action was a winning proposition. An action, in this sense, is always a set of words. Modern pleading boils down to this: the plaintiff makes a statement of the facts and draws from those facts a conclusion as to the defendant's liability. In court the plaintiff's argument then seeks to prove that as a matter of law those facts do justify that conclusion. The old way was to advance a standard winning proposition from the list of forms and in court to attempt to substantiate it.

This can be illustrated schematically, using some simplified examples based on Roman law. Suppose that in a given jurisdiction there is an action which asserts that the thing in question is the plaintiff's and another which asserts that the defendant ought to pay the plaintiff £20. The existence of these actions poses questions: on what factual conditions is it true that a thing of a given description belongs to a person of a given description? On what factual conditions can it be said of a person of a given description that he owes money to another person of a given description? These questions can be answered unscientifically (or, as one might say, evaded), as for instance by asking what the people feel about any given claim, or what the king feels or what some supernatural being wills[22]. But if books begin to be written in answer to these questions, then, as this learning continues to accumulate, the answer will become gradually more scientific.

Let there be another action which asserts that the defendant has committed theft of a silver cup and ought on that account to make a payment to the plaintiff, and another which says that the plaintiff bought a cow from the plaintiff and, arising from that purchase, the defendant ought to do something for the plaintiff. These actions raise their own questions which, once again, must be evaded or answered.

---

22 This theme runs through *S.F.C. Milsom*, Historical Foundations of the Common Law, 2nd ed., London, 1981. See especially at pp. 42-44, and also *S.F.C. Milsom*, Law and Fact in Legal Development, (1967) 17 University of Toronto Law Journal 1.

Once a given society begins to collect answers to some of these actional questions it will begin to answer all of them. A law library will grow up, not suddenly but starting from small beginnings. The law library will take a particular form. It will be focused on the text of the actions and will document the meaning of each claim in terms of the facts which must be adduced to substantiate it. The law will consist of the list of all actions, and the law library will document, action by action, the conditions upon which the plaintiff will win or, in other words, what the plaintiff must show in order to be able to substantiate each of these winning propositions. There is no reason why, within each actional package, the law cannot reach a level of detail and sophistication equal to anything that we know today.

A jurisdiction which lists the claims claimable and works out the range of each can achieve stability without any map of the whole law. The list does the office of the non-existent map. The advantage of a list of claims is that it offers something finite to work on. In effect it breaks up the problem of understanding the law into as many smaller problems as there are claims in the list. If the law is taken to consist in a list of a hundred claims claimable, it is not the whole law that must be made intellectually manageable but rather each of those one hundred claims. The list provides overall stability, and consistency within each actional package is with care quite readily attainable. Rigorous documentation of the scope of every claim – the persons who can bring it, the facts on which it can be brought and the steps to be taken to win it – can produce, action by action, detailed and closely reasoned law. It takes time for all the problems to emerge and for solutions to those problems to be worked through. Over the years, case law builds up within each package.

In England the actions were listed in the formularies, the Register of Writs and pleading manuals such as *Novae Narrationes*, and the cases accumulated in the reports. And the abridgements[23] performed the function of collecting the cases which documented each action. The abridgements represent a combination of two powerful but primitive organizing principles, the list of actions and the alphabet. The alphabet allows the list of actions to be transformed and diversified, but unsystematically. In Roman law the great edictal commentaries of the classical period reveal that kind of law at its highest level of development. The praetor's edict publicly listed every claim claimable. A commentary on every one would yield a complete statement of the law. The abridgements accepted the assistance of the alphabet. The edictal commentaries did not. The order of the edict was historically determined. It was part of the lawyer's training to know his way about the list.

---

23 These originated in private attempts to order the build up of material in the cases. The alphabet gave scope for some departures from the simple list of actions. That is, non-actional headings could be inserted: "A blank volume would be divided up into alphabetical titles – say from abatement to withernam – and the compiler would work through yearbooks, inserting under the appropriate headings a précis or abridged text of each major proposition of law": *J. H. Baker*, An Introduction to English Legal History, 2nd ed., London, 1979, at pp. 158-159, and see p. 168.

This principle of organization – the law as a list of claims, each documented one by one – took both English and Roman law from their pre-law-library days to their classical periods. For Roman law that means through to the 3rd century A.D., and for English law it means down to the mid-19th. In the pre-law-library days there were no scientific answers to the questions posed by the actions. As the library matured, almost every imaginable problem could be discussed and answered from the books. Developed law thus gradually displaces the speculation and ingenious argument which surrounds the core of every proposition and imposes instead scientific order. Philosophers might condemn the artificiality of that order but that artificiality is the price of consistent adjudication.

Both Roman and English law abandoned their forms of action. The question why they had to do so is difficult. The short and over-simplified answer is that, although the list of claims served to stabilize the law, that stability was bought at a high price in sacrifice of rationality. As the documentation of the actions became fuller and more sophisticated, so the sacrifice of rationality became more apparent. In other words, as the law library grew and there was more and more law to know and to know in a scientific way, it became more and more apparent that it was irrational or even absurd to box up that knowledge in the categories inherited from the intuitive past. The taxonomy inherited from the past was manifestly not defensible. Strong pressures to prevent actions from overlapping exacerbated the artificiality, and forensic opportunism sometimes scored curiously disfiguring successes.

Even in our four simple examples above we can see the seeds of intellectual stress. The first two, viewed as legal categories, are categories of consequence. That is, 'The cow, Daisy, is mine!' is a conclusion drawn from facts. The same is true of 'You owe me £20!' But 'I bought a cow from you and therefore ...' and 'You stole a cow from me and therefore ...' are categories primarily of event. Sale and theft are events which trigger consequences. As we have seen, differently based categories tend to intersect. That is the beginning of a rational disaster, at best an impediment to thought and at worst the concealed source of seemingly insoluble problems.

Suppose the buyer does not pay the price of the goods bought. Does his liability arise in the action of debt[24] or the action on sale or both? An artificial answer has to be given, the motive force for which is the attempt to maintain the boundaries of actions or, in other words, the need not to subvert the fundamental organizing principle of a law which is structured on a list of actions: the non-paying buyer's liability arises only in sale, not in debt. But if a lender does not repay a loan, his liability arises in debt, and there is no action on the event 'loan'. Suppose we want to gather up all the events which, like sale, are 'contracts', we will need to depart

[24] 'Debt' here includes the Roman *condictio*, though the two actions were not identical. The example is more Roman than English, since there was no separate action on sale in the common law and, until the action of *assumpsit* began to compete, there was no action under sale except debt or, perhaps one should say, debt-detinue.

from the actional scheme, because loan must come too, but loan is only one cause of indebtedness and, still more annoying, not all the causes of indebtedness are contracts. It follows that the attempt to create a category of 'contract' must break up the actional category of debt[25]. On the other hand, an option to speak only in terms of consequences would have created havoc. Alongside debt for an obligation to pay a *certum*, it would be necessary to devise general actions for obligations to pay different kinds of *incerta*.

This is one kind of stress endemic in a law of actions. There are others, of which we can briefly mention just one. We have assumed that the list of actions is absolutely fixed. It cannot be fixed. It always needs to be supplemented, to cope with grievances which turn out not to have been covered. The supplementary actions threaten the very principle of organization and the value of stability which it protects. To meet that potential damage – that is, to prevent plaintiffs rushing off to supplementary actions as and when they please – more artificiality has to be introduced. In England a great deal of legal history can be explained as a battle to save the rationality of order expressed in the fixed list of actions from being subverted by the supplementary actions. The first-generation actions were to retain their primacy, and the second-generation actions which began as actions on the case (*actiones in factum*) were to accept the principle of subsidiarity: they should not be used even if by the light of nature it seemed that they were suitable to be used unless the facts fell outside the scope of the primary actions[26]. But one by one these defences were knocked down, so that one *actio in factum* after another in effect supplanted the primary action which it was meant to extend. Cumulatively, these stories showed that the list of actions did not in reality provide the immutable foundations of the law.

The reasons why the lists of actions fell into disrepute are very complex. As legal categories the actions were misaligned; supplementation of the list and measures to prevent overlaps caused additional tensions; opportunism and pragmatism introduced curious deformities; lawyerly and linguistic conservatism resisted simplification. All these causes added up, and there were others too. In the end the forms of action had to be abandoned.

---

25 This splitting up, and its difficulties, can be seen in *Gaius*, Institutes, III, 89-91, in which *Gaius* labours to detach from contract the non-contractual causes of indebtedness. In the actional category they did not require to be detached and centuries of usage said they should not be detached, but *Gaius* was committed to a classification of obligations by causative event.

26 The most famous examples are the competition between debt and *assumpsit* focused on in *Slade v. Morley* (1597 - 1602) 4 Coke's Reports 92 (see 1971 C.L.J. 51); and, much later, the competition between trespass *vi et armis* and the action on the case for negligent injury and damage, focused on in *Williams v. Holland* (1833) 10 Bingham's Reports 112. See *J. H. Baker*, An Introduction to English Legal History, 2nd ed., London, 1979, at pp. 282-288, and 342-345.

IV. The Roman Response

It is very difficult to revolutionize legal thought. The law requires continuity. In England *John Austin* tried to classify the law scientifically. He lost his audience. He was too far ahead of the courts[27]. It was impossible in England and impossible equally in Rome for all lawyers with one accord to go over to a brand new way of thinking about the law. Most lawyers most of the time went on thinking in actional packages even after the forms of action had gone. Quite marked traces of that pattern of thought still survive in England well over a century after the forms of actions were abandoned. As *Maitland* said, "[t]he forms of action we have buried, but they still rule us from their graves"[28].

By the time the Romans abandoned their forms of action, they already had a new and better way of looking at the law. For in the late middle of the 2nd century A.D. *Gaius* had brilliantly invented the institutional scheme which has dominated western legal thought ever since. However, we know that the invention and availability of that taxonomy of law did not effect any change in the form of or arrangement of the literature. Even when, more than three centuries later, *Justinian* compacted and reissued the entire law library, he did not arrange it according to the system of the 'Institutes'. On the contrary, he retained an unsystematic ordering of the same kind as, and indeed derived from, the old order of the actions in the edictal list.

However, *Justinian*'s educational scheme placed the Gaian map of the law at, so to say, the very door of the law school. In their first year law students would study the Emperor's new version of the 'Institutes', so that, into whatever depths they were subsequently thrown, they would always know where they were[29]. Everyone who goes to London carries a map of the tube. If you surface into the awesomely detailed reality of, say, Oxford Circus, you still know where you are and how to get back. In the same way, if you came to the law library through the 'Institutes' you could never be completely lost.

It is easy to see what *Justinian* intended. If the minds of young lawyers were formed according to a sound conceptual map, there was no need to rearrange the whole law library. It is less easy to see to what extent lawyers in the previous centuries voluntarily used the institutional scheme to structure their thought. Many no doubt went on thinking in terms of the list of actions, long after the formulary system of litigation fell out of use. But those who were interested in better reasoned

---

27 The story is told in *L.* and *J. Hamburger*, Troubled Lives: John and Sarah Austin, Toronto, 1985, at pp. 53-77.

28 *F. W. Maitland*, The Forms of Action, A. H. Chaytor and W .J. Whittaker, edd., Cambridge, 1965, at p. 2.

29 *Constitutio Omnem* (The Pronouncement 'The Whole Body of the Law'). See the translation in the Pennsylvania Digest: The Digest of Justinian, A. Watson, ed., Philadelphia, 1985, vol. 1, at pp. l-lv.

law and a more intelligible overview must have made more and more use of the institutional scheme. Otherwise one could not account for the ultimate triumph of the Gaian scheme, nor for *Justinian*'s familiar and affectionate reference to its inventor as "our *Gaius*, *Gaius noster*".

V. The English Response

To abandon the forms of action was to shake the foundations of legal thought. One measure which English law soon took was a formal tightening of the doctrine of precedent. That was one obvious way to minimize instability and inconsistency. More recently it has proved possible for the House of Lords to relax that grip[30]. The decision to allow the House to overrule itself was a symptom of a new balance struck between reason and authority. This new deal has been made possible in part by the rise of the university jurist and the transformation of legal literature and legal education. The past century has seen the responsibility for the interpretative development shared between judges and university jurists. The university law schools have indeed become almost wholly responsible for the literature which gives shape and direction to the cases[31].

However, despite the transformation of the law library, there has been a serious failure to give structure to the whole. The alphabetical *Halsbury* dominates the practitioner's research. *Halsbury* represents the old way of doing things; it continues the tradition of the abridgments, much as the form of *Justinian*'s Digest, still disorderly, was continuous with the great edictal commentaries. As for our beginners, the truth is that law students are never made to think about the structure of the law as a whole. Taxonomy is neglected.

The law consists of courses which students and their friends take. That is, each newly qualified lawyer knows that he or she took some courses because they were compulsory and some which were optional. Outside these two circles lie courses they know to have been taken by friends, in the further distance other courses on their own university's menu, others known to be available in other universities and at master's level. But all these units are regarded much as a tourist might regard an archipelago, to be visited in any order and in some cases to be given the miss. And the law schools encourage this view of the law. The courses are presented as an

---

30 Lord Gardiner L.C.'s statement of 26th July 1966 ([1966] 3 All E.R. 77), itself a remarkable law-making pronouncement not easy to classify, recognized the utility of binding precedent as a means to certainty but relaxed the rule that the House of Lords was bound by its own decisions because it could lead to injustice in some cases and "unduly restrict the proper development of the law". The rule which was abrogated went back to the mid-19th century: *Beamish v. Beamish* (1861) 9 H.L.C. 274, esp. at p. 338, per Lord Campbell, confirmed in *London Street Tramways v. London County Council* [1898] A.C. 375.

31 This development is discussed in *P. B. H. Birks*, Adjudication and Interpretation in the Common Law: A Century of Change, (1994) 14 Legal Studies 156-179.

indifferentiated menu. Variations of order and nomenclature as between one university and another add to the impression which is given that there is no structural relation between the many different units. If a university is in experimental mood, changes of order and content may happen even from year to year. This experimentation is not bad, rather the reverse, but it intensifies the perception of the law as inherently fragmentary, a kaleidoscope which can safely be given an occasional twist.

There is now a trend towards shorter courses and more of them. The trend goes under the name 'modularization'. Shorter courses and more courses will mean more fragmentation, more variation between one law school and another. Hence, if we ask upon what principle the law is now organized the answer must be that whereas for centuries it was organized as a list of claims claimable it is now a fluctuating list of courses available, backed up by books marketable.

Where did we go wrong? When the forms of action went, we did have the beginnings of an overview tradition based on the institutional scheme, and the fathers of the modern textbook knew their 'Institutes' and the subsequent history of the classification of law which it spread across Europe. They wrote books which fitted that scheme and they knew how to reconstitute the pattern from the individal units which they contributed. In short they knew the map. If history had worked itself out as it seemed that it must, some version of the institutional scheme would now be dominant in the thought of English common lawyers, and that dominant scheme would be examined, criticized and improved in every law school. Nothing like that is happening. There is no dominant scheme.

VI. The English Overview Tradition

There was English overview literature, but the tradition failed. In the early 18th century *Thomas Wood* wrote an 'Institute of the Laws of England' in the same tradition as that to which *Stair* and the other great institutists of Scotland belonged[32]. That is, he hoped to adapt the Roman institutional scheme to present the law of England – "to show a student a more light, smoother, and nearer way than has hitherto been discovered; tho' not the clearest, smoothest, and nearest that might be made". His preface vividly conveys his conviction that the way to the knowledge of the law was far too "dark and rugged" and far darker and more rugged than it needed to be. "I entertained hopes", he said, "that now it might not be impossible to sort, or to put in some order, this heap of good learning; and that a general and methodical distribution, preparatory to a more large and accurate study of our laws, might now be made"[33].

---

32 *T. Wood*, An Institute of the Law of England, or Laws in their Natural Order, London, 1720.

33 *Wood* (n. 32) pp. ii-iii.

Wood had a predecessor in the person of *Cowell*, Regius Professor of Civil Law at Cambridge. But *Wood*'s book was much larger and more ambitious. Detailed analysis shows that he made only a partial escape from the list of actions, because his Book IV, 'Of the Courts of Justice or the Jurisdiction of Courts' still consists in large measure of a list of actions, each shortly documented (actions on the case, detinue, covenant, debt, trespass *vi et armis*, ejectment, *quare impedit*, waste, replevin).

In retrospect *Wood* appears as a very minor figure. He was overshadowed by *Blackstone*, whose 'Commentaries' were the only really successful English work in the institutional overview tradition. *Blackstone*'s programme had two strings, better legal education and more accessible legal literature. The two go together. Orderly presentation of the law is promoted by proper provision for legal education. As the first ever professor of the common law in an English university, *Blackstone* had a passion for both[34]. He saw that the only way to achieve an improvement in the rational quality of the law was to bring it within the university. He opposed "the custom by some so very warmly recommended, of dropping all liberal education, as of no use to students in the law: and placing them in it's stead, at the desk of some skilful attorney; in order to initiate them early in all the depths of practice". Describing this as an "illiberal path to the profession", he warned of the public danger that would ensue if the interpretation and enforcement of the law were to fall wholly into the hands of "obscure or illiterate men" who could "never aspire to form, and seldom expect to comprehend, any argument drawn *a priori*, from the spirit of the laws and the natural foundations of justice"[35]. His presciption was this:

> "The inconveniences here pointed out can never be effectively prevented, but by making academical education a previous step to the profession of the common law, and at the same time making the rudiments of the law a part of academical education. For sciences are of a sociable disposition, and flourish best in the neighbourhood of each other: nor is there any branch of learning, but may be helped and assistances drawn from the other arts"[36].

In the university he knew that the common law would have to be expounded according to an elegant and rational system, and like so many others he used the

---

[34] *John Cowell*, Institute of English Law – Institutiones Juris Anglicani ad methodum et Seriem Institutionum Imperialium compositae et digestae (1605), translated into English 1655.

[35] *W. Blackstone*, Commentaries on the Laws of England, London, 1765-69, 1, 32.

[36] *Blackstone* (n. 35) 1, 32. *Austin* was occasionally complimentary, as in relation to *Blackstone*'s separation of primary and secondary obligations (albeit not in that language): *J. Austin*, Lectures in Jurisprudence, 4th ed., R. Campbell, ed., London, 1873, at p. 796. On *Blackstone*'s place in the 'institutional' tradition, see *J. W. Cairns*, Blackstone, An English Institutist: Legal Literature and the Rise of the Nation State, (1984) 4 Oxford J.L.S. 318, and *J. W. Cairns*, Blackstone, Kahn-Freund and the Contract of Employment, (1989) 105 L.Q.R. 300.

institutional scheme interestingly and originally adapted by himself[37]. His conception of his task as "an academical expounder of the law" was precisely to convey an intelligible and structured overview, so that the student would see how the subject fitted together. Without a structured overview of that kind, the student would find the study of the law unprincipled, irrational and repulsive. *Blackstone* used the image of a map:

> "You will permit me however very briefly to describe, rather what I conceive an academical expounder of the law should do, than what I have known done. He should consider his course as a general map of the law, marking out the shape of the country, it's connexions and boundaries, it's greater divisions and principal cities: it is not his business to describe minutely the subordinate limits or to fix the longitude and latitude of every inconsiderable hamlet. His attention should be engaged, like that of the readers in *Fortescue's* inns of chancery, 'in tracing out the originals and as it were the elements of the law.' For, if as *Justinian* has observed, the tender understanding of the student be loaded at the first with a multitude and variety of matter, it will either occasion him to desert his studies or will carry him heavily through them, with much labour, delay, and despondence"[38].

This was the task which the Commentaries splendidly discharged[39]. We might say that university law schools should now do more, that they should not ignore even the inconsiderable hamlets. But they certainly ought not to omit the map of the greater divisions and principal cities. *Blackstone's* achievement is easily underestimated. The mud thrown at him by *Bentham* and *Austin* has tended to stick. The 'Commentaries' for the first time gave the world a coherent and reasonably detailed overview of English law, removed from its actional packages[40]. And this view was widely dispersed and, through many editions, was sustained through a long period of time.

The reforms of the 19th century which shook the old foundations of the common law, above all the abolition of the forms of action and the unification of common law and equitable jurisdiction, would not have been possible without the comfort of the 'Commentaries'. They provided a new foundation, the foundation of the new law library which would be built up by jurists such as *Dicey, Pollock, Anson*, and their successors.

However, the books which made the new library were not overview books. They were textbooks on particular areas, written, at least at first, by jurists who knew how they might fit together as parts of some version of the institutional scheme common to the rest of the western legal tradition. The early jurists of the common law, scholars such as *Pollock, Anson* and *Dicey*, did of course know the institu-

---

37 *Blackstone* (n. 35) 1, 35.

38 *Blackstone* (n. 35) 1, 35.

39 *S.F.C. Milsom*, The Nature of Blackstone's Achievement, (1981) 1 Oxford J.L.S. 1, at p. 4.

40 *Milsom* (n. 39) 4.

tional scheme and its history. The books they wrote, so to say, broke off parts of that scheme.

For example, we have seen that one part of that scheme was the law of obligations, divided according to the events from which they arose – contract, wrongs and other events. It is interesting therefore to read in the Preface of the first edition of 'The Law of Tort'[41] that *Pollock* was conscious of the need for writing an English law of obligations. The book is dedicated to *Willes* J. and *Pollock* says that *Willes* J. had always urged the writing of an English law of obligations. *Pollock* then adds that a book on the law of tort added to a book on the law of contract does not of course complete a law of obligations[42]. *Winfield* ventured further[43], but it was not until *Goff* and *Jones* that real headway was made with the obligations arising from miscellaneous events beyond contract and tort[44]. We now have, in different books, an almost complete law of obligations in English. Willes J. and *Pollock*, when they concluded that that was what we must seek to achieve, were thinking immediately of *Pothier*[45] and, more remotely, of Roman law. Nowadays few common lawyers know about the history of legal taxonomy or have any feel for its necessity, but the late 19th century founders of the new juristic profession did know their Roman law and did appreciate the importance of classification.

The overview tradition in England did not completely peter out. *Austin* worked immensely hard on his scientific analysis of the law, but his agonized efforts were too far ahead of the times and, as we have noticed, he had to give up for want of audience[46]. For the rest, overview books fell to a level deemed to be below serious notice, elementary, not suitable for discussion by those pursuing a university education[47]. This was a bad mistake.

---

41 *Pollock* produced his book on contract first, seven years before tort: *F. Pollock*, The Principles of the Law of Contract at Law and in Equity, London, 1876, followed by The Law of Tort, London, 1883.

42 *Pollock*, Tort (n. 41) preface.

43 His study of the nature and boundaries of tort included an important chapter on quasi-contract: *Sir P. H. Winfield*, The Province of the Law of Tort, Cambridge, 1931. That final chapter was later broken off to make: *Sir P.H. Winfield*, The Law of Quasi-Contracts, Cambridge, 1952.

44 *R. Goff, G. Jones*, The Law of Restitution, 1st ed., London, 1966. The force for recognition of this area of law came from the U.S.A. through Professor *Scott* and Professor *Seavey*'s work as reporters of The Restatement of Restitution, American Law Institute, 1937. There had been earlier American work in the field, under the name 'quasi-contract' by *W. A. Keener* (1893) and *F. C. Woodward* (1913).

45 *R. J. Pothier*, Treatise on Obligations, trans. W. D. Evans, London, 1806, published in France, 1761.

46 See text to n. 27.

47 Some of these books have been through many editions and still keep going, as for example *P. S. James*, Introduction to English Law, the first edition of which in 1950 expressly referred the book's vocation to the model of *Justinian*'s Institutes, and *K. Smith, D. Keenan*, English Law, which first appeared in 1963. These books appear to survive because they are found useful in preparing for school exams, as for instance G.C.E. A Level Law.

University jurists such as *Pollock* and *Anson* could never have foreseen how cut off from the institutional scheme and its modern restatements we have become. The reason is, perhaps, that they would never have realized that we would abandon the teaching of the basic first year course in Roman law, based on the 'Institutes'. That course provided the obvious opportunity to keep in touch with the dominant taxonomy of the western legal tradition. No other course could or would take up the weight. Modern jurisprudents have other concerns, and comparative law is simply not strong enough as yet.

In the result, despite *Blackstone*, we have returned to the "heap of good learning" which *Wood* in 1722 hoped could now be sorted[48]. Only, instead of being a heap of actions, it is a heap of books and courses. A very few people manage to keep in touch with the institutional scheme around which the English law library can still be reassembled. But that grip is weakening as the memory fades.

VII. Seven Foundations

It happens that in January 1995 the English professions issued new instructions to law schools on the subject of compulsory courses for those wishing to enter the professions. The new list shows how English law hovers between using the institutional scheme and being completely ignorant of it.

The core subjects have been grandiloquently renamed 'The Foundations of Legal Knowledge'. There are seven such foundations, which the professions list thus: "(1) Obligations I, (2) Obligations II, (3) Foundations of Criminal Law, (4) Foundations of Equity and the Law of Trusts, (5) Foundations of the Law of the European Union, (6) Foundations of Property Law, (7) Foundations of Public Law". The order reveals much. It is not alphabetical, but nor does it have any conceptual coherence. The haphazard sequence is symptomatic of the English indifference to legal taxonomy, and it shows that there was no formulated intention to use civilian categories. Nevertheless, if we re-order the list, we will see that the institutional scheme is present below the surface of this pronouncement.

The law is either public or private. The 'Institutes' deal with public law rather in the manner of a shell surrounding private law. That is, they deal with constitutional matters very briefly at the beginning, and with crime, also very briefly, at the end. Those subjects are represented in the English list at (3) and (7). Something more will be said below about (5), but clearly the law of the European Union is also partly constitutional law and to that extent must also fit here.

Private law concerns persons, things or actions. Of these three the largest is the law of things (or assets). We noted above that the modern restatement of the law of

48 Notice to Law Schools Regarding Full-Time Qualifying Law Degrees, January 1995, discussed in (1995) 111 L.Q.R. 371. More detail can be found in: *P. Birks*, ed., Reviewing Legal Education, Oxford, 1994.

things draws a hard line between obligations and property. Obligations in the institutional scheme is divided according to the event from which the obligation arises, from contract, delict, as though from contract and as though from delict. Nobody admires the *quasi* categories, which were perhaps the least successful creature of Roman jurisprudence[49].

Obligations is fully present in the pronouncement. It has two slots. When the pronouncement first went out to consultation these were called simply Contract and Tort. But the small print under Contract included the words "an outline of the law of restitution", and, since restitution has struggled to escape that wrong label, some of us objected. The consequence was the change to Obligations I and II. The small print under 'Obligations II' shows that it is still concerned with tort. 'Obligations I' includes contract and restitution. Ever since the publication of the American Restatement of Restitution[50] the common law has used the word 'restitution' to denote the law of unjust enrichment and has, except in the work of one or two authors, jettisoned the alternative phrase 'quasi-contract'. The Roman *quasi* categories, unsuccessful as they are, reflected the need to recognize and break down the miscellaneous group of obligations arising from events other than contract and tort. The two units of obligations in the professional pronouncement effectively cover contract, tort and unjust enrichment, though they do not acknowledge the existence of any residual miscellany.

Property is expressly covered lower down the list, in Foundation (5). The small print reveals that Property does not in this context include the law of succession. There is another omission, probably not so deliberately intended. The pronouncement speaks in the heading of 'The Foundations of Property Law' but in spelling out what must actually be done under this head it confines itself to the law of real property. There are very few books on personal property, which has fallen out of almost every law school's curriculum. The routine omission makes it more difficult to understand the law of real property and causes perplexity in the face of very simple problems. How do I make a gift of the silver which I have deposited in my bank? Almost no young common lawyer has ever encountered such a question. That such a gap can open up, not just in one law school but in virtually all law schools, is a symptom of the unsystematic nature of English law. An overview, if there is one, will always warn of a subject's being neglected.

Despite the omission of personal property and the excision of succession, the law of things, subdivided between property and obligations and with obligations

---

49 The category of quasi-contract has been abandoned by all writers in the common law family though it was defended by Professor *Stoljar*: *S. Stoljar*, The Law of Quasi-Contract, 2nd ed., Sydney, 1989, where his choice of terminology is discussed at pp. 1-2. Quasi-delict has never had any role in common law thinking. The modern common law agrees with civilian jurisdictions in dividing obligations as arising from contract, wrongs, unjust enrichment and other events.

50 American Law Institute, 1937.

sub-sub-divided between contract, tort and unjust enrichment, is properly represented in the core. The law of persons is not. *Stair* would have approved, since the elimination of persons was his principal variation of the institutional scheme[51]. It is not clear whether the professions had good reasons for thinking of the law of persons as less than fully foundational. The law of actions is similarly omitted, for the reason that pleading and procedure have traditionally been left until the vocational phase, where they have been starved of the attention they deserve by the practice of the institutions which teach the vocational stage to accept no responsibility for research and writing.

Two foundations have not been discussed, namely (4) Foundations of Equity and the Law of Trusts, and (5) Foundations of the Law of the European Union. As for the former, one might have hoped that the new pronouncement would take another step away from the old dualism of our system by distributing the equitable contribution to the law of obligations to the law of obligations, and, similarly, the equitable contribution to property to property. Finally, the law of the European Union cannot be more than a temporary foundation, if that is not a contradiction in terms. At this time, perhaps it must be studied independently, but in due course it will surely be reabsorbed into constitutional law and into the other substantive subjects which it changes.

In the upshot, (4) and (5) can be put aside as not really independent of the others. What we then find is that the other five fit back into the institutional systematic, with two units of public law corresponding in expanded form to the prefix and suffix of *Justinian*'s 'Institutes' and then three units of private law corresponding to the principal parts of the law of things. Actions is explicably absent. The absence of persons is less easily accounted for.

However little the authors of these provisions were aware of it – and one may be sure that they were completely unaware of it – the conclusion is that the Roman scheme survives in practice just under the surface of our core provisions. This reflects the fact that, in the era when the forms of action were abolished and textbooks began to take the weight of responsibility for stability of the law, books were written and courses were planned by people who knew the institutional scheme and knew where their work belonged in it. *Pollock* knew that contract and tort were parts of the law of obligations found when obligations were divided according to the events which brought them into being. And he knew that contract and tort together did not exhaust the law of obligations. Only in the most recent period has this knowledge begun to be lost. Unless we are careful, out of the resultant chaos will come the painful reinvention of the wheel. Or it would, if time were unlimited. The politico-economic situation will more likely hurry us into a borrowed cure, a code and, in effect, the end of the common law.

---

51 Cf. nn. 15, 17 and text thereto.

An audience cut off from history is vulnerable to curious gospels. In 1974, for example, *Grant Gilmore*, proclaiming and indeed advocating the death of contract and at the same time taking an unjust swipe at university lawyers, said that the academic mind, "usually a generation or so behind the judicial mind in catching on to things", would eventually wake up to the "absurdity of attempting to preserve the 19th century contract-tort dichotomy". He thought that a fusion of contract and tort would occur as 'contract' was reabsorbed into the mainstream of 'tort':

> "Until the 19th century, tort had always been our residual category of civil liability. As the contract rules dissolve, it is becoming so again. It should be pointed out that the theory of tort into which contract is being reabsorbed is itself a much more expansive theory of liability than was the theory of tort from which contract was artificially separated a hundred years ago"[52].

At law students clad in the armour of the 'Institutes' you can safely throw this kind of stuff. Few are so protected. They can be cruelly misled by an *avant garde* indifferent to history.

VIII. Reviving Knowledge of the Roman Institutional Scheme

For the sake of the intellectual order upon which formal justice depends, and for the sake of keeping in touch with the pattern of private law in Europe, and to keep the common law alive, it is essential that English lawyers develop a renewed awareness of the rational structure of the law. Yet, as we saw from the pitiful disorder of the Seven Foundations of Legal Knowledge, even the people in charge of legal education and in a position to issue directions to all the law schools no longer know how to fit the pieces together. *A fortiori* they miss the European dimension. They do not know that the system upon which they fit together gives the key to every continental code and every law library and law bookshop too.

This is the root of the tragedy of the modern common law. The professions can still control the nature and quality of legal education and through that control they can determine the quality of the common law itself and its capacity both to serve its people and to defeat the civilian competition. But, having this power and this

52 *Grant Gilmore*, The Death of Contract, Columbus, Ohio, 1974. Cf. *P. S. Atiyah*, Contract, Promises and the Law of Obligations, (1978) 94 L.Q.R. 193, at p. 194: "I want to suggest that, despite the increasing attacks upon freedom of contract, and the great divide between Contract and Tort, the conceptual apparatus which still dominates legal thinking on these issues is the apparatus of the 19th century". I do not imply that scholars such as *Gilmore* and *Atiyah* ignored or were ignorant of the Roman past, nor of the later elaboration of Roman thought in the age of the *ius commune*, but only that it is unsafe nowadays to serve up such a discussion in terms which assume some similar knowledge in the audience. The impression collected, even if not intended, is that obligations, contract, tort and so on are 19th century ideas.

duty, the professions have proved to have no vision beyond their own short-term interests. So far are they from caring sufficiently about the quality of legal education that they habitually entrust their regulatory powers to people as ignorant of the substance of the common law as they are indifferent to its history and insensible to its modern predicament. Hope comes from an unlikely source. The state's first intervention now means that the professions must at last answer for their stewardship to the Lord Chancellor's Advisory Committee on Legal Education and Conduct, though that Committee still lacks effective powers.

As the 20th century draws to a close the English common law thus finds itself in a degree of intellectual difficulty. It must match the rationality of the civil law if it is to do its duties and retain its own identity. In the universities comparative law is still relatively weak. Roman law courses have all but died out. These points of contact with civilian systematic are therefore not functioning. The memory is fading of the civilian systematic which filled the vacuum left by the forms of action and which still explains the shape of the core categories of our law library and legal education. As that memory fades, reforms in patterns of legal education, especially the craze for modularization, favour more fragmentation and diversification. University lawyers are also driven towards narrower fields of specialization.

If it be true that legal science must make provision for stability and consistency, so that like cases are indeed decided alike, it will not be good to let things fall apart. It is not that the centre will not ultimately hold, but that more peremptory means will be found to ensure that it does. The common law will be killed by an English Civil Code. Neither its character nor its world-wide communion would survive. The choice seems to lie between succumbing to the next wave of enthusiasm for a codification and rapidly improving the unwritten systematic of the law. That means raising the level of attention to the way in which the different parts of the law fit together and, at a higher level of detail, the way in which each part is itself organized internally. This programme requires more thorough, and longer, legal education. The professions' notion that one year or one and half years will suffice belongs in an amateur world which has passed away. Our lawyers need to know more law, and they need to organize it more rationally. The rational overview and internal organization of the parts hang together. They are two parts of one taxonomic exercise. The ordering of the categories of legal thought is a matter for university lawyers and legal education, but it is not at all obvious how, in present conditions and in the light of the indifference of the professions, the English law schools can be persuaded of its importance.

In Scotland it should be easier. The institutional scheme was the very framework of Scots law, and Scots law never had to cope with the mystifying duality of equity and law. And in the Scots law schools *Justinian*'s 'Institutes' are still studied. But the Scots lawyers should be haunted by the ghost of *James Dalrymple*, in whose name, of all names, the alphabet now threatens to triumph. He will only forgive that *iniuria*, if he will forgive it at all, on condition that a book is written, and made compulsory reading, which bears the same relation to the Stair Memorial Encyclopaedia as does *Justinian*'s 'Institutes' to the rest of the *Corpus iuris civilis*. Scots law could still provide the map which might save English law from breaking up in a storm of disorder.

The Civil Law Tradition in Scottish Legal Thought

By John W. Cairns[1]

I. Introduction

Baron *David Hume*, when Professor of Scots Law in the University of Edinburgh, instructed his class thus:

> "Certainly, while I ... refuse allegiance to the Civil Law, as having dominion over us, I have no purpose of discouraging the study of that most enlightened, ingenious and elegant system. Doubtless an acquaintance with it is the best possible instruction for a young man in the general principles of right and wrong, and in the method of reasoning on matters of law; and indeed, as I have already said, the knowledge of it is in many points the knowledge of our own established and municipal practice. In the way of preparation, therefore, for that code which is to be laid before you more in detail here, it cannot be too strongly recommended to your attention"[2].

Some of these remarks clearly echo the views of *Hume*'s teacher *John Millar* on the value of civil law[3]; they also indicate that *Hume* considered the creative reception of civil law into Scots law to be over. It had become, as he put it, "naturalised", and had "been incorporated into our practice, by a long and uniform train of decisions", so that it was "a proper integral part of our common or customary law"[4]. He also stressed that the authority given to civil law was and always had been due to "its agreement with equity and reason", quoting *Thomas Craig* and

---

1 I have benefited from the comments of *George Gretton*, *Hector MacQueen* and *David Sellar*. I gratefully acknowledge my debts, first, to *Angus Stewart* Q.C., Keeper of the Advocates' Library for permission to consult and cite material in the collection of the Advocates' Library and certain Advocates' Manuscripts housed in the National Library of Scotland, secondly to the Keeper of the Records of Scotland for permission to quote from material in the Scottish Record Office, and thirdly to the Trustees of the National Library of Scotland and to the British Library Board for similar permissions. I am also grateful to the Librarians of Edinburgh and Aberdeen University Libraries for permission to quote from material under their care. In all quotations from manuscripts I have preserved the original spelling but expanded common contractions.

2 G. C. H. Paton, ed., Baron David Hume's Lectures 1786-1822, 6 vols., Edinburgh, 1939-58, vol. 1, at p. 14.

3 See, e.g., National Library of Scotland, Adv. MS 20.4.7, fos. 1r-2r, found quoted in *J.W. Cairns*, Rhetoric, Language, and Roman Law: Legal Education and Improvement in Eighteenth-Century Scotland, (1991) 9 Law and History Review 31, at p. 42.

4 *Hume* (n. 2) vol. 1, p. 13.

Viscount *Stair* in support[5]. *Hume*'s mention of both *Stair* and *Craig* in this connection is particularly noteworthy.

The background to *Hume*'s view is complex. He was not simply following the general received wisdom of the ages as may initially appear, but rather, as the echo of *Millar* suggests, his opinion reflected the legal theory of the Scottish Enlightenment. One crucial aspect of the Enlightenment in Scotland was the attempt to develop a science of legislation. By moving away from traditional rationalist views of natural law, the moral sense theory of *Francis Hutcheson* and *Henry Home*, Lord *Kames*, and the theory of moral sentiments found in the work of *David Hume* and, above all, *Adam Smith*, emphasized the connection between law and the history of social life broadly conceived[6]. This had inevitably challenged the value of civil law as a living source of Scots law. While Roman law might be highly regarded as the law of a successful and commercial people, and thus full of examples and lessons, it could now be represented as having lost its value as a living source of Scots law, and its teachers (with the exception of *Millar*) as the practitioners of the pointless, purely antiquarian science excoriated by Lord *Kames*[7]. The Reception was seen as over in Scotland.

The above paragraph may represent an over-generalization and an over-simplification. There was, however, an identifiable trend to devalue civil law in the Scottish Enlightenment. While *Adam Smith* may have placed considerable reliance on the writings and categories of the modern civilians, he saw the introduction of the civil law in Scotland as having disadvantageously disrupted the development of Scots law in contrast with the law of England, the historical continuity of which had ensured it was "more formed on the naturall sentiments of mankind"[8]. Such an

---

5 *Hume* (n. 2) vol. 1, p. 13.

6 The literature on this is growing, and it is impossible to cite it all here. For valuable overviews, see *K. Haakonssen*, Natural Jurisprudence in the Scottish Enlightenment: Summary of an Interpretation, in: N. MacCormick and Z. Bankowski, edd., Enlightenment, Rights and Revolution: Essays in Legal and Social Philosophy, Aberdeen, 1989, p. 36; *idem*, Natural Law and the Scottish Enlightenment, in: (1985) 4 Man and Nature: Proceedings of the Canadian Society for Eighteenth-Century Studies 47; *idem*, Hugo Grotius and the History of Political Thought, (1985) 13 Political Theory 239; *D. N. MacCormick*, Law and Enlightenment, in: R. H. Campbell and A. S. Skinner, edd., The Origins and Nature of the Scottish Enlightenment, Edinburgh, 1982, p. 150. On the rejection of rationalist Natural law, see *V. M. Hope*, Virtue by Consensus: The Moral Philosophy of Hutcheson, Hume, and Adam Smith, Oxford, 1989. On the theme of the development of legislative science, see *K. Haakonssen*, The Science of a Legislator: The Natural Jurisprudence of David Hume and Adam Smith, Cambridge, 1981; *idem*, The Science of a Legislator in James Mackintosh's Moral Philosophy, (1984) 5 History of Political Thought 245; *D. Winch*, Science and the Legislator: Adam Smith and After, (1983) 93 The Economic Journal 501; *J. H. Burns*, Scottish Philosophy and the Science of Legislation, (1985) 2-6 Royal Society of Edinburgh Occasional Papers 11.

7 *H. Home*, Lord *Kames*, Elucidations Respecting the Common and Statute Law of Scotland, Edinburgh, 1777, pp. viii-ix.

8 *A. Smith*, Lectures on Jurisprudence, R. L. Meek, D. D. Raphael, and P. G. Stein, edd., Oxford, 1978, at p. 98.

attitude to civil law was not of course unique to Scotland at this period, and in some other parts of Europe was to bring about pressure for codification, although, in contrast, many Enlightened Scots valued development through case law[9].

The new Scottish attitudes to Roman law exemplified by those of *Hume* that grew out of the Scottish Enlightenment helped determine developments in the 19th century. The teaching of civil law failed in the University of Glasgow and was at a low ebb in that of Edinburgh after 1800[10]. In contrast, in a paper in a volume commemorating the Quincentenary of the University of Aberdeen, it is pleasing to note that, after a gap of some hundred years, lectures on civil law were once again given by the civilist in King's College, *Patrick Davidson*, who was elected in 1833[11]. These lectures, which were given for at least two years in the 1830s, were devoted to "the History and Principles of the Civil Law, as a Branch of general education"[12]. Despite this north-eastern innovation, it is none the less obvious that, until after the Universities (Scotland) Act of 1858, the study of civil law was at a low ebb in the Scottish universities. Much further work needs to be done on this, but the instruction given by *Alexander Irving*, *Douglas Cheape*, and *Alexander Swinton* as Professors of Civil Law in the University of Edinburgh (the only men effectively teaching the subject in this period) seems to have been old-fashioned, ignoring the new developments in the study of Roman law in Germany, although these were well enough known to a number of Scots, who in many ways saw the work of *Hugo* and *Savigny* as a continuation of the Scottish Enlightenment[13].

---

9 *J. W. Cairns*, Adam Smith and the Role of the Courts in Securing Justice and Liberty, in: R. P. Malloy and J. Evensky, edd., Adam Smith and the Philosophy of Law and Economics, Dordrecht, 1994, p. 31; *D. Lieberman*, The Province of Legislation Determined: Legal Theory in Eighteenth-Century Britain, Cambridge, 1989, at pp. 71-175.

10 *J. W. Cairns*, From 'Speculative' to 'Practical' Legal Education: The Decline of the Glasgow Law School, 1801-1830, T.R. 62 (1994) 331, at pp. 341-5.

11 On his election, see Aberdeen University Library, King's College Minutes 1831-47, MS K 51, p. 25. For a discussion of legal education in Aberdeen in the previous era, see *J.W. Cairns*, Lawyers, Law Professors, and Localities: The Universities of Aberdeen, 1680-1750, (1995) 46 Northern Ireland Legal Quarterly 304. This will be completed by a forthcoming further study covering from the latter date to the era of *Davidson*. There had been an abortive attempt under *Davidson*'s predecessor to revive the classes on civil law: see Evidence, Oral and Documentary, Taken and Received by the Commissioners Appointed by His Majesty George IV, July 23rd, 1826; and Re-appointed by his Majesty William IV, October 12th 1830; For Visiting the Universities of Scotland, vol. IV, University of Aberdeen, 1837 Parliamentary Papers, XXXVIII, p. 45.

12 Aberdeen University Library, King's College Minutes 1831-47, MS K 51, pp. 29 (26th Oct. 1833), 57 (1st Sept. 1834).

13 On *Irving*, see *Cairns* (n. 10) 343; on *Cheape*, see *Holtius*, Thémis ou bibliothèque du jurisconsulte et du publiciste 10 (1830-31) 377-86, reviewing *D. Cheape*, An Introductory Lecture on the Civil Law, Delivered in the University of Edinburgh, on Tuesday, 13th November 1827, Edinburgh, 1827; on *Swinton*, see Edinburgh University Library, Mic. M 1366, *J. Lorimer*, The Family Story, p. 147. See also *J. W. Cairns*, The Influence of the German Historical School in Early Nineteenth Century Edinburgh, (1994) 20 Syracuse Journal of International Law and Commerce 191.

Returning to the view of *Hume* that Roman law had been adopted as authoritative due to its agreement with equity and reason, it must be noted that this in fact reflects only one strand of thinking about this topic in the 18th century. Although one should not exaggerate the differences, one can very broadly say that it is possible to identify two rough approaches to civil law and its authority in Scotland by the middle years of that century. The first denied it any authority other than as embodying the *ius naturale*, but stressed the extent to which it in fact was identifiable with the law of nature and nations, which was regarded as authoritative in Scotland. The second saw it as having been adopted historically – perhaps because of the paucity of written law in the Middle Ages – and as validated by customary practice or by statute. This said, it is clear that a range of shades of understanding of this was possible. Moreover, natural law thinking hardly formed a uniform tradition. The approaches of Scots writers to the law of nature and nations were subject to a whole variety of different influences stretching back to *Thomas Aquinas*, *William of Ockham*, and beyond them to the ancient world. If it is impossible to pursue this within the confines of this short paper, it is none the less important to realize that the writers discussed here could have different understandings of natural law.

Hume's linking of *Craig*'s and *Stair*'s views of the importance of civil law is noteworthy. Modern scholars have tended to play down the general importance of *Craig*. The story of the devaluing of the authority of *Craig* is in itself fascinating, and dates back to the era of the Enlightenment[14]. Here one can only speculate as to the reasons for it, though it may be that his strongly royalist political views were unacceptable to Scotland's Enlightened and Hanoverian Whigs, while in more recent years his work has been seen as suspect both because of opinions imputed to him about a legal union with England and because of his legal cosmopolitanism. The view has certainly grown up that he "wrote less as a Scotch lawyer, than as a learned student of the civil and canon and feudal law", as *Cosmo Innes* put it[15]. The context of *Innes*'s remarks is very specifically *Craig*'s account of Scottish legal history – not *Craig*'s account of the law of his own day. More modern authors have generalized this. *A. C. Black* wrote that "it may not be an exaggeration to say that the *Jus Feudale* is not so much a work on Scots law as a legal treatise by a Scots lawyer"[16]. Similar remarks were once made about *Stair*: "The 'Institutions' of Lord *Stair* may be regarded rather as a Treatise of General Jurisprudence, illustrated by reference to the Law of Scotland, than as a mere Digest of Municipal Law"[17]. While this attitude to *Stair* has died away, the view that *Craig* was not

14 See *J. W. Cairns*, The Breve Testatum and Craig's Jus Feudale, T.R. 56 (1988) 311, at pp. 312-3.

15 *C. Innes*, Lectures on Scotch Legal Antiquities, Edinburgh, 1872, p. 2.

16 *A. C. Black*, The Institutional Writers, 1600-1826, in: An Introductory Survey of the Sources and Literature of Scots Law, Edinburgh, 1936, 59, at p. 62.

17 Also: "The great object of Lord *Stair* has been to explain and illustrate the principles of natural justice, with reference chiefly to the law of Scotland". Both are found in J. S. More in: *J. Dalrymple, Viscount Stair*, Institutions of the Law of Scotland Deduced from its Origi-

really writing about Scots law has persisted, and has recently been given renewed currency by *D. M. Walker*[18].

Analysis of the development of this critique of *Craig* with its obvious contradictions must be postponed to elsewhere. But it explains why so much discussion of Scottish legal thought starts with *Stair*. Moreover, *Cooper*'s notion of 'The Dark Age of Scottish Legal History' required depreciation of *Craig*, who wrote within that supposed era. It is no surprise that *Craig*'s *Jus Feudale* was described as "European rather than Scottish", in *Cooper's* essay with that title[19]. In a popular pamphlet, *Cooper*, after depicting the horrors of the 'Dark Age', wrote:

> "Then came *Stair*. The publication of his Institutions in 1681 marked the creation of Scots Law as we have known it – an original amalgam of Roman Law, Feudal Law and native customary law, systematised by resort to the law of nature and the Bible, and illuminated by many flashes of divine metaphysic"[20].

Craig thus could have no place in *Cooper*'s historiography of Scots law. *Cooper*'s disciple Sir *Thomas Smith*, although allowing a greater role for *Craig*, described *Stair* as "the father of Scots law"[21], and also claimed that "[t]he full influence of Roman law was subsequent to the publication of Stair's 'Institutions' in 1681 – which was virtually a Restatement of Scots law"[22].

Cooper was of the view that "[i]n the third quarter of the seventeenth century Scots Law ... suffered a complete transformation" because "[u]p to 1650 its patron saint was David I", who "[a]fter 1681 ... was dethroned by Stair"[23]. This would no longer be accepted. *Stair* drew on what had gone before. Before *Stair* Scots law had already showed itself to be the "original amalgam" described by *Cooper*[24]. Crucial in giving expression to this development was the work of *Craig* in *Jus Feudale*. It was *Craig* who first successfully theorized a system for Scots law within which he explained and justified the use of Roman law.

---

nals, and Collated with the Civil, Canon, and Feudal Laws, and with the Customs of Neighbouring Nations, new [5th] edn., J.S. More, ed., 2 vols., Edinburgh, 1832, vol. 1, at p. xi.

18 *D. M. Walker*, The Scottish Jurists, Edinburgh, 1985, at p. 64.

19 Lord *Cooper of Culross*, The Dark Age of Scottish Legal History, 1350-1650, in: *idem*, Selected Papers, 1922-1954, Edinburgh, 1957, 219, at p. 223.

20 *Cooper*, The Scottish Legal Tradition, in: M. C. Meston, W. D. H. Sellar, Lord Cooper, The Scottish Legal Tradition, Edinburgh, 1991, 65, at p. 69.

21 *T. B. Smith*, Scots Law and Roman-Dutch Law: A Shared Tradition, in: *idem*, Studies Critical and Comparative, Edinburgh, 1962, 46, at p. 49.

22 *T. B. Smith*, A Short Commentary on the Law of Scotland, Edinburgh, 1962, at p. 23. See also *idem*, Strange Gods: The Crisis of Scots Law as a Civilian System, in: *idem* (n. 21) 72, at p. 73.

23 *Cooper*, Cromwell's Judges and their Influence on Scots Law, in: *idem* (n. 19) 111.

24 It is curious to note that the phrase 'original amalgam' is often taken to be referring to the Institutions rather than Scots law. This is, however, understandable given what *Cooper* has just said. See, e.g., *K. Luig*, Stair from a Foreign Standpoint, in: D. M. Walker, ed., Stair

II. The Middle Ages to the 16th Century

By the end of the 16th century, Scots lawyers seem to have been generally agreed that civil law was the proper source to be used when native sources of law – usually considered the Acts of Parliament and *Regiam Majestatem* and the 'Auld Lawes' – failed to give an answer to a legal problem. The position was fairly summarized by Bishop *Leslie of Ross* in his history:

> "Albeit heir sulde be vndirstandet, that this far to the lawis of the Realme we ar astricted, gif ony cummirsum or trubilsum cause fal out, as oft chances, quhilke can nocht be agreit be our cuntrey lawis, incontinent quhatevir is thocht necessar to pacifie this controversie, is citet out of the Romane lawis"[25].

The details of the development of this practice are, however, somewhat obscure[26]. The Middle Ages had seen a reception of Anglo-Norman common law in Scotland, but, as *David Sellar* has pointed out, "it was always Common law with a difference". In part this was because of Scotland's previous legal customs and practices which blended with the Anglo-Norman common law: the Celtic heritage was not rejected. Furthermore, what was gradually borrowed from Anglo-Norman practice was adapted[27]. From the later Middle Ages, Scottish common law continued to prove its "durability and resilience", and to follow its existing path, while English common law developed very rapidly in a somewhat different direction[28]. Moreover, in this era the scholarship of the learned laws – that other *ius commune* – had started already to influence and permeate Scots common law. Thus *Hector MacQueen* has raised the issue of whether academic feudal law affected Scottish legal practice in this period[29], while in litigation involving feudal tenures (the heart of the common law), both the civil and Canon laws are found cited[30].

Tercentenary Studies, Edinburgh, 1981, p. 239; and *D. M. Walker*, The Scottish Legal System: An Introduction to the Study of Scots Law, 6th ed., Edinburgh, 1992, at p. 114.

25 The Historie of Scotland Wrytten First in Latin by the Most Reuerend and Worthy Jhone Leslie Bishop of Rosse, and Translated in Scottish by Father James Dalrymple, Religious in the Scottis Cloister of Regensburg, the Zeare of God, 1596, Scottish Text Society, Edinburgh, 1888, vol. 1, at pp. 119-20.

26 See generally *P. G. Stein*, The Influence of Roman Law on the Law of Scotland, 1963 J.R. 205, at pp. 206-16; *idem*, Roman Law in Scotland, in Ius Romanum Medii Aevi, V. 13b, Milan, 1968; and *idem*, The Source of the Romano-Canonical Part of Regiam Majestatem, (1968) 48 Scottish Historical Review 107.

27 *W. D. H. Sellar*, The Common Law of Scotland and the Common Law of England, in: R. R. Davies, ed., The British Isles 1100-1500: Comparisons, Contrasts and Connections, Edinburgh, 1988, 82, at pp. 86-8; *idem*, Celtic Law and Scots Law: Survival and Integration, (1988) 29 Scottish Studies 1.

28 See generally *H. L. MacQueen*, Common Law and Feudal Society in Medieval Scotland, Edinburgh, 1993. The quotation is from p. 267.

29 *MacQueen* (n. 28) 122.

30 *MacQueen* (n. 28) 78-9, 122.

The significance given to civil law is testified to by the statute of 1496 which required that substantial barons and freeholders send their eldest sons and heirs to school to learn Latin, before attending three years "at the sculis of art and Jure sua that thai may haue knawledge and vnderstanding of the lawis. Throw the quhilkis Justice may reigne universalie throw all the realme. Sua thai that ar schereffis or Jugeis Ordinaris vnder the kingis hienes may haue knawledge to do Justice"[31]. The aim was to reduce the burden on the Lords Auditors, by ensuring that trivial litigation would go to the local courts, whether royal or franchise. The provision is notable, however, for its assumption that it was at "schools" of law that these landholders were to be trained. This can only refer to the universities. These taught civil law and Canon law. The oldest Scottish university, that of St. Andrews, dating from 1411, possessed a Faculty of Canon Law, and had provision in its Bull of Foundation for one of Civil Law, and, though there is no evidence that it came into existence, it is clear that civil law was in fact taught[32]. The University of Glasgow, founded in 1451, also provided some measure of academic education in both these laws[33]. The University of Aberdeen, founded in 1495, had fairly major provision for teaching civil and Canon law, even before the foundation within it of King's College, with its extensive legal establishment[34]. The practical emphasis already given to the teaching of civil law is pointed up by the Papal Bull of 1432 granting a dispensation to Scottish clerics in the University of St. Andrews to study civil law, because "few if any betake themselves to the faculty of civil law, on account of which in [the] kingdom of Scotland, in which there is no other university, there are found few experts in civil law by whom justice can be ministered in civil business"[35]. *James IV* was to petition Pope *Alexander VI* to allow clerics to teach and study civil law because the country was short of civil lawyers. A Papal Bull was duly obtained in 1500[36]. The significance of this is highlighted by the dispute between *James IV* and the *Earl of Buchan* over possession of the Barony of King Edward, in which the Earl's procurator in opposing the King's attempt to reduce the Earl's infeftment cited *Justinian*'s Institutes and Code, and works of the canonists *Nicholas de Tudeschis*, *Joannes de Ferarriis* and *Joannes Andreae*[37]. After the Reformation the need to study civil law continued to be stressed in *John Knox's*

31 T. Thomson and C. Innes, edd., Acts of the Parliaments of Scotland, 12 vols., Edinburgh, 1814-75, [A.P.S.] ii, 238, c. 3.

32 A. I. Dunlop, ed., Acta facultatis artium universitatis Sanctiandree, 1413-1588, Scottish History Society, Third Series, 2 vols., Edinburgh, 1964, vol. 1, pp. xii, cxlix-clvii.

33 *J. Durkan* and *J. Kirk*, The University of Glasgow, 1451-1577, Glasgow, 1977, pp. 127-35.

34 *L. J. Macfarlane*, William Elphinstone and the Kingdom of Scotland, 1431-1514: The Struggle for Order, Aberdeen, 1985, pp. 298-9, 303-4, 320-2, 377-82.

35 A. I. Dunlop and I. B. Cowan, edd., Calendar of Scottish Supplications to Rome [Vol. iii] 1428-1432, Edinburgh, 1970, pp. 210-11.

36 *Macfarlane* (n. 34) 321.

37 A. B. Calderwood, ed., Acts of the Lords of Council. Vol. III: 1501-1503, Edinburgh, 1993, at p. 310 (I am indebted to *Hector MacQueen* for bringing this to my attention).

'First Book of Discipline' of 1561[38]. Underlying this use of the learned laws was a perception that there were many gaps in the statutes and customs of Scotland. Thus, an act of 1473 had claimed that daily before the king came matters for which there "[i]s na law for the decisioune of same"[39]. One aspect of this was the recognition that there were problems with the statutes and the 'auld lawes', not least that of obtaining suitable texts. These difficulties resulted in various attempts to collect the statutes and reform the laws by series of commissions. There was some success in this[40]. The role of civil law was also here recognized by a Parliamentary proposal in 1567 "that ane comissioun be gevin to sufficient personis to mak ane body of the ciuile and Municipale lawis deuidit in heidis conforme to the fassone of the law Romane"[41].

In the 15th century dissatisfaction with the administration of justice increasingly led litigants to attempt to bring their pleas before the King's Council. While various administrative expedients were adopted to deal with this problem[42], we need note that the refounding of the central court already emerging from the King's Council as the College of Justice in 1532[43], with its procedure modelled on that of the church courts, can only have intensified this trend to meld the civil law with the municipal, especially since, by 1600, the majority of those practising before the court had been admitted to do so on the basis of a claim to learning in the civil and Canon law[44]. Moreover, there was a strong preference for the admission of men so trained[45]. Surviving practicks such as those of *Sinclair* confirm that the deficiency in the Scottish statutes and customs was met by the citation of the authorities of civil and Canon law, which had become "the common currency" of those pleading before the Session[46], while in a legal debate in 1548 it had been explicitly argued that "an omitted case remains at the disposal of the common law" (in the sense of *ius commune*)[47]. *James VI*, even if his history was here mistaken, recognized the significance of the College of Justice in this respect, when he told the English Parliament in 1607 that:

---

38 J. K. Cameron, ed., The First Book of Discipline, Edinburgh, 1972, at pp. 140-1, 143-4.

39 A.P.S., ii, 105 (c. 14).

40 See *J. W. Cairns, T. D. Fergus, H. L. MacQueen*, Legal Humanism and the History of Scots Law: John Skene and Thomas Craig, in: J. MacQueen, ed., Humanism in Renaissance Scotland, Edinburgh, 1990, 48, at pp. 50-2.

41 A.P.S., iii, 40.

42 See *A. A. M. Duncan*, The Central Courts before 1532, in: An Introduction to Scottish Legal History, Edinburgh, 1958, 321.

43 A.P.S., ii, 335-6 (c. 2).

44 *R. K. Hannay*, The College of Justice: Essays on the Institution and Development of the Court of Session, Edinburgh, 1933, at pp. 145-6.

45 See *J. W. Cairns*, The Law, the Advocates and the Universities in Late Sixteenth-Century Scotland, (1994) 73 Scottish Historical Review 171.

46 *A. L. Murray*, Sinclair's Practicks, in: A. Harding, ed., Law Making and Law Makers in British History, London, 1980, 90, at pp. 102-3.

47 *Murray* (n. 46) 101.

> "The third [sort of law] is the Ciuill Law. Iames the fift brought it out of France by establishing the Session there, according to the forme of the Court of Parliament of Fraunce ... who occupie there the place of Ciuill Iudges in all matters of Plee or controuersie, yet not to gouerne absolutely by the Ciuill Law as in Fraunce. ... So as the Ciuill Law in Scotland is admitted in no other cases, but to supply such cases wherein the Municipall Law is defectiue"[48].

This comment is especially notable, given that *James* was a believer in the possibility of a union of the laws, and hence unlikely to exaggerate the Scots' reliance on civil law.

Yet, the use of civil law was potentially troubling for the cadre of educated lawyers which now existed in Edinburgh, because of its growing consciousness of a relationship between authority, sources, and political sovereignty[49]. It was difficult to provide a justification for the use of Roman law. Scotland was not part of the Empire; there could be no Lotharian Legend. How was the authority of civil law in Scotland to be justified? The need to justify the use of civil law was to have far-reaching consequences, coming as it did both when ideas of natural law were increasingly influential and when Scots law started to enter its phase of institutional writing. The European institutional tradition worked towards the differentiation of the *ius commune* while drawing on its scholarship. Institutional writers tried to unify national laws by utilizing all the various sources used in determining legal issues in their legal system to present the law as a systematized and synthesized whole organized according to a notion of authority and legitimacy[50]. In this respect it is important to recall that while civil law was extensively cited in Scottish litigation of the 16th century, it was still possible for Sir *James Balfour* to write his 'Practicks' on the basis of the traditional sources of Scottish customary law and statutes, largely ignoring the civil law[51]. This does not mean that *Balfour* rejected the use of civil law or that it was not used in his time, but rather that he was still part of a tradition that considered Scots law, civil law, and Canon law as separate valid sources of rules for deciding legal disputes. This is reinforced by the possibility that the 'Practicks' were the product of a 'law commission' established in 1575 to examine the acts of Parliament, books of the law and decisions of the Session. The aim was to provide a written law by which to judge and decide cases[52]. The civil law was already accessible in written form: it did not need to be included

---

48 J. P. Sommerville, ed., King James VI and I: Political Writings, Cambridge, 1994, at pp. 173-4.

49 *Cairns/Fergus/MacQueen* (n. 40) 60-7.

50 See *K. Luig*, The Institutes of National Law in the Seventeenth and Eighteenth Centuries, 1972 J.R. 193; *J. W. Cairns*, Institutional Writers in Scotland Reconsidered, in: A. Kiralfy and H. L. MacQueen, edd., New Perspectives in Scottish Legal History, London, 1984, p. 76.

51 P. G. B. McNeill, ed., The Practicks of Sir James Balfour of Pittendreich, 2 vols., Edinburgh, 1962.

52 A.P.S., iii, 89.

in the 'Practicks'. The 'Practicks' were intended to stand alongside the civil law. The attempts of the institutional writers to synthesize the law as practised required a quite different approach.

III. The 17th Century

1. Sir Thomas Craig

The late 16th century is when Scots lawyers become articulate for us. The lawyer who provided the first sophisticated explanation of this use of civil law was *Thomas Craig*, and it is with him that an intellectual history of what one might call Scottish legal thought has to begin. *Craig* was forced to confront the issue in writing *Jus Feudale*, because, in that work, he proposed, by comparing Scots forensic custom with the general written Feudal law, to reduce Scots law, which, he claimed, was believed by many to be vague and uncertain, to a structured science[53]. *Craig* in fact used the Ciceronian phrase *in artem redigere*[54]. This scientific aspiration required that he deal with the problems of the sources of Scots law. *Craig*'s brilliant historical insight that much of Scots law was feudal in origin gave him the key to unlock the problem and sort out the difficulties[55]. This realization allowed him to present arguments about the equitable solution to novel problems by a return to the historical origins of Scots law[56]. For *Craig*, this primarily meant a return to the general principles of the *jus feudale*[57]. He recognized, however, that there had been and continued to be widespread use of civil law.

In his first title, *Craig* argued conventionally enough that, in the beginnings of society (which he believed had come into existence through a contract), kings had dispensed justice according to "the reason of natural equity that was inborn in the hearts of men"[58]. The decay of *mores*, however, brought about the writing down of the laws, as justice was no longer dispensed equally. Written law ensured that deci-

---

53 *T. Craig*, Jus feudale tribus libris comprehensum, 3rd ed., Edinburgh, 1732, p. viii. All passages quoted or referred to have been compared with the first edition of 1655. There are no differences of any significance. All translations are my own, although I have generally compared them with the translation by Lord Clyde as 'The Jus Feudale by Sir Thomas Craig of Riccarton with an Appendix containing the Books of the Feus', 2 vols., Edinburgh, 1934.

54 See, e.g., *P. G. Stein*, Legal Humanism and Legal Science, TR 54 (1986) 297, at p. 303.

55 *J. G. A. Pocock*, The Ancient Constitution and the Feudal Law: A Study of English Historical Thought in the Seventeenth Century. A Reissue with a Retrospect, Cambridge, 1987, at pp. 79-90.

56 *Craig* (n. 53) I, viii, 16.

57 *Craig* (n. 53) I, viii, 16. This attitude to feudal law raises interesting and complex issues which I shall discuss elsewhere: here I shall focus exclusively on his treatment of civil law.

58 *Craig* (n. 53) I, i, 5.

sions were rendered justly[59]. In talking of the law used in contemporary Scotland, *Craig* pointed out that the term *jus* had a variety of meanings. It referred to *jus Naturale*, *jus Gentium*, and *jus Civile*. The first of these had two meanings: the first was the common principles of behaviour that nature taught to all living creatures; the second was the natural law nature taught to all human beings. The basic content of this second sense of natural law was:

> "To fear God and honour Him above all else; to embrace those things which are good; to condemn and repress wickedness and crimes; to repulse force with speedy force; to defend oneself and one's property in any way against unjustified attack; to live peacefully and regularly alongside others; to render each person his right; to be unjust to no one; to harm no one: all of which derived from that general and natural doctrine [*naturalis ratio*], that no one should do unto others as they would not have done unto themselves"[60].

He explained that "this natural law is called the good and the just [*bonum et aequum*] from the reason of justice or equity [*juris ratio sive aequitas*] inborn in us", before adding that "neither the legislation of a kingdom, nor prescription of even the longest time, nor custom has force against this law"[61]. Turning to *jus Gentium*, he argued that it chiefly must be followed after the natural law. Not only did it govern international affairs, but "everything all nations observed ought also to have force with us, no matter what the *jus Civile* or *Municipale*" said. The "*jus Gentium* governed purchases and sales, leases, barter" and all nominate and innominate contracts. In dealings with foreigners, the *jus Gentium* had to be followed in spite of any statute of the kingdom, while "among citizens it would have authority unless some statute or specific law opposed it"[62]. *Craig* argued that the term *jus Civile*, though originally referring to the laws of the Romans, now could refer to the laws of each people[63].

These passages of *Jus Feudale* provide the foundation for *Craig*'s explanation of the authority of civil law in Scotland. He thus followed an essentially Thomist view that human beings had the innate capacity to use their reason to know the *aequum et bonum*, and that this exercise of *recta ratio* allowed knowledge of natural law[64]. This reflects the revival of Thomism in the 16th century that took place initially in Paris, and which influenced the Spanish late-scholastics such as *Vitorio*, *de Soto*, and *Suárez*[65]. This view of the issue of the authority of Roman law in

---

59 *Craig* (n. 53) I, i, 11-12.

60 *Craig* (n. 53) I, viii, 6.

61 *Craig* (n. 53) I, viii, 7.

62 *Craig* (n. 53) I, viii, 8.

63 *Craig* (n. 53) I, viii, 9.

64 See, e.g., *J. M. Kelly*, A Short History of Western Legal Theory, Oxford, 1992, at pp. 141-4.

65 *Q. Skinner*, The Foundations of Modern Political Thought, 2 vols., Cambridge, 1978, vol. 2, at pp. 135-73; *J. Gordley*, The Philosophical Origins of Modern Contract Doctrine, Oxford, 1991, at pp. 69-71.

Scotland may derive from *Craig's* education in the University of Paris, although further research would be required to establish this for certain, especially as there were many currents of philosophical thought in Paris at this time[66]. If the revival of Thomism is the correct context in which to understand *Craig's* thinking about law, then he – as did *Grotius* – presumably saw the world as having an inherently moral ordering[67].

It is not possible in the course of this survey to analyse *Craig's* use of civil law in *Jus Feudale*[68]. Here it will suffice to point to his general attitude. *Craig* claimed that after the natural law, and the laws common to all nations, "as many times as some difficulty and more serious controversy happened, recourse had first to be had to our *jus scriptum*, should there be any"[69]. Failing statute, recourse was to be had to the custom of the courts[70]. *Craig* explained that Scots used civil law because there was so little written law in Scotland[71]. By written law he was referring to statutes and perhaps the 'auld lawes', although his attitude to the latter was complex[72]. He stated that in Scotland "we are bound by the Roman laws only in so far as they are congruent with the laws of nature and right reason". He added:

> "Yet surely there is no broader seedbed of natural equity, no more fertile field of articulated reasoning and arguments from those principles of nature than the books of the Roman jurists; from which ought to be drawn, as if from the very fountain, what is equitable and what inequitable by nature and what most agrees and what disagrees with right reason"[73].

We thus find that *Craig* neatly solves the problem of the reference to Roman law in Scotland by arguing that it is accepted not as Roman law but as *ius Naturale* and

66 On *Craig's* studies in Paris, see *Cairns* (n. 14) 316.

67 See *R. Feenstra*, L'influence de la scolastique espagnole sur Grotius en droit privé: Quelques expériences dans des questions de fond et de formes, concernant notamment les doctrines de l'erreur et de l'enrichissement sans cause, in: La seconda scolastica nella formazione del diritto privato moderno, Milan, 1973, p. 377; *D. L. Carey Miller*, Hugo Grotius: Born 1583. The Lasting Impact of a Man of the Seventeenth Century, 1982 Acta Juridica 66.

68 See my forthcoming paper provisionally entitled "Tensions in the Attitude to Roman Law of Thomas Craig". See also *G.D. MacCormack*, The actio communi dividundo in Roman and Scots Law, in *A.D.E. Lewis* and *D.J. Ibbetson*, edd., The Roman Law Tradition, Cambridge, 1994, 159, at pp. 161-2.

69 *Craig* (n. 53) I, viii, 9.

70 *Craig* (n. 53) I, viii, 13-14.

71 *Craig* (n. 53) I, ii, 14.

72 *Cairns/Fergus/MacQueen* (n. 40) 61-4. *Craig* initiated a debate on the authority of the 'auld lawes' which had important historical consequences. See *H. L. MacQueen*, Glanville Resarcinate: Sir John Skene and Regiam Majestatem, in: A. A. MacDonald, M. Lynch, I. B. Cowan, edd., The Renaissance in Scotland: Studies in Literature, Religion, History and Culture Offered to John Durkan, Leiden, 1994, 385; *idem*, Regiam Majestatem, Scots Law, and National Identity, (1995) 74 Scottish Historical Review 1; and *C. Kidd*, Subverting Scotland's Past: Scottish Whig Historians and the Creation of an Anglo-British Identity, 1689-c.1830, Cambridge, 1993, at pp. 148-50. This later debate may have some link with attitudes to Civil law in the 18th century, but this cannot be explored here.

the product of *recta ratio*. The Thomist philosophy that *Craig* learned as a student thus provided him with a justification for Scottish use of civil law. He argued that, although Scotland had "shaken off the papal yoke", none the less when there was a conflict between Canon law and civil law, the Canon law was preferred, especially in those areas under the jurisdiction of the Commissary Courts[74].

Craig thus established in Scottish legal thought the position that the civil law was authoritative in so far as it was identifiable with the *ius Naturale*. This was of tremendous importance. If his view was scarcely original, none of his Scottish contemporaries – such as *Skene*, *Balfour*, or *Welwood* – appear to have articulated the authority of civil law in Scotland in quite this way. Moreover, he stressed that civil law was followed because there was so little written law in Scotland. The civil law was above all *jus scriptum*, and provided *leges certae*, both of which he thought very important for justice. Absent Scottish statutes or custom, civil law gave the Scots a rule to follow, one which was likely to be inherently just. It is perhaps worth recollecting here that Dr. *Murray* has pointed out that it was rare for Scottish statutes to be cited before the Session: the lack of written law may have seemed greater to 16th-century Scots than we are now inclined to think[75]. Moreover, *Craig*'s French education would have made him aware of the codification of the customary law there[76]. This may have made Scotland seem particularly devoid of written law. *Craig* thus wrote:

> "We accordingly follow the decisions or rules of the civil law chiefly in the administration of moveable property, granted that each nation will have employed its own particular forms of process. And we use our own forms of actions which are not entirely different from the civil law; we state, however, that the civil law must entirely be followed, in pacts, transactions, restitution, decisions or (as we now say) arbitrations, servitudes, contracts both *bonae fidei* and *stricti iuris* as well as nominate and innominate, evictions, pledges, tutory, legacies, actions, exceptions, obligations, and finally in the punishing of wrongs: and to say truly, this civil law so permeates all our law suits and about all business that scarcely no issue or no type of case arises in which its authority and particular practice is not plainly obvious: whenever anything difficult arises in court or law suits, the solution of it is sought thence"[77].

The scope for the use of Roman law, justified by natural law, was thus very wide.

---

73 *Craig* (n. 53) I, ii, 14.

74 *Craig* (n. 53) I, iii, 24; I, viii, 17.

75 *Murray* (n. 46) 101.

76 See *R. Filhol*, The Codification of Customary Law in France in the Fifteenth and Sixteenth Centuries, in: H. J. Cohn, ed., Government in Reformation Europe, 1520-1560, Glasgow, 1971, at p. 265; *J.P. Dawson*, The Codification of the French Customs, (1940) 38 Michigan L.R. 765.

77 *Craig* (n. 53) I, ii, 14.

2. *Viscount Stair*

Even before the publication of the printed text of *Jus Feudale* in 1655, *Craig's* views were influential, as Sir *Thomas Hope* in his 'Practicks' quoted *Craig's* views on the authority of civil law as natural law[78]. When *Stair* came around 1660 to write his 'Institutions', his approach to the authority of Roman law in Scotland was very similar to that of *Craig*[79]. He wrote:

> "The Law of each Society of People under the same Soveraign Authority, is called *The Civil Law,* or the Law of the Citizens of that Common-wealth; though that now be appropriat to the Civil Law of the *Roman* Common-wealth or Empire as the most excellent. And because of that Affinity that the Law of *Scotland* hath with it, as have also the Laws and Customs of the Chief Nations, to which the victorious Arms of the *Romans* did propagate it, and its own worth, even after the ruine of the *Roman* Empire which hath so commended it, that though it be not acknowledged as a Law, binding for its Authority, yet being, as a Rule, followed for its equity, it shall not be amiss here to say something of it"[80].

Alan Watson has pointed out that the phrase "as a rule" has to be interpreted as meaning "as a code of conduct"[81]. This view of the authority of Roman law is in part the result of *Stair's* reading of *Craig*, as comparison shows that, in writing his brief account of the development of Roman law, *Stair* had in front of him *Craig's* paragraphs on the same from which *Stair* largely culled his version, abbreviating and translating *Craig's* Latin into English[82]. The extent to which *Craig's* history of

---

78 J. A. Clyde, ed., Hope's Major Practicks, 1608-1633, 2 vols., Edinburgh, 1937, vol. 1, at pp. 1, 2 (I, i, 2 and 5).

79 A point already noted by *W. D. H. Sellar* in A Historical Perspective, in: Meston/Sellar/Cooper (n. 20) 29, at p. 49. We lack a good scholarly edition of *Stair.* I shall therefore cite the 2nd edition as the last prepared by the author: *J. Dalrymple, Viscount Stair,* The Institutions of the Law of Scotland Deduced from its Originals, and Collated with the Civil, Canon and Feudal Laws, and with the Customs of Neighbouring Nations, Edinburgh, 1693. Comparison shows that in the passages here relied on the commemorative edition edited by D.M. Walker, Edinburgh, 1981, is identical other than in punctuation and spelling. Other editions will be cited as necessary.

80 Stair (n. 79) I, i, 12. Cf. Craig (n. 53) I, viii, 9.

81 *A. Watson,* The Rise of Modern Scots Law, in: La formazione storica del diritto moderno in Europa, Atti del Terzo Congresso Internazionale della Società Italiana di Storia del Diritto, 3 vols., Florence, 1977, vol. 3, 1167, at p. 1175.

82 *Craig* (n. 53) I, ii, 1-11; *Stair* (n. 79) I, i, 12. For example: "Tarquinii Superbi tempore fuit Sextus Papyrius, qui leges omnes Regias in unum contulit, et ejus liber jus civile Papyrianum dicebatur", "The *Romans* were first govern'd by Kings who gave them Laws, which, being Collected by *Papirius* in the time of *Tarquinius Superbus*, were therfore called the *Papirian* Law"; "placuit tandem ut Triumviri in Graeciam mitterentur … Missi sunt Sp. Posthumius, A. Manlius, et P. Sulpitius, jussique inclitas Solonis leges describere, et aliarum civitatum Graeciae instituta et mores cognoscere …", "they sent the *Triumviri, Posthumus, Manlius* and *Sulpitius*, to the Greek Republicks, to understand the Laws of these Commonwealths", "per eundem Tribonianum et alios delectos ad rem tantam viros, Codicem ex responsis Caesarum confici curavit. Isque codex Theodosianus primo dictus; sed cum plera-

Roman law was *Stair's* primary source is vividly demonstrated by the later author's statement, based on a mistranslation or perhaps misreading of the relevant passage in *Craig*, that *Phocas*, rather than *Justinian*, died in 565[83]. Given that the same error is found in the first edition of the 'Institutions', and in both manuscript stems, it must originate in the work of *Stair* himself[84]. Subsequent editors of the 'Institutions' altered the text here, so that *Stair* did not write nonsense[85]. The discovery of this use of *Craig* is unsurprising when we consider that *Stair* greatly relied on *Craig* for his account of land law, stating indeed that he would only deal in detail with the alterations in the law since *Craig* wrote[86]. Moreover, while *Stair*

---

que responsa Imperatorum quotidie in manus venirent, ipseque Justinianus novas aliquot decisiones adjecisset, sub incudem revocatus est Codex Theodosianus, et longe locupletior factus sub nomine Justiniani ipsius exiit", "he did also by *Tribonian* and others, collect the Rescripts, Decrees, and all the Edicts of the Emperors, which before were more imperfectly compiled in their *Theodosian Codex*, and which thereafter he perfected, and named the *Justinian Codex*"; "Postea in juniorum gratiam adjecit Justinianus quatuor libros Institutionum, prima totius juris civilis elementa continentes", "*Justinian* did also cause frame the four Books of the *Institutes*, as the Sum and Elements of the whole Law".

83 *Craig* (n. 53) I, ii, 11: "Justiniano cum nepos Justinus successisset, et post eum Tiberius et Mauritius, paulatim cum majestate Romani imperii jus etiam Civile in Italia oppressum est armis Gothorum et Longobardorum, praecipue temporibus Phocae, qui quartus erat a Justiniano: adeo ut post Justiniani mortem (qui obiit anno salutis 565) pene perierint leges Romanae: nec spatio quingentorum annorum et ampliius in pretio erant; donec Lotharii secundi imperatoris tempore, quae diu latuerunt, in lucem tandem emergere coeperunt"; Stair (n. 79) I, i, 12: "But as nothing human is stable, shortly after this greatest perfection of the *Roman* Law, in the time of *Phocas* the Emperor, who reigned fourth after *Justinian*, and died in the year 565, The *Roman* Empire being opprest by the Irruption of the *Goths* and *Longobards*, the *Roman* Law did also ly under Ashes above the space of five hundred years, until a new shape of the *Roman* Empire being set up in *Germany*, *Lotharius* the Emperor, who flourished in the eleventh Century, did again revive and restore the *Roman* Law".

84 See *Stair*, The Institutions of the Law of Scotland, 1st ed., I, i, 12 (I am indebted to the Faculty of Advocates and the Keeper of its Library for permission to examine one of its copies of the first edition). Not only is the same problem found in manuscripts of both the 1662 and 1666 stems, but some of them also introduce further nonsense (having 567 rather than 565, or even some wildly improbable years – such as 1065 – or reporting that Phocas reigned for four years or that he reigned four years after Justinian). I examined National Library of Scotland, Adv. MS 24.2.10, fo. 3r; Adv. MS 25.1.5, p. 4; Adv. MS 25.1.11, fo. 6v; Adv. MS 25.1.12, fo. 3r; Adv. MS 25.4.17, fo. 4v; National Library of Scotland, MS 5434, fo. 6r; MS 7116 p. 10. *Stair's* mistaken version of *Craig* is not derived from one of the existing standard compends of *Jus Feudale* in English: see, e.g., National Library of Scotland, Adv. MS 25.6.2, fo. 2r, nor from any surviving irregular versions of this compend that I have been able to consult.

85 See J. Gordon and W. Johnstone, edd., *Stair*, The Institutions of the Law of Scotland, 3rd ed., Edinburgh, 1759, I, i, 12, p. 7; G. Brodie, ed., 4th ed., 3 vols., Edinburgh, 1826-31, I, i, 12, vol. i, at p. 7; J.S. More, ed., new [5th] edn., 2 vols., Edinburgh, 1832, I, i, 12, vol. i, at p. 9. John Gordon in his n. q on p. 7 notes that the original text was different and that he has altered "and" to "who". More, p. 9 n. q does likewise. The original reading has been restored in the commemorative edition: D.M. Walker, ed., Edinburgh, 1981, I, i, 12, at p. 81 with a correcting n. 21 on p. 95.

86 *Stair* (n. 79) II, iii, 3.

makes several explicit references to *Craig*, *Gordon* has pointed out that *Stair*'s account of land law may be more reliant on *Craig* than he acknowledges[87]. For his admission to the Faculty of Advocates in 1648, *Stair* offered a public lesson on feudal law for which he drew on *Craig*'s as yet unprinted work[88]. That he should turn to it for assistance in writing the 'Institutions' is hardly remarkable, though it raises questions about the depth of *Stair*'s personal knowledge of the civilian literature[89].

It has long been recognized that *Stair's* account of natural law was much influenced by *Grotius*'s *De jure belli ac pacis* (1625) and followed the Dutch author's reformulation of the scholastic tradition based on *Vitoria* and *Suárez*[90]. There are, however, crucial differences. *Stair* retained a greater sense of the importance of the Divine will in natural law than did *Grotius*, and was also strongly influenced in his account by Presbyterian thought[91]. Without exploring further the sources of *Stair*'s views on the nature of law, it is clear that *Stair*'s reading of *Craig* and his reading of *Grotius* would have been mutually reinforcing. The underlying reliance on the late scholastics of both of these important sources must have determined *Stair*'s attitude. As *Gordon* has pointed out, *Stair* accordingly regarded civil law as authoritative in Scotland only so far as it embodied equity or the law of nature[92]. *Gordon* also shows that, while *Stair*'s use of Roman law was complex and varied, he generally treated it as embodying natural equity, and therefore a valid source on which to draw in an exposition of Scots law[93]: "Where our antient Law, Statutes, and our recent Customs and Practiques are defective, recourse is had to Equity, as the first and universal Law" as *Stair* himself put it[94].

---

87 *W. M. Gordon*, Stair, Grotius and the Sources of Stair's Institutions, in: J.A. Ankum, J.E. Spruit, F. B. J. Wubbe, edd., Satura Roberto Feenstra sexagesimum quintum annum aetatis complenti ab alumnis collegis amicis oblata, Fribourg, 1985, 571, at p. 582.

88 See Scotstarvet's 'Trew Relation', (1916) 13 Scottish Historical Review 380, at p. 387. For his admission, see Scottish Record Office, Books of Sederunt of the Lords of Council and Session, CS. 1/5, fo. 182v, where he is recorded as having been admitted after making 'ane publict lessoune' upon the 'Civill law'. This may just be a clerk following a version of the common formula, or may represent a view that the *Libri feudorum*, as the *decima collatio* of the *Authenticum* in the *Volumen parvum* were properly described as part of the civil law.

89 For another instance of *Stair's* reliance on *Craig*, see *H.L. MacQueen*, Stair's Later Reputation as a Jurist: The Contribution of William Forbes, in: *W.M. Gordon*, ed., Miscellany Three, Edinburgh, 1992, 173, at p. 194, n. 52.

90 See, e.g., *P. G. Stein*, Legal Thought in Eighteenth Century Scotland, 1957 J.R. 1, at pp. 3-5; *A. H. Campbell*, The Structure of Stair's Institutions, Glasgow, 1954, at pp. 20-1.

91 *J. D. Ford*, Stair's Title 'Of Liberty and Servitude', in: Lewis and Ibbetson (n. 68) 135; *Stein* (n. 90) 4-5.

92 *W. M. Gordon*, Stair's Use of Roman Law, in: A. Harding, ed., Law Making and Law Makers in British History, London, 1980, at p. 120; *idem*, Roman Law as a Source, in: Walker (n. 24) 107.

93 *Gordon*, Stair's Use of Roman Law (n. 92) 126.

94 *Stair* (n. 79) I, i, 16.

3. *Sir George Mackenzie*

Craig's and *Stair*'s approach was not the only possible way of explaining the authority of civil law in Scotland. A number of important different strands of thought can be discerned woven together in the writings of Sir *George Mackenzie*. *Mackenzie* had studied both civil and Canon law for two years in Bourges and, as his many writings show, was a learned civilian[95]. Thus, at the end of his life, he was working in the Bodleian Library in Oxford on "Observations ... upon the *Digests*, and some illustrious Questions, which have in this last Age employed and divided the best Lawyers and Statesmen in *Europe*"[96]. Since *Mackenzie*'s thinking on law and politics has not yet been properly investigated, it is impossible to give anything approaching an adequate consideration of it here, but a few remarks may be ventured.

Mackenzie seems to have given systematic attention to legal theory only shortly before his death[97], when he put forward his most coherent account of it in his manuscript 'Discourse on the 4 First Chapters of the Digest'[98]. The account of natural law is slight and pedestrian. *Mackenzie* claimed that human beings innately know what natural law is through God "darting it upon our harts". He could not "understand how that can be properly called a Law that derives not its authority from a superiour power", and concluded "that God almighty must be the Law giver and that the Laws of Nature are dictates written in our harts by him rather then any conclusions drawne by us"[99]. He stressed that "Wee may doubt how farr Right Reason may be looked on as the fountaine of the Law of Nature"[100]. The principle on which the law of nature was founded was that of preservation of the universe[101]. In reaching these conclusions, *Mackenzie* disputed *Cumberland*'s founda-

95 See Archives Départementales du Cher, Livre Matricule des Ecoliers, Série D.9, fo. 5v (I owe this citation to the kindness of *Mme. Marie-Claude Tucker*).

96 *G. Mackenzie*, The Moral History of Frugality, with its Opposite Vices, in: Works of that Eminent and Learned Lawyer, Sir George Mackenzie of Rosehaugh, 2 vols., Edinburgh, 1716-22, vol. 1, 141, at p. 142. *Idem*, A Discourse on the 4 First Chapters of the Digest, to Shew the Excellence and usefullnesse of the Civill Law, British Library, Additional MS 18,236 is presumably the fruit of this project.

97 *Mackenzie*, The Moral History (n. 96) 141-2: "Finding such various Opinions concerning the first and fundamental Rules of Justice, urged with great Animosity, and that the Laws of Nations were alleg'd by all Sides; I resolved, after having studied the Roman Laws, and the Municipal Law of our own Nation Forty Years, to spend some Time enquiring into the Laws of Nations."

98 British Library, Additional MS 18,236. This important MS contains the fullest contemporary account of the sources of Scots law, with an especially interesting and detailed account of statutory interpretation by a man who was a master of the Scottish statute book. I shall cite it by the modern foliation (which accidentally omits a folio numbered 21, jumping from 20 to 22).

99 Ibid., fo. 8r-v.

100 Ibid., fo. 8r.

101 Ibid., fo. 6r.

tion of natural law on benevolence, *Hobbes*'s of it on self love, and *Locke*'s view that it was discoverable through the exercise of human reason alone[102]. He was evidently concerned to argue against those who saw natural law purely as useful convention, and to emphasize the importance of God and divine authority and intervention[103]. When he turned to municipal law, *Mackenzie* again focused on the role of the legislator. For England and Scotland, the legislator was the king[104]. *Mackenzie* derived the absolute authority of the king from his divinely appointed right to govern. Each individual king derived his personal right through an indefeasible hereditary right[105]. It was this right that gave him authority to legislate. Furthermore, "God Almighty was the first and great Lawgiver"[106]. By legislating, kings were just acting as God's representatives on earth. On the other hand, "all Kings and Parliaments are subordinate to the Laws of God, the Laws of Nature, and the Laws of Nations"[107]. While there is evident tension in *Mackenzie*'s thinking on these matters, his emphasis on legislation (whether by God or king) as the primary source of law does suggest he would have rejected *Grotius*'s, *Craig*'s, and *Stair*'s views of natural law as deriving from a moral order in the world. Without pressing this too far, it is a plausible suggestion that had *Mackenzie* read *Pufendorf*'s works on natural law (which he does not seem to have done), while he would there have found much with which to disagree, he would have been inclined to agree with the German author's deduction of all law from the will of a sovereign[108].

Mackenzie characterized the Civil law thus:

> "[I]t seems that God Almighty did inspire the Romans to digest the principles of Reason into a Body of their positive Law, to the End Nations might have common principles wherein they might agree, and it is therefore called by the French and us and by most of all other Nations, the Common Law"[109].

---

102 Ibid. fos. 4v-7r.

103 Ibid., fos. 7v-8r; *Mackenzie*, The Moral History (n. 96) pp. 141-2: "But after I had with all Diligence I could, instructed myself, as far as I thought was possible, I clearly found, that these Debates were not so much occasion'd by the Laws of Nations, as fed by Luxury and Avarice, which of late have given Authority to that which some Men think a more obliging Law, call'd Conveniency: and therefore I resolved to attack likewise this powerful Enemy of Law and Justice."

104 British Library, Additional MS 18,236, fos. 18r-20v.

105 See, e.g., *G. Mackenzie*, Observations on the Acts of Parliament, Edinburgh, 1686, at pp. 298-9, 393, and more generally, *idem*, Jus Regium: Or, The Just and Solid Foundations of Monarchy in General; and more especially of the Monarchy of Scotland, London, 1684.

106 *G. Mackenzie*, The Religious Stoic, in: *idem*, Works (n. 96) vol. 1, 39, at p. 58.

107 *Mackenzie*, Jus Regium (n. 105) 152 [The Right of Succession Defended].

108 For some perceptive remarks on the differences between *Grotius* and *Pufendorf* on these issues, see *Haakonssen*, Natural Jurisprudence in the Scottish Enlightenment (n. 6) 40-1.

109 British Library, Additional MS 18,236, fo. 18r.

When he came to consider the authority of the civil law in Scotland, he turned to an historical approach. He saw each nation, when it first came to make laws, as borrowing the laws of another. Thus, after a discussion of Jewish law, he claimed "that most of the other Nations have borrowed their Laws from the Romans". In turn, Roman law was originally borrowed from the Greeks, and Greek law from the Egyptians. The ultimate foundation of all laws were the laws of *Noah*[110]. That he saw law givers as borrowing from earlier laws, supports the argument implicit in the previous paragraph that, although civil law might embody a universal justice, for *Mackenzie* it would become positive law in Scotland only because it was *willed* to be such either expressly or tacitly. Thus he wrote: "The Old Customs of Scotland are originally derived from the Roman Law in what Concerns moveables; From the Feudall in what Concerns heritage, and the Cannon, in what Concerns Ecclesiasticall matters"[111]. On the basis of this customary foundation, he saw further statutory and other development – often by borrowing from other nations – as having taken place[112]. Given his focus on statutes, it is unsurprising to find that he to some extent related the authority of Roman law to Scottish statutes. In his treatise on criminal law he wrote: "We follow the Civil Law in judging Crimes, as is clear by several Acts of Parliament, wherein the Civil Law is called the Common Law"[113]. He made similar remarks in his 'Institutions'[114]. This opinion derived from his view that all law receives its authority ultimately from the monarch, and his consequent preference for statutes (which he argued were enacted by the king alone with Parliament only consenting) over custom (which he thought acquired its authority from the tacit consent of king and people)[115]. While *Mackenzie* recognized that "the *Romans,* [had] studied with great exactness, the principles of Equity, and Justice"[116], he did not claim that the authority of Roman law existed only so far as it was an embodiment of natural law, and instead put forward the rather vague proposition that "this Civil law is much respected generally, so it has great influence in *Scotland,* except where Our own express Laws, or Customes, have receded from it"[117]. Elsewhere he wrote more positively that "the Civil Law ... is the great Foundation of our Laws and Forms", arguing that "tho' the *Romans* had some Customs or Forms peculiar to the Genius of their own Nation; yet their

110 Ibid., fos. 11r-12v. He has a lengthy debate on whether the Egyptians copied Jewish law or *vice versa.*

111 Ibid., fo. 16v.

112 Ibid. fos. 16v-17r.

113 *G. Mackenzie*, Laws and Customs of Scotland, in Matters Criminal, in: *idem*, Works (n. 96) vol. 2, 49, at p. 54.

114 *G. Mackenzie* Institutions of the Law of Scotland, 2nd ed., Edinburgh, 1688, at pp. 3-4.

115 *Mackenzie* (n. 114) 5, 6-7 (in the first edition of the Institutions, *Mackenzie* forgot to mention the king in connection with the authority of custom); *Mackenzie*, Observations on the Acts of Parliament, sig. A4r, pp. 6-7, 94, 153.

116 *Mackenzie* (n. 114) 3.

117 *Mackenzie* (n. 114) 3-4.

Laws, in undecided Cases, are of universal Use"[118]. In a discussion of statutory interpretation, he dealt with the issue of a crime that had no penalty attached, arguing that "wee ought to recurr to the Civill Law, as being indeed the Generall Supplement of our Law"[119]. This last confirms that he considered the use of civil law in Scotland as primarily validated by custom and statutory endorsement – even if indirect – since he went on to stress that if the statute were derived from another system of law, and the Civil law were silent, then the other system of law was the best source of interpretation[120].

It is telling that no place was given to writers on legal theory in *Mackenzie*'s idealized account of the structure of the Advocates' Library, and scorn was pored on the fashion in which "the body of Roman law became overlaid with philosophy, as with a leprosy", as a result of the work of the scholastics: a disease he saw cured by the Humanists of the Renaissance[121]. Furthermore, while *Mackenzie*'s works have the conventional allusions to the laws of nature and nations, the reference at the end of his life to a new intention to study the laws of nations in order to investigate theories of justice, if true, suggests his thinking was not much influenced by them[122]. This tendency not to confront the laws of nature and nations was probably the product of *Mackenzie*'s education at Bourges, as the study of natural law had as yet made no impact on the French law faculties, which, except for the introduction of classes on municipal law in 1679, remained thirled to the traditional curriculum of civil and Canon law[123]. There *Mackenzie* would have learned an eclectic mix of historical and rational exegesis of the civil law texts as a living tradition[124]. Moreover, his approach was also to some extent historicist, as his views of the authority of the king would suggest. He argued that "Laws do ordinarly show the Genius of the Nation; so do they likewise show the Genius of the Time wherein they are made"[125]. One is left with a strong sense that *Mackenzie*'s approach to the authority of civil law in Scotland was mixed. He saw it as reasonable and universal, as validated by references in Scottish statutes, and as justified by the fact of historical

---

118 *G. Mackenzie*, Observations Upon the 18th Act of the 23d Parliament of King James the Sixth Against Dispositions made in Defraud of Creditors, in: *idem*, Works (n. 96) vol. 2, p. 1, at p. 7.

119 British Library, Additional MS 18,236, fo. 33v.

120 Ibid.

121 *G. Mackenzie*, *Oratio inauguralis in aperienda jurisconsultorum bibliotheca*, J.W. Cairns and A.M. Cain, edd., Edinburgh, 1989, at pp. 66-67.

122 See *Mackenzie* (n. 96) 141-142: "Finding such various Opinions concerning the first and fundamental Rules of Justice, urged with great Animosity, and that the Laws of Nations were alleg'd by all Sides; I resolved, after having studied the *Roman* Laws, and the Municipal Law of our own Nation Forty Years, to spend some Time enquiring into the Laws of Nations."

123 *L. W. Brockliss*, French Higher Education in the Seventeenth and Eighteenth Centuries: A Cultural History, Oxford, 1987, at pp. 277-9.

124 *Brockliss* (n. 123) 289-92.

125 *Mackenzie*, Observations on the Acts of Parliament (n. 105) 461.

use. He did not relate its authority in Scotland to the laws of nature and nations as higher law binding in Scotland as *Craig* and *Stair* had more rigorously done, while his references to the 'genius' of nations being expressed through their laws, does suggest the extent to which he was influenced by French legal Humanism of the 16th century, and its realization of links between law and history[126].

While in practice the difference of the approach of *Mackenzie* to that of *Craig* and *Stair* might not be important, *Mackenzie*'s stress that "the Civil Law ... is the great Foundation of our Laws and Forms" seems closer to a claim that there was a Roman-Scotch law analogous to the Roman-Dutch Law, even though we can also find *Stair* stating that *"[o]ur Customs,* as they have arisen mainly from Equity, so they are also from the Civil, Canon and Feudal Laws from which the Terms, tenors and Forms of them are much borrowed"[127]. Moreover, to claim that civil law had become Scots law directly through custom, practice, and statute was to make a stronger claim than that asserting that it could be adopted so far as congruent with Natural law and right reason. It is difficult to conceive of *Stair* claiming that the calling of an advocate was based on Roman law, and that "we may justly assert that it were fit the Lords of Session understood exactly the Civil Law"[128]. Given that by the end of the 17th century, the Faculty of Advocates had adopted policies which ensured that virtually all advocates had an academic training in civil law, *Mackenzie*'s attitude must have been widely shared[129].

---

126 See, e.g., *D. R. Kelley*, François Hotman: A Revolutionary's Ordeal, Princeton, 1973, at pp. 192-7.

127 *Mackenzie* (n. 118) 7; *Stair* (n. 79) I, i, 16. Though Scots or Scottish is the usual modern adjective, 'Roman-Scotch' has a nice euphony with 'Roman-Dutch'. See now also *R. Zimmermann* and *J.A. Dieckmann*, Das schottische Privatrecht im Spiegel seiner Literatur, ZEuP 3 (1995) 899, who at p. 899 write that "[d]ie Publikation von Stairs Institutionen im Jahre 1681 konstituierte schließlich das römisch-schottische Recht in ähnlicher Weise wie *Grotius*'s Inleidinge fünfzig Jahre zuvor das römisch-holländische", and at p. 909 discuss "Der römisch-schottische usus modernus". In coining the term 'Roman-Scotch Law', I do not mean to deny the significance of the contribution of Canon law as part of the *ius commune*, but rather to emphasize the significance of the blending of the Roman and Scots laws. Though the significance of Canon law, especially in consistorial matters, cannot be denied, it is clear that, *pace Craig*, Civil law was regarded as the pre-eminent influence. The matter requires further research, of course, and a proper assessment of the significance for this of the continuance of the separate consistorial jurisdiction.

128 *Mackenzie* (n. 121) 65; *idem* (n. 118) 7.

129 *J. W. Cairns*, The Formation of the Scottish Legal Mind in the Eighteenth Century: Themes of Humanism and Enlightenment in the Admission of Advocates, in: N. MacCormick, P. B. H. Birks, edd., The Legal Mind: Essays for Tony Honoré, Oxford, 1986, 253, at pp. 255-61.

IV. The 18th Century

By 1700, it is easy to identify two complementary trends in Scottish legal scholarship. First, the institutional tradition of writing on national law exemplified by *Stair* and *Mackenzie* was well established. It continued to make accounting for the authority accorded to civil law particularly imperative[130]. Secondly, scholars had now firmly located Scots law within the framework of the law of nature and nations. This had practical as well as theoretical importance, legitimating arguments as to what *was* Scots law by reference to Natural law and the law of nations in both civil and criminal cases[131]. There has as yet been little systematic research through the records of the courts that might help establish the doctrinal history of Scots law[132], but in so far as one can rely on the writings of Scots lawyers of the period, it is evident that there had been a substantial reception of Roman law in Scots law by the end of the 17th century. The legacy of thinking on the role of civil law from 17th-century Scotland was drawn upon by those attempting in the next century to make sense of the practical reliance on civil law in Scottish litigation. To explore this, it is useful first of all to examine the work of those who successfully taught Scots law in the early years of the 18th century, all initially using *Mackenzie*'s 'Institutions', that archetypal institutional work, as their textbook. This was the period when the influence of scholarship on Natural law was at its greatest in Scotland, especially the voluntarist approach popularized by *Samuel Pufendorf*, whose textbook was to become the primary vehicle for the teaching of ethics and moral philosophy[133].

1. John Spotswood

From 1702 to around 1705, and again from 1710 to around 1722, *John Spotswood* taught Scots law privately in Edinburgh[134]. After training with a Writer to

130 See *Luig* (n. 50); Cairns (n. 50).

131 See *J. W. Cairns*, Hamesucken and the Major Premiss in the Libel, 1672-1770: Criminal Law in the Age of Enlightenment, in: R.F. Hunter, ed., Justice and Crime: Essays in Honour of the Right Honourable The Lord Emslie, Edinburgh, 1993, p. 138; *idem*, Scottish Law, Scottish Lawyers, and the Status of the Union, in: J. Robertson, ed., A Union for Empire: Political Thought and the British Union of 1707, Cambridge, 1995, 243, at p. 254-67.

132 But see, e.g., *H. L. MacQueen* and *W. D. H. Sellar*, Unjust Enrichment in Scots Law, in: E. J. H. Schrage, ed., Unjust Enrichment: The Comparative Legal History of the Law of Restitution, Berlin, 1995, p. 289; *MacCormack* (n. 68); R. Evans-Jones, The History of the *Actio Quanti Minoris* in Scotland, 1991 J.R. 190; *idem*, Unjust Enrichment, Contract and the Third Reception of Roman Law in Scotland, (1993) 109 L.Q.R. 663.

133 See, e.g., *J. Moore and M. Silverthorne*, Gershom Carmichael and the Natural Jurisprudence Tradition in Eighteenth-Century Scotland, in: I. Hont and M. Ignatieff, edd., Wealth and Virtue: The Shaping of Political Economy in the Scottish Enlightenment, Cambridge, 1983, p. 73; *P. G. Stein*, From Pufendorf to Adam Smith: The Natural Law Tradition in Scotland, in: Europäisches Rechtsdenken in Geschichte und Gegenwart: Festschrift für Helmut Coing zum 70. Geburstag, Munich, 1982, 667.

the Signet in Edinburgh (where he had graduated M.A. from the University), *Spotswood* studied law in the University of Leiden under Professors *Vitriarius* and *Noodt*[135]. In his classes, *Spotswood* gave a systematic account of justice and law based on the writings of the modern school of natural law[136]. Here a few points only will be mentioned. After a conventional account of justice, he explained that with respect to law it was divided into "Naturall, which is these dictats Imprinted on our minds by God, and Civill, which is principally formed from and founded on the Law of Nature", adding later that "Equity, though not different from Naturall Justice, yet many times it is contrair to Law, and where they differ, if the Mind of the Legislator be plain, it is to be followed, but if not, Equity is Cheifly to be noticed"[137]. *Spotswood* gave a voluntarist definition of law as "a rule prescribed by God or any subaltern Sovereign by which subjects are to Govern their actions"[138]. If this may suggest the influence of *Pufendorf*[139], *Spotswood* added that "the grand Rule by which Laws are formed is the Law of Nature and Nations", of which his account is not at all reminiscent of that of the German author. Indeed, he cited *Grotius* for some of his exposition[140]. In turning to the authority of civil law, *Spotswood* stressed that it is followed as the law of nations and because of its equity or conformity to natural justice, though, like *Mackenzie*, emphasizing its mention in Scottish statutes: "the Civill Law of the Romans ... [is] common to all Nations in Generall, so by the common Law in our acts of Parliament is meant the Civill law"; "The Civill Law, or ... the Roman Law, which was the particular laws and customs of the City of Rome, and which, for its equity and excellency, was received as Law by the most Civilized nations in the World". In Scotland "we follow the Civill Law principallie in decisions of matters annent moveables and Executries where our own Law is deficient"[141].

2. *John Cuninghame*

Similar views on the nature of law were expressed by *John Cuninghame* who taught Scots law between 1705 and 1710[142]. *Cuninghame* told his class:

---

134 See *J. W. Cairns*, John Spotswood, Professor of Law: A Preliminary Sketch, in: Gordon (n. 89) 131.

135 *Cairns* (n. 134) 135-8.

136 I have not identified the source of his views on the laws of nature and nations which are conventional enough, but it is worth pointing out that they do not seem particularly influenced by those of his teacher *Vitriarius*: compare the remarks in National Library of Scotland, MS 3412, pp. 1-5 with those in *P.R. Vitriarius*, Universum jus civile privatum ad methodum institutionum Justiniani compositum, Leiden, 1697, I, i.

137 *J. Spotswood*, in: National Library of Scotland, MS 3412, at pp. 3-4.

138 *Spotswood* (n. 137) 4.

139 See, e.g., *S. Pufendorf*, On the Duty of Man and Citizen According to Natural Law, J. Tully, ed., Cambridge, 1991, at p. 27.

140 *Spotswood* (n. 137) 5-7.

141 *Spotswood* (n. 137) 7-9.

"Before Sir George comes to speak of our municipal Law he speaks of two sorts of Laws which make up a part of our Laws, viz. the Civill Law and the Cannon Law, by the Civill Law we understand the Laws of the Romans which because of the equity and exactness beyond all other Laws is in our acts of Parliament frequently called the Common Law, for its commonly received not only in Scotland but likewise in many other places of Europe such as in Holland, Germany, France and Spain and even in England though many are of the contrair opinion"[143].

He went on to list, in the manner of *Craig*, the areas of Scots law in which it was,

"of great use in our Law as to the matter of Tutors and Curators, in all Contracts and obligations, and as to the ways of acquiring and extinguishing them, as to the manner of restitution in integrum, as also for crimes and servitudes and Testaments and all sorts of actions, and therefore it may be said to be of general use in our Law, and moreover its out of the Civill Law that all our reasoning and Topicks are taken"[144].

He did not appear to see civil law as having a statutory authority in Scotland, but as simply being accepted as part of Scots law. His use of the rhetorical term 'topic' is particularly interesting as indicating that advocates commonly drew on civil law for propositions and maxims on which to found arguments in pleading[145]. In other words, use of civil law was pervasive in legal practice.

3. Alexander Bayne

Alexander Bayne, the first Professor of Scots Law in the University of Edinburgh, holding the chair from 1722-37, is perhaps the most important of these early figures, and it is he who provides the most interesting explanation of the authority of Roman law. In his 'Notes' on *Mackenzie*'s 'Institutions', based on his lectures to his class, he wrote that civil law was known in Scotland by the beginning of the 13th century. He explained:

"It is owing to our Churchmens studying the Canon Law, which was formed from the Civil Law, and to the original Penury of any written Law of our own, that our Law participates so much of the Civil Law: For having no written Law of our own to be fond of, Want made us search; and we naturally drew from the nearest Source, and the best known"[146].

---

142 See *J. Cuninghame*, National Library of Scotland, MS 3413, at pp. 1-3; Edinburgh University Library, MS Gen. 1735, at pp. 1-5.

143 *Cuninghame*, Edinburgh University Library, MS Gen. 1735, p. 5.

144 *Cuninghame* (n. 143) 5-6.

145 See also *Cuninghame*, National Library of Scotland, MS 3413, p. 3: "By the Civil Law is often meant the Law of the Romans, for its Excellency, and it is Called the Common Law because it is Commonly received through all Europe, It is usefull in regard we borrow all our Topicks from it, in pleading." On topical reasoning: see *I. Maclean*, Interpretation and Meaning in the Renaissance: The Case of Law, Cambridge, 1992, at pp. 75-82.

Bayne developed these few statements in his 'Discourse on the Rise and Progress of the Law of Scotland'. There he wrote of Scots law that it "participates in a large Measure of the Spirit of those excellent Laws of Antiquity" and that "it is a Happiness that the Study of it is rendered so much the more agreeable by its borrowed Lustre from the *Roman* Law"[147]. *Bayne* went on to give a history of Scots law, claiming:

> "It would appear that of old there was a great Penury of any written Law with us, and in that I think we have been very happy; for having no written Law of our own, besides a few of our ancient Customs, blended with what we have got from the Feudal Law, which in part may have been reduced into Writing, we have the more naturally had Recourse to the Civil Law ... I consider therefore the Civil Law, as having become for some Time our proper written Law ..."[148].

This development was attributed to the influence of churchmen both in the Middle Ages and after the founding of the College of Justice[149]. *Bayne*'s use of the term 'proper written Law' is of great significance. Behind it is the Latin *ius proprium*, which was a term used in contrast to *ius commune*. *Bayne* is explicitly stating that Roman law became Scots law. Moreover, the phrase also echoes the Latin *ius scriptum*. This suggests the influence of *Craig*'s idea that the Scots turned to Roman law because of the lack of *written* Scots law. Civil law filled the gap. *Bayne* explained:

> "Thus the Civil Law was at first introduced, and by these Steps it has become so considerable a Part of our Law, so that we not only follow its Rules and Decisions, chiefly in what relates to Moveables, as Sir *Thomas Craig* says; but also in Pactions, Transactions, Restitutions, Arbitrations, Servitudes, Contracts of all Kinds, Evictions, Pledges, Tutories, Actions, Exceptions and Obligations. I say, we not only make use of it in all these Contracts and Obligations, but by the Help of it we have given a just Temperament to many of the Severities and Hardships in other Parts of the Law, and have made them more conformable to right Reason and natural Equity. Thus in many of our Decisions, we find the severities of Feudal Penalties justly mitigated, from Reasons which the Civil Law had inspired. ... Herein, I say, was our great Happiness, that having no written Law of our own, we had naturally Recourse to the Civil Law; for if, as in other Nations, our own ancient, and perhaps barbarous Laws and Customs, had been committed to Writing, we had like them been tenaciously addicted to our own Laws, and partially fond of what had been handed down to us by our Ancestors, we had disdained to adopt the Laws of another nation, how much soever preferable to our own. Thus our Want of written Law

---

146 *A. Bayne*, Notes for the Use of the Students of the Municipal Law in the University of Edinburgh: Being a Supplement to Sir George Mackenzie's Institutions, Edinburgh, 1731, at pp. 2-3.

147 *A. Bayne*, A Discourse on the Rise and Progress of the Law of Scotland, and the Method of Studying it. For the Use of the Students of the Municipal Law, in: T. Hope, Minor Practicks, A. Bayne, ed., Edinburgh, 1726, at p. 152 (the pagination is defective – this is the second p. 152).

148 *Bayne* (n. 147) 162.

149 *Bayne* (n. 147) 163.

> was our great Felicity, and thus the Civil Law became our written Law for a course of many Years"[150].

Because Scotland was "therefore plentifully supplied from the Pandects and Code with Laws touching private Right", there had been little need for legislation on this topic, so that "the Civil Law [was] the Rule of Judgment in all Cases, wherein our own particular Statutes and consuetudinary Laws were silent: So that the Civil Law was in old Times our proper written Law"[151].

If *Bayne* did not exactly claim that this was still the case, he came very close to doing so, arguing that, as the courts developed, "our Law gradually received Improvements; and what we borrowed from the Civil Law, was either adopted simply without any Alteration, or was varied a little according as our different Manners and Genius made an Alteration necessary". This development was achieved partly by the statutes of *James VI*, and partly by the decisions of the Session, so that "by a long Tract of Time [it was] made the proper and peculiar Law of our Country". Yet, he added, as new cases emerged, recourse was still had to civil law except in so far as it was inconsistent with our statutes and practick – a practice endorsed by various acts of Parliament: "From all which it manifestly appears, that the Civil Law has all along been considered as our Law, and is justly made the rule of Judgment in all Cases wherein our Law is silent; and when such decisions will prove nowise derogatory to our own proper Laws and Customs"[152]. *Bayne* thus seems to argue that civil law became Scots law by customary practice, adopted to serve as the written law of Scotland. He seems to accept that there was a Roman-Scotch law. It may be that civil law could be identified with natural equity and right reason, but this, according to *Bayne*, was not the reason it had been adopted in Scotland. It had been used to compensate for the lack of any written law – with the resulting creation of a Roman-Scotch law – while it could still be used to resolve new issues.

If *Bayne* did not justify the authority of civil law by reference to the law of nature, but gave a solely historical explanation of its use, it is none the less obvious that he was heavily influenced by *Craig*, whom he indeed cites. He followed the earlier author's contention that lack of written law induced the Scots to turn to civil law, while also inverting it to suggest that the use of civil law ensured they felt no need to legislate. He avowedly gave *Craig*'s list of topics in which Roman law was used.

---

150 *Bayne* (n. 147) 164-5. It is specially notable that while a few years later *Smith* and others were to be fascinated by the continuity of English law as an indicator of its formation on just principles, *Bayne* here identified it with a tenacious clinging to possibly barbarous laws.

151 *Bayne* (n. 147) 165-6.

152 *Bayne* (n. 147) 166-8.

4. William Forbes

Roughly contemporary with *Spotswood* and *Bayne* was *William Forbes*, the first Professor of Civil Law in the University of Glasgow, holding the chair from 1714-46. At least some of the time *Forbes* taught Scots law, initially on the basis of *Mackenzie*'s 'Institutions'[153]. In 1722, he published his own textbook[154]. In it he gave a relatively conventional voluntarist theory of law, emphasizing that "[t]he very Notion of a Law implies that of a Lawgiver"[155]. He commented that there was "no authoriz'd Collection of the Laws of Nature and Nations any where, save in the Books of the *Roman* Law"[156]. Turning to Scots law, he commented that it was "raised upon eleven Foundations", one of which was Civil law[157]. Like *Bayne*, he saw Civil law as having become Scots law:

> "The Civil Law ... is effectually naturaliz'd in Scotland. 'Tis the great Foundation of our Laws and Forms, so twisted therewith, that our Judges have recourse to that excellent Fountain of Equity and Justice, where our own Customs and Statutes are silent and defective. The Parliament doth, in some Statutes, expressly own it to be our Law; and the general Revocations of our Princes are founded upon it. In other Statutes, the Force and Authority of the Civil Law with us, is tacitly acknowledged; and Students are admitted Advocats upon Trial of their Knowledge of it"[158].

Forbes's concept of "naturalization" effectively avoided the issue of what made civil law authoritative. His allusions to statutes suggest that he saw them as recognizing that civil law was already in force.

5. Lord Bankton

There were two major statements of Scots law later in the 18th century, both of which show the increased influence of the systematic thinking on Natural law that developed through the century. The first we should consider is that of *Andrew McDouall*, Lord *Bankton*. In the first volume of his 'Institute' published in 1751,

---

153 *J. W. Cairns*, The Origins of the Glasgow Law School: The Professors of Civil Law, 1714-61, in: P. B. H. Birks, ed., The Life of the Law: Proceedings of the Tenth British Legal History Conference, Oxford, 1991, London, 1993, 151, at pp. 177-9.

154 *W. Forbes*, The Institutes of the Law of Scotland. Volume First. Comprehending the Private Law, Edinburgh, 1722. See also *idem*, The Institutes of the Law of Scotland. Volume Second. Comprehending the Criminal Law, Edinburgh, 1730.

155 *Forbes* (n. 154) vol. 1, pp. 1-3.

156 *Forbes* (n. 154) vol. 1, p. 4.

157 *Forbes* (n. 154) vol. 1, pp. 4-5: "1. Upon the Law of Nature. 2. Upon the reveal'd Law of God. 3. Upon the Law of Nations. 4. Upon the Civil Law. 5. Upon the Canon law. 6. Upon the Feudal Law. 7. Upon some old Books. 8. Upon Acts of Parliament, and of Convention of Estates. 9. Ancient Customs. 10. Acts of Sederunt. 11. By-Laws or Statutes of particular Corporations, or Bodies Politick."

158 *Forbes* (n. 154) vol. 1, pp. 8-9.

he argued that it "is only a superior that can give laws, for none other has power to command or forbid, which is the proper business of laws". On the basis of this strong emphasis on legislative sovereignty, he accordingly claimed that "the civil, canon and feudal laws [are] ... in some measure sources of our law, but ... are only to be regarded as law with us, so far as they are received by our statutory or consuetudinary law, that is, by express or tacite consent of the legislature". He summed up the position thus:

> "From many of our statutes it appears, that our legislators had great regard to the civil and canon laws, which therein are termed the common law, as being common to most nations: this indeed shews, that our lawgivers followed these laws as an example, in framing those statutes for their reasonableness and expediency; and therefore, it may from thence be concluded, that our judges ought to direct themselves by the civil and canon laws, as a rule, where our own statutes and customs fail, or where the question, tho' concerning a feudal subject, is not decided by our feudal customs"[159].

This last point shows that he disagreed with *Craig*'s view of the need to rely on the general *jus feudale*, which he elsewhere specifically stated[160]. Thus, though *Bankton* saw the civil law as "compiled for the most part from the laws of nature and nations"[161], the former of which, termed "the law or dictate of reason", was to be discovered "by the use of reason, duly improv'd"[162], its authority in Scotland was derived, not from this, but historically from statute or custom. *Bankton*'s attitude in this respect seems to resemble that of *Mackenzie* rather than that of *Stair* or *Craig*, although it is much more rigorously systematic. It must also reflect the views of *Pufendorf* and his school on the nature of law.

6. John Erskine

Alexander Bayne's successor in the chair of Scots Law in the University of Edinburgh was *John Erskine*, who held the office from 1737 to 1765. In 1754 he published 'Principles of the Law of Scotland' in Edinburgh. This was a short work intended to act as a textbook for his classes. It reveals his support for a voluntarist view of law: "Law is the command of a sovereign, containing a common rule of life for his subjects. It is divided into the law of nature, the law of nations, and civil or municipal law"[163]. He defined the law of nature as "that which God, the Sover-

---

159 *A. McDouall*, Lord *Bankton*, An Institute of the Laws of Scotland in Civil Rights: with Observations upon the Agreement or Diversity Between them and the Laws of England, 3 vols., Edinburgh, 1751-53; reprinted, 3 vols., Edinburgh, 1993-5, vol. 1, at p. 2, 4-5, 19. Note that *Bankton* is using the phrase 'as a rule' in the same sense as *Stair* already had, that is 'as a code of conduct' or 'as a set of norms': see text *supra* at n. 81.

160 *Bankton* (n. 159) vol. 1, p. 13 note.

161 *Bankton* (n. 159) vol. 1, p. 11.

162 *Bankton* (n. 159) vol. 1, p. 7.

163 *J. Erskine*, Principles of the Law of Scotland, Edinburgh, 1754, I, i, 1. I have compared these passages in all the editions prepared by *Erskine*. He did not change the text.

eign of the universe, has prescribed to all men, not by any formal promulgation, but by the internal dictate of reason alone"[164]. He conventionally said: "Civil or municipal law is that which every sovereign kingdom or state has appropriated to itself"[165]. Turning to the issue of the authority of Roman law, he wrote:

> "The civil and canon laws, though they are not perhaps to be deemed proper parts of our written law, have undoubtedly had the greatest influence in *Scotland.* The powers exercised by our sovereigns and our judges, have been justified upon no other ground, than that they were conformable to the civil and canon laws ... but the *Roman* continues to have great authority in all cases, where it is not derogated from by statute or custom, and where the genius of our law suffers us to apply it"[166].

He thus allowed great scope for civil law, but is not precise about the nature of its authority, other than in stressing that neither it nor Canon law were "proper parts of our written law" – which alludes to the notion put forward by *Bayne* that Civil law was *ius proprium* as the written law of Scotland – and in referring to statutory recognition. In his *magnum opus*, 'An Institute of the Law of Scotland', published posthumously in Edinburgh in 1773, he did attempt to flesh this out further. Once more *Erskine* emphasized that law was the command of a superior and stressed legislative sovereignty[167]. He now alleged that *Mackenzie* had claimed Roman law as the written law of Scotland[168]. This remark is incorrect and rather puzzling. It may derive from *Erskine*'s familiarity with the works of *Bayne*, who, as we have seen, did say this. He also stated that *Stair* rejected the authority of the civil law[169]. Given the attitude of *Stair*, following *Craig* in viewing Roman law as followed as authoritative in so far as it exemplified the *aequum et bonum*, this is instructive as to *Erskine*'s own focus on legislative sovereignty. *Erskine* put forward his detailed opinion of the authority of Roman law thus:

164 *Erskine* (n. 163) I, i, 2.

165 *Erskine* (n. 163) I, i, 4.

166 *Erskine* (n. 163) I, i, 15.

167 *J. Erskine*, An Institute of the Law of Scotland, Edinburgh, 1773, I, i, 2; I, i, 19.

168 *Erskine* (n. 167) I, i, 41.

169 *Erskine* (n. 167) I, i, 41. In the 4th edition, Edinburgh, 1805, the editor, J. Gillon, has added in the text to *Erskine*'s reference to *Stair*: "also Craig, *De Feudis*, lib. I. Dieg. 2. No. 14". It is not noted as an editorial addition, and contradicts Gillon's statement (p. [v]) that "the Editor has been careful to preserve the original text without alteration". Subsequent editions continue this additional reference. In making this addition, *Gillon* was probably influenced by the lectures of *David Hume*, as *Hume* by this date was already pointing out to his students that *Craig* and *Stair* agreed on this point. See, e.g., National Library of Scotland, Adv. MS 7.2.4, fos 7r-8r (dating from 1797-8). *Gillon*'s addition to the text of *Erskine* would have been prompted by his recognition that *Hume* in this part of his lecture evidently had *Erskine* (n. 167) I, i, 41 in mind. *Gillon* had attended *Hume*'s lectures on Scots law over two years: Edinburgh University Library, MS Matriculation Roll of the University of Edinburgh, Arts-Law-Divinity. Transcribed by Dr. Alexander Morgan 1933-1934, 3 vols., vol. 1, at pp. 495 (1789-90), 508 (1790-91).

> "Without offering any precise opinion upon this point, an observation or two drawn from our statutes may not be improper. *First,* The powers exercised, both by our sovereigns and judges, have been justified by parliament on this single ground, That they were conformable to the Roman law. ... *2dly,* A special statute was judged necessary, soon after the Reformation, for abrogating such of the laws, either Civil or Canon, as were repugnant to the Protestant doctrine ...; and the abrogation of a law is generally understood to import, that the law abrogated had formerly been in force. These observations prove at least, that great weight is to be laid on the Roman law in all cases not fixed by statute and custom, and in which the genius of our law will suffer us to apply it: and as we have few statutes in the matter of contracts, transactions, restitutions, servitudes, tutories, and obligations, the knowledge of it must be singularly useful in determining controversies arising from those heads of the law. Yet where any rule of the Roman law appears to have been founded on a subtilty peculiar to their system, it were absurd to pay the smallest regard to it"[170].

Erskine here somewhat fudges the issue of what gives authority to Roman law in Scotland, although hinting at the significance of statutory recognition by his (somewhat forced) allusion to the Act 1567, c. 2[171]; it is clear, however, that in practice his view of the scope of the potential use of Roman law is much the same as that of the other authors examined. Again we find a list of areas of law in which Scots law followed Roman law derived ultimately from that given by *Craig*, and an acceptance of *Craig*'s claim that Scots law drew so much on civil law because of its lack of an adequate written law.

V. Conclusion: From Practical to Educational Value

Towards the end of *Erskine's* tenure of the chair of Scots law in the University of Edinburgh, the teaching of law, especially of civil law, started to undergo a revolution in the University of Glasgow, as *John Millar*, Baron *David Hume*'s teacher, brought Smithian jurisprudence to bear on all his courses[172]. Roman law was recognized as having in the past been received: its main value now was to teach legislative science through explaining the links between history, society, and law. There was some reaction against *Millar*'s views from *John Wilde* in Edinburgh, who argued that the civil law had a value in itself, and put forward views on teaching similar to those of the German Historical School[173]. *Wilde's* successors did not follow his example, and education in civil law in Edinburgh resumed its old track, taught by *Alexander Irving* from the outmoded textbooks of *Heineccius*, which had

---

170 *Erskine* (n. 167) I, i, 41.

171 A.P.S., ii, 548.

172 See *J. W. Cairns*, 'Famous as a school for Law, as Edinburgh ... for medicine': Legal Education in Glasgow, 1761-1801, in: A. Hook and R. B. Sher, edd., The Glasgow Enlightenment, Phantassie, East Linton, 1995, p. 133.

173 *Cairns* (n. 3) 43-6; *idem* (n. 13) 193-4.

been superseded by the new German scholarship[174]. *Irving* agreed with *Hume*'s views on Roman law and told his class:

> "The Civil Law is not now so much studied as it has been our own code being much enlarged – But the Study of it is important for affording a Knowledge of the principle on which Law in general is founded and preventing the study of it from degenerating into a mere matter of Memory"[175].

Already by 1780, Lord *Kames* could tell *Boswell* that while once civil law had been used to resolve points of Scots law, now "a Man would be laughed at were he to quote Civil law now that they are settled"[176]. Indeed, there was general consensus by the end of the 18th century that the reception of Roman law was over in Scotland[177]: the era of the Roman-Scotch law had passed. This is not to say that it was denied that there could be recourse to civil law in Scottish litigation: "and to this day, on a doubtful point, without precedent, there is no authority equal to the Roman law", *Hume* told his students in 1797[178]. Instead, as Professor *Irving* reported to the Commission visiting the Scottish universities in 1826:

> "Those branches of the Civil Law which have been admitted as of authority with us, after they have entered into the works of our Institutional writers, and are confirmed by judgments and decisions of the courts, become part of the Scotch Law, and are studied in the Class of Scotch Law, so the student has less occasion to resort to the Civil Law than originally"[179].

His successor in the Chair of Civil Law agreed, stating that if the authority of Civil law remained "it is very different in degree", so that "to say nothing of the statutes which have been enacted, and the legal authors who have appeared since its first introduction, its influence has been superseded by the very precedents which have been founded on it"[180].

When there was an intellectual revival of the study of Roman law in Scotland after 1860, what was taught was the historical civil law as its study had developed on the Continent, especially in Germany, since the beginning of the 19th century. *James Muirhead*, Professor of Civil Law in the University of Edinburgh, 1862-88, educated in Heidelberg, expounded Roman law historically to the time of *Justi-*

---

174 See, e.g., *A. Irving*, Edinburgh University Library, MSS Gen. 1389-90; National Library of Scotland, MSS 24611-12.

175 *A. Irving*, National Library of Scotland, MS 24612, fo. 104r.

176 G. Scott and F. A. Pottle, edd., Private Papers of James Boswell from Malahide Castle, 18 vols., New York, 1928-34, vol. 15, at pp. 290-1.

177 See *Cairns* (n. 129) 267-8, 276-7.

178 *Baron David Hume*, National Library of Scotland, Adv. MS 7.2.4, fo. 7r.

179 *A. Irving*, in: Evidence, Oral and Documentary, Taken and Received by the Commissioners Appointed by His Majesty George IV, July 23rd, 1826; and Re-appointed by his Majesty William IV, October 12th 1830; For Visiting the Universities of Scotland. Volume I. University of Edinburgh, 1837 Parliamentary Papers XXXV, p. 183.

180 *Cheape* (n. 13) 30-1.

nian, initially within a Pandectist systematics[181]. His pupil and successor *Henry Goudy*, educated at Königsberg, appears to have done likewise. The content of *Muirhead*'s classes is well indicated by his books[182]: that he should have produced an edition of *Gaius*'s 'Institutes' as a textbook for his class is particularly telling[183]. *Goudy* is best known for his study of the law of bankruptcy[184]. It is notable, however, that his work on Roman law was on the ancient world[185]. When he looked at modern Scots law, he saw the Reception as over. He argued that "after the Reformation the Roman law became *jus receptum* in Scotland to quite as great an extent as it did in Germany, Holland, and other continental countries", but now:

> "No doubt in the Scotch Reports of the present century citations of Justinian's texts and of the Civilians will be found to be comparatively rare, but that is due mainly to the fact that a wealth of decided cases has accumulated, and that, in matters of commercial law, the well-furnished storehouses of the English Reports have been largely resorted to"[186].

There seemed to be no need now to return to the sources drawn on to create the Roman-Scotch Law. The focus of these professors on the classical Roman law is perfectly understandable. They – and other Scots – had studied law in Germany in the heyday of the 'Pandektenrecht'. The 'Pandektenwissenschaft' was an attempt to create a universal modern law drawing on the principles of Roman law. And if there was some variation in this among authors, it is broadly true to say that the sources of the old *ius commune* tended to be ignored in this task. Roman law and 'Pandektenrecht' had become different studies[187]. The example of Germany would have taught these Scots that modern law – even if inspired by the civil law – was something different from the Roman law, while it also encouraged these men to look to codification[188].

Before *Craig* gave a theory to Scots law, there existed a pragmatic realization that Roman law provided useful material when there were gaps in Scots law. It is notable, however, that civil law (and for that matter Canon law) were looked upon as something separate from Scots law: statutes and writers talk of municipal law,

---

181 For his curriculum, see The Edinburgh University Calendar during his period of office.

182 *J. Muirhead*, Historical Introduction to the Private Law of Rome, Edinburgh, 1886.

183 J. Muirhead, ed., The Institutes of Gaius and Rules of Ulpian. The Former from Studemund's Apograph of the Verona Codex, Edinburgh, 1880.

184 *H. Goudy*, A Treatise on the Law of Bankruptcy in Scotland, Edinburgh, 1886.

185 See, e.g., *H. Goudy*, Trichotomy in Roman Law, Oxford, 1910.

186 *H. Goudy*, An Inaugural Lecture on the Fate of Roman Law North and South of the Tweed, London, 1894, at p. 27.

187 See *K. Zweigert* and *H. Kötz*, An Introduction to Comparative Law, trans. *T. Weir*, 2nd ed., Oxford, 1992, at pp. 145-6; *A. F. Rodger*, Scottish Advocates in the Nineteenth Century: The German Connection (1994) 110 L.Q.R. 563, at pp. 572-9; *O. F. Robinson*, *T. D. Fergus*, and *W. M. Gordon*, European Legal History: Sources and Institutions, 2nd ed., London, 1994, at pp. 262-8.

188 *A. F. Rodger*, The Codification of Commercial Law in Victorian Britain (1992) 109 L.Q.R. 570.

civil law, and Canon law. In a sense it is almost as if a claim was being made that these are three separate valid sources for formulating rules to decide causes. After *Craig*'s time there is a more self-conscious use of civil law, and thereafter the municipal law and the civil law as used in Scotland become progressively integrated: here it is useful to recall *Robert Burnet*'s remark about Sir *Alexander Gibson of Durie* that he regularly read the civil law and the Doctors of Law, while having the Scots law shelved in his heart so that, as *Burnet* conjectured, *Gibson* was marrying the civil law to the Scots law[189]. Given that *Gibson* (who was *Craig*'s son-in-law) was Lord President in the first half of the 16th century and that *Burnet* (who was married to *Craig*'s grand-daughter) was an advocate and later a Senator as Lord *Crimmond*[190], this is particularly valuable evidence, especially since *Burnet* goes on to stress that: "Civil Law has no authority among us, but, in the absence of our own Municipal Law, the *ratio juris Civilis* is highly appreciated by us, and is greatly valued by the learned and the judges skilled in the laws who often follow this *ratio* in deciding causes"[191]. Likewise the Lords of Session in 1620 issued an Act of Sederunt ratified the next year by Parliament as "[m]eaning to follow and practize the guid and Commendable lawis Civill and Cannone"[192]. It is this attitude that created what has here been christened the Roman-Scotch law. In the institutional period proper of Scots law, the writings of men such as *Mackenzie*, *Bayne*, *Stair*, *Erskine*, and *Bankton* expounded this Roman-Scotch law, but in doing so, they of course helped differentiate Scots law from the *ius commune*, especially in the context of the new orientations and understandings to which the Enlightenment had given rise. This would no doubt have been facilitated by the failure of Scotland to develop any specific literature adapting Roman law to the *hodiernum ius*, presumably because legal education in the Scottish universities had failed at the end of the 16th century, while its revival in the 18th was in the context of the pre-eminence given to natural law. Moreover, the ever-increasing focus on legislative sovereignty in the 18th century continued to marginalize Civil law. By 1800, the Reception was seen to be over. After the reform and renewal of legal education in the Scottish universities in the 1860s, a new role had to be found for civil law. Its value was now considered to be a variation of that for which *Millar*, *Hume*, and *Irving* had already argued. It still had some practical relevance, and was referred to in the courts from time to time. But its main importance was now seen as educational – with education in it considered to be best pursued in the ancient Roman law. Roman-Scotch law had given way to Scots law and Roman law as different disciplines.

---

189 *Craig* (n. 53) xi.

190 *G. Brunton* and *D. Haig*, An Historical Account of the Senators of the College of Justice From its Institution in M.D.XXXII., Edinburgh, 1836, at p. 264; F. J. Grant, ed., The Faculty of Advocates in Scotland 1532-1943 with Genealogical Notes, Edinburgh, 1944, at p. 25.

191 *Craig* (n. 53) xi.

192 Act 1621, c. 18, in A.P.S., iv, 615.

The Use of the Civil Law in Scottish Courts

By Alan Rodger

I. Introduction

In this short article I do not propose to give a systematic account of the cases in which civil law – in which I include both Roman law and the later developments culminating in the *ius commune* – has been cited in the Scottish courts since that matter has been discussed repeatedly over the years. Instead I shall look at a number of more general issues which are suggested by the material.

The basic theoretical position with respect to Roman law is, of course, long since settled: the Scottish courts are always concerned to discover or to determine what is the Scots Law on any topic and civil law is simply one of the sources to which the courts may have regard. So the Scottish courts may choose to follow the civil law, but it is not binding upon them. Lord *Dunedin* put the point succinctly when he said that "[a]fter all, however, the Roman law, though interesting, is only of service as showing the foundation on which the Scots law rests. The real question must always be what is the law of Scotland"[1]. One can go rather further. By this stage in the development of Scots Law most areas are occupied by existing authority. Where that is so, the courts will not readily be persuaded to depart from that authority and to introduce a brand new doctrine from civil law[2]. Equally, even if that authority is ultimately based on the civil law, the courts will usually be able to decide a new point by reference to that existing authority without feeling any need to explore the civil law authority which may have been its original foundation[3].

That being so, there may seem to be little room for the actual use of civil law in our courts. A glance through the Scottish law reports certainly seems to confirm

1 *Cantiere San Rocco v. Clyde Shipbuilding and Engineering Co.* 1923 S.C. (H.L.) 105, at p. 123. This well-accepted approach was reaffirmed recently by Lord *McCluskey* in some remarks which Dr. *Evans-Jones* has noted as "sensible things": *Connelly v. Simpson* 1993 S.C. 391, at p. 403B. Cf. *R. Evans-Jones*, Roman Law in Britain (sic) Scotland, Rechtshistorisches Journal 13 (1995) 494, at p. 502. For a brief account of the present position of Roman Law, see *A. Rodger*, Roman Law in Practice in Britain, Rechtshistorisches Journal 12 (1994) 261.

2 *Drummond's Judicial Factor v. H. M. Advocate* 1944 S.C. 298, at pp. 301 sqq.

3 Cf. already *D. Cheape*, An Introductory Lecture on the civil law delivered in the University of Edinburgh on Tuesday, 13th November 1827, Edinburgh and London, 1827, at p. 31.

that impression since there are very few references to the civil law. Similarly if you go into the Advocates Library you will find that books on civil law are not shelved in a prominent position – because they are not consulted regularly by advocates giving opinions or preparing arguments for court. Indeed much of the work of the Court of Session is concerned with areas where civil law is not relevant. So, presently at least, civil law does not play a large part in everyday practice.

II. The 19th Century

This is no new phenomenon. For the last two hundred years at least Scottish practitioners have shown little taste for the detailed study of civil law. The inaugural lecture of Professor *Cheape* at Edinburgh University in 1827 contains passages which show that he well knew that even then civil law was not immediately attractive to students[4]. Nor is this surprising since it must have been an unspeakably dull subject, to be got up mainly from the dry pages of *Heineccius*. Indeed it is worth stressing that it is the historical study of civil law which develops and which is interesting. If all that was on offer to students today were, say, the rules on the *lex Aquilia* as presented apparently higgledy piggledy in Digest title 9, 2, in the Institutes of *Justinian* and in the tedious pages of *Heineccius*, then the subject would be totally dead. It is not surprising therefore that by the start of the 19th century civil law did not attract teachers of distinction in Scotland or that the Faculty of Advocates' examination was little more than a farce. When in typically forthright and unrepentant manner *Henry Brougham* pointed this out, his remarks were resented and it was quite rightly – if not altogether relevantly – said that, if anything, the position in England was worse[5]. None the less the defence to his attack was weak since in truth the study of civil law was moribund. It was only when the German Historical School gave birth to the modern historical study of the subject that it became a field in which, for those with a taste for such things, there were discoveries to be made and progress to be achieved. But it was not until 1862 that a Scottish university found a scholar of distinction in Professor *James Muirhead* who was familiar with the continental literature of the subject and pursued it in a thoroughly modern way.

Presumably the Faculty of Advocates was prepared to tolerate a somewhat inadequate standard in civil law partly because many members would never practise law anyway and partly because in any event there was not much recourse to it in practice. Contemporaries certainly thought that this was the case[6] and if one looks

---

4 *Cheape* (n. 3) e.g. at p. 35.

5 The controversy is most easily studied in *J. Browne*, Remarks on the Study of the civil law, Edinburgh, 1828.

6 Cf. *A. Rodger*, Scottish Advocates in the Nineteenth Century: the German Connection, (1994) 110 L.Q.R. 563, at p. 574. See also *Cheape* (n. 3) 29 sqq., esp. at 31. Of course, the standards in Scots Law were not high either.

through the Session Papers of the early 19th century, argument from the civil law does not feature prominently. There are exceptions, of course, such as the slightly earlier (1795) *Gardner v. Fergusons*, in which for the first time a pursuer recovered damages for personal injuries caused by non-criminal negligence and in which the argument was largely based on civil law[7]. But for the most part the advocates refer to passages from writers such as *Stair* or *Erskine* and to previous decisions of the Court. Moreover many of the cases concern questions of feudal law in which civil law writers would not be expected to feature prominently and do not indeed do so. The overall impression is of a system which had got beyond the stage where it felt the need to refer regularly to the old civil law. If that is correct, then the position of Scots Law with respect to the civil law may not have changed fundamentally over the last two hundred years.

III. Individual Contributions

Since questions involving recourse to civil law occur only comparatively rarely, most counsel and judges are not particularly familiar with either the concepts or the literature. Therefore, more than in the commoner areas of practice, personal factors will come into play and some counsel and judges may perform with greater confidence than their colleagues. For instance, as was recognized in Parliament House at the time, in the Outer House of the Court of Session that excellent classicist Lord *Stott* enjoyed his excursion into the world of *Justinian* in *Sloans Dairies*, whereas in the Inner House Lord *Wheatley* was not at ease in handling the material[8]. Similarly in *Cantiere San Rocco*[9] it was the scholarly Mr. *Normand*, the appellants' junior counsel and a future president of the Classical Association of Scotland, who presented the House of Lords with an argument based on the *condictio causa data causa non secuta*. Throughout his life Lord Chancellor *Birkenhead* was understandably proud of having beaten *Holdsworth* to the Vinerian Scholarship with his Roman law papers in the 1896 B.C.L. examination[10]. Not surprisingly therefore he seems to have felt quite happy dealing with the general thrust of the appellants' (technically incorrect) argument from Roman law. By contrast on this occasion Lord *Dunedin* chose not to become too involved in the detailed argument from Roman law but to rest more generally on the approach in the existing Scottish writers and cases, while distinguishing the Coronation Cases which were the cornerstone of the respondents' argument.

---

[7] See *H. M'Kechnie*, Reparation, in: Encyclopaedia of the Laws of Scotland, vol. 12, Edinburgh, 1931, p. 517.

[8] 1977 S.C. 223. On the case see *A. Rodger*, Roman Law comes to Partick, in: R. Evans-Jones, ed., The Civil Law Tradition in Scotland, 1995, 198 sqq.

[9] 1923 S.C. (H.L.) 105.

[10] Cf., e.g., *The Second Earl of Birkenhead*, The Life of F. E. Smith First Earl of Birkenhead, London, 1959, p. 56.

In his speech Lord *Birkenhead* refers briefly to *Roby*'s 'Roman Private Law'[11], while Viscount *Finlay* cites *Mackeldey* and *Ortolan*[12]. When wrestling with the problem of a sentence in *Erskine* based on D. 12, 4, 5, 4, *Ulpian 2 disputationum*, Lord *Shaw* quotes quite extensively from *Roby*[13]. Especially since this reliance on *Roby* has been the subject of comment[14], it is interesting to notice that none of these works was cited by the appellants either in their printed case or in the oral argument. Perhaps Lord *Finlay* was referring to books with which he had been familiar when studying law. But that cannot be the explanation for Lord *Shaw*'s use of *Roby*'s work on Roman private law which was not published until 1902, long after Lord *Shaw*'s student days were over. His reference to *Roby* is therefore at first sight a little surprising since nothing which we know of Lord *Shaw* would suggest that a Roman law textbook would have been his favourite bed-time reading.

So why *Roby*? The clue lies in Lord *Shaw*'s language: "I am happy to cite, in connexion with this topic, the views of that great scholar and latinist, Mr. *Roby*"[15]. This tells us that the citation is not of some remote authority who is unknown to Lord *Shaw*, but rather of someone whose qualities he knows and admires. That deduction is confirmed by a glance at the careers of *Roby* and Lord *Shaw*. Although *Roby* is nowadays remembered mainly for his works on Latin grammar and Roman law, he was in fact very much a public figure in the world of education and business. After a long career in these fields he became the Liberal Member of Parliament for the Eccles Division of Lancashire from 1890 to 1895. In 1892 Lord *Shaw* joined him on the Liberal benches as the member for Hawick District which he was to represent until he became a Lord of Appeal in 1909. *Roby* and *Shaw* were therefore M.P.s on the same side for 3 years. It is easy to infer that they would have been acquaintances. But there is no need for speculation since Lord *Shaw* tells us elsewhere[16]: "The late Dr. *Roby* was a friend and colleague of my own in Parliament, and surely one of the most erudite men who ever sat in the House of Commons". We may safely infer that Lord *Shaw* chose to quote "the quite remarkable exposition of the condiction which Mr. *Roby* gives"[17] because he admired him and thought of him as a friend. It is therefore all the more unfortunate that Lord *Shaw* should have chosen to cut short his old friend's exposition just before the sentence where he correctly recorded the effect of the passage of *Ulpian* which the House was considering[18].

---

11 1923 S.C. (H.L.) at p. 109.

12 1923 S.C. (H.L.) at pp. 114-115.

13 1923 S.C. (H.L.) at p. 117.

14 *Evans-Jones* (n. 1) 497 and 500. See also *R. Evans-Jones*, Unjust Enrichment, Contract and the Third Reception of Roman Law in Scotland, (1993) 109 L.Q.R. 663.

15 1923 S.C. (H.L.) at p. 117.

16 The Law of the Kinsmen, London, 1923, at pp. 84-85.

17 1923 S.C. (H.L.) at p. 117.

18 *H. J. Roby*, Roman Private Law, vol. 2, Cambridge, 1902, p. 78.

There are signs elsewhere of a similar tendency for judges to find for themselves passages from civil law authorities which they think will serve their purposes. So, for instance, in the *Edinburgh and District Tramways* case[19], when speaking of recompense, Lord *Dunedin* refers to an unspecified passage from *Pothier* and says, "I notice that that [*sc.* the brocard *nemo debet locupletari ex aliena jactura*] is the basis of *Pothier's* definition of it, his definition being really practically no more than a translation of the brocard"[20]. The form of the remark indicates what the report of the argument confirms, *viz.* that *Pothier* was not cited to the court and that this was something which Lord *Dunedin* found for himself. Indeed he appears to have had a certain penchant for *Pothier* since in his well-known frolic on the civil law in *Sinclair v. Brougham*[21] – a passage which was certainly very much his own production and not derived from the argument presented to the Judicial Committee in that very English appeal – in addition to texts of *Ulpian* from the Digest Lord *Dunedin* quoted sections from *Pothier*'s 'Traité des obligations'[22]. Since he had an excellent knowledge of French[23], it is not at all surprising that Lord *Dunedin* should have found *Pothier* a convenient and attractive source of information about civil law matters. It may even be that he had his own copy[24].

Since the Digest texts do not on the whole contain detailed discussions of legal principle, but rather a multitude of decisions on individual cases, the material does not readily lend itself to formulating the theoretical basis for an area of our law, even where the civil law material forms the ultimate bedrock. This is particularly clear in the area of unjust enrichment. If it be the case that "Scots law still lacks a clear and coherent structure in this field"[25], or that "[t]he taxonomy of the quasi-contractual remedies which are afforded by the law of Scotland is not in a wholly satisfactory state"[26], then some at least of the blame can be laid at the door of the compilers of the Digest who took and adapted texts from many different areas of the law to produce titles which are incoherent and often well-nigh impossible to understand. Starting from that base, later civil law writers did not produce a clear structure either and so until recently little progress had been made in producing a

19 *Edinburgh and District Tramways v. Courtenay* 1909 S.C. 99.

20 1909 S.C. at p. 105.

21 [1914] A.C. 398.

22 [1914] A.C. at pp. 434 sqq. Lord *Dunedin* referred to this passage in his speech in *Cantiere San Rocco*: 1923 S.C. (H.L.) at p. 126. For another example of reference to civil law authority which would not have been cited, see the speech of Lord *Macmillan* in the case referred to in n. 48 infra.

23 See, for example, the article on *Andrew Graham Murray, Viscount Dunedin*, Dictionary of National Biography 1941-1950 (*Lord Macmillan*).

24 There is no copy of the French text of the 'Traité des obligations' in the House of Lords Library.

25 *Morgan Guaranty Trust v. Lothian Regional Council* 1995 S.C. 151, at p. 155D per Lord President *Hope*.

26 1995 S.C. at p. 173H *per* Lord *Cullen*. The reference to taxonomy is very much à la mode in discussions of enrichment law.

satisfactory analysis of the various elements which go to make up the Scots Law on the topic. Although that is now changing, the discussion in *Royal Bank of Scotland p.l.c. v. Watt*[27], as to the basis on which a bank might recover money paid out as the result of the presentation of a fraudulently altered cheque, suggests that we have some way still to go.

IV. Civilian Aspects of Scots Law

Unjustified enrichment is an excellent example[28] of an area of our law which owes so much to the civil law that no-one can understand or hope to develop the modern law coherently without a proper knowledge of its civil law foundations. Unless our law on unjustified enrichment were to be codified – a suggestion which met with little support and much vigorous opposition at a seminar organized by the Scottish Law Commission in October 1994 – then we have to try to understand the law and the cases which we have. They are peppered with Latin terminology which points unmistakably to the civil law doctrines lurking just below the surface. Although it might be wise not to exaggerate the depth of civilian learning of even the 18th century judges, none the less many of the decisions cannot be interpreted without some grasp of the civil law to which the arguments alluded. So even if the Court of Session were one day tempted to adopt some version of the German analysis which features prominently in modern academic writing[29], this could not alter the simple fact that in the existing cases the Scottish courts had not adopted an analysis of that kind. So anyone wishing to understand the reasoning and distinctions which are actually to be found in the cases would still require to be familiar with the civil law. In this area it is too entrenched to be removed.

None the less the need to understand the underlying civil law basis presents difficulties for practitioners who may have no training in civil law and no knowledge of the Latin used in the texts mentioned in the older decisions and institutional writers. This is, of course, simply a particularly acute example of a much wider problem which confronts Scots lawyers. However useful they may be, the institutional writers do not provide an answer for every problem even in those areas which they cover. Naturally they supplemented their discussion by referring to authorities such as *Voet* or *Vinnius*. They wrote moreover for an audience of whom many could have been expected to be familiar with those writers. Indeed these references form such an integral part of the institutional books that we can no more understand or evaluate them without consulting the works cited than we could use a modern textbook on contract without consulting the cases referred to in the footnotes. In short there is a danger – which can be detected, for example, in *Royal Bank of Scotland*

---

27 1991 S.C. 48.

28 There are, of course, many others such as barter, loan and hire.

29 Cf., e.g., *N. R. Whitty*, Issues in Scots Enrichment Law, 1994 J.R. 127, at p. 133; *idem*, Die Reform des schottischen Bereicherungsrechts, ZEuP 3 (1995) 216 sqq.

p.l.c. v. Watt – that passages from the institutional writers may be quoted in isolation, without reference to the wider civil law context in which they were writing and which really provides the key to what they are saying. The danger is not hard to identify. It is much more difficult to prescribe a remedy – especially with the decline in the attention which is paid to civil law in training our future practitioners.

There is a further real difficulty which would persist even supposing that somehow we produced a generation of practitioners who could handle the civil law materials. After the death of Lord *Macmillan* in 1952, in his memory the Pilgrim Trust agreed to pay for the refurbishment of a collection of civil law works. The intention was to encourage their use in legal and historical research[30]. They now stand gleaming on their shelves in the Advocates' Library, a sight to be shown to visitors, a monument to the civil law tradition of our law, but unread and unused by the advocates who practise it in the Court of Session and beyond. At least, however, the works would be on hand for advocates to consult if they wished. But nowadays most practitioners of Scots law are not advocates and they practise far from Edinburgh. For them the civil law sources would be extremely difficult to find. Moreover most litigation today is conducted in the Sheriff Court rather than in the Court of Session. It follows that questions which might raise civil law issues would be at least as likely to surface in the sheriff courts as in the Court of Session and to be handled by a solicitor, say, in Dumfries rather than by an advocate in Edinburgh. That being so, the sources of our law should really be accessible throughout Scotland. But what access would a practitioner in Dumfries have to the views of *Voet*? Against this modern background it would indeed be strange, I believe, if our system now deliberately chose to adopt a policy of attaching increased importance to works of which perhaps only one copy exists in Scotland and that copy is in the Advocates' Library. At the very least it would increase the time which lawyers would need for research – time for which their clients would pay. In truth a vision of our legal system deliberately attaching increased importance to the views of Latin authors of the 18th century or earlier, contained in books which are not readily available, is a vision of a system which would not work in the interests of clients.

Nor indeed should we yearn to make Scots law into some kind of civil law theme park in which visitors can inspect the last working model of an *actio communi dividundo*[31]. There is after all no particular virtue in using civil law materials to develop our law unless they happen to fit better into the existing scheme. Otherwise they carry with them no special hallmark of excellence. For example, although the late Sir *Thomas Smith* argued that the use of civil law authorities might help to advance our law on delictual liability for economic loss[32], not only

30 The Lord Macmillan Memorial, 1957 S.L.T. (News) 122.

31 Cf. *Upper Crathes Fishings Ltd. v. Bailey's Exrs.* 1991 S.C. 30.

32 *T. B. Smith*, Strange Gods: Crisis of Scots Law as a Civilian System, in: T. B. Smith, Studies Critical and Comparative, Edinburgh and New York, 1962, 72, at pp. 81 sqq.

has that not happened, but it is also obvious that the civil law is not necessarily the high road to extended liability in this field since German law, impeccably civilian in all its ways, protects a very much narrower range of interests than our law[33].

V. The South African Way

It may reasonably be argued that in recent years the South African courts have made much use of civilian materials and that this shows that such an approach can be made to work in a modern legal system. (The position is inevitably changing with the changes in the character of the Bar since black majority rule.) But even there, with judges and counsel who have a considerable familiarity with the old sources, one can detect certain real practical difficulties. In *Phame (Pty.) Ltd. v. Paizes*[34], for instance, the Appellate Division were required to rule on the scope of the aedilician remedies in sale in modern South African law. The arguments and judgment are replete with references to the Digest and to a multitude of later civilian writers. For the translation of the former the Court relies on the infamous *Scott* translation, while for the later authorities the Court had the good fortune that junior counsel for the respondents happened to be a former lecturer in Latin who had produced translations acceptable to both sides. There are no former lecturers in Humanity at the Scottish bar, and perhaps not even the Cambridge Regius Professor of civil law could match the counsel "who reads Latin as facilely as Afrikaans and English"[35]. Even with that help at hand not everything goes smoothly.

The Appellate Division are concerned to trace the development of a seller's liability for statements made about the object being sold and they begin their consideration of the ancient Roman law by looking at the aediles' edict which had a provision about such statements – the exact scope and effect of which are not entirely clear[36]. *Holmes* J.A. refers to various passages of the Digest and quotes *Scott's* translation of D. 21, 1, 1, 1, *Ulpian* 1 *ad edictum aedilium curulium* for the text of part of the aediles' edict, dealing with a slave who is sold "contrary to what has been said and promised"[37]. Having done so, he goes out of his way to say: "the words translated 'said and promised' are *dictum et promissum*. They appear sometimes in the works of writers as *dictum promissumve* or, in the plural, *dicta promissave*". But in truth the words in the Digest which *Scott* translates as 'said and pro-

33 Cf. *R. Zimmermann*, The Law of Obligations: Roman Foundations of the Civilian Tradition, 1990, at pp. 1036 sqq. with references.

34 1973 (3) SA 397 (A).

35 1973 (3) SA 397 (A) at 410H describing J. C. de Wet who was counsel for the appellant. On the hearing, see *E. Kahn*, A Trimestrial Potpourri, (1992) 109 S.A.L.J. 344, at pp. 345 sqq.

36 Cf. *R. Monier*, La garantie contre les vices cachés dans la vente romaine, Paris, 1930, pp. 50 sqq.

37 Emphasis added by *Holmes* J.A.

mised' are not *dictum et promissum* at all but *dictum promissumve*[38]. And that this was indeed the wording of the edict itself is confirmed by other texts taken from the commentaries on it[39]. On one view it might be said that the court's mistake is just a trivial slip. But in reality it is more than that since, whether in ancient or in modern law, there is all the difference in the world between a provision which imposes liability for something 'said or promised' and one which imposes liability for something 'said and promised'. Indeed the development of this branch of the law would have been different if the provision had read *dictum et promissum*. If the Appellate Division could make such a mistake despite the judges' wealth of experience in handling civil law material, similar difficulties would doubtless lie in wait for courts in Scotland if they were to embark on a series of adventures among the original Roman law sources.

VI. Civilian Texts and the Courts' Decisions

In *Phame* the judges' consideration of the equities of the situation led them to the same conclusion as their understanding of the relevant authorities[40]. It is therefore not entirely clear to what extent in that case the Appellate Division would have felt free to reject the doctrine in the old authorities which they examined with such great care, though one gets a strong impression that in the end they were concerned above all to lay down law which was suitable for a modern society.

In much the same way one cannot help wondering whether the decision of the Court of Session in *Morgan Guaranty* – to allow the *condictio indebiti* even where the error was one of law – really should be seen as resting on the decision of the Court of Session in *Stirling v. Earl of Lauderdale*[41] in 1733 which meant, according to Lord *Clyde*, that the question "was not technically open to decision, as was taken to be the situation in 1959"[42]. Suppose that, when uncovered, the papers in *Stirling* had revealed that the decision had been misreported and that the case had been decided in the opposite sense after full argument on the civilian authorities. Is it really to be supposed that the Court of Session would have felt itself constrained to stand back from all the modern developments in other jurisdictions and hold that

38 "Quodsi mancipium adversus ea venisset, sive adversus quod dictum promissumve fuerit cum veniret fuisset..." Not only is the translation of "dictum promissumve" wrong, but there are serious errors in the rest of the short extract.

39 For the text of the edict, see *O. Lenel*, Das Edictum Perpetuum, 3rd ed., Leipzig, 1927, p. 555 and on *dictum promissumve* see n. 9. Aspects of the text are by no means free from difficulties. See, for example, the discussion in *F. Pringsheim*, The Decisive Moment for Aedilician Liability, in: F. Pringsheim, Gesammelte Abhandlungen, vol. 2, Heidelberg, 1961, 171, at pp. 172 sqq.

40 1973 (3) SA 397 (A) at 416B-E.

41 (1733) Mor. 2930.

42 1995 S.C. at p. 172A.

error in law could not found an action of repetition? One rather suspects not – which simply suggests that *Stirling* was a convenient peg on which to hang the decision which the five judges wished to adopt, but that the Court really reached its view not because the judges had settled the law in 1733 but because "there were good reasons for doing this on logical grounds as well as on grounds of equity"[43]. A proper consideration of the civil law writers may indeed be a way of ensuring that any new decision is taken on a basis which fits in with the rest of the law relating to that subject-matter. For the rest, precisely because they are in no sense binding on the Court, the views of those writers, even supposing that they actually relate to the particular problem being considered by the Court, are perhaps unlikely in themselves to be decisive one way or the other, unless they happen to coincide with the view which the Court is minded to adopt on the merits.

Certainly there is no sign in the judgments in *Morgan Guaranty* that their Lordships were concerned with the detail of the Roman law texts. The Lord President mentioned the well-known fact that the Digest texts on the *condictio indebiti* do not distinguish between errors of law and errors of fact[44]. But he also quoted the first sentence of C. 1, 18, 10, a constitution of *Diocletian* and *Maximian* of 294 A.D. which does make the distinction and says that repayment is available only when the payment was made due to an error of fact. Having quoted the text, however, the Lord President does not refer to it again except in so far as it features in one of the extracts from the pleadings in *Stirling* set out later in his opinion[45]. So – wisely – the judges do not attempt to explain the development of the doctrine in Roman law, nor do they claim to be able to reconcile the various approaches. It would have been an unrewarding task at best, if only because the argument about the relevance of the distinction between errors of law and errors of fact has raged over the centuries partly at least because the Roman texts are inconclusive. *Morgan Guaranty* therefore tends to confirm the observation[46] that our courts are most likely to be asked to look at Roman law texts in those cases where they do not actually provide an answer. If they had provided an answer, the point would probably not have been litigated today because it would have been settled long ago.

VII. Brocards and Maxims

Because much of the detail of the civil law is either rather inaccessible or else is all too obviously inappropriate for a modern system, practitioners and judges have always attached importance to Latin tags or brocards which encapsulate some as-

43 1995 S.C. at p. 164F per Lord President *Hope*.

44 1995 S.C. at p. 157H.

45 1995 S.C. at p. 162D.

46 Cf. *Rodger* (n. 8) 210.

pect of the law[47], e.g. *nasciturus pro jam nato habetur*[48], *nemo debet locupletari ex aliena jactura, periculum rei venditae nondum traditae est emptoris*[49], *ignorantia juris haud excusat.* But such rules are little more than leading strings for infants. Only rarely will they provide a worthwhile guide to the solution of a problem which is troubling a court. One such exceptional case perhaps was *Sharp v. Thomson*[50] where the brocard *traditionibus non nudis pactis rerum dominia transferuntur,* which comes ultimately from C. 2, 3, 20, a constitution of 293 A.D., was a useful reminder in a hard case of the path of virtue from which the courts were being urged to stray[51]. But, on the whole, matters are more complicated. For instance, it is not usually[52] the enrichment principle as such which is in issue but rather whether in the particular circumstances anyone is unjustifiably enriched, nor the principle that risk passes on the perfection of a sale but rather whether in the particular circumstances the sale is perfect[53]. On such points the brocards tell us nothing. Even where they are Roman in origin, they will often have been taken from a limited context and refashioned in a way which may have suppressed some of the qualifications which would have applied in practice[54]. Others date from a later period[55] and again, by reason of their brevity and apparent simplicity, may achieve a prominence which serves to obscure rather than to illuminate the correct development of the law. On one approach the key to the decision in *Morgan Guaranty* was the judges' determination to drive the non-Roman brocard *ignorantia juris haud excusat* from an area in which it should never have been applied[56].

---

47 Cf. *Cheape* (n. 3) 22 sqq.

48 Cf. *Elliot v. Joicey* 1935 S.C. (H.L.) 57, an appeal from the Court of Appeal in England which turned on the construction of a Scottish will. Lord *Macmillan* quotes D. 1, 5, 7 and Lord *Clyde*'s translation of *Craig*, Jus Feudale, 2, 13, 15, the last part of which seems to have no connexion with the Latin original. For a disrespectful review of the Scottish Law Commission's use of the brocard, see *A. Rodger*, Report of the Scottish Law Commission on Antenatal Injury, 1974 J.R. 83, at pp. 88 sqq.

49 *Sloans Dairies v. Glasgow Corporation* 1977 S.C. 223 discussed in *Rodger* (n. 8).

50 1995 S.L.T. 837.

51 The result was, of course, far from universally welcome. Interestingly enough, one practitioner described the Outer House decision which was affirmed in the Inner House as "an affront to any civilised – as opposed to civilian – legal system": *I. Doran*, Letter to the Editor, 1995 S.L.T. (News) 101, at p. 102.

52 See, however, *Royal Bank of Scotland p.l.c. v. Watt* (n. 27).

53 *Sloans Dairies Ltd. v. Glasgow Corporation* (n. 49).

54 See, above all, *D. Daube*, Zur Palingenesie einiger Klassikerfragmente, in: D. Cohen and D. Simon, edd., Collected Studies in Roman Law, Frankfurt am Main, 1991, 789; also *P. Stein*, Regulae Iuris, Aberdeen, 1967, esp. at pp. 118 sqq.

55 For an account of some of the later developments, see *Stein* (n. 54) esp. Chaps. 8 and 9.

56 1995 S.C. at p. 164F *per* Lord President *Hope*; at p. 172B *per* Lord *Clyde*; and at pp. 174-175 *per* Lord *Cullen*.

VIII. Classical Roman Law

Where a rule of law has been fashioned in a short formula, use of that short formula may give rise to methodological questions: should one use it in some loose way or should one pay some attention to the context in which it was originally set down? This question can be presented as involving a choice between concentrating on the ancient Roman law and looking at the whole development of the civil law since the Middle Ages[57]. It is said that "delving into the pure classical law" cannot be justified by "the utility of modern writings on classical Roman law in assisting with current legal problems"[58]. To the somewhat monotonous complaints about anglicisation of Scots law there is now added a complaint about the dominance of English professors of civil law with a fixation on "classical Roman law as the apogee of achievement"[59]. There are echoes of battles long ago in Germany before codification confined the professors of Roman law to their classrooms and re-echoes of controversies in Germany today[60].

Undeniably the doctrines of ancient Roman law were developed and often altered in the centuries after the Digest was discovered and those developments will often be of importance in understanding the basis for some aspect of Scots law. An obvious example is the transformation of the *actio de in rem verso* so that it came to shape a whole area of our law of unjustified enrichment. It is partly because the fact of this development was not properly appreciated that our law of unjustified enrichment seemed so confusing[61].

But the work of modern Romanist writers should not simply be swept aside. They are after all concerned actually to understand what the texts say and why they say it. Drawing attention to their results may make you unpopular but may at the same time be of some value even to practitioners. So, if the House of Lords has stated the law on an aspect of potestative conditions too widely, it would seem churlish to suppress that information simply because the point was clarified in a

57 Cf. *D. L. Carey Miller*, The Use of Roman Law in Scotland: A Reply, 1975 J.R. 64.

58 *D. L. Carey Miller* (n. 57) 69.

59 *Evans-Jones* (n. 1) 500. It is noteworthy that, contrary to the tenor of Dr. *Evans-Jones*' remarks, Professor *Stein* and Professor *Birks* both made extremely important contributions to thinking on problems in Scots Law.

60 Cf., for instance, *B. Windscheid*, Das römische Recht in Deutschland, in: P. Oertmann, ed., Reden und Abhandlungen, Leipzig, 1904, 25 which was recently cited by Professor *Zimmermann* in "Heard melodies are sweet, but those unheard are sweeter ...": Condicio tacita, implied condition, und die Fortbildung des europäischen Vertragsrechts, AcP 193 (1993) 121, at pp. 172 sq. *Zimmermann* heightens his effect by a certain cutting of *Windscheid*'s original. On the reception given to *Zimmermann*'s lecture see *W. Wiegand*, Back to the Future, Rechtshistorisches Journal 12 (1993) 277 and *R. M. Kiesow*, Anfang und Ende eines Kongresses, Rechtshistorisches Journal 12 (1993) 485, at pp. 486 sqq.

61 See *H. L. MacQueen, W. D. H. Sellar*, Unjust Enrichment in Scots Law, in: E.J.H. Schrage, ed., Unjust Enrichment: The Comparative Legal History of the Law of Restitution, Berlin, 1995, 289, at pp. 300 sqq.

brilliant and accessible article on classical Roman law[62]. Similarly if, in a passage examined by the House of Lords[63], *Bell* refers to an apparently puzzling statement of the Roman jurist *Paul*[64] about the law of pledge and to *Voet*'s criticism of it, then even practitioners might find it useful to know that *Paul* was actually writing about *fiducia* and that interpolation accounts for the particular form of the statement found in the Digest[65]. Certainly no explanation of the text which ignores this fact will be persuasive[66]. Equally there seems to be little harm in drawing attention to the origins of D. 22, 6, 7, *Papinian* 19 *quaestionum*[67] as a factor[68] in any argument that our courts should not treat that text as helpful in considering remedies for the recovery of property which has been transferred in error[69]. After all it is usually regarded as good practice to consider legal propositions in their appropriate context and as bad practice to apply them in different contexts for which they may not have been framed.

If indeed then the Scottish courts are to be asked to look at material from Roman law, it seems only sensible to do everything necessary to explain any difficulties since the judges can hardly be expected to adopt blindly what is not binding on them and what truly moreover cannot be understood without the insights of modern scholarship. More generally, to urge that courts should look at civilian materials but disregard the results of modern Romanist scholarship is like urging doctors to study biochemistry but to disregard the results of the discovery of D.N.A. In neither case would such an approach be the best recipe for success.

---

62 *D. Daube*, Condition Prevented from Materializing, in: *D. Daube*, Collected Studies (n. 54) 995 referred to in *A. Rodger*, Potestative Conditions, 1991 S.L.T. (News) 253.

63 *North-Western Bank v. Poynter, Son and Macdonalds* (1894) 22 Rettie (H.L.) 1, at p. 8.

64 D. 13, 7, 37, *Paul 5 ad Plautium.*

65 *O. Lenel*, Quellenforschungen in den Edictcommentaren, in: O Behrends and F. D'Ippolito, edd., Gesammelte Schriften, vol. 1, Naples, 1990, p. 456. Cf. *O. Lenel*, Palingenesia Iuris Civilis, vol. 1, Leipzig, 1889, col. 1153, fragment 1111.

66 Cf. *A. Rodger*, Pledge of Bills of Lading in Scots Law, 1971 J.R. 193, at p. 206.

67 *Lenel*, Palingenesia (n. 65) vol. 1, col. 853, fragment 280, comparing D. 31, 79.

68 For others see *Zimmermann* (n. 33) 868 sqq. with references.

69 Cf. *Morgan Guaranty*, 1995 S.C. at p. 172B-C *per* Lord *Clyde*.

Placing the Civilian Influence in Scotland: A Roman-Dutch Perspective

By Daniel Visser

I. Through Panes of Slightly Irregular Glass, Or: Can the Civil Law Influence in Scotland and South Africa Be Compared?

> "The duet that he knew from the concert halls of Europe came to Versluis in that living room in the interior of Africa, performed by an aged missionary and his son, as something strangely transformed, like a landscape seen through panes of slightly irregular glass or an image slightly distorted by its reflection in an antique mirror. A mixture of doubt and recognition was evoked in its perception, so that there was a tenuous moment of uncertainty in which one asked oneself, is it or is it not?"

This passage from *Karel Schoeman*'s taut novel of displacement, 'Another Country'[1], may serve as a metaphor of the inevitable distortions that the civilian tradition has undergone in South Africa. In the same way that Roman law itself was transformed during its reception into the pre-existing legal systems of the various regions of Europe, the importation into South Africa of the result of that process of reception, namely the Roman-Dutch version of the *ius commune*, quite naturally came to reflect the outcome of the intellectual, social and economic currents that have shaped this continent. Here in South Africa the settlers were far removed from the concerns that determined the nature of civil society in Europe. We need only remind ourselves that when Holland experienced the apex of her golden age of achievement, the small settlement at the Cape was a forlorn victualling station for the mother country; when the enlightenment spread across Europe, when Scots such as *Adam Smith* and *David Hume* "changed the whole current of European thought and life"[2], the now considerably larger settlement at the southern tip of Africa remained a slave society; when the industrial revolution swept Europe into the modern age the settler community in South Africa was essentially agricultural; when Europe turned to social democracy after World War II and set its face against racial discrimination, South African law retained much of its 19th century

[1] Translated into English by David Schalkwyk and published by Sinclair-Stevenson, London, in 1991.

[2] *Kenneth Clark*, Civilisation: A Personal View, 1969, at p. 259.

character, and at the same time became the tool of the State in implementing a system of institutionalized discrimination. (Clearly South Africa was not completely isolated from European trends; it is just that its geographical isolation often led to the intellectual mood not being synchronized with that of Europe – and that frequently at critical junctures.) Of considerable importance, furthermore, is the fact that the civil law lives on in South Africa in an uncodified form (albeit spatially displaced), while it manifests itself in codified form on the continent of Europe. In addition, the transformation that the heavy influence of English law has wrought on the Roman-Dutch law since the beginning of the 19th century is central to the cast of the civil law in South Africa[3]. It should, therefore, not elicit any surprise that in the end the civilian tradition in South Africa came to be rather different from the European variation.

Scotland, on the other hand, is a part of Europe, and its legal system could, in the course of its development, always draw on the intellectual and social movements that made themselves heard across the North Sea. And it did indeed do so – in varying degrees, depending on the socio-political climate of the time. At the same time, the Scottish intellectual tradition was an important force in the shaping of the European mind. Of course Scotland is a unique part of Europe and its empathy with continental thinking has varied from time to time, but essentially it is a European country. Yet, despite this concord, the civilian tradition in Scotland, too, is very different from that of the Continent. *David Sellar* has written that two features in particular distinguish the history of Scots law from that of other systems in Europe: first, its great antiquity and continuity, reaching back as it does through Anglo-Norman influence to Celtic and Saxon law of a time before written records

---

3 On the mixed legal system in South Africa see generally *B. Beinart*, The English Legal Contribution in South Africa: The Interaction of Civil and Common Law, 1981 Acta Juridica 7; *Reinhard Zimmermann*, Das römisch-holländische Recht in Südafrika, 1983, pp. 1 sqq.; *idem*, Synthesis in South African Private Law: Civil Law, Common Law and usus hodiernus pandectarum, (1986) 103 S.A.L.J. 259; *idem*, Roman Law in a Mixed Legal System: The South African Experience, in: Robin Evans-Jones, ed., The Civil Law Tradition in Scotland, 1995, pp. 41 sqq.; *D. L. Carey Miller*, South Africa: A Mixed System subject to Transcending Forces, in: Esin Orücü, Elspeth Attwooll and Sean Coyle, edd., Studies in Legal Systems: Mixed and Mixing, 1996, pp. 165 sqq.; *D. P. Visser*, Daedalus in the Supreme Court – The Common Law Today, (1986) 49 T.H.R.H.R. 127; *O. D. Schreiner*, The Contribution of English Law to South African Law: and the Rule of Law in South Africa, 1967, at pp. 5 sqq.; *C. F. Forsyth*, In Danger for their Talents: A Study of the Appellate Division of the Supreme Court of South Africa 1950-80, 1985, at pp. 182 sqq.; *H. J. Erasmus*, Roman Law in South Africa Today, (1989) 106 S.A.L.J. 666, at pp. 669 sqq.; *H. B. Fine*, The Administration of Criminal Justice at the Cape of Good Hope 1795-1828, unpublished Ph.D. thesis, University of Cape Town, 1991, at pp. 1-106 ; *Stephen D. Girvin*, The Influence of a British Legal Education and Practice at the Bar on the Judges appointed to the Supreme Courts of Southern Africa 1827-1910, unpublished Ph.D. thesis, University of Aberdeen, 1990; *Edwin Cameron*, Legal Chauvinism, Executivemindedness and Justice: L. C. Steyn's Impact on South African Law, (1982) 99 S.A.L.J. 38; *Adrienne van Blerk*, The Irony of Labels, (1982) 99 S.A.L.J. 365; *idem*, The Genesis of the "Modernist-Purist" Debate, (1984) 47 T.H.R.H.R. 255; *H. J. Erasmus*, Thoughts on Private Law in a Future South Africa, 1994 Stellenbosch L.R. 105.

(without having been interrupted by any significant revolution or codification); and, secondly, its equivocal position between the common law and the civil law[4]. The influence of English law has meant that the received civil law acquired a distinctive character in Scotland, so that whenever one observes a particular rudiment of Roman law in Scots law, one is often prompted to wonder: Is it, or is it not?

Scots law and South African law have, therefore, both important similarities and dissimilarities. The differences between the two legal systems indicate that one has to proceed with caution when comparing Scots and South African law, and the question is whether the resemblance between the two systems is of sufficient substance to make comparison of these systems particularly meaningful. That is to say, are the twin facts that there are (differently configured) vestiges of Roman law in both Scots and South African law, and that each owes a debt to the common law for its present shape, sufficiently unusual so as to offer a special opportunity for each of these systems to learn more about itself by looking at the other? Or do claims that Scots and South African law share a special affinity merely amount to another device in the repertoire of nationalists with ulterior motives? One may move some way towards answering these questions, I believe, by considering, first, certain aspects of the structure of these legal systems and how that structure impacts on the development of the law.

II. The Structure of Scots and South African Law

1. Institutional Writings as a Source of Law

There are not many legal systems in the world that exhibit the unusual feature of having been shaped by both the great legal traditions of the Western world. Just how much of the civil law forms part of the present Scots law, or how much formed part of it in the past, is much debated in Scotland, but that debate is not of central importance to my argument[5]. First, I am interested in *the fact that there has been civilian influence*: for once any legal system has had such influence it is seldom completely removed; sublimated, perhaps, but not removed. The fact that chickens were first domesticated in India, leading to the regular ingestion of the eggs of these birds, is hardly uppermost in our minds at the breakfast table, but the

---

4 *W. D. H. Sellar*, A Historical Perspective, in: Michael C. Meston, W.D.H. Sellar, and the Rt. Hon. Lord Cooper, The Scottish Legal Tradition, Scott C. Styles, ed., 1991, p. 29.

5 For and overview of the debate, see *Niall R. Whitty*, The Civilian Tradition and Debates on Scots Law, 1996 T.S.A.R. 227. See further *H. L. MacQueen*, Common Law and Feudal Society in Medieval Scotland, 1993, pp. 2 sqq.; *A. McCall-Smith*, Scots Law in a Comparative Context, in: J. P. Grant, ed., Independence and Devolution. The Legal Implications for Scotland, 1976, pp. 153 sqq., at p. 157; *R. Evans-Jones*, Some Reflections of the condictio indebiti in a Mixed Legal System, (1994) 111 S.A.L.J. 759; *idem*, Roman Law in Britain (sic) Scotland, Rechtshistorisches Journal 13 (1994) 494; *idem*, Unjustified Enrichment, Contract and the Third Reception of Roman Law in Scotland, (1883) 109 L.Q.R. 663.

sublimation of the history of this bit of acculturation can never take away that our way of doing things contains this fragment, amongst many others, of Indian culture. Secondly, I am interested in the fact that the two countries do not only share a civilian influence, but that there were *similar patterns of reception* of Roman law into early Roman-Dutch and Scots law, while the resultant mix was *captured in the same way* in "great synthesizing works"[6] that were destined to be extremely influential in the later development of each system: the 'Introduction to Dutch Jurisprudence' by *Hugo Grotius*[7] in the Netherlands and the 'Institutions of the Law of Scotland' by *James Dalrymple*, Viscount *Stair* in Scotland[8]; also, Scots law was strongly influenced by Dutch law in the crucial period when some of the most important of these institutional treatises were written[9]. Thirdly, I am interested in the fact that each system has, as an important part of its constituent elements, a large measure of common law principles; and the particular civilian/common law mix of each system has in important ways been determined by similar forces[10].

The close links of each system to the Roman-Dutch law in the crucial period of the 17th and 18th centuries as well as the shared common law experience have resulted in the two systems being peculiarly intelligible to each other. It is true that English law has had a far longer and far more intense influence on Scots law than it has had on South African law, and that, consequently, the civilian basis of South African law is much broader than that of Scots law. But nevertheless the approach to the law and indeed the substantive law in regard to a great many issues in one of the systems are more often than not instantly recognizable to a lawyer from the

6 *T. B. Smith*, Scots Law and Roman-Dutch Law: A Shared Tradition, 1961 J.R. 32, at p. 34. On Roman-Dutch law generally see *Reinhard Zimmermann*, Römisch-holländisches Recht – ein Überblick, in: Robert Feenstra and Reinhard Zimmermann, edd., Das römisch-holländische Recht: Fortschritte des Zivilrechts im 17. und 18. Jahrhundert, 1992, pp. 9 sqq. and the other contributions to that volume.

7 *Hugo de Groot*, Inleidinge tot de Hollandsche Rechts-geleerdheid, F. Dovring, H.F.W.D. Fischer, E.M. Meijers, edd., Leiden, 1965.

8 The 2nd ed., 1693, should be used.

9 See e.g. *T. B. Smith*, Strange Gods: The Crisis of Scots Law as a Civilian System, 1959 J.R. 119, at p. 128; *idem* (n. 6) 39; *Peter Stein*, The Influence of Roman Law in the Law of Scotland, 1963 J.R. 205; *Robert Feenstra*, Scottish-Dutch Legal Relations in the 17th and 18th Centuries, in: H. de Ridder-Symeons and J.M. Fletcher, edd., Academic Relations between the Low Countries and the British Isles 1450-1700 [Proceedings of the First Conference of Belgian, British and Dutch Historians of Universities held in Ghent, 30th September – 2nd October 1987], 1989, at pp. 25 sqq.

10 On mixed systems generally see *Peter Stein*, Relationships among Roman Law, Common Law and Modern Civil Law, (1992) 66 Tulane L.R. 1587; *Joachim Zekoll*, Zwischen den Welten – Das Privatrecht von Louisiana als europäisch-amerikanische Mischrechtsordnung, in: Reinhard Zimmermann, ed., Amerikanische Rechtskultur und europäisches Privatrecht: Impressionen aus der neuen Welt, 1995, pp. 11 sqq.; *Reinhard Zimmermann*, Roman Law in a Mixed Legal System: The South African Experience (n. 3); *Reinhard Zimmermann* and *Daniel Visser*, South African Law as a Mixed Legal System, in: Reinhard Zimmermann and Daniel Visser, edd., Southern Cross: Common Law and Civil Law in South Africa, 1996, pp. 1 sqq.; *D. L. Carey Miller* (n. 3) 165 sqq.

other system. Indeed, the very fact that the debates within the systems are so similar (e.g. whether Scots law is a mixed system or not, or how much South African law owes to English law) indicates the affinity of the two systems.

I want to use the improbable fact of the institutional writers being a source of law (at least formally) as a basis for illustrating this affinity. This fact is, of course (except on rare occasions), unimportant to the daily application of the law in both countries, but at the same time it can tell us important things about the nature of law as it is practised in Scotland and South Africa[11].

With the clarity and conciseness that is characteristic of his work, Professor *Neil MacCormick*[12] argues that the notion of legislation being the primary source of valid law[13] is a rather modern view and that this notion brought in its wake the recasting of precedent as a source of law. It led to the view that "if all law is legislated law, then case law is legislated law and it is the judges who legislate it"[14]. *Stair* and *Grotius*, on the other hand, approached law from the opposite point of view, namely that Natural law is the primary source of law and that "long custom, especially 'learned custom' evolved by those experienced in handling practical problems (judges in particular), will more securely indicate what are sound deductions from basic principles than will most instant legislation"[15]. The judges in Scotland (and South Africa, it should be added) have turned the approach of the institutional writers on its head by also casting their works as an independent source of law, as a kind of legislation. *MacCormick* puts it thus:

> "The final irony is that the institutional writers' own works, works which could only have been written on the basis of a natural law theory which authorizes asserting as already law all principles conformable with 'reason', themselves come to be reclassified as 'sources of law' in the positivistic sense"[16].

---

11 On the Scots institutional writers, see *D. M. Walker*, Principles of Scottish Private Law, 3rd ed., 1982, at pp. 25 sqq.; *idem*, The Scottish Legal System, 5th ed., 1981, at pp. 452 sqq.; *T. B. Smith*, Scotland: The Development of its Laws and Constitution, 1962, at pp. 32 sqq.; *John W. Cairns*, Institutional Writings in Scotland Reconsidered, (1983) 4 J.L.H. 76. On the institutional writers that are authoritative in South Africa, see *H. R. Hahlo* and *Ellison Kahn*, The South African Legal System and its Background, 1973, at pp. 543 sqq.; *D. H. van Zyl*, Geskiednis van die Romeins-Hollandse Reg, 1979, at pp. 290 sqq.; *J. C. de Wet*, Die Ou Skrywers in Perspektief, 1988, at pp. 125 sqq.

12 *N. D. MacCormick*, Legal Reasoning and Legal Theory, 1978, at pp. 58 sqq.

13 The reasons for such a view are twofold, he explains: "Legislation is a unique source of law in that it yields what have been felicitously called 'rules in fixed verbal form', rules which have a uniquely authoritative formulation in the *ipsissima verba* of the legislature; and just because legislative power and legislative procedure are formally defined, we have in this case more or less exact criteria of validity which make it possible to distinguish reasonably clearly what is from what is not duly enacted law": *MacCormick* (n. 10) 58.

14 *MacCormick* (n. 10) 60.

15 *MacCormick* (n. 10) 59.

16 *MacCormick* (n. 10) 61.

Why has this happened? And why do the courts, in a modern age where the past is not a particularly popular guide to the future, continue to retain this source? I believe that there are clearly identifiable reasons (both content-based and content-independent) that explain why the courts in South Africa and Scotland have taken this path.

2. Content-Based Reasons

Despite the fact that in theory the institutional writers are regarded by the courts like some kind of legislation[17], they are in fact often cited for the common-sense solutions that their works tend to offer[18]: like *Stair*'s Natural law (which was in fact influenced by the work of *Grotius*)[19], *Grotius*' approach to Natural law rests on the notion that the principles of the *recta ratio* may be identified with reference to rational deduction from human nature and the general social organization of human beings, which reveals the basic precepts according to which one may determine whether conduct is right or wrong[20]. One should not overestimate the Natural law content of the 'Inleidinge', but *Grotius* clearly did not confine Natural law principles to the sphere of international law. He relied on these principles in formulating the principles of private law, not only to close the gaps that existed in the positive law, but also to effect a synthesis of the various local laws and the received Roman law[21].

One does not have to share the jusnaturalist approach of *Grotius* and *Stair* to realize that, since there are rarely more than two or three possible solutions to any

17 See e.g. *D. P. Visser* and *D. B. Hutchison*, Legislation from the Elysian Fields: The Roman-Dutch Authorities Settle an Old Dispute, (1988) 105 S.A.L.J. 630.

18 The intrinsic merit of these works was, after all, the reason why the institutional writers, over time, acquired special status (although they were not intended to have this status by their authors): see generally *Cairns* (n. 11) 98 sqq. In regard to the relative authoritativeness of institutional writers in Holland and South Africa, see *R. Feenstra* and *C. J. D. de Waal*, Seventeenth Century Leyden Law Professors and their Influence on the Development of the Civil Law, 1975, at pp. 52 sqq., 99 sqq., and *passim*.

19 *P. G. Stein*, Stair's General Concepts, in: Stair Tercentenary Studies, David M. Walker, ed., 1981, p. 181.

20 *J. D. Van der Vyver*, Die Regsfilosofie van Hugo de Groot, (1983) 46 T.H.R.H.R. 151; *D. L. Carey Miller*, Hugo Grotius: Born 1583: The Lasting Impact of a Man of the 17th Century, 1982 Acta Juridica 66.

21 See generally *Karl Wellschmied*, Zur Inleidinge tot de Hollandse Rechts-geleerdheid des Hugo Grotius, T.R. 20 (1952) 415; *H.F.W.D. Fischer*, Book Review of *Wellschmied*'s Hugo Grotius' Inleidinge tot de Hollandse Rechts-geleerdheid und das Recht seiner Zeit, doctoral thesis, University of Göttingen, 1950, T.R. 20 (1952) 189; *Robert Feenstra*, Grotius' Doctrine of Unjust Enrichment as a Source of Obligation: Its Origin and Its Influence in Roman-Dutch Law, in: Unjust Enrichment. The Comparative Legal History of the Law of Restitution, Eltjo J.H. Schrage, ed., 1995, p. 197; *D. P. Visser*, Die Invloede op Hugo de Groot, (1993) 56 T.H.R.H.R. 136, at pp. 141 sqq.; *Zimmermann* (n. 6) 26 sqq.

given problem, their works (as well as those of the other institutional writers who took their lead from these authors) often contain solutions that could serve as the basis for modern judgments. It follows then that this inherent, content-based persuasiveness is probably an important reason for the institutional writers being maintained as a source of law. The recent decisions in South Africa and Scotland on the question of error of law in the context of the *condictio indebiti* offer a convenient basis to illustrate this fact.

In *Morgan Guaranty Trust Company of New York v. Lothian Regional Council*[22] the Inner House of the Court of Session held that money paid under a so-called 'swap agreement', which had been declared void, was recoverable with the *condictio indebiti* even though it was made in error of law. Somewhat earlier, the South African Appellate Division had, in a case involving the overpayment of tax – *Willis Faber Enthoven (Pty.) Ltd. v. Receiver of Revenue*[23] – likewise ruled that an error of law was in principle not a bar to the *condictio indebiti*. For present purposes I will confine myself to an investigation of the way in which both courts justified their decisions.

(a) The *Morgan Guaranty* Case

In the *Morgan Guaranty* case Lord *Hope*, noting the long history of uncertainty and controversy in regard to the question of whether an error of law could found a claim for the return of a payment that was not due, stated that, of all the past cases on this question, three – each a century removed from the other – were particularly relevant: the early 18th century decision of *Stirling v. Earl of Lauderdale*[24], the case of *Wilson and McLellan v. Sinclair*[25] some hundred years later, and the 1959 judgment in *Glasgow Corporation v. Lord Advocate*[26]. In *Stirling v. Earl of Lauderdale* the Court had allowed the *condictio indebiti* in an instance in which there had been an error of law; in *Wilson and McLellan v. Sinclair* the *Earl of Lauderdale* case was considered not to constitute binding authority and the Court disallowed a claim for the return of an erroneous payment made in error of law; and in *Glasgow Corporation v. Lord Advocate* the Court confirmed this view. In his erudite judgment, Lord *Hope* reveals that *Wilson and McLellan v. Sinclair* was based on an erroneous assumption by Lord *Brougham* about the value of the *Earl of Lau-*

22 1995 S.C.L.R. 225. On this case see *Graeme T. Laurie*, Error of Law and Unjust Enrichment in Scotland, (1995) 112 L.Q.R. 379; *Mike Oldham*, Payments Made under Mistake of Law: A Legal Error Exposed in Scotland, (1995) 54 C.L.J. 246; *Niall R. Whitty* and *Daniel Visser*, Error of Law, Excusability and Unjustified Enrichment in South Africa and Scotland, (forthcoming).

23 1992 (4) S.A. 202 (A).

24 (1733) Mor. 2930.

25 (1830) 4 W. & S. 398.

26 1959 S.C. 203.

derdale case as a precedent. Because of the brevity of the report (one line in 'Morison's Dictionary') Lord *Brougham* had not attached any weight to it. Due to the diligence of counsel in the present case, however, it was revealed that the matter had been fully argued before the Court in the *Earl of Lauderdale* case and that all the authority, both pro and contra, had been put before the court. C. 1, 18, 10 as well as the Humanists *Cujacius*, *Perezius* and *Donellus* were referred to as disallowing the recovery of a payment made in error of law. The other side had relied on the fact that, in the whole of the rubric in the Digest devoted to the *condictio indebiti*, not one text limited the action to instances where the payment had been made in error of fact; furthermore, counsel had cited *Hugo Grotius*, *Van Leeuwen* and *Stair* as approving of the view that no such limitation should be placed on the recovery of erroneous payments. In the course of his judgment Lord *Hope* showed that, although the opinions of the judges in the *Earl of Lauderdale* case were not recorded, it is clear that, apart from having made their decision after very full argument on the matter, the judgement was in fact regarded, both in the subsequent works of institutional writers and in the court decisions that followed it, as having settled the matter. Thus *Erskine*[27] relied on this decision for his view that "the Court of Session has justly sustained action even where the payment had proceeded upon an error of law" while a later edition of *Stair*[28] noted, with reference to (amongst other authority) *Stirling v. Earl of Lauderdale*, that, although *Stair* had not directly expressed himself on this point, the *condictio indebiti* would lie for a payment made under a mistake of either fact or law[29]. (Lord *Hope* also recorded that *Bankton*[30] had clearly stated that payment made in error of law "must be restored, where there is just cause to support it".) Therefore, Lord *Hope* held, that *Glasgow Corporation v. Lord Advocate* was a departure from established authority. In any event, his lordship added, the reasons given by Lord *Brougham* for his decision were not convincing: equity actually favoured allowing the recovery of a payment made *errore juris* rather than the converse, as Lord *Brougham*, Lord *Clyde* (whose son also delivered a judgment in the case) and certain judges in subsequent cases seemed to think.

In his judgment Lord *Hope* used the institutional writers in three different ways. First, to establish what the law was at the time of the decision in *Stirling v. Earl of Lauderdale* and during the century between this decision and the *Glasgow Corporation* case[31]; secondly, to give substance to *Stirling v. Earl of Lauderdale* as a precedent, by showing that it was reached after a thorough consideration of the institutional writers (and other civilian authorities)[32]; and, thirdly, to underscore the

27 *J. Erskine*, The Institutes of the Laws of Scotland, Edinburgh, 1775, 3, 3, 54.

28 *Viscount Stair*, Institution of the Law of Scotland, 3rd ed., J. S. More, ed., Edinburgh, 1832.

29 Note to *Stair* (n. 24) 1, 7, 9, cited in the opinion of Lord *Hope*, at 233A.

30 *Lord Bankton*, An Institute of the Laws of Scotland, Edinburgh, 1751-1753, 1, 8, 23 and 24, cited in the opinion of Lord *Hope*, at 232B.

31 See the opinion of Lord *Hope*, at 232A-233C.

equity of the decision reached by the Court in the present case[33]. In particular, it is important to note that, in overruling *Glasgow Corporation v. Lord Advocate* and reinstating *Stirling v. Earl of Lauderdale*, Lord *Hope* stressed the equitable basis of the decision not to apply the *ignorantia iuris* rule in relation to the *condictio indebiti*, and that he did so with specific reference to *Bankton*[34]. Put simply: the Court took the institutional writers seriously because their solution to problems before the Court commended itself both for its logic and its equitable nature[35].

(b) The *Willis Faber* Case

The same sentiment appears from the South African case. The position in South Africa had originally been determined by the 1888 case of *Rooth v. The State*[36], in which the relevant civilian authority, reflecting the centuries-old debate in regard to *error iuris* in the context of the *condictio indebiti*, had been fully, albeit unsystematically, reviewed. In that case, *Kotzé* C.J. held that error of law was a bar to the *condictio indebiti*; and this approach was followed (even if often reluctantly) until the *Willis Faber* case in 1992. In *Willis Faber* the Court once again surveyed the old authorities and said:

> "The fact of the matter is that the Court was faced with a situation where the Roman-Dutch writers whom we usually turn to for an exposition of the law were not in agreement. As Van den Heever J.A. explained in *Tjollo Ateljees (Eins) Bpk. v. Small* 1949 (1) S.A. 856 (A) at 874, in such a situation 'we may choose to rely upon those opinions which appear to us to be more conformable to reason' (and, I would add, more in conformance with the law and requirements of our time)"[37].

---

32 At 236A-237C.

33 At 238D.

34 At 238D. The reference was to *Bankton* (n. 26) 1, 8, 31. Lord *Hope* attached great importance to the consideration that equity demands that the parties in an action based on the *condictio indebiti* should be treated equally. He cited statements to this effect by counsel for the Earl of Lauderdale as well as by Lord *Ivory* in *Dickson v. Halbert* (1854) 16 D. 586 and concluded that "the absolute nature of the rule [i.e. *ignorantia iuris neminem excusat*] leaves no room for considerations of equity between the parties. It is out of place in a discussion about private rights, where a party is not seeking to be excused from his ignorance but is seeking to show merely that his payment was a mistaken one and not to be taken as a gift: see *Bankton* 1, 8, 31" (at 238D); later he added: "By removing the error of law rule, we will be providing a remedy which will *prima facie* be available in these cases, but whether it will or will not be given will depend in each case on considerations of equity" (at 238G).

35 Of course, not all references to the institutional writers are defensible: see generally *Alan Rodger*, Lord MacMillan's Speech in *Donoghue v. Stevenson*, (1992) 108 L.Q.R. 236.

36 (1888) 2 S.A.R. 259.

37 *Willis Faber Enthoven (Pty.) Ltd. v. Receiver of Revenue* 1992 (4) SA 202 (A) at 219I-J. On this case, see *Daniel P. Visser*, Error of Law and Mistaken Payments – A Milestone, (1992) 109 S.A.L.J. 177; *C.-J. Pretorius*, The condictio indebiti, Error of Law and Excusability, (1993) 56 T.H.R.H.R. 315.

Hefer J.A. after noting the fact that there is no logic in the distinction between error of law and error of fact for the purposes of the *condictio indebiti*, held as follows:

> "Considered as a matter of simple justice between man and man, there is no conceivable reason why the receiver of money received in error of fact should in the eyes of the law be in a better position than one who has received money paid in error of law"[38].

The learned judge continued and said that in *Rooth*'s case *Kotzé* C.J. had followed *Voet* and the other authorities that disallowed the *condictio indebiti* where payment had been made *errore iuris* because he had regarded that view as conforming to equity[39]. Since in the opinion of *Hefer* J.A. the converse was true, he felt free to follow *Grotius* and the others that allowed an action in these circumstances.

Once again the Court used the old authorities for three different purposes. Firstly, to establish what the Roman-Dutch law itself was in regard to this matter[40], secondly to undermine the authority of *Rooth*'s case by highlighting the fact that there was no unanimity amongst the Roman-Dutch writers, and, thirdly, to underscore its own view that the equities are in favour of allowing the reclamation of payments *errore iuris*. The fact is that the Court found the reasoning of a particular institutional authority convincing and adopted that reasoning.

3. Content-Independent Reasons – South Africa

But why do the courts choose to search in the works of the institutional writers for the first principles in terms of which to decide a new issue, or in terms of which to re-look at an old issue? It seems to me that one of the reasons why the courts have, in the course of the development of the law, instituted these works as sources of law, was to create an agreed starting point to consider new issues, or to reconsider old issues that have become controversial. Of course it would be possible to find principles for the development of the law in a variety of differently constituted sources, but the ingrained conservatism of lawyers and, more importantly, the fact that the principles that are found in sources that have moulded the law over a long period are likely not to disrupt the coherence of the legal system as a whole[41]. (And concern for coherence was an important concern for many of the judges who championed Roman-Dutch law. The professors at the universities of Cape Town,

38 At 221A-B.

39 At 265: "I can discover no equity in favour of the applicants, but rather the reverse; and here I wish to point out that the rule 'ignorance of the law is no excuse', and disallowing an action for the recovery of that which had been unduly paid, do not conflict with the principles of the *aequum et bonum* ...".

40 At 216H-219J.

41 *MacCormick* (n. 10) 52 sqq.

Stellenbosch and Pretoria have over many years emphasized the value of the systematics of civilian legal thought in producing a workable system. Quite naturally, when their students were eventually appointed to the bench, they began to shape the law in accordance with the ideals of symmetry and order that they were taught during their studies[42].) It did not matter, furthermore, that the particular authority dates from a period considerably removed in time from the present, for that is the way of the law: it accepts the appropriateness of a particular rule until there is convincing justification to remove it. (After all, in England the persuasiveness of the opinions of their own [Scots!] 'institutional writer' Lord *Mansfield* is not questioned merely because he wrote his judgments a long time ago.) But this school did not rely exclusively on the traditional authorities of the 17th and 18th centuries which they knew had to be reformed and adapted to modern needs. As *Forsyth* explains:

> "[I]nstead of finding that reforming influence in the reception of English law, as the pragmatists did, they [i.e. the so-called 'purists'] found it in Continental legal writing. The classical Roman-Dutch law was the starting point, but the ancient rules as well as existing precedents were to be subjected to extensive historical and comparative analysis. Only if that analysis revealed the established rule to be logically and systematically correct, should it be followed. The purist attitude did not seek, with the antiquarians, a legal system in which the pedigree of each rule was historically legitimate, but a system in which each rule was fitted into a single logically coherent framework of legal principle. The classical Roman-Dutch law was the purists' starting point, not their end point"[43].

Often, then, these writers, using the institutional writers as a front, brought the terminology, taxonomy and even solutions of modern Dutch, German and (to a lesser extent) French law into the South African law. When this happened the continental approach was often presented as the logical extension of that of the Roman-Dutch writers. Thus, for instance, authors on the law of delict and criminal law structured their textbooks around the continental approach to these subjects, which approach filtered into the case law as these authors gained prominence. In this way principles of Dutch and German law found their way into South African law, without the courts having had to refer directly to sources relating to the law of these countries. This practice brought much modern civilian learning into South African law, a process greatly facilitated by virtue of the fact that the Afrikaans-speaking academics enjoyed a linguistic affinity to at least two of the most influential European countries[44].

---

42 *Forsyth* (n. 3) 184.

43 *Forsyth* (n. 3) 184. On the influence of continental legal thought on South African academic lawyers see generally *Hugh Corder* and *Dennis Davis*, Law and Social Practice: An Introduction, in: Hugh Corder, ed., Essays on Law and Social Practice in South Africa, 1989, p. 9; *Reinhard Zimmermann* and *Charl Hugo*, Fortschritte der südafrikanischen Rechtswissenschaft im 20. Jahrhundert: Der Beitrag von J. C. de Wet (1912-1990), T.R. 60 (1992) 157.

44 See generally *Zimmermann* and *Visser* (n. 10) 1 sqq.

However, the very extent to which the pendulum has swung in favour of Roman-Dutch law in South Africa during the second half of this century indicates clearly that there must have been another, far more powerful, reason than mere concern for coherence that lay behind the concentrated attention devoted to the Roman-Dutch authorities: for the innate conservative approach of lawyers means that judges have to be specifically motivated to embark on a large scale revision of the law. Any judicial programme to reform the law that is as extensive as that which South Africa experienced since the 1950s, but especially in the 1960s and 1970s, must therefore inevitably give rise to the question: What force was driving it? And the answer is: nationalism[45].

Nationalism as a force in South African law has been around for a long time. The superimposing of English law onto the existing Roman-Dutch law after the occupation of the Cape in 1806 was motivated only partly by the derelict state in which the new colonialists found the administration of justice at the Cape[46]; and the renewed resurgence of English law after the Anglo-Boer war was also not entirely the result of the unconscious bias of English-trained judges[47]; and in the second half of this century the restoration of Roman-Dutch law was very much part of a wider political agenda[48]. Of course, the fortunes of Roman-Dutch and English law waxed and waned for a variety of reasons other than nationalistic tendencies of one kind or another. For example, Lord *De Villiers*, Chief Justice of the Cape Colony and later the first Chief Justice of the Union of South Africa was clearly inspired by nothing more sinister than a deep respect for Roman-Dutch law as a system when he did his part to mould a distinctive South African law out of the laws of both colonial powers[49]; and in the Transvaal, during the period directly after the Anglo-Boer war, one of the most impressive benches in the history of the country (led by Sir *James Rose-Innes* and hand picked by the British authorities) applied and adapted the Roman-Dutch law to the needs of the time in a way which

---

45 See in regard to the influence of nationalism in the development of South African law *Eduard Fagan*, Roman-Dutch Law in Its South African Context, in: Zimmermann / Visser (n. 10) 33 sqq.; *Forsyth* (n. 3) 223. See generally also *Alan Watson*, Legal Transplants: An Approach to Comparative Law, 1974, at p. 51.

46 See generally in regard to the anglicization policies of the British government after 1806, *Fine* (n. 3) 1 sqq.

47 Which is underlined by the fact that the University of Leiden considered it necessary to create a chair in South African law in order that young Afrikaners may study their law and the law of South Africa remain orientated towards the civil law tradition. The first – and only – incumbent was *Melius de Villiers*, brother of Lord *de Villiers*, the first Chief Justice of the Union of South Africa in 1910.

48 See generally *Forsyth* (n. 3) 1 sqq.; *Carey Miller* (n. 3) 165 sqq.

49 On Lord de Villiers see generally *E.A. Walker*, Lord de Villiers and His Times, 1925, at pp. 1 sqq.; *H. Corder*, Judges at Work, 1984, at pp. 34 sqq.; *M. M. Corbett*, Lord de Villiers of Wynberg, (1994) 111 S.A.L.J. 373; *Reinhard Zimmermann*, De Villiers, John Henry, in: Juristen: Ein biographisches Lexikon, Michael Stolleis, ed., 1995, pp. 160 sq.; *Stephen D. Girvin*, The Architects of the Mixed Legal System, in: Zimmermann / Visser (n. 10) 119 sqq.

did much to preserve its influence[50]. But, that having been said, over the years nationalism was the strongest force that influenced the vicissitudes of Roman-Dutch and English law in South Africa. As it happened, when the Afrikaner nationalist movement managed to win political power in 1948 English law held a particularly strong position in South African law. The agenda of the new government included appointing an increased number of Afrikaans-speaking judges to the Supreme Court and many of them shared, of course, the nationalist ideals of the government of the day and saw the courtroom as an arena of struggle against, as they saw it, English hegemony in all fields, including the law – and the result was a civilian revolution of considerable proportions. Although the Roman-Dutch law had always had some of its most distinguished exponents amongst the English judges[51], the competing ideologies in relation to the composition of South African law were now firmly part of the political struggle between Afrikaans and English speaking South Africans (which for a long time in our history was what was meant when the 'racial question' was referred to).

The outcome of the notorious *bellum juridicum*[52] between 'purists' and 'pragmatists' for the soul of South African law was a mixed one. On the one hand the increased influence of the civilian tradition meant that important parts of the law that had hitherto been rather less than transparent, were transformed into systematized, coherent systems – one thinks immediately of the areas of contract, delict and criminal law, where the theories of *J. C. de Wet*[53], *W. A. Joubert*[54], *N. J. J. van der Merwe*[55] and others were transformed into judgments by judges such as *Lucas Steyn*[56] and *Frans Rumpff*[57]. On the other hand, these reforms often included changes on the basis of Roman-Dutch law that were made seemingly for the sole reason to remove the influence of English law – more often than not with less than happy results. At the same time the pre-occupation of so many judges with the structure of the law, rather than with justice, meant that the admiration for their achievement was marred by human rights abuses that went uncensured by the court[58].

---

50 On Sir James Rose-Innes see generally *Corder* (n. 49) 35 sq.; *Reinhard Zimmermann*, Innes, James Rose, in: Juristen: Ein biographisches Lexikon, Michael Stolleis, ed., 1995, pp. 312 sq.; *Girvin* (n. 49) 121.

51 See generally *Girvin* (n. 49) 95 sqq.

52 Cf. the works quoted above (n. 3).

53 In regard to the work of Professor *J. C. de Wet* see generally *Zimmermann* and *Hugo* (n. 43) 157 sqq. and *Edwin Cameron*, Lawyers, Language and Politics – In Memory of J. C. de Wet and W.A. Joubert, (1993) 110 S.A.L.J. 51.

54 In respect of the work of Professor *W. A. Joubert*, see *Cameron* (n. 53) 51 sqq.

55 See *P. Q. R. Boberg*, The Law of Delict, Volume I: Aquilian Liability, 1984, ix.

56 On *Steyn*, see *Cameron* (n. 3) 38 sqq.

57 On *Rumpff*'s influence see *P. Q. R. Boberg*, Defamation South African Style – The Odyssey of *animus iniuriandi*, in: Coenraad Visser, ed., Essays in Honour of Ellison Kahn, 1989, p. 35.

4. Content-Independent Reasons – Scotland

In Scotland, too, nationalism (albeit with a different content) has played a role in the formation of the law. Scots law, like Roman-Dutch law, came to exist as an identifiable entity at least partly because of the nationalizing tendencies that emerged in European legal systems since the 17th century[59]. And in the 20th century *T.B. Smith*'s "neo-civilian crusade against uncritical anglicisation"[60] evidences the fact that also in Scotland nationalism could spill over into the making of the law. But there is an important difference between the developments in Scotland and South Africa: *Sir Thomas*'s campaign (and that of Lord *Cooper* before him) did not strike a chord with the judiciary. No doubt there are a variety of reasons why this was so, but it must at least partly be because he did not work out the details of how the renewed exploitation of the civil law – in the service of Scots law – should take place. Nor could he have done so alone, as he himself realized: "More urgent than material means" he said, "is the need for men and women willing and qualified to take their part in those heavy labours of scholarship which alone can achieve this end [i.e. to preserve Scots law as a civilian system]"[61]. And without any basis for the courts to use in developing the law along civilian lines, and indeed without the inspiration that such materials could bring to do so, no large scale revival was likely to take place. For the South African experience to have had an exact counterpart in Scotland a partnership between academic writers and the judiciary would have been necessary.

5. Summary

Although Scots and South African law have important points of similarity, and are therefore particularly intelligible to one another, the differing nationalist forces have left South Africa with a more overtly civilian system; and this difference in the structure of the law has, as we shall presently see, produced a dramatic dissimilarity in the way in which courts are able to approach the solution of problems before them.

---

58 See *Forsyth* (n. 3) 129 sqq.; *Adrienne van Blerk*, Judge and be Judged, 1988, at pp. 1 sqq; *John Dugard*, Human Rights and the South African Legal Order, 1978; *A.S. Matthews*, Freedom, State Security and the Rule of Law, 1986; and *Stephen Ellman*, In a Time of Trouble, 1992; *Reinhard Zimmermann*, "Turning and Turning in the Widening Gyre ...": Gegenwartsprobleme der Juristenausbildung in Südafrika, in: Verfassungsrecht und Völkerrecht: Gedächtnisschrift für Wilhelm Karl Geck, 1989, pp. 985 sqq.; *Carey Miller* (n. 10) 165 sqq.

59 See *Peter Stein*, The Influence of Roman Law on the Law of Scotland, 1963 J.R. 205; *T. B. Smith*, The Influence of the 'Auld Alliance' with France on the Law of Scotland, in: *T.B. Smith*, Studies Critical and Comparative, 1962, p. 27; *Whitty* (n. 5).

60 *Niall R. Whitty*, Some Trends and Issues in Scots Enrichment Law, 1994 J.R. 127.

61 *T. B. Smith*, Strange Gods: The Crisis of Scots Law as a Civilian System, 1959 J.R. 119, at p. 141. This point was made by *Niall Whitty* in a lecture at the University of Cape Town in September 1995: see *Whitty* (n. 5).

III. The Effect of the Structure of the Law on its Development

1. Mixed Legal Systems

In my view the main value in comparing the two systems is to be found in the process by which the 'complex component'-structure of the law in the two countries has been a factor in the application and development of the law. This process may be illustrated by considering how in South Africa, much more than in Scotland, the structure of the law has created an extraordinary flexibility in the law.

Of course precedents may be overruled with an appeal to a number of different kinds of justification, but if one has at one's disposal an alternative source of law which theoretically has the same authority as a precedent, such justification is much easier. Let me attempt to explain: A very important fact about these two systems is that their civilian component is not codified, but imbricated into the case law and the other authoritative sources, namely the old authorities and (on rare occasions) specific legislation. In any codified mixed system that consists of both common law and civil law components, the civilian component (as indeed any other component) will be firmly entrenched, but will tend to be static, simply because the reform of a codified system is likely to be a very slow process – if indeed any reform is undertaken. Furthermore the power of judges to adapt the law is normally particularly constrained by the words of a code. In uncodified mixed systems of the same kind, on the other hand, the civilian component is encapsulated both in the precedents of the courts and in books by certain canonized authors, which the courts have declared to be authoritative. The extent of the civilian content of the law is therefore dependent on the attitude of judges. This means that the civil law element is likely to be less entrenched than in codified systems, but at the same time also less static: we know that in any legal system based on *stare decisis* a strong judge can make an important difference to the direction of the law; we know, too, that in systems that take academic writing seriously, authors can, likewise, have a major impact on the content of the law and the approach to problem-solving[62]. Comparing uncodified 'mixed' systems like Scots and South African law highlights the phenomenon (which I have described elsewhere[63]) that in such systems 'reception' remains a dynamic process and that powerful judges and compelling authors (often in combination with one another) are able to continue to oust the current rules (that hail from one of the constituent systems) and replace them by those of the other constituent system, sometimes even on a large scale. When a judge finds a principle laid down in a precedent to be in conflict with how he would prefer to decide the case, a system where the only source of law (apart from

---

62 In regard to the influence of academic writing on South African law generally, see *Reinhard Zimmermann*, Das römisch-holländische Recht in Südafrika, 1983, at pp. 41 sqq. and pp. 70 sqq.; *Zimmermann / Visser* (n. 10) 19 sqq.; but see *Susan Scott*, To burden or not to burden?, (1991) 54 T.H.R.H.R. 264.

63 (1986) 49 T.H.R.H.R. 127.

legislation) is precedent, that principle could probably be jettisoned only if the judge could present 'incontrovertible reasons' to justify the change; or, as Professor *MacCormick* says, a judge may normally adopt a solution that appeals to him on consequentialist grounds only if in doing so he does not break the "fundamental judicial commandment: Thou shalt not controvert established and binding rules of precedent"[64]. However, in a system which has institutional writers as a 'third source' the judge is able to appeal to the fact that the new rule which he seeks to introduce is already part of the body of the law, in that it is to be found in a work of one of the institutional writers; or vice versa he may appeal to English law in order to oust a civilian precedent embedded in the law.

2. The Effect of the Complex Component Structure – South Africa

In South Africa this possibility has indeed been utilized fully and the phenomenon has worked both ways, even if in the latter half of the 20th century established English principles were mostly replaced by Roman-Dutch ones. I mention only two examples. The jettisoning of the doctrine of 'nuisance' in *Regal v. African Superslate (Pty.) Ltd.*[65] is a prominent instance of the South African Appellate Division replacing established principles within the system by relying primarily on the fact that they were not of Roman-Dutch origin. Ever since *Holland v. Scott*[66] and *Austen Bros. v. Standard Diamond Mining Co. Ltd.*[67] it had been accepted that Roman-Dutch law and English law concerning the relations between neighbours were substantially the same and this led the English principles relating to 'nuisance' to dominate this field of law. In the *Regal* case, however, the Court produced the *deus ex machina* of the Roman-Dutch law as being the residual law of South Africa and ruled that it had not been superseded by English law[68]. On the other hand, the courts have also on many occasions, where a particular situation had been governed by a principle derived from Roman-Dutch law, invoked the English counter-principle as justification for changing the law. Thus the decision in *S.A.U.K. v. O'Malley*[69] (confirmed in *Pakendorff v. De Flamingh*[70]) featured a dramatic ousting of the Roman-Dutch based fault requirement in certain defamation claims. In *O'Malley* the then Chief Justice, Mr. Justice *Rumpff*, held *obiter* that, due to the powerful position of the press vis à vis the individual, *animus iniur-*

---

64 *MacCormick* (n. 10) 195 sqq. and 106-7.

65 1963 (1) S.A. 102 (A).

66 (1882) 2 E.D.C. 307.

67 (1882) 1 H.C.G. 363.

68 At 106E-G. See generally in regard to this saga *Forsyth* (n. 3) 198 sqq., and *Derek van der Merwe*, The Law of Neighbours, in: Zimmermann / Visser (n. 10) 759 sqq.

69 1977 (3) S.A. 394 (A); see, in this regard, *Forsyth* (n. 3) 204 sqq.

70 1982 (3) S.A. 146 (A).

iandi need not be proved in claims against the media[71]. The learned judge likened the South African common law[72] to a cord made up of different strands and explained that although the Roman-Dutch strand provided generally that there is no liability for defamation without the proof of *animus iniuriandi*, an English law strand had been absorbed in respect of claims against the media, making it unnecessary to plead and prove the existence of intention in such instances. In *Pakendorff*'s case the *obiter dictum* of *O'Malley*'s case became *ratio decidendi*. It is submitted that were it not for the device of being able to rely on the authority of English law as residual authority, the Court would have had to weigh the value of the reputation of the individual against the competing value of the freedom of press. However, since the Court could rely on English law in this way it could dispense with 'incontrovertible reasons' and freedom of the press was not even mentioned[73].

3. The Effect of the Complex Component Structure – Scotland

Scots law, in contrast, experienced this phenomenon in a more sublimated way and it has (at least since the 19th century) essentially been a one-way street – as might be expected, seeing that the House of Lords is the final Court of Appeal for Scotland. The approach of the Scots courts[74] has, of course, been far more subtle than that of the Lord Chancellor, Lord *Cranworth*, in *Bartonshill Coal Company v. Reid*[75], where he said that "in England the doctrine [i.e. of common employment] must be regarded as well settled; but if such be the law of England, on what ground can it be argued not to be the law of Scotland?" Nevertheless, there has been a steady accretion of English law to Scots law in the last two centuries based on an assumption that the two systems are the same – and as a result they have become increasingly the same. The Scots courts of course often do not follow English law. Thus, for example, Lord Justice-Clerk *Scott Dickson* said in *Copland v. Brogan* (a case dealing with a gratuitous mandatory)[76]:

---

71 At 407H.

72 In the sense of 'residual law'.

73 *Rumpff* C.J. was aware that English law in this regard was ameliorated by section 4 of the United Kingdom Defamation Act of 1952, which prescribes a procedure by which 'innocent' defamers may escape liability for defamation (and through which the edge is taken off the strict liability of the press for defamation), but said that if the legislature were to be of the opinion that innocent defamers (including the press and the radio) needed further protection, it would provide such protection at the appropriate time (at 158F). The new consitutional dispensation in South Africa has already seen to it that the freedom of the press will indeed be taken into account in the future: see the judgment of *Cameron* J. in *Holomisa v. Argus Newspaers Ltd.* 1996 (2) S.A. 588 (W) and *Du Plessis v. De Klerk*, 1996 (3) SA 850 (CC).

74 See in regard to this topic *Lord Roger of Earlsferry*, Roman Law in Britain, Rechtshistorisches Journal 12 (1993) 494, at p. 501.

75 (1858) 3 Macq. 266, at 285.

76 1916 S.C. 277.

"With regard to the English authorities which have been quoted, I have difficulty in accepting them as being in conformity with the law of Scotland, and I do not agree that the same rule of law as applies to gratuitous obligations under English law can be held as applying in this case".

(In this instance, it should be said, Scots law happened to differ not only from English law, but also from Roman law. Therefore, it represents one of the many cases of Scots law asserting its independence without reference to the civilian tradition.)

Furthermore, it is trite that the fabric of Scots law had in a significant measure been orientated towards English law by the style of legislation emanating from Westminster, although, it would seem, there is nowadays an increased awareness of the distinctiveness of Scots law[77].

The possibility of a legal system being able to 'pick and choose' from more than one residual law to solve new problems or to reconsider existing solutions to old problems, is able to produce a situation where the courts are able to approach judicial law-making in a rather more flexible and open-ended way than is usual in systems that take precedent seriously. In South Africa the courts have seized the opportunity to develop the law by making full use of the 'alternative' residual law as justification when they saw a need to change the law. In this way they have made (whatever their underlying motives might have been) the tension between the two legal traditions into an engine of change. In fact, at times the South African courts seemed to cross the threshold of tolerance that a legal system is able to show for the disregard of the value of consistency.

In Scotland, on the other hand, because the judiciary had not become part of the movement to revive the civilian tradition in the same way that so many of the South African judges did, the dual tradition did not lead to the value of consistency being taxed as much as it has been in South Africa. Of course the fact that the civil law and the common law have combined in the creation of Scots law has brought with it perhaps a greater degree of uncertainty than in purely common law systems. However, the point is that this 'natural' uncertainty was not compounded by an activist court choosing, sometimes somewhat recklessly, between the two systems; and thus we see that the differing levels of success of nationalism in the law produced very different approaches to judicial law-making in the two systems.

IV. And What About the Future?

South Africa's first democratic elections in April 1994 marked the beginning of a fundamental transformation of the country as a whole, including its laws. Already much has been done: important legislation has been passed and every month

---

77 See *Sellar* (n. 4) 53 sqq.

the law reports bring news of decisions in terms of the new (interim) Constitution that reinterpret the existing law in order to ensure that it conforms to the spirit of that document. Section 35 of the interim Constitution lays down that the courts should, in applying the common law (and here I use the term to mean 'residual law') as well as African customary law, have regard to the values laid down in the interim Constitution[78]. That means that the Constitution now becomes the paradigm within which the law will develop in the future. We can expect, for instance, that the negation of the freedom of the press, as evidenced in *Pakendorff v. De Flamingh*[79], will be reconsidered. And there will be many other challenges. The interim Constitution also makes it clear that African customary law should be accorded an increased status in South Africa and this is likely to lead to further changes. Thus, while the legal revolution brought about by the Purists found its inspiration in the *ius commune*, the current transformation takes the Constitution as its guiding light.

What, then, does this mean for the civilian tradition in South Africa? In the first place, one should keep in mind that the law, even in times of great change, is essentially a conservative discipline. When one sees Mr. Justice *Ismail Mahomed*, one of the leading civil rights lawyers during the Apartheid era, boldly extending the operation of the *Placaet van den Staten van Hollandt, tegens de Pachters ende Bruyckers van den Landen* of 26 September 1658 (which regulates the rights of tenant farmers and users of land to claim compensation)[80], or Mr. Acting Justice *Dikgang Moseneke*, former Vice-President of the Pan Africanist Congress, giving an erudite judgment on the *condictio indebiti*, in which he cites the Digest and the old authorities, one receives a powerful reminder of the durability of legal tradition[81]. Obviously the South African common law will be adapted in many ways, but it is now clear that it will be adapted only to conform to the needs of the present and not for the sake of a symbolic new beginning. In 1989 Albie Sachs (now Mr. Justice Sachs of the South African Constitutional Court) gave the lead when he argued that there is not much value in trying to oust the entire South African common law merely because of its colonial heritage. As it happens, our law, he said, came to us from Holland and Britain. If the pattern of colonial domination in Africa had been somewhat different, we might conceivably have ended up with law that was essentially French or Italian. Now all of this does not matter: the law of the colonial powers has been transformed into South African law and our energies should be directed at shaping it in a way that will increase its usefulness for all South Africans[82]. This view is widely accepted today. Of course, the new gen-

78 Act 200 of 1993. Section 35 reads: "In the interpretation of any law and the application and development of the common law and customary law, a court shall have due regard to the spirit, purport and objects of this chapter [chapter 3 on fundamental rights]".

79 *Supra*, n. 70.

80 *Palabora Mining Co. Ltd. v. Coetzer* 1993 (3) S.A. 306 (T).

81 See *Standard Bank of SA Ltd. v. ABSA Bank Ltd.* 1995 (2) S.A. 740 (T).

82 *Albie Sachs*, The Future of Roman-Dutch Law in South Africa, 1989, at p. 7.

erations of judges that will be appointed in the next few decades will not be going to the old authorities all too often for guidance, but the civilian component of the law is already anchored in the judgments of the courts and, in that way, will forever be part of our law.

In Scotland important forces are at work as well. In the first place the unfolding saga of the European Union and the possibility of legal integration will obviously be a major factor in the future development of Scots law. It has been suggested that this process might strengthen the civilian component of Scots law. I do not know whether that will indeed turn out to be the case, but it certainly is a possibility. Secondly there is a growing body of very impressive academic literature which is readily accessible to any person brought up in a civilian system and which doubtlessly will influence the future shape Scots law[83].

Once again different forces are shaping the destinies of Scots and South African law, but this time these forces might, unlike those of the 19th and 20th century, bring the two systems closer together. Each system remains a window to the civilian tradition with its own irregularities, and when we look at one another there is a double warp, but in spite of that, when we look through these windows, we see the same landscape.

83 See, e.g., *D. L. Carey Miller*, Corporeal Movables in Scots Law, 1991; *Kenneth G.C. Reid*, Property, in: Stair Memorial Encyclopaedia, vol. 18, 1993; *idem*, Unjustified Enrichment and Property Law, 1994 J.R. 167; *George Gretton*, Unjustified Enrichment in Scotland, 1992 Journal of Business Law 108; *Evans-Jones*, (1993) 109 L.Q.R. 663; *Hector L. MacQueen*, Unjustified Enrichment and Breach of Contract, 1994 J.R. 137; *Niall Whitty*, Some Trends and Issues in Scots Enrichment Law, 1994 J.R. 127; *idem*, Die Reform des schottischen Bereicherungsrechts, ZEuP 3 (1995) 216 sqq. For a general overview, see *Reinhard Zimmermann, Johann A. Dieckmann*, Das schottische Privatrecht im Spiegel seiner Literatur, ZEuP 3 (1995) 898 sqq.

The Civil Law in European Codes

By Reinhard Zimmermann

I. The European Codes: Background and Significance

I have been asked to talk about the civil law in European codes. This is not as straightforward a task as it may appear at first glance. We should, at the outset, therefore spend some minutes reflecting on the background, scope and significance of the terms used in the title of my lecture. A code, or codification, in the modern technical sense of the word, is a peculiar kind of statute. Like all other statutes, it is enacted by a legislature, and its application is therefore backed by the authority of the state for which that legislature is competent to make laws. Its characteristic features are, firstly, that a codification must aim at being comprehensive. It has to provide a regulation not only for a number of specific issues but has to cover a field of law in its entirety. Secondly, a codification constitutes an attempt to present its subject matter as a logically consistent whole of legal rules and institutions. It provides both the conceptual framework and intellectual fulcrum for any further doctrinal refinement and judicial or legislative development of the law.

Codification, as outlined in these few sentences[1], is a specific historical phenomenon that originated in late 17th and 18th century legal science[2]. It was an enormously influential idea, that managed, within hardly more than 150 years, to recast the entire legal tradition on the European continent. It was much less successful in England[3]. Hence, for the modern legal mind, European private law and codification have become inseparably linked to each other. In reality, however, there is nothing intrinsically self-evident about that connection. Before the age of codification European private law flourished, for many centuries, as a 'common law'[4].

---

[1] For a more detailed analysis, see *Reinhard Zimmermann*, Codification: History and Present Significance of an Idea, (1995) 3 European Review of Private Law 95 sqq.; for another recent assessment, see *Pierre Legrand*, Strange Power of Words: Codification Situated, (1994) 9 Tulane European and Civil Law Forum 1 sqq.

[2] Cf., e.g., *J. H. A. Lokin, W. J. Zwalve*, Hoofdstukken uit de Europese Codificatiegeschiedenis, 1990; *Helmut Coing*, Europäisches Privatrecht, vol. 1, 1985, pp. 67 sqq.; *idem*, Europäisches Privatrecht, vol. 2, 1989, pp. 7 sqq.

[3] Cf., e.g., *J. H. Baker*, An Introduction to English Legal History, 3rd ed., 1990, pp. 249 sqq.

[4] Cf. *Helmut Coing*, Europäisches Privatrecht, vol. 1, 1985, pp. 34 sqq., 124 sqq.; and see, most recently, *Reinhard Zimmermann*, Roman Law and European Legal Unity, in:

Moreover, it was ultimately based on Roman law, and Roman law itself was never codified. On the contrary, it was characterized by many features which a modern observer would associate with the English common law rather than the (modern) continental private law[5].

The two oldest codifications still in force today are the French 'code civil' of 1804 and the Austrian General Civil Code ('Allgemeines Bürgerliches Gesetzbuch') of 1811. They were preceded by the Prussian Code of 1794[6]. All three are usually referred to as the 'Natural law codes': their purpose was to put the entire law into systematic order in pursuance of a general plan for society[7]. During the 19th century, the idea of codification became intimately linked to the emergence of the modern nation-states[8]. This is particularly obvious in Germany[9], where the preparation of a German Civil Code immediately became a matter of great – practical as well as symbolic – significance in the years after the creation of the German Reich. By the time the German Civil Code ('Bürgerliches Gesetzbuch') came into effect (1st January 1900), just about all the other states of central, southern and eastern Europe had codified their private law[10]. In most instances, the French code civil provided the main source of inspiration. It continued to apply in Belgium and became the basis of the Dutch 'Burgerlijk Wetboek' of 1838. It provided the point of departure for the Italian 'codice civile' of 1865 (which could thus be enacted a mere four years after the kingdom of Italy had come into being), for the Portuguese 'código civil' of 1867, the Spanish 'código civil' of 1888/1889 and the Romanian Civil Code of 1865. The Serbian Civil Code of 1844, on the other hand, was influenced mainly by the Austrian codification.

The enactment of the German Civil Code, in turn, stimulated a revision of the Austrian code (which took effect in three stages during the years of the First World

---

A. S. Hartkamp, M. W. Hesselink *et al.*, edd., Towards a European Civil Code, 1994, pp. 67 sqq.; *Harold J. Berman, Charles Reid*, Römisches Recht in Europa und das ius commune, ZEuP 3 (1995) 3.

5 See *Peter Stein*, Roman Law, Common Law, and Civil Law, (1992) 66 Tulane L.R. 1591.

6 For an important new assessment, see *Andreas Schwennicke*, Die Entstehung der Einleitung des Preußischen Allgemeinen Landrechts von 1794, 1993. Cf. also the evaluation by *Gerhard Dilcher*, Die janusköpfige Kodifikation – das preußische Allgemeine Landrecht (1794) und die europäische Rechtsgeschichte, ZEuP 2 (1994) 446.

7 For a detailed discussion, now available in English, see *Franz Wieacker*, A History of Private Law in Europe, translated by *Tony Weir*, 1995, pp. 257 sqq.

8 Cf., e.g., *Franz Wieacker*, Der Kampf des 19. Jahrhunderts um die Nationalgesetzbücher, in: *idem*, Industriegesellschaft und Privatrechtsordnung, 1974, pp. 79 sqq.; *Reiner Schulze*, Vom ius commune zum Gemeinschaftsrecht, in: *idem*, ed., Europäische Rechts- und Verfassungsgeschichte, 1991, pp. 18 sqq.

9 See *Wieacker/Weir* (n. 7) 363 sqq.; *Michael John*, Politics and Law in Late Nineteenth-Century Germany, 1989.

10 For a general overview, see *Carlos Bollen, Gerard-René de Groot*, The Sources and Backgrounds of European Legal Systems, in: Hartkamp, Hesselink *et al.* (n. 4) 97 sqq.

War[11]) and it prompted the Greeks to codify their law; the Greek Civil Code, promulgated in 1940 but effective only from 1946, is generally considered to be part of the German legal family. Another member of that family is Switzerland, although both its Civil Code of 1907 and its revised code concerning the law of obligations of 1911 are in certain respects highly original and cannot be said to be modelled on the German code[12]. The Swiss experiences influenced the draftsmen of the new Italian Civil Code of 1942 without, however, inducing them to break radically with the French tradition[13]. A wholesale reception of the Swiss codes occurred in Turkey. Indeed, the idea of codification has shaped the civil law in many countries outside Europe, including regions as diverse as East Asia and Latin America; it managed to gain a foothold even in British India[14] and the United States of America[15]; and it asserted itself under radically different social and political conditions such as those prevailing in the former socialist states[16].

Even today, and in spite of gloomy visions usually associated with the term 'decodificazione'[17], codification is not a spent force. More than 50 states have codified their private law since 1945[18]. The most recent example in Western Europe are the Netherlands. Core parts of the Dutch Civil Code came into force on 1st January 1992, other parts had already been enacted in 1970, 1976 and 1991[19]. Many of the states of Eastern Europe have, since the fall of the 'Iron Curtain', embarked on ambitious recodification schemes[20]. On an international level we have the 'Convention on Contracts for the International Sale of Goods', concluded in

---

11 Cf. *Barbara Dölemeyer*, Die Teilnovellen zum ABGB, in: Herbert Hofmeister, ed., Kodifikation als Mittel der Politik, 1986, pp. 49 sqq.

12 *Wieacker/Weir* (n. 7) 387 sqq. More specifically on the relationship between the Swiss and German codes, see *Rudolf Gmür*, Das Schweizerische Zivilgesetzbuch verglichen mit dem Deutschen Bürgerlichen Gesetzbuch, 1965. On the influence of pandectist legal learning in 19th century Switzerland, cf., most recently, *Pio Caroni*, Die Schweizer Romanistik im 19. Jahrhundert, Zeitschrift für Neuere Rechtsgeschichte 16 (1994) 243 sqq.

13 For a recent evaluation, see *Giorgio Cian*, Fünfzig Jahre italienischer codice civile, ZEuP 1 (1993) 120 sqq.; and see the contributions in I Cinquant'Anni del Codice Civile, 2 vols., 1993.

14 *Bijay Kisor Acharyya*, Codification in British India, 1914 (Tagore Law Lectures).

15 For a recent analysis, see *Shael Herman*, Schicksal und Zukunft der Kodifikationsidee in Amerika, in: Reinhard Zimmermann, ed., Amerikanische Rechtskultur und europäisches Privatrecht: Impressionen aus der Neuen Welt, 1995, pp. 45 sqq.

16 For an overview, see *Konrad Zweigert, Hein Kötz*, Einführung in die Rechtsvergleichung auf dem Gebiete des Privatrechts, vol. I, 2nd ed., 1984, pp. 355 sqq.

17 *Natalino Irti*, L'età della decodificazione, 3rd ed., 1989.

18 Cf. *Rodolfo Sacco*, Codificare: modo superato di legiferare?, 1983 Rivista di diritto civile 117 sqq.; *Konrad Zweigert, Hans-Jürgen Puttfarken*, Allgemeines und Besonderes zur Kodifikation, in: Festschrift für Imre Zajtay, 1982, pp. 569 sqq.

19 Cf. the contributions in Franz Bydlinski, Theo Mayer-Maly, Johannes W. Pichler, edd., Renaissance der Idee der Kodifikation, 1991.

20 Cf., e.g., the report by *Miroslav Libuda*, ZEuP 3 (1995) 672 sqq. (focusing on Czech law); *Oleg Sadikov* Das neue Zivilgesetzbuch Rußlands, ZEuP 4 (1996) 259 sqq.

Vienna in 1980, which provides a codification of a particularly important area of international trade law. It has, to date, been adopted by close on 40 states[21]. And as far as the 'approximation' of the laws of the member states of the European Union in terms of the E.C. Treaty is concerned, the European Parliament has called for the preparation of a code for the entire European private law[22]. Code-like 'Principles of International Commercial Contracts' have been published by the 'International Institute for the Unification of Private Law' in 1994[23], and this year (1995) the first part of the 'Principles of European Contract Law', prepared by a 'Commission on European Contract Law', have appeared in print[24]. An express purpose of the latter initiative is to provide a basis for a future European Code of Contract Law.

II. Civil Law and the Civilian Tradition

1. The Meaning of Civil Law

Civil law, the other key term in the title to this lecture, is somewhat ambiguous. The Oxford Companion to Law, for instance, lists ten different meanings[25]. It may refer to the law applied to Roman citizens (as opposed to the *ius gentium*) or to the traditional core of Roman law, based on the XII Tables and on subsequent legislative enactments (as opposed to the *ius honorarium*, i.e. the body of law developed by the praetors). Sometimes it means Roman law at large, but it is also used as a synonym for private law. Civil law (as the entire body of state law) can be opposed to Canon law, but it can also (as a common denominator of the continental European legal systems) be contrasted to the English (or Anglo-American)[26] common law. These are probably the most important variations of the term in legal history, comparative law and modern jurisprudence. In the context of the present confer-

---

21 See *Ulrich Magnus*, Aktuelle Fragen des UN-Kaufrechts, ZEuP 1 (1993) 97 sqq.; *idem*, Stand und Entwicklung des UN-Kaufrechts, ZEuP 3 (1995) 202 sqq.; and Appendix I to *v. Caemmerer/Schlechtriem*, Kommentar zum Einheitlichen UN-Kaufrecht, 2nd ed., 1994.

22 For a discussion, see *Winfried Tilmann*, Eine Privatrechtskodifikation für die Europäische Gemeinschaft?, in: Peter-Christian Müller-Graff, ed., Gemeinsames Privatrecht in der Europäischen Gemeinschaft, 1993, pp. 485 sqq.; *idem*, Zweiter Kodifikationsbeschluß des Europäischen Parlaments, ZEuP 3 (1995) 534 sqq.

23 For a discussion, see *Klaus Peter Berger*, Die UNIDROIT-Prinzipien für Internationale Handelsverträge, Zeitschrift für Vergleichende Rechtswissenschaft 94 (1995) 217 sqq. and the contributions by *Michael Joachim Bonell, Alejandro M. Garro, Hernany Veytia, Luiz Olavo Baptista* and *Franco Ferrari* in (1995) 69 Tulane L.R. 1121 sqq.

24 For a discussion, see *Reinhard Zimmermann*, Konturen eines europäischen Vertragsrechts, Juristenzeitung 1995, 477 sqq.; *idem*, Die "Principles of European Contract Law", Teil I, ZEuP 3 (1995) 731 sqq. A German translation appears in ZEuP 3 (1995) 864 sqq.

25 *David M. Walker*, The Oxford Companion to Law, 1980, p. 222.

26 On this notion see, critically, *Reinhard Zimmermann*, 'Common law' und 'civil law', Amerika und Europa, in: *idem*, ed., Amerikanische Rechtskultur und europäisches Privatrecht, 1995, pp. 1 sqq.

ence, and particularly in light of the three preceding papers presented by *Professor Birks*, *Dr. Cairns* and *Lord Rodger*, we should probably use the last meaning as a point of departure. Civil law and common law are usually taken today to designate the two major legal traditions of the Western world[27]. In the civil law, so it is said[28], large areas of private law are codified. It has already been pointed out that this was not always the case. Codification is merely a specific condition in which the civil law currently presents itself. But there is a second distinctive feature. The civilian legal tradition originated in medieval Bologna with the rediscovery and intellectual penetration of the most important body of Roman legal sources, *Justinian*'s Digest. The English common law, on the other hand, developed more independently from Roman law (though neither in complete nor noble isolation)[29]. Here we have the historical connection between civil law as Roman law and civil law as continental European private law. This connection is based, historically, on a process usually referred to as 'reception': it was the reception of Roman law that is widely seen as having constituted European civil law[30].

2. Characteristic Features of the Civil Law

European civil law, in the sense of continental European private law at large, exhibits a number of attributes distinguishing it from the laws of other cultures[31]. It is, in many complex ways, related to moral norms, religious beliefs and political evaluations. At the same time, however, it is quite distinct from morality, religion and politics. It is administered by a body of professional experts who have received a specialized training that qualifies them for their task. The central institution providing such training is typically a university. As a university subject, law is submitted to methodical reflection and analysis: it is the object of a legal science. European legal science, in turn, attempts to demonstrate how indiviudal rules and

---

27 Cf., e.g., *James Gordley*, Common law and civil law: eine überholte Unterscheidung, ZEuP 1 (1993) 498 sqq.

28 *Arthur Taylor von Mehren, James Russèll Gordley*, The Civil Law System, 2nd ed., 1977, p. 3.

29 For details, see *Peter Stein*, The Character and Influence of the Roman Civil Law, 1988, pp. 151 sqq.; *R.H. Helmholz*, Continental Law and Common Law: Historical Strangers or Companions?, 1990 Duke Law Journal 1207 sqq.; *Reinhard Zimmermann*, Der europäische Charakter des englischen Rechts, ZEuP 1 (1993) 4 sqq.

30 The authoritative analysis is still the one provided by *Franz Wieacker*; see *Wieacker/Weir* (n. 7) pp. 71 sqq. He emphasizes the intellectualization and rationalization of law and public affairs in general, and the creation of a European *ius commune*, as the core features of the impact of Roman law on European legal thinking.

31 For a succinct summary, see *Harold J. Berman*, Law and Revolution: The Formation of the Western Legal Mind, 1983, pp. 7 sqq.; *Franz Wieacker*, Foundations of European Legal Culture, (1990) 38 American Journal of Comparative Law 1 sqq.; *Peter Häberle*, Europäische Rechtskultur, in: *idem*, Europäische Rechtskultur, 1994, pp. 9 sqq. The following paragraph is based on my foreword to *Wieacker/Weir* (n. 7) V sqq.

the decisions of individual cases can be derived from general propositions, and how they can thus be understood and related to each other. A determined effort is made to rationalize the application of the law. Moreover, European law possesses an inherently dynamic character. It is always developing. But it is developing within an established framework of sources and methods, of concepts, rules and arguments. It constitutes a tradition that is constantly evolving. And in spite of many differences in detail, that tradition is characterized by a fundamental unity. It is based on the same sources, has been moving with the same cultural tides, reflects a common set of values and uses common techniques[32].

3. Civil Law and Civil Code

It is important to realize that codification has not brought about an entirely new era within the history of the European civil law. Of course, there have been certain fundamental changes, but they relate to attitude and ideology rather than to substance. The German Civil Code, as has been emphasized already, was drafted in the wake of German national unification and it was taken, at least by some, to be a characteristic expression of the German national spirit. Also, and more importantly, it marked the point where discussion of Roman private law and modern doctrinal scholarship parted company[33]. The codification was attributed sole, supreme and unquestioned authority, and all the energies of those legal academics interested in the application and development of private law were channelled into the task of expounding the code and of discussing the court decisions based on its provisions. As a result, legal scholarship has undergone a process of nationalistic particularization (which has been denounced, emphatically, as 'undignified' and 'humiliating')[34].

On the other hand, the codification movement was itself a European phenomenon affecting the private law in Germany or Austria as profoundly, and in essentially a similar manner, as in France or Italy. The Prussian Code apart[35], all European codifications are characterized by a considerable built-in flexibility which has, by and large, made them stand the test of time[36]. Their draftsmen took to heart *Porta-*

---

32 Cf., most recently, *Reinhard Zimmermann*, Civil Code and Civil Law, (1994/95) 1 Columbia Journal of European Law 82 sqq.

33 This is elaborated in more detail in *Reinhard Zimmermann*, Roman and Comparative Law: The European Perspective, (1995) 16 J.L.H. 21 sqq.

34 For examples of this kind of 'national legal science', see (1994/95) 1 Columbia Journal of European Law 63 sqq. (with reference to the sharp criticism of this state of affairs by *Rudolf von Jhering*).

35 See *Jan Schröder*, Das Verhältnis von Rechtsdogmatik und Gesetzgebung in der neuzeitlichen Privatrechtsgeschichte (am Beispiel des Privatrechts), in: Okko Behrends, Wolfram Henkel, edd., Gesetzgebung und Dogmatik, Abhandlungen der Akademie der Wissenschaften in Göttingen, Philologisch-historische Klasse, Dritte Folge, n. 178, 1989, pp. 43 sqq.

36 This point is further elaborated, as far as the German Civil Code is concerned, in (1994/95) 1 Columbia Journal of European Law 89 sqq.

lis' famous observation[37] that the task of legislation is to determine, "par de grandes vues", the general maxims of law. It has to establish principles rich in implications rather than descend into the details of every question which might possibly arise. The *application* of the law belongs to the magistrate and lawyer, "pénétré de l'esprit général des lois".

Thus, the scene was set for an alliance, not for confrontation, between legislation and legal science[38]; and, as a result, it appears to be generally recognized today that a code has to be brought to life, and has to be kept in tune with the changing demands of time, by active and imaginative judicial interpretation and doctrinal elaboration[39]. In spite of the code, the civilian tradition is still evolving. And it is indeed, fundamentally, still the civilian tradition that is evolving. For while judicial interpretation and doctrinal elaboration have certainly produced some odd quirks of national jurisprudence, they have proceeded from the provisions of the various codes they were supposed to apply. These codes, however, have grown on the same legal soil. Thus, it is well known that those who drafted the German Civil Code did not, by and large, intend their code to constitute a fresh start, a break with the past. On the contrary: they generally aimed at consolidating the contemporary version of the Roman common law: pandectist legal doctrine. Not inappropriately, therefore, the 'Bürgerliches Gesetzbuch' has been referred to as the "statute book of the historical school of jurisprudence"[40].

But even the French 'code civil', carried by the élan of a revolutionary movement, subscribed to traditional conceptions of private law, that were, as *James Gordley*[41] puts it very pointedly, almost old-fashioned when the code was enacted.

---

37 As cited in *Konrad Zweigert, Hein Kötz*, An Introduction to Comparative Law, 2nd ed., 1987, translated by *Tony Weir*, paperback edition 1992, p. 92. Cf. also the comments by *Herman* (n. 15) 52 sqq.

38 Cf. *Okko Behrends*, Das Bündnis zwischen Gesetz und Dogmatik und die Frage der dogmatischen Rangstufen, in: Behrends/Henkel (n. 35) 9 sqq.

39 This point is also emphasized by *Karsten Schmidt*, Die Zukunft der Kodifikationsidee: Rechtsprechung, Wissenschaft und Gesetzgebung vor den Gesetzeswerken des geltenden Rechts, 1985, pp. 67 sqq. For further elaboration see, as far as German law is concerned, *Reinhard Zimmermann*, An Introduction to German Legal Culture, in: Werner Ebke, Matthew W. Finkin, edd., An Introduction to German Law, 1996, pp. 16 sqq. As far as the French and Austrian codes are concerned, see the famous clauses in art. 4 c.c. and § 7 ABGB. For details concerning the relationship between the code and judicial development of the law in France and Austria, see *Heinz Hübner*, Kodifikation und Entscheidungsfreiheit des Richters in der Geschichte des Privatrechts, 1980, pp. 33 sqq.; *Zweigert/Kötz/Weir* (n. 37) 91 sqq., 164 sqq. The Swiss code has, from the beginning, been renowned for its "deliberate reliance ... on judicial amplification" (*Zweigert/Kötz/Weir* (n. 37) 181). Its draftsmen made extensive use of 'general clauses'; cf. e.g. *Gmür* (n. 12) 50 sqq. Significantly, the new Dutch Civil Code relies more widely on general clauses than the old one; cf. *Hartkamp*, Diskussionsbeitrag, in: Bydlinski/Mayer-Maly/Pichler (n. 19) 63. Concerning good faith, see, most recently, *Zimmermann*, Juristenzeitung 1995, 490 sq.; *Friedrich K. Juenger*, Listening to Law Professors Talk about Good Faith: Some Afterthoughts (1995) 69 Tulane L.R. 1253 sqq.; Jack Beatson, David Friedman, edd., Good Faith and Fault in Contract Law, 1995.

40 *Paul Koschaker*, Europa und das römische Recht, 4th ed., 1966, p. 291.

The draftsmen found them in the 17th and 18th century treatise writers, such as *Domat* and *Pothier*. The same is true, *mutatis mutandis*, of the other two great 'Natural law codes'[42]. For the impact of natural law on the actual content of private law was rather limited[43]. It could be used to make a choice between two or more conflicting solutions, to streamline traditional doctrines or to generalize and round off trends of legal development that had been going on for centuries. But the *ratio naturalis* of Natural law did not normally oust the *ratio scripta* of Roman law[44]. Nor, of course, did a code like the Austrian General Civil Code attempt to incorporate the local and regional laws prevailing in the various parts of the monarchy; after all, it was intended to constitute a code that was universally applicable[45]. Predominantly, at least, it is an emanation neither of local custom nor of abstract, universal thought patterns, but of traditional civil law doctrine. The same has remained true of more recent codifications, including the new Dutch civil code[46]. They all carry an unmistakably civilian imprint, and the common tradition thus provides the background for an evaluation of their differences and similarities. They all, in a way, used the same legal grammar and, as a result, it is not difficult for those who have learnt that grammar to understand their content. 'Civil Law in European Codes': this topic, therefore, in essence concerns the fundamental intellectual unity within a diversity of modern legal systems. We will confine our attention to the law of obligations, the most characteristically 'European' of the coreareas of private law[47], although an investigation into property law and testate succession would probably yield similar results. (Family law and intestate succession

---

41 Myths of the French Civil Code, (1994) 42 American Journal of Comparative Law 459 sqq.; cf. also *Reiner Schulze*, Französisches Recht und Europäische Rechtsgeschichte im 19. Jahrhundert, in: *idem*, ed., Französisches Zivilrecht in Europa während des 19. Jahrhunderts, 1994, pp. 12 sqq.

42 *Andreas Schwennicke* (n. 6) *passim*, has emphasized the extent to which the draftsmen of the Prussian code followed (and merely rationalized) traditional patterns of the *ius commune*. As far as the Austrian code is concerned, see the evaluation by *Werner Ogris*, Zur Geschichte und Bedeutung des österreichischen Allgemeinen bürgerlichen Gesetzbuchs (ABGB), in: Liber Memorialis François Laurent, 1989, pp. 381 sqq.

43 This has been emphasized, in particular, by *Klaus Luig*, Der Einfluß des Naturrechts auf das positive Privatrecht im 18. Jahrhundert, ZSS (GA) 96 (1979) 38 sqq.

44 *Luig*, ZSS (GA) 96 (1979) 54.

45 *Wilhelm Brauneder*, Vernünftiges Recht als überregionales Recht: Die Rechtsvereinheitlichung der österreichischen Zivilrechtskodifikationen 1786 – 1797 – 1811, in: Reiner Schulze, ed., Europäische Rechts- und Verfassungsgeschichte, 1991, pp. 121 sqq. The same is true, of course, of the French code civil; cf. *Schulze* (n. 41) 23 sqq.

46 Which even contains a whole variety of instances where its draftsmen, consciously or unconsciously, have reverted to principles of Roman law even though the old code had departed from them; cf. *Hans Ankum*, Principles of Roman Law Absorbed in the New Civil Code, lecture delivered at the International Conference on European Legal Traditions and Israel in Jerusalem (April 1994) and to be published in the proceedings of that conference (ed. A.M. Rabello).

47 For an explanation see *Reinhard Zimmermann*, The Law of Obligations: Character and Influence of the Civilian Tradition, (1992) 3 Stellenbosch L.R. 5 sqq.

may not share as much common ground.) And we will take Roman law as our central point of reference. For if it was the 'reception' of Roman law that constituted European civil law, it must also have played a pivotal role in rendering the European civil codes civilian.

III. Roman Roots I: Common Origins

It is not easy to think of a legal rule expressed in exactly the same way in all European codes. One possible candidate, one would have thought, is the rule that legally or morally offensive contracts must be void. And indeed, the codes invariably tackle this problem by way of general clauses, which (also invariably) use the key concepts of illegality and immorality[48]. All these rules are based on Roman law: the *lex Non dubium* of Emperor *Theodosius*[49], which elevated all statutory prohibitions to the status of a *lex perfecta*, and the suppression of transactions *contra bones mores* by the Roman jurists and Emperors[50]. But if one looks more closely at the various codes one finds subtle variations. Art. 20 I of the Swiss 'Obligationenrecht' (OR) refers to "contracts with an illegal content", § 134 BGB to "legal acts violating a statutory prohibition". The French and Italian codes relate the invalidity of illegal and immoral contracts to their famous doctrines of 'cause' or *causa*[51] (which in turn derive from medieval jurisprudence but can be traced back ultimately to two fragments in the Digest[52]). The German, Swiss and Austrian codes contain specific provisions dealing with 'usurious' transactions[53], the Austrian code also still retains the institution of *laesio enormis*[54] (derived from C. 4, 44, 2)[55]. French law does not deal with 'usury' but has a rather different version of *laesio enormis*[56]. Art. 1133 c.c. does not only refer to transactions prohibited by law and contrary to the *boni mores* but also mentions those against public policy. The Dutch Civil Code contains a similar provision[57]. As far as legal consequences are concerned, most codes simply declare the contract to be void. German law,

---

48 For a comparative overview, see *Zweigert/Kötz/Weir* (n. 37) 407 sqq. and, most recently, *Hein Kötz*, Die Ungültigkeit von Verträgen wegen Gesetz- und Sittenwidrigkeit, RabelsZ 58 (1994) 209 sqq.

49 *Nov. Theod.* 9.

50 For all details, see *Reinhard Zimmermann*, The Law of Obligations: Roman Foundations of the Civilian Tradition, 1990, paperback edition 1996, pp. 697 sqq., 706 sqq.

51 Cf. art. 1133 code civil; art. 1343 codice civile.

52 Law of Obligations (n. 50) 549 sqq.

53 § 138 II BGB (on its historical background, see Law of Obligations (n. 50) 175 sqq., 268 sqq.); Art. 21 OR; § 879 II n. 4 ABGB.

54 § 934 ABGB

55 See Law of Obligations (n. 50) 259 sqq.

56 Art. 1674 c.c.

57 Art. 3:40 I BW.

however, displays a somewhat greater degree of flexibility concerning illegal contracts. The transaction is void, unless a contrary intention appears from the statute[58]. A similar, though not identical rule was introduced by the Dutch legislature[59]. This flexible approach, incidentally, is quite in tune with that adopted in classical Roman law before *Theodosius* enacted the *lex Non dubium*[60].

IV. Roman Roots II: Two Sets of Rules

1. Duties and Liability of a Seller

Not infrequently the Roman sources contain two different sets of rules dealing with one and the same problem. Both may have found their way into our modern codifications. Under a contract of sale, for instance, the vendor was under no obligation to transfer ownership of the object sold. He merely had to grant the purchaser undisturbed possession and was thus responsible for *vacuam possessionem tradere* and for sustaining the continued enjoyment of the *res*. Thus, there was an implied warranty of peaceable possession (*habere licere*), for as soon as the true owner, by asserting his title, evicted the purchaser, the latter could hold the vendor responsible[61]. This liability for eviction, as we find it in the law of *Justinian*, became part and parcel of the *ius commune* and it was also adopted by the 'code civil'[62]. The situation was different, as far as *certam rem dare* obligations (for instance, the promise to deliver a certain slave) were concerned. Here the promisor had to transfer ownership and was liable as soon as he was unable to do so[63]. This is the regime that obtains today in modern German law (§ 433 sqq., 440 BGB). It is as 'civilian' as, but nevertheless quite different from, the liability for eviction, no matter that the draftsmen of the German code had not in fact taken their inspiration from the *obligationes dandi*, but thought (wrongly) that the new regime had organically evolved from the liability for eviction[64]. This explains why, though requiring the vendor to transfer ownership, they still made his liability to pay damages dependent upon eviction[65].

---

58 § 134 BGB (on which see the discussion by *Hans Hermann Seiler*, Über verbotswidrige Rechtsgeschäfte (§ 134 BGB), in: Gedächtnisschrift für Wolfgang Martens, 1987, pp. 719 sqq.).

59 Art. 3:40 II BW.

60 Law of Obligations (n. 50) 697 sqq.

61 For the details, see Law of Obligations (n. 50) 293 sqq. and, most recently, *Wolfgang Ernst*, Rechtsmängelhaftung, 1995, pp. 7 sqq.

62 Artt. 1626 sqq. c.c. Cf. also the comparative remarks by *Andreas Wacke*, Die verschuldete Eviktion, in: Festschrift für Hubert Niederländer, 1991, pp. 141 sqq.

63 For details, see *Ernst* (n. 61) 91 sqq.

64 See *Ernst* (n. 61) 123 sqq.

65 § 440 II BGB.

2. *Breach of Contract*

Breach of contract presents another example of a significant discrepancy between French and German law. The 'Bürgerliches Gesetzbuch' distinguishes between different types of breach of contract. Of central significance is a highly artificial concept of (supervening) impossibility devised by *Friedrich Mommsen*, and inspired largely by the Roman regime applicable to *certam rem dare obligationes*[66]. Although, by the time of *Justinian*, this concept had lost its function, it still featured in the *Corpus iuris civilis* and has puzzled subsequent generations of lawyers[67]. On the one hand, *Mommsen* wanted to be faithful to the sources; on the other hand, he attempted on that basis to devise a neat and logically consistent scheme of liability for breach of contract. It is hardly surprising that, under these circumstances, 'impossibility' became a very broad conceptual abstraction and, as such, a common systematic denominator for a whole range of situations. What *Mommsen* could not (given the framework of authoritative sources within which he operated) take into consideration, was the fact that the modern general law of contract derives from the consensual contracts of Roman law, not from the law of stipulations entailing *certam rem dare*[68]. With regard to the former, liability had to be assessed according to the standard of good faith (*ex fide bona*), and there was thus no need for a strict categorization of specific types of breach of contract[69]. More particularly, supervening impossibility did not have to be dealt with separately. Of central importance was the question whether, and under which circumstances, the failure to perform, or to perform properly, was attributable to the debtor, before he could be made liable for *id quod interest*; and this question was indeed the very question that preoccupied the authors of the older *ius commune*. Following this pattern of the *ius commune* is the French 'code civil'[70]. Its art. 1147 refers to 'inexécution', a broad concept which covers all forms of breach of contract (that is, those cases where one of the parties "ne satisfera point à son engage-

---

66 *Friedrich Mommsen*, Die Unmöglichkeit der Leistung in ihrem Einfluß auf obligatorische Verhältnisse, 1853. For a discussion, see *Christian Wollschläger*, Die Entstehung der Unmöglichkeitslehre: Zur Dogmengeschichte des Rechts der Leistungsstörungen, 1970, pp. 123 sqq.; *Susanne Würthwein*, Zur Schadensersatzpflicht wegen Vertragsverletzungen im Gemeinen Recht des 19. Jahrhunderts: Grundsätze des Leistungsstörungsrechts im Gemeinen Recht in ihrer Bedeutung für das BGB, 1990; Law of Obligations (n. 50) 783 sqq., 809 sqq.

67 For a modern example of the confusion obtaining in a legal system based directly on the Roman sources, see *W.A. Ramsden*, Supervening Impossibility of Performance in the South African Law of Contract, 1985, pp. 55 sqq.

68 Cf. *Klaus-Peter Nanz*, Die Entstehung des allgemeinen Vertragsbegriffes im 16. Jahrhundert, 1985; John Barton, ed., Towards a General Law of Contract, 1990; Law of Obligations (n. 50) 537 sqq.; *Reinhard Zimmermann*, Roman-Dutch Jurisprudence and its Contribution to European Private Law, (1992) 66 Tulane L.R. 1689 sqq.; *Robert Feenstra*, Die Klagbarkeit der pacta nuda, in: Robert Feenstra, Reinhard Zimmermann, edd., Das römisch-holländische Recht: Fortschritte des Zivilrechts im 17. und 18. Jahrhundert, 1992, pp. 123 sqq.

69 Law of Obligations (n. 50) 788 sqq., 807 sqq.

70 Cf., e.g., *Zweigert/Kötz/Weir* (n. 37) 532 sqq.

ment"). The debtor is liable wherever such non-performance is not due to *vis maior* or *casus fortuitus*[71].

3. Initial Impossibility of Performance

As far as initial impossibility of performance is concerned, most modern codes appear to be squarely based on the famous principle that has come down to us under the name of *Iuventius Celsus*: *Impossibilium nulla obligatio est*[72]. Thus, for instance, § 306 BGB provides that a contract, the performance of which is impossible, is void. Similar provisions can be found in Swiss[73] and Italian law[74], and, confined to the law of sale, also in the 'code civil'[75]. We appear to be dealing here with a rule, not only of venerable antiquity, but also of obvious and even axiomatic validity. However, *impossibilium nulla obligatio est* merely encapsulates the obvious idea that nobody can be obliged to perform what he cannot perform. This is not identical with the assertion that a contract, the performance of which is impossible, is void; and in the eyes of the Roman lawyers the one did indeed not necessarily follow from the other[76]. Thus, as far as the contract of sale is concerned, we find some fragments in the *Corpus iuris* where a contractual action for what we would call the positive interest is granted, and where the contract, to that extent, appears to have been regarded as valid. Stipulations concerning an impossible performance, however, were invariably held to be void by the Roman lawyers. This was probably based neither on logic nor on policy; it simply followed from the way in which the applicable *formula* was phrased: for condemnation presupposed the existence of an object, the value of which could sensibly be estimated[77].

Thus, the modern codes perpetuate a rule solely applicable to a type of contract which has not been adopted by any of them. The responsibility for this odd anachronism rests in the first place on the Natural lawyers[78]. Discarding the 'subtleties' of Roman law, they found an altogether new starting point for determining the

71 A similarly streamlined set of rules, centred around a uniform concept of breach of contract, has been developed in English law. The Vienna 'Convention on the International Sale of Goods', the German Commission charged with the reform of the law of obligations, the Unidroit 'Principles of International Commercial Contracts' and the 'Principles of European Contract Law' drafted by the 'Commission on European Contract Law' all follow the same approach. Cf. *Zimmermann*, Juristenzeitung 1995, 480 sqq.

72 D. 50, 17, 185.

73 Art. 20 OR.

74 Artt. 1346, 1418 II *codice civile*.

75 Art. 1601 c.c.

76 For details, see Law of Obligations (n. 50) 686 sqq.; cf. also pp. 241 sqq.

77 See the references in Law of Obligations (n. 50) 689 sq.

78 For details, see *Christian Wollschläger*, Die willenstheoretische Unmöglichkeitslehre im aristotelisch-thomistischen Naturrecht, in: Sympotica Franz Wieacker, 1970, pp. 154 sqq.; Law of Obligations (n. 50) 692 sq.

effect of initial impossibility on contractual obligations in the idea that their content may be attributed to the promisor only if it is based on the exercise of his free will. The promisor must have chosen to be bound, and as a rational being he can choose only what he is able to carry out. A person can will only what lies within the reach of his volition. The law of contract is based on freedom of will. *Ergo*: a contract directed at something impossible must be invalid. This reasoning could not fail to commend itself to the Pandectists, and thus we find the (partial) concurrence of views, mentioned above, between the draftsmen of codifications from both the 'Germanic' and 'Romanistic' legal families. More recently, however, the rule embodied in § 306 BGB has been regarded as unsound and unfortunate[79]. Textbooks and commentaries are therefore full of exhortations to apply it restrictively and to try wherever possible to avoid the harshness inherent in the unequivocal verdict of invalidity. Quite in line with these developments, the new Dutch Civil Code has completely abandoned the rule[80]. One can hardly refuse the label 'civilian' to this solution. For we are dealing here with the return towards a more flexible regime espoused, already, by the Roman lawyers[81].

V. Roman Roots III: Interpreting the Sources

In other cases, considerable variations in the solutions presented by the modern codes are based on the fact that the relevant Roman sources, which have for centuries informed our discussion, are either unclear, or even contradictory. This is not at all a rare phenomenon, since the Digest is not a systematically-structured piece of legislation but a compilation of fragments from classical Roman legal writings, put together under *Justinian* in the 6th century A.D. It constitutes a gigantic torso of Roman law, which contains case decisions, legal opinions and rules, commentary, disputes, and excerpts from textbooks and monographs. Its overall character is casuistic. Much of it reflects the contemporary position at the various stages of Roman legal history, while other parts were altered to suit the requirements of the 6th century. In addition, we have to take account of the Imperial legislation contained in the *Codex Iustiniani* and of the rules contained in an elementary textbook invested with statutory force: *Justinian*'s 'Institutes'.

---

79 Cf., e.g. *Ernst Rabel*, Unmöglichkeit der Leistung (1907) and Über Unmöglichkeit der Leistung und heutige Praxis (1911), both today in: *Ernst Rabel*, Gesammelte Aufsätze, vol. 1, 1965, pp. 1 sqq., 56 sqq.; *Zweigert/Kötz/Weir* (n. 37) 526 sq.; *Ulrich Huber*, Leistungsstörungen, in: Gutachten und Vorschläge zur Überarbeitung des Schuldrechts, vol. 1, 1981, pp. 813 sqq.

80 Cf. *A. S. Hartkamp*, Mr. C. Asser's Handleiding tot de Beoefening van het Nederlands Burgerlijk Recht, Verbintenissenrecht, Part 1, 9th ed., 1992, n. 25.

81 Cf. also § 878, 1 ABGB ("What is *downright* impossible, cannot be the object of a valid contract") and the interpretation placed on this rule by *Ernst Rabel*, Zur Lehre von der Unmöglichkeit der Leistung nach Österreichischem Recht (1911), in: Gesammelte Aufsätze, vol. 1, 1965, pp. 79 sqq.

1. Vicarious Liability

Digesta 19, 2, 25, 7[82] is one of those ambiguous fragments which have been used as the textual foundation for two contradictory solutions. A contractor has undertaken the transport of a column. He uses some servants to carry out that obligation. They drop the column and break it. Is the contractor liable not only for his own fault but also for theirs? Or is his liability dependent upon whether he himself was at fault (for instance, in selecting and supervising his servants)? This depends on the interpretation of the clause "si qua ipsius eorumque, quorum opera uteretur, culpa occiderit"; or, more precisely, on whether the particle *que* in "eorumque" has to be understood conjunctively ('and') or disjunctively ('or'). According to the latter interpretation, we would be dealing with an instance of vicarious liability *stricto sensu*, i.e. liability based (merely) on the fault of others. This is indeed how modern Romanists would tend to read the text, for only this interpretation would seem to fit in with the conductor's *custodia* liabilty[83]. It is this solution that we find, within a delictual context, in art. 1384 c.c.: one is responsible, not only for the injury which one causes by one's own action, but also for that which is caused "par le fait des personnes dont on doit répondre"[84].

Digesta 19, 2, 25, 7 (the *que* interpreted conjunctively), on the other hand, was one of the key sources upon which 19th century German legal writers relied in order to reject the notion that one person could be held strictly responsible for the acts of others[85]. 'No liability without fault' was one of the great axioms of Pandectist doctrine[86], and the Roman texts tended to be read in such a way as to conform thereto. By the time the BGB was drafted the idea of vicarious liability had gained ground[87], though it ultimately managed to establish itself only in the contractual context[88]. But when it came to the law of delict, the forces of tradition – a tradition only supposedly going back to the Roman sources! – largely had their way, strongly supported by lobbyists representing the interests of trade, industry and

---

82 "Qui columnam transportandam conduxit, si ea, dum tollitur aut portatur aut reponitur, fracta sit, ita id periculum praestat, si qua ipsius eorumque, quorum opera uteretur, culpa acciderit".

83 *Rolf Knütel*, Die Haftung für Hilfspersonen im römischen Recht, ZSS (RA) 100 (1993) 419 sqq.; Law of Obligations (n. 50) 397 sqq. *Contra*: *Geoffrey MacCormack*, Culpa in eligendo, RIDA 18 (1971) 541 sq.

84 On the origin of this provision (*Domat* and *Pothier*) cf. *Alan Watson*, Failures of the Legal Imagination, 1988, pp. 6 sq., 15 sqq.; on its application, see *Zweigert/Kötz/Weir* (n. 37) 676 sqq.

85 Cf., for example, *Bernhard Windscheid*, *Theodor Kipp*, Lehrbuch des Pandektenrechts, 9th ed., 1906, § 401, n. 5.

86 Cf., e.g., the analysis by *Hans-Peter Benöhr*, Die Entscheidung des BGB für das Verschuldensprinzip, T.R. 46 (1978) 1 sqq.

87 For details of the development, see *Hans Hermann Seiler*, Die deliktische Gehilfenhaftung in historischer Sicht, Juristenzeitung 1967, 525 sqq.

88 § 278 BGB.

agriculture. The principle laid down in art. 1384 c.c. was curtly rejected by the second Commission drafting the BGB as being entirely alien to traditional 'German' notions of justice and fairness[89]. According to § 831 BGB, therefore, liability for the unlawful acts of employees hinges on *culpa in eligendo vel custodiendo vel inspiciendo*[90]. This rule has turned out to be a major source of embarrassment, and has largely been responsible for the extravagant encroachment of contractual remedies on the law of delict, which is such a characteristic feature of the modern German law of obligations[91].

We are obviously dealing here with an important difference between French and German law. Yet, both solutions will have to be labelled 'civilian', for both of them derive from the same intellectual tradition. That tradition has shaped the parameters within which the legal discourse has taken place: the distinction between contractual and delictual liability; the relevance, in principle, of fault as the basis for liability; the possibility of acting through others and the problem, under these circumstances, of how to attribute fault; and the definition of the range of such other persons for whose fault one may be held responsible. Texts like D. 19, 2, 25, 7 and others deriving from the same intellectual tradition[92] did not, of course, 'determine' whether a legal system opted for vicarious liability or for a strict implementation of the fault principle, but they provided the framework of concepts and arguments for rationalizing that decision.

2. *Transfer of Ownership and Payment of Purchase Price*

For another example we may turn to *Justinian*'s 'Institutes'. They contain an enigmatic rule relating to the transfer of ownership resulting from a contract of sale[93]. Ownership, according to the first sentence of *Inst.* 2, 1, 41, will pass only once the purchase price has been paid (or security given). In the very next sentence, however, the rule appears to be rendered more or less nugatory: for here it is said to be sufficient that the vendor "puts his trust in the purchaser". It is likely that we are dealing with an attempt to reconcile generally accepted notions and prac-

89 Protokolle, in: *Benno Mugdan*, Die gesammten Materialien zum Bürgerlichen Gesetzbuch für das Deutsche Reich, vol. 3, 1899, p. 1094.

90 There is, however, as far as this fault requirement is concerned, a reversal of the *onus* of proof.

91 *Zweigert/Kötz/Weir* (n. 37) 670 sqq.; *B.S. Markesinis*, A Comparative Introduction to the German Law of Torts, 3rd ed., 1994, pp. 676 sqq.

92 For example, *Robert-Joseph Pothier*, Traité des obligations, nn. 121, 456.

93 *Inst.* 2, 1, 41: "Sed si quidem ex causa donationis aut dotis aut qualibet alia ex causa tradantur, sine dubio transferuntur: venditae vero et traditae non aliter emptori adquiruntur, quam si is venditori pretium solverit vel alio modo ei satisfecerit, veluti expromissore aut pignore dato. quod cavetur quidem etiam lege duodecim tabularum: tamen recte dicitur et iure gentium, id est iure naturali, id effici. sed si is qui vendidit fidem emptoris secutus fuerit, dicendum est statium rem emptoris fieri".

tices of *Justinian's* time with the principles of classical Roman law. Painstaking modern research has revealed the significance and development of both the rule and its fatal qualification within the history of Roman law[94]. The lawyers of the *ius commune*, on the other hand, had to accept the text as they found it. Yet, they could never be quite sure how to understand its content[95]. Considerable uncertainty persisted, as is reflected in the fact that all three Natural law codes contain a different version of the rule[96]. The draftsmen of the BGB, who at first intended to abandon *Inst.* 2, 1, 41, finally opted for yet another solution (the justification for which is, however, regarded as questionable)[97].

VI. Roman Roots IV: Different Layers of Tradition

If *Inst.* 2, 1, 41 provides an example for a notoriously unclear rule, we have only to look at the question of transfer of ownership in general to find two entirely different regimes, both of which can be traced back to – and have in fact been derived from – a contradictory set of sources from Roman law.

1. The Abstract and the Causal System

In classical Roman law, transfer of ownership[98] was effected by *mancipatio* for *res mancipi*, by *traditio* for *res nec mancipi*, alternatively by *in iure cessio* for both categories of things. *Mancipatio* and *in iure cessio* were 'abstract', i.e. their validity did not depend on whether they were based on a legal ground motivating and justifying such transfer. *Traditio*, on the other hand, was (probably) causal in that it did require a *iusta causa traditionis* (such as a valid contract of sale)[99]. *Justinian* retained only *traditio*[100]. But he incorporated into the *Corpus iuris civilis* a text by

---

94 Cf. Law of Obligations (n. 50) 272 sqq.

95 For all details, see *Robert Feenstra*, Reclame en Revendicatie, 1949, pp. 98 sqq., 255 sq.; *Coing* (n. 4) 307 sqq.; *Klaus Luig*, Übergabe und Übereignung der verkauften Sache nach römischem und gemeinem Recht, in: Satura Roberto Feenstra oblata, 1985, pp. 445 sqq.; *Robert Feenstra*, Eigendomsovergang bij koop en terugvorderingsrecht van de onbetalde verkoper: Romeins recht en Middeleeuws handelsrecht, T.H.R.H.R. 50 (1987) 134 sqq.

96 § 224 sqq. I 11 PrALR; art. 1582 sq. c.c.; § 1063 ABGB.

97 § 454 BGB. For all details, see the historical discussion by *Klaus Luig*, Das Verhältnis von Kaufpreiszahlung und Eigentumsübergang nach deutschem Recht, in: Letizia Vacca, ed., Vendita e trasferimento della proprietà nella prospettiva storico-comparatistica, 1991, vol. 1, pp. 225 sqq.

98 For a general overview of the historical development, see *J.H. Dondorp, E.J.H. Schrage*, Levering krachtens geldige titel, 1991 (on which, see ZSS (RA) 11 (1994) 703 sqq.).

99 *Max Kaser*, Das römische Privatrecht, Erster Abschnitt, 2nd ed., 1971, pp. 412 sqq.

100 *Max Kaser*, Das römische Privatrecht, Zweiter Abschnitt, 2nd ed., 1975, pp. 282 sq.

Julian (D. 41, 1, 36), which appears to have dispensed with this requirement; and in a key text of the 'Institutes' (2, 1, 40) he merely stressed the intention to transfer.

For a long time, the *ius commune* was dominated by the causal system: transfer of ownership was seen to depend on what the jurists of the German *usus modernus* referred to as *titulus* (= *iusta causa traditionis*) and *modus* (= the different forms of *traditio*)[101]. This regime was incorporated into the Austrian General Civil Code[102]. It was not difficult to trace it back to Roman law. *Friedrich Carl von Savigny*, on the other hand, took his cue from texts like *Iul.* D. 41, 1, 36 and *Inst.* 2, 1, 40, and managed, on the basis of a reinterpretation of the Roman sources, to establish his doctrine of the abstract dispositive legal act[103]: transfer of ownership was based on an agreement between the owner and the acquirer that ownership be transferred. This agreement constituted a legal transaction that was completely separate from, and independent of, the underlying obligatory act, and it replaced the *titulus* of the older doctrine. Eventually, this proposition found its way into the BGB[104], where it contributes to the famous (or infamous) 'abstract' character of the German Civil Code[105]. The differences between the abstract and the causal systems of transfer of ownership are not inconsiderable; thus, for instance, the *condictio indebiti* acquires much greater practical significance within a system which allows the transferor to lose his title and requires him to argue that this change of title may have been unjustified. Yet, at the same time, both systems are undoubtedly civilian.

2. *The Consensual System*

The same is true even of a third system that we find in modern continental codes. It does not require a separate act of conveyance at all, but allows ownership to pass upon conclusion of a sale[106]. The French 'code civil' provides a fine exam-

---

101 For all details, see *Coing* (n. 4) 302 sqq.; *Italo Birocchi*, Vendita e trasferimento della proprietà nel diritto comune, in: Vacca (n. 97) 139 sqq.; *Dondorp/Schrage* (n. 98) 31 sqq.

102 § 380 ABGB; on which see *Theo Mayer-Maly*, Kauf und Eigentumsübergang im österreichischen Recht, in: Vacca (n. 97) 275 sqq.

103 For details, see *Wilhelm Felgentraeger*, Friedrich Carl von Savignys Einfluß auf die Übereignungslehre, 1927; *Filippo Ranieri*, Die Lehre von der abstrakten Übereignung in der deutschen Zivilrechtswissenschaft des 19. Jahrhunderts, in: Wissenschaft und Kodifikation des Privatrechts im 19. Jahrhundert, vol. 2, 1977, pp. 90 sqq.; *Coing* (n. 2) vol. 2, pp. 393 sqq.; *Götz Landwehr*, Abstrakte Rechtsgeschäfte in Wissenschaft und Gesetzgebung des 19. Jahrhunderts, in: Karsten Schmidt, ed., Rechtsdogmatik und Rechtspolitik, 1990, pp. 173 sqq.

104 Cf. the discussion by *Rolf Knütel*, Vendita e trasferimento della proprietà nel diritto tedesco, in: Vacca (n. 97) 287 sqq.

105 *Folke Schmidt*, The German Abstract Approach to Law, (1965) 9 Scandinavian Studies in Law 133 sqq.; *Konrad Zweigert*, *Hartmut Dietrich*, System and Language of the German Civil Code 1900, in: S.J. Stoljar, ed., Problems of Codification, 1977, pp. 34 sqq.; *Zweigert/Kötz/Weir* (n. 37) 150 sqq.

ple. Its art. 1583 reads: "Elle (sc.: the contract of sale) est parfaite entre les parties, et la propriété est acquise de droit à l'acheteur à l'égard du vendeur, dès qu'on est convenu de la chose et du prix, quoique la chose n'ait pas encore été livrée, ni le prix payé". This doctrine was propagated most forcefully by *Hugo Grotius*[107] and other Natural lawyers of the 17th and 18th centuries[108]. But it can already be found in *Leonardus Lessius*[109], and even at the time of the Commentators it had been foreshadowed by the introduction of a routine clause into notarial sales instruments which stipulated that the vendor would henceforth possess on behalf of the purchaser[110]. This was interpreted as *traditio per constitutum possessorium.* Similar constructions paved the way to the consensual principle in French law[111]. Thus, the new approach was partly the product of notarial practice and possibly also of the French *droit coutumier.* It was also based on biblical authority: because thought is to be equated to deed, a promise to transfer ownership must have the same effect as the alienation of property itself[112]. Significantly, however, the consensual theory was couched in terms of traditional civilian learning and thus woven into the fabric of the learned law. *Grotius* even drew on Roman law in order to provide doctrinal support – both on its *usus modernus* and on the classical law as restored by contemporary legal humanism[113].

VII. Roman Roots V: More Ambiguity

1. Mora Creditoris

There are many more examples of this phenomenon: two distinctly different regimes prevailing in the European codes and both of them tracing their pedigree back to Roman law. *Mora creditoris*, for instance, is unknown in some modern legal systems as a specific legal institution. The creditor is liable, in the same way as

---

106 For comparative evaluations of the different regimes regulating the transfer of property in Europe (abstract, causal and consensual; on the latter cf. the next paragraph in the text), see *Franco Ferrari*, Vom Abstraktionsprinzip und Konsensualprinzip zum Traditionsprinzip, ZEuP 1 (1993) 52 sqq.; *Andreas Roth*, Abstraktions- und Konsensprinzip und ihre Auswirkungen auf die Rechtsstellung der Kaufvertragsparteien, ZVglRW 92 (1993) 371 sqq.; *Ulrich Drobnig*, Transfer of Property, in: Hartkamp, Hesselink (n. 4) 345 sqq. Neither the abstract nor the consensual system are carried through in practice without exception. Thus, there seems to be a trend among the modern legal systems towards a convergence (once again) on the basis of the causal system.

107 De jure belli ac pacis, Lib. II, Cap. VI, 1.

108 Cf., e.g., *Samuel Pufendorf*, De jure naturae et gentium, Lib. IV, Cap. IX.

109 *William M. Gordon*, Studies in the Transfer of Property by Traditio, 1970, pp. 172 sq.

110 *Dondorp/Schrage* (n. 98) 49 sqq.

111 *Dondorp/Schrage* (n. 98) 83 sqq.

112 *Dondorp/Schrage* (n. 98) 70 sqq.

113 *Gordon* (n. 109) 173 sq.

the debtor, for breach of contract[114]. This was, *mutatis mutandis*, also the view taken by the authors of the *ius commune*: they saw *mora creditoris* as a counterpart, or twin image, of *mora debitoris*[115]. Both were based on fault, and both required the breach of a duty (to deliver in the one case, to receive performance in the other). The concept of *mora creditoris* underlying the provisions of the BGB is quite a different one[116]. For fault as a requirement for *mora creditoris* had lost its basis when it came to be recognized in the second half of the 19th century that the creditor is not *obliged* to receive performance but merely *entitled* to do so. The institution of *mora creditoris* is merely designed to relieve in certain respects the position of a debtor who has done whatever he could reasonably be expected to do. This doctrine goes back to *Friedrich Mommsen*[117]; it was emphatically reasserted by *Josef Kohler*[118] and it impressed the fathers of the BGB[119]. Of course, both *Mommsen* and the earlier authors of the *ius commune* claimed that their views were derived from, or at least reconcilable with, the sources of Roman law. Contemporary Romanist doctrine tends to side with *Mommsen* and to attribute the modern, objective construction of *mora creditoris* to the Roman lawyers[120]. Again, however, not all our sources conform to such a general pattern[121].

2. Set-off

Or one may look at set-off as a convenient way of satisfying mutual debts. The *magna quaestio* has always been how set-off becomes effective. Modern legal systems deriving from Roman law generally fall into two groups in this regard. § 388 BGB represents a good example of the one, when it states that "[t]he set-off is made by declaration to the other party". This rule is based on a tradition dating back to the Glossator *Azo*[122]. Both French[123] and Austrian[124] law, on the other

---

114 Cf., as far as French law is concerned, the discussion by *Uwe Hüffer*, Leistungsstörungen durch Gläubigerhandeln, 1976, pp. 61 sqq., 87 sqq.

115 Cf., e.g., *Christian Friedrich Glück*, Ausführliche Erläuterung der Pandekten, vol. 4, 1796, pp. 401 sqq.; *Carl Otto von Madai*, Die Lehre von der Mora, Dargestellt nach Grundsätzen des Römischen Rechts, 1837, pp. 227 sqq.

116 § 293 sqq. BGB.

117 Die Lehre von der Mora nebst Beiträgen zur Lehre von der culpa, 1855, pp. 133 sqq.

118 Annahme und Annahmeverzug, Jherings Jahrbücher für die Dogmatik des bürgerlichen Rechts 17 (1879) 261 sqq.

119 Motive, in: *Mugdan* (n. 89) vol. 2, 1899, pp. 37 sqq.; cf. also *Hüffer* (n. 114) 14 sqq.

120 Cf. *Kaser*, Römisches Privatrecht, Erster Abschnitt (n. 99) 517 sq.; *Wolfgang Kunkel, Heinrich Honsell*, Römisches Recht, 4th ed., 1987, pp. 247 sq.

121 For a discussion see Law of Obligations (n. 50) 819 sqq.

122 For details, see *Heinrich Dernburg*, Geschichte und Theorie der Kompensation, 2nd ed., 1868, pp. 284 sq.

123 Art. 1290 c.c.

124 § 1438 ABGB.

hand, do not require any such declaration. As soon (and as far) as two debts capable of being set off confront each other, both of them are extinguished *ipso iure*; no account is taken of the will of the two parties concerned. Again, this conception of a set-off can be traced back to the Glossators[125]. How did this dichotomy arise? Because it was not entirely clear how *Justinian*'s compensation worked. "... ut actiones ipso iure minuant", say the 'Institutes'[126], and in the 'Codex', too, it is emphasized that "[c]ompensationes ex omnibus actionibus ipso iure fieri"[127]. That is, however, in strange contrast to the language used in other places ("compensationis obici", "opponi compensationem")[128] and also to the fact that the *ipso iure* effect of *compensatio* is not stressed more strongly in the Digest. And what is the reason for this amibiguity in our sources? It lies in the distinctly procedural flavour which was one of the most characteristic features of set-off in classical Roman law. Whether, and if so, in which manner and under which circumstances a set-off could be effected, depended entirely on the nature of the formula applicable in a given situation[129]. Thus, the Roman lawyers never developed a uniform and systematic approach to the problem of set-off, and *Justinian* was faced with a formidable task when he recognized the need to devise a generalized doctrine, that was no longer dictated by procedural niceties. After all, the formulary procedure had been abandoned. In spite of all his efforts, however, he did not manage to eradicate all traces of the older legal layers.

VIII. The Process of Generalization

Generalization of rules and institutions, concepts and criteria of Roman law is a characteristic feature of the civilian tradition. Often, that process had already been started by the classical Roman lawyers, who built on the foundations of the ancient *ius civile*; it was carried on by *Justinian*; and it was further advanced by the jurists of the *ius commune*. Sometimes a reaction occurred against these too far-flung generalities. The codifications, of course, reflect the results of these developments. Set-off provides a rather inconspicuous example. The evolution of the law of delict is much more spectacular.

---

125 *Dernburg* (n. 122) 283 sq.

126 *Inst.* 4, 6, 30.

127 C. 4, 31, 14 (*Iust.*); cf. also C. 4, 31, 4 (*Alex.*); *Paul.* D. 16, 2, 4; *Paul.* D. 16, 2, 21 (all interpolated).

128 C. 4, 31, 14, 1. Cf. further *Siro Solazzi*, La compensazione nel diritto romano, 2nd ed., 1950, pp. 166 sqq.

129 For details, see Law of Obligations (n. 50) 761 sqq.

1. The Evolution of the Law of Delict

The point of departure was a quaintly worded enactment from the 3rd century B.C. Even in Roman law this statute had been extended, adapted and modernized in so many ways that a jurist from the time of its enactment would hardly have recognized the late classical (or Justinianic) delict of *damnum culpa datum* as specifically Aquilian; and any legal advice based merely on the wording of the *lex* would have been hopelessly inadequate. *Urere frangere rumpere* had been superseded by the all-embracing term *corrumpere*[130]; remedies were granted in cases of indirect causation[131] and even in situations where the substance of the object concerned was not at all affected[132]; fault in the broadest sense of the word became a sufficient basis for liability[133]; the injured party could recover his full *quod interest*[134]; the role of plaintiff was no longer confined to the owner of the object killed or damaged[135]; and the ambit of Aquilian protection had even been extended to damage to freemen[136].

This process of extension, adaptation and modernization was carried on by courts and writers of the *ius commune*: almost imperceptibly at first, with small and hesitating steps, but leading, eventually, to the far-ranging, popular and comprehensive remedy described by writers like *Samuel Stryk*[137]. The famous Enlightenment lawyer, *Christian Thomasius*, even set out to pull down 'the Aquilian mask' from the contemporary *actio de damno dato*, which, he said, differed from the Aquilian action as much as a bird from a quadruped[138]. At the same time, however, it was still distinctively civilian. So was the famous general clause of the French[139] and Austrian codes[140] in which the development culminated. It constituted the statutory version of the 'Natural' law of delict as propounded most prominently by *Hugo Grotius*[141]. "Ex ... culpa obligatio naturaliter oritur, si damnum

130 Law of Obligations (n. 50) 984 sqq.

131 Law of Obligations (n. 50) 978 sqq.

132 Law of Obligations (n. 50) 986 sq.

133 Law of Obligations (n. 50) 1005 sqq.

134 Law of Obligations (n. 50) 969 sqq., 973 sq.

135 Law of Obligations (n. 50) 994 sqq.

136 Law of Obligations (n. 50) 1014 sqq.

137 "Tituli praesentis usus amplissimus est, cum omnium damnorum reparatio ex hoc petatur, si modo ulla alterius culpa doceri possit": Usus modernus pandectarum, Lib. IX, Tit. II, § 1. For details of the development, see *Law of Obligations* (n. 50) 1017 sqq.; *Jan Schröder*, Die zivilrechtliche Haftung für schuldhafte Schadenszufügungen im deutschen usus modernus, in: La responsabilità civile da atto illecito nella prospettiva storico-comparatistica, 1995, pp. 142 sqq.

138 Larva legis Aquiliae detracta actioni de damno dato, 1703, § 1.

139 Art. 1382 c.c.

140 § 1295 ABGB.

141 On the development from *Grotius* to the 'code civil', see *Robert Feenstra*, Vergelding en vergoeding, 2nd ed., 1993, pp. 15 sqq.; Law of Obligations (n. 50) 1036, n. 248. On the

datum est, nempe ut id resarciatur", he had postulated[142], using terms and concepts that were thoroughly familiar to anybody even vaguely acquainted with the tradition of Aquilian liability.

One of the core features of 'Natural' law theories concerning delictual liability was, of course, their readiness to provide compensation for purely patrimonial loss. Both § 1295 ABGB and art. 1382 code civil reflect this way of thinking. Even this, however, was not a revolutionary novelty. For a somewhat equivocal phrase in *Inst.* 2, 3, 16 i.f.[143] could, if taken out of context, be read to imply that according to Roman law any *damnum* was recoverable, irrespective of whether it had flowed from damage to the plaintiff's property or person. This wide interpretation had gained ground in the Middle Ages, and, as a result, Aquilian protection had become available in cases of purely patrimonial loss long before the Natural lawyers[144]. The Pandectists of the 19th century, on the other hand, predominantly advocated a return to the more limited scope of Aquilian liability in Roman law[145], and it was this view which found expression in § 823 I BGB: a certain number of specific rights and interests are listed[146], and it is only by violating one of them that a person may become liable in delict. Neither the German nor the French codes have conclusively settled the thorny issue of liability for pure economic loss. Courts and legal writers in the one country have had to restrict the range of application of an all too liberal provision[147], while in the other country they are devising strategies of extending the scope of an all too narrowly conceived liability regime[148]. While

history of the relevant provision in the Italian 'codice civile' (art. 2043) see *Guido Alpa*, Unjust Damage and the Role of Negligence: Historical Profile, (1994) 9 Tulane European and Civil Law Forum 147 sqq.

142 De jure belli ac pacis, Lib. II, Cap. XVII, § I. On *Grotius*' general clause of delictual liability, see, most recently, *Robert Feenstra*, Das Deliktsrecht bei Grotius, insbesondere der Schadensersatz bei Tötung und Körperverletzung, in: Feenstra/Zimmermann (n. 68) 429 sqq.

143 "[S]ed si non corpore damnum fuerit datum neque corpus laesum fuerit, sed alio modo damnum alicui contigit ... placuit eum qui obnoxius fuerit in factum actione teneri".

144 See *Horst Kaufmann*, Rezeption und usus modernus der actio legis Aquiliae, 1958, pp. 46 sqq., 62 sqq.; Law of Obligations (n. 50) 1023 sq.; *Schröder* (n. 137) 147 sqq. Cf. also, for instance, *Thomas Kiefer*, Die Aquilische Haftung im "Allgemeinen Landrecht für die Preußischen Staaten" von 1794, 1989, *passim*, who draws attention to the continuity between the doctrines of the *usus modernus* and the generalized form of delictual liability in the Prussian Code.

145 Cf., for example, *Johann Christian Hasse*, Die Culpa des Römischen Rechts, 2nd ed., 1838, pp. 26 sq.; *Windscheid/Kipp* (n. 85) § 451, 455; RGZ 9, 158 (163 sqq.); *Hans Hermann Seiler*, Römisches deliktisches Schadensersatzrecht in der obergerichtlichen Rechtsprechung des 19. Jahrhunderts, in: Festschrift für Hermann Lange, 1992, pp. 256 sqq.; *Ruth Bilstein*, Das deliktische Schadensersatzrecht der Lex Aquilia in der Rechtsprechung des Reichsgerichts, 1994, pp. 19 sqq., 28 sqq.

146 The list contained in § 823 I BGB can, incidentally, also be traced back to *Grotius*; cf. *Feenstra* (n. 141) 17.

147 Cf., most recently, *Canadian National Railway Co. v. Norsk Pacific Steamship Co. Ltd.*, (1992) 91 D.L.R. (4th) 289 (320 sqq.) and *Peter Gotthardt*, Landesbericht Frankreich, in: Christian von Bar, ed., Deliktsrecht in Europa, 1993, p. 16.

starting from two opposing principles, both systems in actual practice therefore tend to converge[149].

2. The Evolution of the Law of Contract

Ever since *Gaius*, contract is perceived to be the other main branch of the law of obligations. Here we find a similar development from unimposing origins towards the modern general law of contract, that constitutes a central feature of all civilian jurisdictions[150]. In this case, not even the Pandectists attempted to reverse the position. The Roman rule was *nuda pactio obligationem non parit*[151]. But by the time of *Justinian*, a whole variety of agreements had in one way or another become legally recognized. First, there were the four famous consensual contracts, already well established in classical Roman law. Then there were the contracts *innominati* (*innominati* even though some of them had actually acquired individual names). Furthermore, consensual agreements were enforceable, if they had been attached to one of the recognized contracts and had been concluded at one and the same time as the main contract (*pacta in continenti adiecta*). Then, again, there were two groups of agreements, which were not classified as contracts, but which were nevertheless enforceable: the so-called *pacta praetoria* and *pacta legitima*. Other informal arrangements, which did not fall into these categories, could be raised by way of defence; apart from that they could at least be regarded as *obligationes naturales*.

The *Corpus iuris* thus presented a somewhat patchy picture; it was marked by haphazard distinctions and internal inconsistencies. These inconsistencies, of course, presented an intellectual challenge to Glossators, Commentators and the later generations of learned lawyers and triggered off their efforts to establish a more rational scheme. Canon law, the law merchant, supposedly 'Germanic' notions of good faith, Spanish scholasticism inspiring 16th century courts and treatise writers in the Southern Netherlands, Natural law theories: many factors contributed to the ultimate recognition of the principle *ex nudo pacto oritur actio* (or: *pacta* [*nuda*] *sunt servanda*). In a way, one can say that it was a triumph of Roman law in spite of Roman law. That contracts based on nothing more than formless consent are, as a rule, actionable is recognized (though no longer always specifically spelt out[152]) in all modern Continental codes.

---

148 Cf., most recently, *Karl Larenz, Claus-Wilhelm Canaris*, Lehrbuch des Schuldrechts, vol. II/2, 13th ed., 1994, § 75 I 3, 4.

149 For a similar conclusion, see *Helmut Koziol*, Generalnorm und Einzeltatbestände als Systeme der Verschuldenshaftung: Unterschiede und Angleichungsmöglichkeiten, ZEuP 3 (1995) 359 sqq.; cf. also J. Spier (ed.), The Limits of Liability, 1996.

150 For details of what follows, see the literature quoted above (n. 68).

151 *Ulp.* D. 2, 14, 7, 4.

152 It is usually taken to be implicit in § 305 BGB. But see, as far as France is concerned, art. 1134 c.c.

3. The Evolution of the Law of Unjustified Enrichment

The move towards a general law of contract was bound to have consequences for the law of unjustified enrichment. The Roman system of *condictiones* tied in with and supplemented the contractual system[153]. Particularly important was the *condictio indebiti*, for it covered the paradigmatic situation of *indebitum solutum*[154]. Recognition of *ex nudo pacto oritur actio* was bound to extend its range of application even further. The main function of the *condictio indebiti* is still to supplement the law of contract. It has to be available whenever a transfer fails to achieve what it is supposed to achieve: the discharge of an obligation that the transferor had incurred towards the transferee. Not surprisingly, therefore, in all continental legal systems we find general rules dealing with the restitution of benefits conferred by transfer[155]. The significance of these rules within a given legal system may vary. But whether they subscribe to a consensual, a causal or an abstract system of transfer of ownership, all legal systems provide enrichment remedies, and they all specifically emphasize, and single out, the claim of enrichment by transfer.

Historically, this uniformity of approach is based on the common Roman heritage, for we are dealing here with the modern, extended version of the *condictio indebiti*. Even the new Dutch Civil Code devotes nine sections to 'onverschuldigde betaling', before it deals with other cases of unjustified enrichment[156]. Characteristically, the modern version of the *condictio indebiti* has abandoned, step by step, certain idiosyncrasies of its Roman ancestor; characteristically, too, this gradual development is still reflected in the different codes[157].

Apart from that, however, there have been, over the last 300 years, repeated attempts to formulate a general enrichment action – a magic formula comprising all instances of unjustified retention even apart from *indebitum solutum*. In France and Germany the decisive advances were launched from two completely different points of departure. The French courts[158] recognized a general enrichment action on the basis of the *actio de in rem verso utilis*, a claim based historically on a sin-

---

153 For details, see *Berthold Kupisch*, Ungerechtfertigte Bereicherung: Geschichtliche Entwicklungen, 1987, pp. 4 sqq.; Law of Obligations (n. 50) 841 sqq.

154 For details, see Law of Obligations (n. 50) 834 sqq., 848 sqq. In both *Gaius*'s and *Justinian*'s 'Institutes' *indebitum solutum* is the only form of enrichment liability dealt with: *Gai.* 3, 91 (and see *Gai.* D. 44, 7, 5, 3 read in conjunction with *Gai.* D. 44, 7, 1 *pr.*); *Inst.* 3, 27, 6.

155 For all details, see *Reinhard Zimmermann*, Unjustified Enrichment: The Modern Civilian Approach, (1995) 15 Oxford J.L.S. 403 sqq.

156 Artt. 203:6 BW. For an analysis of the historical development see *Eltjo J.H. Schrage*, The Law of Restitution: The History of Dutch Legislation, in: *idem*, ed., Unjust Enrichment: The Comparative Legal History of the Law of Restitution, 1995, pp. 323 sqq.

157 See the discussion in (1995) 15 Oxford J.L.S. 408 sqq.; as far as the law of unjustified enrichment under the *usus modernus pandectarum* is concerned, see *Berthold Kupisch*, Ungerechtfertigte Bereicherung, in: Schrage (n. 156) 237 sqq.

158 Arrêt *Boudier*, 15. 6. 1892, Recueil Dalloz 1892 (première partie), p. 596.

gle passage in *Justinian*'s Code[159], accepted by the 'code civil' – at best – in a vestigial form, and generalized by a German professor writing a textbook on French private law[160]. *Friedrich Carl von Savigny*, on the other hand, chose the *condictio sine causa* (*generalis*) as the most suitable means to overcome the Roman fragmentation[161]. But even before the *Cour de Cassation* and *Savigny*, *Hugo Grotius* had drawn together the different threads spun by his predecessors from the material available within the *Corpus iuris*, and had woven them into a single, crisp and comprehensive formula[162]. Even for this formula the Digest, of course, provided a convenient model; it was the general equitable principle enunciated by Pomponius: "... hoc natura aequum est neminem cum alterius detrimento fieri locupletiorem"[163].

IX. The Ambivalence of Generalization

The modern general concept of contract is, ultimately, derived from the consensual contracts of Roman law. On the other hand, one could also describe the modern regime of *ex nudo pacto oritur actio* as a reversal of the Roman rule of *nuda pactio obligationem non parit*. This kind of ambivalence is typical of the civilian tradition. One can think of a variety of examples where the second aspect (the gradual erosion of a central principle of Roman contract law by means of Roman learning and, usually, even on the basis of a handful of sources from the *Corpus iuris*) comes out even more strongly.

---

159 C. 4, 26, 7, 3 (*Diocl. et Max.*).

160 See *Karl Salomo Zachariä von Lingenthal*, Handbuch des Französischen Civilrechts, 1808, vol. II, § 399 sqq. The astonishing career of the *actio de in rem verso* has been described by Berthold *Kupisch*, Die Versionsklage, 1965. See further *John P. Dawson*, Unjust Enrichment, 1951, pp. 85 sqq.; *Robert Feenstra*, Die ungerechtfertigte Bereicherung in dogmengeschichtlicher Sicht, (1972) 29 Ankara Üniversitesi Hukuk Fakültesi Dergisi 298 sqq.; *Coing* (n. 4) 498 sqq.; Law of Obligations (n. 50) 878 sqq.

161 System des heutigen römischen Rechts, vol. 5, 1841, pp. 503 sqq. For an analysis, see *Horst Hammen*, Die Bedeutung Friedrich Carl v. Savignys for die allgemeinen dogmatischen Grundlagen des Deutschen Bürgerlichen Gesetzbuches, 1983, pp. 187 sqq.

162 De jure belli ac pacis, Lib. II, Cap. X, II. For details, see *Robert Feenstra*, De betekenis van De Groot and Huber voor de ontwikkeling van een algemene actie uit ongerechtvaardigde verrijking, in: Uit het recht, Rechtsgeleerde opstellen aangeboden aan mr. P.J. Verdam, 1971, pp. 137 sqq.; *idem*, L'influence de la scolastique espagnole sur Grotius en droit privé: quelques expériences dans des questions de fond et de forme, concernant notamment les doctrines de l'erreur et de l'enrichissement sans cause, in: Fata Iuris Romani, 1974, pp. 338 sqq.; Law of Obligations (n. 50) 885 sqq.; *Daniel Visser*, Das Recht der ungerechtfertigten Bereicherung, in: Feenstra/Zimmermann (n. 68) 370 sqq.; *Robert Feenstra*, Grotius' Doctrine of Unjust Enrichment as a Source of Obligation: Its Origin and Its Influence in Roman-Dutch Law, in: Schrage (n. 156) 197 sqq.

163 *Pomp.* D. 12, 6, 14; cf. also *Pomp.* D. 50, 17, 206. On the origin and background of this principle and its reception into the legal system, see *Christian Wollschläger*, Das stoische Bereicherungsverbot in der römischen Rechtswissenschaft, in: Römisches Recht in der europäischen Tradition, Symposion für Franz Wieacker, 1985, pp. 41 sqq.

1. Specific Performance

Omnis condemnatio pecuniaria was one such principle. It had been of fundamental importance in classical Roman law[164]. Closely connected with the formulary procedure, it was largely discarded during the ascendancy of the postclassical *cognitio* procedure, but not completely abandoned by *Justinian*. The *Corpus Juris*, therefore, leaves considerable doubt as to how much ground the principle of specific performance had actually gained in practice. Glossators and Commentators introduced subtle and elaborate distinctions in order to provide some sort of systematic framework for the confusing casuistry of the sources, and even until the days of the *usus modernus* the question continued to be embroiled in disputes. *Nemo potest praecise cogi ad factum* remained the general maxim applicable for *facere*-obligations. Via *Pothier*[165] it even found its way into the French 'code civil'[166]. In Germany, the last vestiges of *omnis condemnatio pecuniaria* were ultimately overcome in the course of the 19th century, and parties to a contract are entitled, as a matter or course, to demand performance of their respective obligations *in specie*. This is implicit in § 241 BGB. By and large, the position in German law is representative of the contemporary civilian approach, for even in France art. 1142 c.c. has, for all practical purposes, been rendered nugatory[167].

2. Contracts in Favour of Third Parties

Alteri stipulari nemo potest is another principle of Roman law that took a long time and much intellectual effort to overcome[168]. It was taken to prevent the recognition of a contract in favour of third parties. *Justinian*'s compilers, however, not only retained, and even emphasized, this principle but also took over, extended or introduced a number of situations in which it did not apply[169]. Thus, they provided convenient levers, which sufficiently imaginative lawyers could use to unhinge the principle altogether. In the course of the 17th century, and under the combined auspices of *usus modernus* and Natural law, the contract in favour of third parties came to be very widely accepted, albeit on the basis that the third party was re-

---

164 For what follows, see *Coing* (n. 4) 432 sqq.; Law of Obligations (n. 50) 770 sqq.; *Karin Nehlsen-von Stryk*, Grenzen des Rechtzwangs: Zur Geschichte der Naturalvollstreckung, AcP 193 (1993) 529 sqq.; *Wilhelm Rütten*, Zur Entstehung des Erfüllungszwangs im Schuldverhältnis, in: Festschrift für Joachim Gernhuber, 1993, pp. 939 sqq.; *Tilman Repgen*, Vertragstreue und Erfüllungszwang in der mittelalterlichen Rechtswissenschaft, 1994.

165 Traité des obligations, n. 160.

166 Art. 1142 c.c.

167 For a comparative discussion, see *Zweigert/Kötz/Weir* (n. 37) 504 sqq.

168 For all details of the development, see Law of Obligations (n. 50) 34 sqq.; and see also *Hein Kötz*, Rights of Third Parties: Third Party Beneficiaries and Assignment, in: International Encyclopedia of Comparative Law, vol. 7, chapter 13, 1992, nn. 4 sqq.

169 Cf., for example, C. 8, 54, 3 (*Diocl. et Max.*); *Ulp.* D. 13, 7, 13 *pr.*; C. 3, 42, 8 (*Diocl. et Max.*). The latter texts are probably interpolated.

quired to accept the right which was to be conferred on him. This was a consequence of the emphasis that Natural lawyers, and most notably *Hugo Grotius*[170], placed on will and consensus as the essential elements of contract law. Even before *Grotius*, incidentally, *Antonius Perezius* and *Covarruvias* had drawn attention to the fact that recognition of contracts affecting third parties followed from the endorsement of *ex nudo pacto oritur actio*[171].

It was in the garb of this consensual construction that the contract in favour of a third party made its way into the Prussian, Bavarian, and Saxonian codifications. The Austrian Code was more conservative in this respect and retained the *alteri stipulari nemo potest* principle[172]. So did, under the influence of *Robert-Joseph Pothier*[173], the French 'code civil'[174]. It made provision for only two narrowly defined exceptions in art. 1121: a 'stipulation au profit d'un tiers' is valid, "losque telle est la condition d'une stipulation que l'on fait pour soi-même ou d'une donation que l'on fait à un autre". It is not difficult to discover the sources from the *Corpus iuris* on which these exceptions were based. French courts have managed to prize open this back door and to introduce into French law – *contra legem*, as it were – the modern contract in favour of third parties[175]. According to the 'théorie de la création directe de l'action' the third party acquires the right directly at the time when promisor and promisee conclude their contract; his own declaration does not have a constitutive effect. This has brought French law into line with modern German law; the "mature"[176] solutions found in § 328 BGB sqq. are due to the conceptual clarity achieved by the Pandectists[177]. The Austrian code, as a result of a revision in 1916, follows a very similar pattern.

X. Intellectual Unity Beyond Codification

1. Roman Law, Natural Law and Pandectist Legal Science

The historical development of the contract in favour of third parties gives rise to two further observations. Firstly, contrary to what is often alleged, the BGB is not necessarily more 'Roman' in its content than the so-called Natural law codes. The main thrust of Natural law was not directed against the rules and institutions of Ro-

170 De jure belli ac pacis, Lib. II, Cap. XI, § 18.

171 See *Coing* (n. 4) 425; and see *Antonius Perezius*, Praelectiones in duodecim libros codicis, Lib. VIII, Tit. LV, n. 9.

172 § 881 ABGB.

173 Traité des obligations, nn. 57 sqq.

174 Art. 1165 c.c.

175 Cf. *Zweigert/Kötz/Weir* (n. 37) 494 sqq.

176 *Zweigert/Kötz/Weir* (n. 37) 502.

177 Cf. especially *Windscheid/Kipp* (n. 85) 316.

man law as such, but rather against the complexity of sources, the lack of system and transparency, and the great number of intractable doctrinal disputes that had for centuries enveloped its application and bedevilled its comprehensibility. The 19th century Pandectists[178], on the other hand, who prepared the ground for the BGB were often quite happy to endorse, perpetuate and further refine a development that was clearly moving away from the ancient Roman sources. In essence, they advocated organic development rather than sterile historicism; and whilst it is easy, today, to criticize their methodology one must not, at the same time, forget that they created a legal framework not only of unequalled sophistication but also suited to the requirements of the first one hundred years of the 'Modern'[179].

For another illustration of this point we may turn to the problem of the determination of price. Article 1108 c.c. requires every contract to have "un objet certain". 'Objet' in terms of this rule, and in terms of art. 1129 c. c., is also the counterperformance to be given for the performance of services, the transfer of an object, etc. As far as a contract of sale is concerned, art. 1591 c.c. specifically determines that the price has to be "déterminé et désigné par les parties". These rules are based, unmistakably, on Roman law. Article 1591 is the codified version of the *certum pretium* requirement for the Roman contract of sale[180]. The more general rule of art. 1108, on the other hand, appears to represent an intermediate stage within the grand development from the fragmented Roman law of contracts (which focused on individual types of contract, the constituent elements of which, as a matter of course, had to be the object of the agreement of the parties) towards the modern, general concept of contract, which emphasizes the freedom of the parties to design their own contract[181]. Thus, according to the modern point of view, it has only to be ascertained whether the parties had intended to be bound[182]. This is, indeed, the approach adopted by the BGB[183]. Thus, in particular, determination of the price may be left to one of the contracting parties, be it that he has to decide 'in an equitable manner' or even in his free discretion[184]. This obviously represents a deviation from Roman law. It is based on Pandectist doctrine[185] which had managed to

---

178 For an overview in English, see *Mathias Reimann*, Nineteenth Century German Legal Science, (1990) 13 Boston College Law Review 837 sqq. and now also *Wieacker/Weir* (n. 7) pp. 341 sqq. For a vindication of their leading representative, *Bernhard Windscheid*, see *Ulrich Falk*, Ein Gelehrter wie Windscheid, 1989.

179 Cf. *Paul Johnson*, The Birth of the Modern-World Society 1815 – 1830, 1991.

180 It is discussed in a number of interesting fragments; see Law of Obligations (n. 50) 253 sqq.

181 Cf. *Barry Nicholas*, The French Law of Contract, 2nd ed., 1992, pp. 115 sq.

182 Cf. *Wolfgang Witz*, Der unbestimmte Kaufpreis, 1989, pp. 89 sqq., 155 sqq. and the comparative discussion by *Barry Nicholas*, Certainty of Price, in: Comparative and Private International Law, Essays in Honor of J. H. Merryman, 1990, pp. 247 sqq.; *A.T. van Mehren*, The Formation of Contracts, in: International Encyclopedia of Comparative Law, vol. 7, chapter 9, 1992, nn. 50 sqq.

183 315 sqq. BGB.

184 § 315 I BGB.

venture, in *Jhering*'s famous words, beyond Roman law by means of Roman law. In sharp contradistinction to the strict requirements of arts. 1129, 1591 c.c. which have given rise to a complex casuistry[186], § 315 sqq. BGB appear to have stood the test of time. It is therefore hardly surprising that these more liberal principles are also gaining ground internationally[187].

2. *Factors Counterbalancing the Nationalistic Isolation*

The second point relates to the intellectual unity of the civilian tradition. We have emphasized that it existed until the end of the 18th century; and that it has greatly been threatened by the nationalization of law and legal science resulting from the introduction of codifications within the confines of the modern nation states. But there have been factors counterbalancing this nationalistic isolation. The most important of them, of course, provides the basis for the present paper: all these codifications are, and have remained, emanations of one and the same tradition. Characteristically, therefore, neither the French 'code civil' nor the Austrian codifications were intended to be codes of national, specifically French or Austrian law. They were universalistic in spirit, approach and outlook[188]. The same is true of the German BGB, even if it was caught up in a surge of nationalistic sentiment. For it was only in exceptional instances that this nationalistic attitude, reinforced by a specifically anti-French bias, left its mark on the content of the code[189].

The common tradition underlying the modern codifications also contributed to the continued existence of a network of intellectual contacts between them. The 'code civil', in particular, was able to maintain its dominant position in large parts of Europe even after Napoleon had been defeated[190]. Down to the end of the

---

185 For details, see *Hans-Joachim Winter*, Die Bestimmung der Leistung durch den Vertragspartner oder Dritte (§ 315 bis 319 BGB) unter besonderer Berücksichtigung der Rechtsprechung und Lehre des 19. Jahrhunderts (unpublished Dr. iur. thesis, Frankfurt, 1979).

186 See *Witz* (n. 182) 21 sqq.; *Christian Larroumet*, Droit Civil, vol. 3, 2nd ed., 1990, nn. 386 sqq.

187 Cf. Artt. 2.101 sqq. of the 'Principles of European Contract Law' (on which see *Zimmermann*, Juristenzeitung (1995) 477 sqq.); cf. also Art. 5.7 of the 'Principles of International Commercial Contracts' (Unidroit). In the meantime, even the Assemblée plénaire of the Cour de cassation has adopted a much more liberal approach to long term supply agreements and has reversed its previous interpretation of art. 1129 c.c.: Dalloz 1996, 13; and see the analysis by *Claude Witz, Gerhard Wolter*, Das Ende der Problematik des unbestimmten Preises in Frankreich, ZEuP 4 (1996) 648 sqq.

188 Cf. *supra*, n. 45. Interestingly, *H. Kooiker* even draws attention to a "third renaissance" of Roman law (after the introduction of the French and Dutch codifications!): Lex scripta abrogata, 1996.

189 Cf. the examples provided in (1994/95) 1 Columbia Journal of European Law 87 sq.

190 Cf. *Elmar Wadle*, Französisches Recht und deutsche Gesetzgebung im 19. Jahrhundert, in: Reiner Schulze, ed., Europäische Rechts- und Verfassungsgeschichte, 1991, pp. 201 sqq.;

19th century, for instance, it remained in force in the Prussian Rhine-Province and in other German areas on the left bank of the Rhine. The Grand Duchy of Baden adopted the 'Badisches Landrecht', which was based on a translation of the 'code civil'[191]. One entire division of the Imperial Supreme Court, the second 'senate', dealt with the appeals involving French law. Of course, one did not refer to French but to Rhenish law[192], and the second senate was therefore dubbed the 'Rhenish' one. Pandectist legal learning, on the other hand, was influential all over Europe: from Sweden[193] to the Netherlands[194] and Italy[195], and not least of all in France[196]. This reception was not confined to methodology and system, we also find impulses penetrating to the level of private law doctrine. *Rudolf von Jhering*'s famous *culpa in contrahendo*, based on the rather shaky foundations of a handful of Roman sources concerning the sale of *res publicae*, *res divini iuris* and *liberi homines*[197], provides just one example[198].

In view of the similarity of language, German influence on Austrian legal science and on Austrian law was, of course, particularly strong[199]. Thus, for instance, the general clause of delictual liability in § 1295 ABGB was reduced, by

Reiner Schulze, Französisches Recht und Europäische Rechtsgeschichte im 19. Jahrhundert, in: *idem*, Französisches Zivilrecht in Europa während des 19. Jahrhunderts, 1994, pp. 23 sqq.; and the other contributions to the same volume.

191 According to *Helmut Coing*, Einleitung, in: Staudinger, Kommentar zum Bürgerlichen Gesetzbuch, 12th ed., vol. 1, 1980, n. 24, 16,6% of the population of the German Reich (i.e. more than 8 million persons) of 1890 lived according to French law. Cf. also the map in *Hans Schlosser*, Grundzüge der Neueren Privatrechtsgeschichte, 7th ed., 1993, p. 118.

192 Cf. e.g. *Hans-Jürgen Becker*, Das Rheinische Recht und seine Bedeutung für die Rechtsentwicklung in Deutschland im 19. Jahrhundert, Juristische Schulung (1985) 338 sqq.

193 *Jan-Olof Sundell*, German Influence on Swedish Private Law Doctrine 1870-1914, 1991 Scandinavian Studies in Law 237 sqq.

194 Cf. *J. H. A. Lokin*, Het NBW en de pandektistiek, in: Historisch vooruitzicht, Opstellen over rechtsgeschiedenis in burgerlijk recht, BW-krant jaarboek 1994, pp. 125 sqq.

195 Cf., e.g., Reiner Schulze, ed., Deutsche Rechtwissenschaft und Staatslehre im Spiegel der italienischen Rechtskultur während der zweiten Hälfte des 19. Jahrhunderts, 1990.

196 See the comprehensive study by *Alfons Bürge*, Das französische Privatrecht im 19. Jahrhundert: Zwischen Tradition und Pandektenwissenschaft, Liberalismus und Etatismus, 1991, pp. 150 sqq.; cf. also *idem*, Der Einfluß der Pandektenwissenschaft auf das französische Privatrecht im 19. Jahrhundert: Vom Vermögen zum patrimoine, in: Reiner Schulze, ed., Französisches Zivilrecht in Europa während des 19. Jahrhunderts, 1994, pp. 221 sqq.

197 Cf. Law of Obligations (n. 50) 241 sqq.; *Erich Schanze*, Culpa in contrahendo bei Jhering, Ius Commune 7 (1978) 326 sqq.; *Dieter Medicus*, Zur Entdeckungsgeschichte der culpa in contrahendo, in: Iuris Professio, Festgabe für Max Kaser, 1986, pp. 169 sqq.

198 *Stephan Lorenz*, Die culpa in contrahendo im französischen Recht, ZEuP 2 (1994) 218 sqq.

199 Cf., e.g., *Werner Ogris*, Die Wissenschaft des gemeinen römischen Rechts und das österreichische Allgemeine bürgerliche Gesetzbuch, in: Helmut Coing, Walter Wilhelm, edd., Wissenschaft und Kodifikation des Privatrechts im 19. Jahrhundert, vol. 1, 1974, pp. 153 sqq.; *Wilhelm Brauneder*, Privatrechtsfortbildung durch Juristenrecht in Exegetik und Pandektistik in Österreich, Zeitschrift für Neuere Rechtsgeschichte 5 (1983) 22 sqq.

way of interpretation, into a kind of condensed version of § 823 I, 823 II BGB. In 1916 the legislature even added, totally unnecessarily one would have thought, a second subsection to § 1295 ABGB which corresponds to § 826 BGB[200].

Similarly important was the rise of comparative law as a new and independent branch of legal science in the course of the 19th century[201]. Comparative research provided a rich source of inspiration for draftsmen of 19th and 20th century legislation[202].

XI. New Legal Rules

We have been referring to instances where the general current of civilian opinion was drifting away from a principle of Roman law. In other cases new legal doctrines were developed and grafted onto the traditional law of obligations. But although they were new, these doctrines were often crafted of Roman substance. Thus, for example, the medieval lawyers could avail themselves of some building stones hewn from the Digest[203] in order to establish the notion that only those agreements which rest upon a lawful *causa* are actionable. This was a crucial step facilitating the transition from *nuda pactio obligationem non parit* to the counter-rule *ex nudo pacto oritur actio*[204].

Fidem frangenti fides frangitur was a principle of medieval Canon law[205] which was transformed by virtue of a suspensive condition read into the contract: "subintelligitur conditio 'si fides servetur'"[206]. People usually promise a performance in

200 For a critical evaluation of the assimilation between the German and Austrian law of delict, see *Rudolf Reischauer*, in: Peter Rummel, ed., Kommentar zum ABGB, vol. 2, 1984, § 1294, n. 16; for a different view, see *Friedrich Harrer*, in: Michael Schwimann, ed., Praxiskommentar zum ABGB, vol. 5, 1987, § 1295, nn. 1 sqq. Very much the same development, interestingly, appears to have occurred in Swiss law (with regard to the general clause of Art. 41 I OR); cf. *Peter Gauch*, Deliktshaftung für reinen Vermögensschaden, in: Festschrift für Max Keller, 1989, p. 136.

201 Cf. *Zweigert/Kötz/Weir* (n. 37) 47 sqq.; *Max Rheinstein*, Einführung in die Rechtsvergleichung, 2nd ed., 1987, pp. 37 sqq.

202 Cf., in particular, *Helmut Coing*, Rechtsvergleichung als Grundlage von Gesetzgebung im 19. Jahrhundert, Ius Commune 7 (1978) 168 sqq. Cf. also, for instance, the preparatory drafts for the various parts of the BGB: Werner Schubert, ed., Die Vorlagen der Redaktoren für die erste Kommission zur Ausarbeitung des Entwurfs eines Bürgerlichen Gesetzbuches, 1980 sqq.

203 In particular *Aristo/Ulp*. D. 2, 14, 7, 2; *Ulp*. D. 2, 17, 7, 4; *Ulp*. D. 44, 4, 2, 3; further details in Law of Obligations (n. 50) 549 sqq.

204 Cf. *supra*, n. 68.

205 *Georges Boyer*, Recherches historique sur la résolution des contrats, 1924, pp. 220 sqq.; *J. A. Ankum*, De voorouders van een boze fee, 1964, pp. 10 sqq., *Friedrich Merzbacher*, Die Regel 'Fidem frangenti fides frangitur' und ihre Anwendung, ZSS (KA) 99 (1982) 339 sqq.

206 Cf., e.g., Decretales Gregorii IX, Lib. II, Tit. XXIV, Cap. XXV and *Boyer* (n. 205) 220 sqq., 240 sqq.

order to obtain a counterperformance. If the other party fails to perform, they do not, presumably, want to be bound either. A general right of rescission in case of breach of contract was never recognized in Roman law[207]. Suspensive conditions and the skilful use of legal fictions, however, were[208]. The Natural lawyers took up this line of development[209], which eventually led to the incorporation of a rule into the 'code civil' according to which "[l]a condition résolutoire est toujours sousentendue dans les contrats synallagmatiques, pour le cas où l'une des deux parties ne satisfera point à son engagement"[210]. The draftsmen of the BGB availed themselves of a tacit *lex commissoria* when they granted the creditor a unilateral right of rescission in cases of impossibility of performance and *mora debitoris*[211].

The device of an implied condition also stood at the cradle of the *clausula rebus sic stantibus*: a proviso according to which a contract is binding only as long and as far as matters remain the same as they were at the time of conclusion of the contract[212]. It became part and parcel of the *usus modernus* as well as of the systematic endeavours of the Natural lawyers, and it attained great prominence in the field of private law and far beyond. And if, technically, the *clausula* took the form of a *conditio tacita*, even its substance was inspired by the Roman sources, though in this case not the legal ones. Moral philosophers like *Seneca*[213] and *Cicero*[214] had been the first to draw attention to the change of circumstances and thus to sow the seed for a legal principle of great importance.

XII. Main Features of a European Law of Obligations

The main theme of what has been said, so far, was that of considerable diversity within a fundamental intellectual unity – a unity created largely by a common tra-

---

207 *Fritz Schulz* very pointedly refers to an "iron rule of Roman law which the classical lawyers unflinchingly observed". But see Law of Obligations (n. 50) 578.

208 Cf. generally 'Heard melodies are sweet, but those unheard are sweeter ...': Condicio tacita, implied conditions und die Fortbildung des europäischen Vertragsrechts, AcP 193 (1993) 121 sqq.

209 For details, see *Karl Otto Scherner*, Rücktrittsrecht wegen Nichterfüllung, 1965, pp. 92 sqq.; *Coing* (n. 4) 444.

210 Art. 1184 c.c. On this rule, and its history, see *Boyer* (n. 205) 381 sqq., 11 sqq.; *Hans-Georg Landfermann*, Die Auflösung des Vertrages nach richterlichem Ermessen als Rechtsfolge der Nichterfüllung im französischen Recht, 1968; *Scherner* (n. 209) 135 sqq.

211 For details, see *Hans G. Leser*, Der Rücktritt vom Vertrag, 1975, pp. 16 sqq.

212 For details, see Law of Obligations (n. 50) 579 sqq. and, since then, *Ralf Köbler*, Die 'clausula rebus sic stantibus' als allgemeiner Rechtsgrundsatz, 1991; *Michael Rummel*, Die 'clausula rebus sic stantibus', 1991; *Zimmermann* (n. 208) 134 sqq.; *Klaus Luig*, Dogmengeschichte des Privatrechts als rechtswissenschaftliche Grundlagenforschung, Ius Commune 20 (1993) 193 sqq.

213 De beneficiis, Lib. IV, XXXV, 3.

214 De officiis, 3, XXV – 95.

dition. If we finally try to assess the main features of a common European law of obligations, as derived from Roman law and embodied in the modern codes, we may include the following points[215].

The law of obligations constitutes a body of law that is distinct from property law. The one deals with *iura in personam*, the other with *iura in rem*. Within the law of obligations there is a fundamental distinction between contract and delict. This distinction does not, however, represent an exhaustive basis for the systematic analysis of the law of obligations. In particular, unjustified enrichment and *negotiorum gestio* are recognized as independent sources of obligations. Delictual liability, as a rule, is based on fault. There are, however, also cases of purely risk-based liability. We have a general remedy for the restitution of benefits conferred without obligation, the core features of which are the notions of 'transfer' and 'without legal ground'. Unjustified enrichment also has to be skimmed off, if it has come about in other ways. Taking care of someone else's affairs may lead to a claim for compensation.

There is a general law of contract, and contracts are based, as a rule, on the informal consent of the parties (established by means of offer and acceptance). Only in exceptional situations, and for specific policy reasons, does the law require the observation of certain formalities. The parties are free to decide whether they want to enter into a contract or not, and it is up to them to determine the content of their transaction. Such content may not, however, be illegal or immoral. Equality in the

---

215 There is not, to my knowledge, any comprehensive comparative investigation of this nature. As far as German law is concerned, cf., however, *Max Kaser*, Der römische Anteil am deutschen bürgerlichen Recht, Juristische Schulung (1967) 337 sqq.; *Eduard Picker*, Zum Gegenwartswert des Römischen Rechts, in: Hans Bungert, ed., Das antike Rom in Europa, 1985, pp. 289 sqq.; *Rolf Knütel*, Römisches Recht und deutsches Bürgerliches Recht, in: Walter Ludwig, ed., Die Antike in der europäischen Gegenwart, 1993, pp. 43 sqq.; for Dutch law, see *Robert Feenstra*, Romeinsregtelike grondslagen van het Nederlands privaatreg, 5th ed., 1990. Cf. also, under more general aspects, *Heinz Hübner*, Sinn und Möglichkeiten retrospektiver Rechtsvergleichung, in: Festschrift für Gerhard Kegel, 1987, pp. 235 sqq.; *Heinrich Honsell*, Das rechtshistorische Argument in der modernen Zivilrechtsdogmatik, in: Dieter Simon, ed., Akten des 26. Deutschen Rechtshistorikertages, 1987, pp. 305 sqq.; and, under the auspices of European legal unity, *Reiner Schulze*, Allgemeine Rechtsgrundsätze und europäisches Privatrecht, ZEuP 1 (1993) 442 sqq.; *Reinhard Zimmermann*, Roman Law and European Legal Unity, in: Hartkamp, Hesselink *et al.* (n. 4) 65 sqq.; *Rolf Knütel*, Rechtseinheit in Europa und römisches Recht, ZEuP 2 (1994) 244 sqq. More specifically on the question of a common system of European law, see *Bruno Schmidlin*, Gibt es ein gemeineuropäisches System des Privatrechts?, in: *idem*, Vers un droit privé européen commun?, Skizzen zum gemeineuropäischen Privatrecht, 1994, pp. 33 sqq.; *Berthold Kupisch*, Institutionensystem und Pandektensystem: Zur Geschichte des res-Begriffes, (1990-1992) 25-27 The Irish Jurist 293 sqq. (published in 1994); *Eltjo Schrage*, Das System des neuen niederländischen Zivilgesetzbuches, Juristische Blätter (1994) 501 sqq. As far as specific areas of substantive law within the field of obligations and property are concerned, cf. also chapters 8 - 22 in A.S. Hartkamp, M.W. Hesselink *et al.*, edd., Towards a European Civil Code, 1994. They do not, however, merely deal with the civil law jurisdictions but mainly revolve around the civil law/common law dichotomy.

values exchanged is largely immaterial. A party is not bound by his agreement, if he has given it while labouring under a defect of the will (based on or induced by *error*, *metus* or *dolus*). The parties to a contract are entitled to demand performance of their respective obligations *in specie*. Apart from that, the general law of contract contains rules concerning legal capacity, the interpretation of contracts, the requirements for breach of contract and the remedies available (damages, the right to withhold performance and termination), agency, contracts in favour of third parties and cession, penalty clauses, time, place and other modalities of performance, termination of contractual obligations by means other than *solutio propria* (most notably set-off), extinctive prescription, plurality of debtors and creditors. Most of these rules constitute *ius dispositivum*, i.e., they are not mandatory.

The legal system also makes available to the parties specific contractual paradigms. They range from sale, exchange, donation, *locatio conductio rei*, *operis* and *operarum*, to suretyship, mandate, deposit and two different types of loan (for use and for consumption). Again, most of the statutory rules concerning these contract types (like the aedilitian remedies in sale) are not mandatory. Also, the parties are free to conclude atypical (or, in traditional civilian terminology, 'innominate') contracts.

Even apart from the structural foundations and the main rules and institutions of the law of obligations, most of the key-concepts which we use in order to express ourselves are Roman in origin and belong to the common civilian heritage: obligation, contract and delict, debtor and creditor, *dolus*, *culpa* and *diligentia quam in suis*, risk and *vis maior*, gratuitous and onerous, bilateral and unilaterally binding transactions. The civilian tradition has also seeped into the interstices of the codes: where they do not deal with a matter at all, where they contain a blanket clause, or where the solution to a specific problem has expressly been left to legal science[216]. *Casum sentit dominus, interpretatio contra eum qui clarius loqui debuisset, venire contra factum proprium, dolo agit qui petit quod statim redditurus est, nemo auditur turpitudinem suam allegans*: these phrases still belong to the standard repertory of modern private lawyers all over Europe.

And, finally, it has to be remembered that no codification is perfect. Thus, there are bound to be drafting mistakes. In other cases a specific view, espoused by 18th or 19th century legal science, turns out to be, in retrospect, one-sided and unbalanced, somewhat idiosyncratic or too firmly rooted in outdated ideological or doctrinal premises. In many of these cases, courts and legal writers have been able to redress the situation; they have found ways and means to assert more modern views, even in the face of the code. Oddly enough, however, the doctrines thus developed have precursors in the older *ius commune*. Yet, this experience is odd only for those who are caught up in the simplistic illusion that a codification can be entirely cut off from the continuity of historical development. For even in a codified

216 For details and examples, see *Reinhard Zimmermann*, Civil Code and Civil Law, (1994/95) 1 Columbia Journal of European Law 89 sqq., 94 sqq.

legal system the re-appearance of ideas is by no means a rare – although it is usually an unacknowledged – phenomenon[217]. In the process, many of the jagged edges and time-bound eccentricities of the codes are worn away. In Germany, for instance[218], the courts have been prepared to award financial compensation for non-pecuniary harm in all cases where a person's 'general personality right' has been seriously infringed. This is clearly *contra legem*, for the BGB not only does not recognize a 'general personality right', it also explicitly confines the aggrieved plaintiff to a claim for the pecuniary loss that he has suffered. It is, however, in conformity with the civilian tradition as established, in this case, on the basis of the Roman *actio iniuriarum*[219].

Given some insight into historical background and comparative context, it is not at all difficult for a modern private lawyer from one jurisdiction to understand the rules contained in other civil codes, to recognize similarities and to evaluate differences, and to identify the common foundations underlying all of them. It should not, in principle, be more difficult to devise a European codification today than it was to draft the French or German codes – not, at any rate, if one confines one's attention, as was the brief of this paper, to the European continent. What one may well question, however, is the vocation of our time for this ambitious kind of legislation. The 'code civil' would have been unimaginable without the treatises of *Domat* and *Pothier*, the BGB equally inconceivable without the work of *Savigny* and *Windscheid*. The lesson is obvious. Once again, the essential prerequisite for a truly European private law would appear to be the emergence of an 'organically progressive' legal science[220], which would have to transcend the national boundaries and to revitalize a common tradition[221].

---

217 *Theo Mayer-Maly*, Die Wiederkehr von Rechtsfiguren, Juristenzeitung (1971) 1 sqq. Cf. also *Peter Stein*, Judge and Jurist in the Civil Law: A Historical Interpretation, in: *idem*, The Character and Influence of the Roman Civil Law, 1988, pp. 142 sqq.; and, most recently, *David Johnston*, The Renewal of the Old, Inaugural Lecture, Cambridge, 1996.

218 For more examples concerning German law, see (1994/95) 1 Columbia Journal of European Law 101 sqq.

219 For all details, see Law of Obligations (n. 50) 1050 sqq., 1090 sqq.; *Helge Walter*, Actio iniuriarum: Der Schutz der Persönlichkeit im südafrikanischen Privatrecht, 1996.

220 *Friedrich Carl von Savigny*, Vom Beruf unserer Zeit für Gesetzgebung und Rechtswissenschaft, 1814, in: Hans Hattenhauer, ed., Thibaut und Savigny: Ihre programmatische Schriften, 1973.

221 For a programmatic statement, see *Reinhard Zimmermann*, Savigny's Legacy, (1996) 112 L.Q.R. 576 sqq.

Civilian Elements in European Civil Procedure

By Jeroen M. J. Chorus

I. Common Historical Roots

Most lawyers will probably, at first sight, subscribe to the idea that English and Scottish civil procedures are very different from continental systems. This is not helped by a deeply rooted British consciousness of being so very distinct. Today, however, the argument is gaining ground that this idea is in need of fundamental revision. As put elegantly by Professor *Markesinis*[1], common lawyers and civil lawyers, though different, are not as different as common mythology considers them to be. Let me briefly sketch some historical aspects of this argument.

Baron *van Caenegem* has shown that it is possible, and justified, to treat the history of civil procedure in a European framework. There is no need to remain within national boundaries, not even to keep Britain, or England, separated from the rest of Europe. I can do no better than borrow largely here from *van Caenegem*'s exemplary History of European Civil Procedure published in 1973[2].

The chronological differences in the diffusion of 'learned procedure', the romano-canonical procedure, on the Continent and in the British Isles, conspicuous as they are, must not mislead us. For there appear basic similarities in the main stages through which all European courts and their practice have passed and these are so striking as to justify a common treatment.

This view is easily defended for the medieval and early modern times. Baron *van Caenegem* points here to such fundamental features as the rationalization of evidence, the judicial centralization, and the rise of learned and professional judges. Though in very diverse forms and at most varying times these developments appear all over Europe, including the British Isles. The practice of a number of British courts, until well into the 19th century, offers further firm ground for *van Caenegem*'s view. We must think of the former civilian courts of Britain such as the Scottish Court of Session, the English Courts of Chancery and of Admiralty and the ecclesiastical courts. All these important and lesser courts maintained romano-canonical procedure until the great reforms during the 19th century.

---

1 *B. S. Markesinis*, Litigation-mania in England, Germany and the U.S.A.: Are we so very Different?, (1990) 49 C. L.J. 233, at p. 276.

2 *R. C. van Caenegem*, History of European Civil Procedure, in: International Encyclopedia of Comparative Law, vol. 16, c. 2, 1973, at pp. 6, 87, 101 sq., 104 sqq., 110.

Even after the changes of the post-*Bentham* era there remains a strong case for *van Caenegem*'s thesis of a basic similarity of much of civil procedure both in England and Scotland and on the Continent. No doubt measures like the introduction of the civil jury, of the examination of witnesses by the party adducing them (and no longer by the judge), of the taking of proof by the court which is to decide the case (and no longer by commissioners), suggest that Scotland drifted away from the Continent. And English civil procedure shows even more elements which are distinctly non-civilian.

In England, however, the new forms of process, as laid down in the Judicature Acts of 1873 and 1875 and in the Rules of Court which came to supplement these Acts, must be regarded as the triumph of chancery, and thus the triumph of civilian ideas. Modern English civil procedure is much closer to the old chancery than to the old common law procedure. Of the old chancery practice the exaggerations of cumbersome paperwork and secrecy, especially in the examination of witnesses, were discarded. It is also true that the public and oral central part of the common law process, the trial, was now extended to equity cases. But of the old common law procedure far more elements had to give way as obsolete. The archaic forms of action were abolished just as the abstruse technicalities connected with each of them. The absence of forms of actions was a chancery characteristic. The role of the civil jury, which had never existed in chancery, was reduced. In evidence interrogatories with written testimony and affidavits became common practice. The role of the court, especially of the masters, in directing procedure before trial was much strengthened. The mode of pleading of the new High Court of 1875 was modelled on the uses of the former Admiralty Court, so it also assumed civilian features.

It is not exceptionable, therefore, to agree that the various European systems of civil procedure, on both sides of the Channel, in large measure share common historical roots.

II. Recent Steps Towards Harmonization

1. Harmonization of Procedural Law within the European Union

If we feel persuaded that modern European forms of civil procedure are in fact built on decidedly common historical foundations, this should assist in reviewing the idea that Anglo-Scottish procedural law is all too different from other European laws. It may then be hoped that comparative study could be of practical utility. Even harmonization in the field of civil procedure would no longer seem a delusion.

The issue of harmonization of procedural law was, after some hesitation, raised within the European Union in recent years. The ideal is no less than that of a single system for the judicial resolution of disputes arising out of business conducted in the European market. It is difficult to avoid the conclusion that this ideal is, in fact, instantly required by the precept of a single European 'internal market'. It is, however, obvious that it will be achieved only through major effort.

In 1987 a 'working group', chaired by the indefatigable Professor *Storme*, and consisting of expert representatives from the then twelve Member States of the European Communities, started work on 'the approximation of the civil procedural law in Europe'. The working group was committed by the Commission of the European Communities and it produced its report at the end of 1993[3]. Within the working group agreement was achieved on a common European practice in respect of a substantial number of aspects. The published drafts are certainly not in any definitive shape but they do represent documents from which further progress can be made.

Surely, the first swallow cannot be taken to announce the summer. In the meantime numerous major difficulties remain to be resolved. Professor *Tony Jolowicz*, who succeeded Sir *Jack Jacob* as a representative of the United Kingdom in the working group, testifies of his initial scepticism concerning the practical utility of the work undertaken[4]. He recalls the differences between the civil law and the common law systems, each taken as a group, and he mentions especially one of these differences, obviously in his opinion a very material one. The matter in question is, of course, the common law trial, at which witnesses are examined and cross-examined by counsel, at which argument is presented orally to the judge and at the end of which judgment is delivered. The common lawyer finds it almost impossible to envisage a procedural system which has no such trial. Yet there is not even a word in any of the other European languages which gives an adequate translation of this trial; there is no need for a word by which to refer to an institution which is unknown[5].

2. *Civilian and Common Law Procedure*

Indeed, as *Zweigert* and *Kötz*[6] put it, the needs met by civil procedure are met in ways decidedly different under common law and civil law. Turning to the preparation and progress of a civil suit, the way the facts are presented to the court, especially the way witnesses and experts are selected and examined, one cannot but

3 See Marcel Storme, ed., Rapprochement du droit judiciaire de l'Union européenne. Approximation of Judiciary Law in the European Union, Bibliotheek van gerechtelijk recht, vol. 19, 1994.

4 See his preface in Storme (n. 3).

5 See also *J. A. Jolowicz*, Fact-finding: A Comparative Perspective, in: D. L. Carey Miller and P.R. Beaumont, edd., The Option of Litigating in Europe, U.K. Comparative Law Series, vol. 14, 1993, p. 133, at p. 134.

6 *Konrad Zweigert, Hein Kötz*, Introduction to Comparative Law, transl. *Tony Weir*, 2nd ed., repr. 1993, at pp. 280 sqq.

admit that the two great western traditions appear to have developed quite differently. These learned writers regard as perhaps the most striking differences those connected with fact-finding. Common law systems assign almost exclusively lawyers, civil law systems assign besides lawyers also, or even predominantly, judges to examine witnesses and experts. In this respect, as in others, the tasks and functions of the court and the parties and their lawyers are dealt with in quite different ways by both groups of systems of civil procedure[7].

It would appear to be not entirely superfluous to warn, once again, against oversimplifying the contrast and in this way sacrificing accuracy[8]. British and United States comparatists have not abandoned their habit of identifying two models of taking evidence, or even of procedure generally, in civil causes: the 'adversarial', also called 'accusatorial', model and the 'inquisitorial' one. The first is said to be characteristic only of English law and of those systems which adhere to the common law tradition, whereas the second, the inquisitorial model, is supposed to be universal in the civilian laws[9]. I expect no disapproval if I list contemporary Scottish procedure, despite its considerable differences from the English, for present purposes among the common law tradition.

Now what is wrong with this way of contrasting? The suggestion is that civilian proceedings are conducted by the judge, and the judge only, and that Anglo-Scottish proceedings are conducted by the parties, and the parties only. That suggestion is quite misleading[10]. In general in civil litigation, in both British and in continental courts, the parties determine what issues will be raised, what evidence will be introduced, and what arguments will be made. The parties, via their lawyers, not the judge, motivate the proceedings. At the same time judges (and here must be included the English High Court masters and registrars) have certain powers to take initiatives in the course of proceedings, if need be even of their own motion, without being prompted by a party or counsel to do so. This is valid for English, Scottish and civilian judges, though not all powers of an Anglo-Scottish judge are open to his civilian brethren, and the other way round; equally, the instances where those powers are in fact made use of, vary greatly. Differences on this scale, however, abound also as between French, Dutch, German and Austrian judges, and so

---

7 See *Hein Kötz*, Zur Funktionsteilung zwischen Richter und Anwalt im deutschen und englischen Zivilprozeß, in: Festschrift für Imre Zajtay, 1982, p. 277. See also the same author's The Role of the Judge in the Court-room: The Common Law and Civil Law Compared, 1987 T.S.A.R. 35.

8 *Jeroen M. J. Chorus*, The Judge's Role in the Conduct of Civil Proceedings: Some Continental and Scottish Ideas from before 1800, in: D. L. Carey Miller and D. W. Meyers, edd., Comparative and Historical Essays in Scots Law: A Tribute to Professor Sir Thomas Smith Q.C., 1992, p. 32.

9 See *Peter Stein*, Legal Institutions. The Development of Dispute Settlement, 1984, at pp. 36 sqq.; Sir *Jack I. H. Jacob*, The Fabric of English Civil Justice, The Hamlyn Lectures, 1987, at pp. 5-19 and 264 sq.; *Markesinis* (n. 1) 251 sq.

10 See *Kötz* (n. 7); see also *Jolowicz* (n. 5) 140.

on. In most systems there coexist, apart from the ordinary form of procedure, special modes (e.g. in family law cases) wherein judges must fulfil very active roles. The same is true of Britain. The ordinary form of civil procedure, however, anywhere in Europe, is largely adversarial or accusatorial[11]. In this respect the civilian systems do not differ from the Anglo-Scottish ones[12].

At the outset we must forget this inquisitorial label. It is an unfortunate label because to lawyers of today it no longer refers to the great traditions of continental romano-canonical procedure and, indeed, those of the old Court of Chancery and the Court of Session of the 17th and 18th centuries, which might, with greater justification, be styled inquisitorial (with a positive connotation). Today lawyers will hear the word inquisitorial as derogatory and it will stir their vague notions of the Spanish inquisition, heretic-hunt, and the Star Chamber.

As may be clear from what has been said so far, I am not denying that there are important and numerous differences between various European procedural systems. We will have occasion to come back to these differences. They are, however, not of such magnitude that comparison would be useless[13] or that harmonization would be a hopeless issue. This is what the shared historical roots suggest and, perhaps, what the results of the working group for the approximation of European civil procedure law point to. The differences come from tradition and from prevailing views of principle and policy, rather than from the nature of things[14].

I cannot even think of attempting a survey of differences existing between the various European systems of civil procedure, not even those of civilian and common law systems, each taken as a group. The present paper is devoted to 'taking stock' and I have been made to understand that concern should be preferably with the civilian part of stock. This entails inevitably an undeserved neglect of the non-civilian content of European laws and, presumably a lesser sin, the tendency to annex to the civilian mass all that is not of manifest common law origin. However, if a person knowingly participates, he has only himself to blame, as *Ulpian* recognized in his discussion of the slave who entrusted himself to a barber shaving where people were playing at ball[15].

---

11 See *Arthur Taylor von Mehren*, The Significance for Procedural Practice and Theory of the Concentrated Trial: Comparative Remarks, in: Europäisches Rechtsdenken in Geschichte und Gegenwart: Festschrift für Helmut Coing, vol. 2, 1982, p. 361; *John H. Langbein*, The German Advantage in Civil Procedure, (1985) 52 University of Chicago L.R. 823.

12 But see *Jolowicz* (n. 5) 141 sqq.

13 See *A. E. Anton*, Scottish Thoughts on French Civil Procedure, 1956 J.R. 158, at p. 158.

14 See *J. A. Jolowicz*, On the Nature and Purposes of Civil Procedural Law, in: International Perspectives on Civil Justice: Essays in Honour of Sir Jack I. H. Jacob Q.C., 1990, p. 27, at p. 44.

15 D. 9, 2, 11 *pr.*

III. Civilian Stock in European Civil Procedure

1. Characteristics of Civilian Procedure

The issue of civilian elements in modern civil procedure does not appear, at first blush, to have attracted much attention. The vivid discussion of the fundamental rights laid down, or held to be implied, in Art. 6 of the European Convention on Human Rights, to mention only this busy field, is not usually concerned with detecting civilian elements in these rights. The rights to a fair and public hearing, to be held within a reasonable time and by an independent and impartial tribunal established by law, and to a publicly pronounced judgment, would probably be claimed by all European systems as belonging to their stock – something which might be defended successfully for the period since about 1800, the times of the French revolution. In a similar way the European Communities Convention on Jurisdiction and Judgments does not readily offer points of departure for a search of civilian elements. Considering, though, the original number of Member States and the relative paucity of changes required after the accession of the United Kingdom and Ireland it might be arguable that the private international law of all Member States contains something of the relevant civilian elements.

Upon closer inquiry we discover a number of studies, written by American, German, and English comparatists, which are helpful for present purposes. In these works certain devices of civilian procedure are being individualized and subsequently either accepted or rejected as worthy of being considered with a view to reform of the common law. In recent years relevant material has been published by authors like *von Mehren*, *Kaplan*, *Langbein*, *Schlesinger*, *Kötz*, *Mann*, *Markesinis* and *Jolowicz*[16]. A fair selection of civilian devices singled out in these writings might run as follows (here I am relying heavily on *Kötz*).

The interrogation of witnesses in civilian procedure is conducted mainly by the court. It is the court which invites the witness to tell what he knows about the matter on which he has been called. After the witness has told his story the court will ask questions designed to test, clarify and amplify it. It is only then that counsel and the parties have their turn to ask pertinent questions but often there is little questioning by counsel or the parties. There is no full stenographic transcript of the testimony. Instead the judge himself will dictate a note of the sum and substance of what the witness has said. Counsel may insist on having particular parts of the testimony recorded verbatim in the minutes[17]. Under this system there is no need to prepare the witness for the questioning in court and the problem of 'coaching' witnesses is avoided[18].

---

16 See nn. 11; 7; 1; 5, 14, 27; *Benjamin Kaplan*, Civil Procedure – Reflection on the Comparison of Systems, (1959-1960) 9 Buffalo L.R. 409; *Rudolf B. Schlesinger et al.*, Comparative Law, Cases – Text – Materials, 5th ed., p. 337, at pp. 525 sqq; *F. A. Mann*, Fusion of the Legal Professions?, (1977) 93 L.Q.R. 367.

17 In Norway, Sweden and Finland oral proof is recorded in full; see Storme (n. 3) 98 sqq.

Experts hired by the parties are rarely brought in a civilian court though their written statements may, and will, be adduced as evidence. Suppose, for instance, that expert evidence is necessary in an action for damages brought by a patient against a medical specialist on the ground of the defender's failure to exercise the required care in the treatment of the claimant. As a rule the expert will then be selected and appointed by the court, after the parties have had the opportunity to suggest names. The written questions to be responded to by the expert will be finally formulated by the court, also after consultation. The expert's report may or may not lead to an oral examination in court and in the former case it is, again, the judge who will conduct that examination, allowing, clearly, more or less substantial additional questioning by counsel for both sides. The expert, appointed by the court, other than a party-expert, will feel loyal rather to the court than to either party and this factor may promote independence and impartiality[19].

It is the duty of most continental courts to find and apply the law[20]: *jura novit curia*. Though it is good practice for counsel to submit legal argument, and this will be more complete and reliable the better or the more specialized the lawyer, yet (except in Spain) counsel is under no duty to do so. In most cases, as long as the case is not brought in the highest tribunals, counsel will restrict himself to stating the facts, listing the evidence and possibly drawing some lines of legal argument. The responsibility for the law is not his but the court's. The court must, of its own motion, carry out research; in the large majority of cases it does so – far more comprehensively than the lawyer concerned. The court is also perfectly entitled to decide on legal grounds entirely different from those put forward by either of the parties. But it should preclude the more glaring surprises and so invite the parties to comment on grounds of law which the court thinks potentially decisive but which were not invoked[21].

The three devices so far mentioned have in common that the civilian judge performs tasks which the Anglo-Scottish judge may safely, or, indeed, must, expect counsel to fulfil. Here we meet one, not the only, reason for the conspicuous need in continental countries for more judges than is necessary in Britain. According to statistical information collected by Professor *Markesinis*[22] in 1987 in England and Wales there were 16.8 judges per one million of population; in what was then West Germany the figure was 278 judges per million of population. The figure for England and Wales is suspect in so far as it does not include deputy judges and deputy registrars, High Court masters and members of tribunals. Nor does it include the

---

18 See *B. C. Punt*, Fact-finding: A Dutch Perspective, in: D.L. Carey Miller and P. R. Beaumont, edd., The Option of Litigating in Europe (n. 5) 109, at pp. 118 sq.

19 See *Punt* (n. 18) 119 sq.; *Jolowicz* (n. 5) 139 sq.

20 French courts are not subject to a duty to, but may, supplement legal grounds.

21 Some systems make the court subject to a duty to hear the parties in this situation, others do not; see generally Storme (n. 3) 94 sqq.

22 *Markesinis* (n. 1) 244.

very great number of magistrates but these (mainly lay) judges are concerned with criminal cases only. It should also be kept in mind that Germany is not representative of continental countries; in all other European countries the number of judges *per capita* is smaller than in Germany. We may note the figure for the Netherlands, where the number of judges *per capita* is the smallest of all continental countries. In 1988/89 the Netherlands had 82 and West-Germany 294 judges per one million of population[23]. It would seem that the other continental countries are somewhere between the Dutch and German positions. It may then be safely assumed that in civil litigation for each English judge there are roughly four Dutch, sixteen German, and between four and sixteen other continental judges *per capita*. I do not know the figure for Scotland but will take it that the situation may be rather like the English[24]. So at least there is more than meets the eye in Professor *Markesinis'* sally that *jura novit curia* is an expensive compliment to pay to a judge[25]. Conveniently, however, he is silent upon the costs of trial-lawyers.

A final civilian device may be considered: the *astreinte*[26]. This well-known special coercive technique was developed originally by the French courts during the 19th century. It is used as a means of enforcing judgments for performances in kind. On issuing a judgment requiring the defender to do something other than pay money, or refrain from performing a specific act (e.g. not take up employment with a rival of his former employer) an order may be added that the defender must pay a specific sum of money – the *astreinte* – to the pursuer if he does not comply with the judgment. The *astreinte* goes into the pocket of the claimant but is not classified as a payment of damages; any amount paid is not to be deducted from damages awarded. Other continental systems 'received' some kind of *astreinte*: the Benelux countries, Greece and Denmark in the form as just described. Germany and Portugal know of similar institutions but subject to the proviso that in Germany the *astreinte* must be paid entirely to the state, while in Portugal half must be paid to the state. The respective English and Scottish remedies of specific performance and specific implement and the doctrine of contempt of court cover part of the same ground.

The four civilian devices now singled out cannot be dealt with here in any but the most superficial fashion. In a general way, and with regard only to the first three, Professor *Kötz* has this to say. Every foreign observer will express unreserved admiration for the versatile skills and dynamic presentation of the best counsel at trial, carefully examining and effectively cross-examining witnesses and

---

23 See *E. Blankenburg*, Rechters en advocaten in Nederland en beide Duitslanden, in: Role and Organization of Judges and Lawyers in Contemporary Societies, Netherlands National Reports, Ninth World Conference on Procedural Law, vol. 5, Procesrechtelijke reeks NVvP, 1992, p. 85.

24 But Professor *M. C. Meston*, in his oral intervention, suggested that Scotland has about two judges for each English judge *per capita*.

25 *Markesinis* (n. 1) 251.

26 See *Zweigert* and *Kötz* (n. 6) 511 sqq.

tendering skilled argument on the facts and the law of a case; all before a detached judge whose only function appears to be to ensure that the advocates conduct themselves in a seemly fashion, but who will then go on to deliver an eloquent, highly persuasive judgment. This common law procedure must be ideal for certain cases which are concerned with important problems of public interest, or questions of great impact on an individual litigant, or assets of very high value. It is the Rolls Royce of civil procedures.

Kötz continues, however, that just as impressive as Rolls Royces are, it is undisputed that the continental Volkswagen in most cases does safely reach its destination. Other big cases, of a more complicated character, such as large anti-trust, product liability, or mass disaster cases, are less suitable for trial on the basis of the British model but require more judicial control over the conduct of the action. And in the very large number of small cases there is even more to be said in favour of 'managerial judging' in the civilian way. In fact, in common law jurisdictions the development is going in this direction with respect to small claims litigation.

The judge conducting the latter type of cases will have to use wider powers and to perform wider duties than his brother presiding over a classical trial. That judge must, indeed, largely take over the conduct of the case from the parties, and must be free to base his decision on facts which he has elucidated for himself, by his own examination of the parties and the witnesses. This judge, when examining a witness, necessarily descends into the arena and is liable to have his vision clouded by the dust of conflict. All modern societies, however, want to provide effective justice for the ordinary members of the public and it is questionable whether that need can be satisfied without judges pursuing a more active and dominant course[27].

2. Draft Rules of the Storme Working Group

I shall round off by investigating what place is devoted to the specific civilian devices here discussed, in the results of the working group on civil procedure in Europe[28]. With regard to evidence – apart from an important, extensive regulation of discovery and one rule providing for recording by mechanical means of oral proceedings – there is only Art. 5 of their draft which lays down the duty to appear before court and give evidence. The comments on this article state that the court which takes the evidence may consist of only one judge, also when judgment will be pronounced by several judges. There is no suggestion that the judge taking evidence should be one of the judges passing judgment. But it is said, explicitly, that

27 See *Jolowicz*, Some Twentieth Century Developments in Anglo-American Civil Procedure, in: Studi in onore di Enrico Tullio Liebman, vol. 1, 1979, p. 217, at pp. 265 sqq.; and Jolowicz (n. 5) 144 sqq.

28 See Storme (n. 3).

the court which hears the testimony may be another court than the one passing judgment; examples are a lower court (this is not restricted to cases of appeal) and a court in another country. The manner in which a witness shall be questioned in court is left to the discretion of the Member States. The general introductory report[29] underlines the very cautious attitude of the working group in matters of evidence. It follows that we will look in vain for drafted rules on the interrogation of witnesses or on experts.

Arts. 3.5-7 concern the law to be applied by courts. The – tacit – basic rule, of course, requires that the relevant law if invoked by a party must be applied. Rules or principles of law not so invoked may – in virtue of Art. 3.5 – nevertheless be applied (the court then acting of its own motion) provided that all parties have had the opportunity to be heard thereon. A duty to apply laws in point not invoked is not imposed. The comments on the articles explain that it should be left to the discretion of the Member States either to impose a duty on the courts, or merely – as in French law – to grant a power to the court to apply of their own motion laws not invoked by the parties.

The working group has paid much attention to the application of foreign laws by courts. The basis here is apparently the same as for domestic laws, as set out above, under the same proviso[30]. But here the court may also invite the parties to cooperate in the determination of the content and interpretation of the relevant foreign law[31]. In this event, according to the comments, the hearing of the parties should extend to both the interpretation to be given to the relevant conflict of laws rule, and the content and interpretation of the relevant foreign law; the national laws are left free to provide for such further rules as may seem required in this context. It follows further that it is equally left to the discretion of the national laws to provide for the modalities of the eventual cooperation between the court and the parties.

With regard, however, to the law of another Member State there is a stricter provision in Art. 3.6. If a national rule of conflict of laws requires the application of the law of another Member State, the court has a duty to apply, of its own motion, that foreign law. It seems likely that the idea is that this (national) conflict of laws rule itself must also be applied by the court of its own motion.

In Arts. 13.1-4 a form of *astreinte* is offered, modelled after the relevant existing Benelux uniform statute. It is expressly stated that the national laws may impose yet other sanctions for non-performance of an order of the court. The working group felt that it would be impossible to have contempt of court here substituted by *astreinte* and therefore both are allowed cumulatively. It is suggested, however (in the explanatory memorandum), that the Member States concerned empower the courts to choose between the two and not let the claimant have this option. Though

---

29 See Storme (n. 3) 66.

30 As follows from Art. 3.7, para. 1.

31 Art. 3.7, para. 2.

the articles do not seem to state explicitly that the remedy is not available with regard to an order for the payment of money, there can be no doubt that this restriction should obtain. Further discussion of the drafted rules, comments, and explanation may here be omitted.

IV. Conclusion

If anything this taking stock of civilian elements in European civil procedures offers additional argument for strengthening attempts at harmonization. It seems useful, even necessary, to proceed from the results of the European working group.

Such a conclusion must sound familiar in Scotland. It recalls the day in July 1946 when that eminent Scottish judge, Lord *Cooper of Culross*, Lord Justice-Clerk of the Court of Session as he then was, delivered his famous address to the Summer School of Edinburgh University[32]. Lord *Cooper* gave a brief analysis of the social and economic revolution "which is upon us", as he then felt, so shortly after the war. It may be that his analysis has not in all parts proved right in later years. But right he certainly was in stressing that public respect for law "depends upon the law's ability to satisfy the average man's feeling for common justice visibly done". To satisfy this test, he urged, "the civilian will have to abate something of his worship of the Roman genius for jurisprudence ... and the common lawyer will have to recognise that his methods and their fruit are not necessarily the final perfection of human wisdom". Lord *Cooper* felt convinced that we should "need both the civilian and the common lawyer to tide us over the great transition" of our age, and he went on to say that we shall need above all the civilian method of legal thinking. If all of us concur with the former part of this statement we may also, occasionally, be attracted by the latter.

32 Lord *Cooper of Culross*, The Common and the Civil Law – a Scot's View, (1950) 63 Harvard L.R. 468, also in: *idem*, Selected Papers, 1957, p. 201.

The Future: The Civilian Tradition in European Community Law

The Role and Relevance of the Civil Law Tradition in the Work of the European Court of Justice

By David A. O. Edward[1]

I. Introduction

It is now 500 years since civil law was first taught at the King's College of Aberdeen. As a way of celebrating this achievement, we were invited to celebrate the civilian tradition which, throughout those 500 years, has been a basic building block and inspiration for most of the legal systems of Europe. Though the legal map has become ever more complex and densely filled, civil law rightly remains a core subject in the Aberdeen law degree.

At the other end of the historical spectrum, the newest addition to the core subjects, not only in Aberdeen but in all the Scottish law degrees, is European Community law. Though it has emerged only in the last 45 years, Community law has fast become the focus of a rather different European legal tradition. So Judge *Thijmen Koopmans* and other commentators speak of "a new *ius commune* for Europe". There may be those who are perturbed by that idea, but I suspect that the first teachers of civil law at King's College would have regarded it as normal, natural and desirable.

The question I have been asked to address is whether the civilian tradition – the old *ius commune* – has had an influence on the way in which the Court of Justice has developed the new *ius commune*?

Put briefly, my answer is that, if you look for obvious traces of the civil law in the Court's judgments, you will find very few. The main reason is that Community law and the civil law deal with different kinds of problem.

On the other hand, if the civilian tradition is today, as Professor *Zimmermann* puts it, "a fundamental intellectual unity created by a common tradition" – an attitude of mind rather than a set of rules or principles – that tradition could be said to permeate the work of the Court at the deepest level. I suspect that common lawyers find some of the Court's case law difficult to understand precisely because the

---

[1] Particular thanks are due to *Nicolas Lockhart*, Legal Secretary at the Court of Justice, both for his help and his insights. The opinions expressed are those of the author alone.

Court is, in a deep though not immediately obvious sense, profoundly civilian in outlook.

I propose to address three points. First, why does the substantive civil law have so little influence on the work of the Court? Second – perhaps a sub-point of the first – why does the Court seem to avoid civilian solutions in cases under the Brussels Convention, the very field where it might have been expected to find them useful? Third, in what sense, nevertheless, can the Court be said to be profoundly civilian in outlook?

II. Why the Civil Law is *Not* an Influence

Lord *Mackenzie Stuart* has pointed out in his paper some of the reasons why there are relatively few traces of the civil law, as such, in Community law. I would add a further reason.

One has only to remember what the European enterprise is all about. It was conceived after the Second World War as a means of cementing the new peace by creating a zone of economic (and therefore political) stability in western Europe. The aim was to tackle, by legal and institutional means, the economic problems of the latter part of the 20th century – and beyond.

It would be demanding a great deal of foresight from those first teachers at King's College, and even more so from the Romans, to expect their civilian system to provide many of the answers to the problems of today's global economy. To take one example, how would they have reacted to, never mind resolved, the problem that the number of fish in the sea is not, as we were always told, unlimited?

Indeed, so much of the Community legal system is entirely new that not even the national systems provide many answers to the issues with which it has to deal. The institutional structure is unique, the constitutional framework is still evolving and attempts to channel its development in the direction of national preconceptions have almost always failed.

At a more technical level, new Community concepts and terminology are needed to tackle problems, such as the elimination of non-tariff barriers to trade in goods or mutual recognition of professional diplomas, precisely because such issues simply do not arise in national law which (except, in a sense, in the United Kingdom) is concerned with problems internal to a single State, rather than those arising between states.

It does not even enter our heads that Baxters' soup from Speyside might not, for legal reasons, be as marketable in Edinburgh or London as in Aberdeen. Far otherwise when it comes to marketing the same soup in Helsinki or Athens. What is the Finnish or Greek consumer to make of a tin labelled 'Cock-a-Leekie'? And what insights as to ingredients and preparation would the couthy accents of Grampian offer to the harassed housewife of Brindisi?

States (apart from our own) do not have an internal problem of mutual recognition of diplomas but they are very chary of recognizing other peoples'. Even the proud possessor of an Edinburgh LL.M. may find himself in difficulties if he puts it on his visiting card in Baden-Württemberg[2].

Community law is late-20th-century law to deal with late-20th-century social and economic problems on a transnational basis. So it is not surprising that national systems provide few clues to the solution of questions which, almost by definition, go beyond the scope of national law.

That is not to say that Community law finds nothing to borrow from pre-existing national law. The members of the Court – Judges and Advocates General – see problems through the spectacles of their own training and practice. Instinctively, they reach for the tools they would normally use to solve them. Since most of them come from what could broadly be called a civilian background, it would be astonishing to find no civilian influences at all in the working of the Court.

But, as Professor *Zimmermann*'s paper shows, there is no single civilian tradition. Each national legal system has undergone a reception peculiar to itself, frequently dictated by its own history, and has evolved the civilian concepts it has received in a more or less different way. Their lawyers and judges have delved into the civil law toolbox only to the extent that the tools they found there seemed useful or appropriate. It would, I think, be mere antiquarian romanticism to suppose that there exists – somewhere 'out there' – a collection of pure civilian principles, unalloyed by national adaptations, which lie ready to hand as useful tools to solve the problems of a late 20th-century economic community. Moreover, such Platonic idealism, with its appeal to a 'purer' past, is a denial, rather than an affirmation, of the living civilian tradition.

There is, however, one field in which one might have expected to find civilian influences actively at work. That is the interpretation of the Brussels Convention on civil jurisdiction and the recognition and enforcement of judgments.

III. The Brussels Convention on Jurisdiction and the Recognition and Enforcement of Judgments

The Brussels Convention was originally concluded in 1968 when all the Member States were 'civil law countries'. Although it has been modified at the time of subsequent accessions, much of the terminology remains recognizably civilian.

The Court's approach to Brussels Convention cases may, at first blush, seem like a stubborn rejection of outside influence. After all, the Convention is concerned

---

2 See Case C-19/92 *Kraus v. Land Baden-Württemberg* [1993] E.C.R. I-1663.

with the very stuff of what national courts do: civil and commercial courts are constantly having to ask themselves whether they have jurisdiction and whether their judgments are effective. Yet, even in this field, there is a positive effort on the part of the Court to ensure that the language it employs does not identify the case-law with any system, civilian or otherwise, but rather to look for autonomous concepts or independent definitions.

Why abstraction rather than borrowing? Why not use grammar that lies ready to hand? Some examples will illustrate the reason.

In the first *Reichert* case[3] the Court was asked whether a claim under the French Civil Code, known as the *action paulienne*, fell within Article 16(1) of the Convention. That Article confers exclusive jurisdiction on the *forum situs* "in proceedings which have as their object rights *in rem* in immovable property". A civil lawyer would probably disclaim attribution of the *action paulienne* to the learned civilian whose name it bears. But a Scots lawyer would have no difficulty in recognizing the proceedings between the Reichert family and the Dresdner Bank as an attempt by a creditor to reduce a disposition to conjunct and confident persons. Probably all legal systems have a similar remedy, but not all systems have the same form of action.

In his opinion Advocate General *Mischo*, referring explicitly to the French notion, proposed that the Court should rule that an action "such as the *action paulienne* under Article 1167 of the French civil code" does not come within Article 16(1) of the Convention[4]. But in the operative paragraph of its judgment, the Court avoided any direct reference to the French terminology. Instead it stated that "an action whereby a creditor seeks to have a disposition of right *in rem* in immovable property rendered ineffective as against him on the ground that it was made in fraud of his rights by his debtor" does not fall within Article 16(1). The ruling was thus neutral, abstract or "non-system-specific".

One can see a similar approach in the Court's very recent ruling in *Danværn*[5] which was concerned with interpretation of Article 6(3) of the Convention, which limits "reconventional jurisdiction" in counterclaims.

Sued in the court of his own domicile, the Danish defender sought by way of defence to set off a debt allegedly due by the German pursuer to him. The question was whether "set-off as a defence" was to be treated as a counterclaim falling under Article 6(3) of the Convention. If it was, the defender would not be entitled to set-off his debt against a pursuer not domiciled in Denmark since the debt in question did not "arise from the same contract or facts on which the original claim was based".

---

3 Case 115/88 *Reichert & Kockler v. Dresdner Bank AG* [1990] E.C.R. I-27. See subsequently Case C 381/89 *Reichert & Kockler v. Dresdner Bank A.G.* [1992] E.C.R. I-2149.

4 [1990] E.C.R. I-27, at p. I-37, point 27(2).

5 Case C-341/93 *Danværn Production A/S v. Schuhfabriken Otterbeck GmbH & Co* [1995] E.C.R. I-2053.

What was the nature of the defender's claim and how did it fit with the language of Article 6(3)?

The French text of Article 6(3) refers to *une demande reconventionnelle*, thus putting the emphasis on the necessity to establish jurisdiction by reconvention. French law, like Scots law, distinguishes between *compensation légale*, where one debt cancels another out by simple operation of law, and *compensation judiciaire*, where the second debt must be judicially constituted and *then* set off against the first. Since it is necessary to establish jurisdiction by reconvention in the second case but not in the first, the very terms of the French text suggest that "set-off as a defence" does not fall within the scope of Article 6(3).

However, the law of set-off has developed differently in Germany and France – see Professor *Zimmermann*'s paper. The German text of the Convention refers to *eine Widerklage*, and a German court had (in an earlier case) held that set-off as a defence did fall within Article 6(3).

Other language versions neither clearly cover, nor clearly rule out, set-off as a defence. The English text refers to "a counter-claim" which puts the emphasis on procedure rather than jurisdiction. The Danish text is equally inconclusive since the word used in Article 6(3) – *modfordringer* – covers both types of claim.

In order to solve the problem, it would have been possible for the Court to rely on the precisely developed conceptual distinctions of French law, importing into Community law the notions of "set-off by operation of law" and "judicial set-off". The looser terminology of English, Danish and possibly German law could perhaps have been ignored as anomalous and/or unimportant.

The Court's approach, however, was to begin by describing the two possible situations by reference to the procedural context in which they arise. In a sense, it combined the French approach (distinguishing between the legal effects of the two types of claim) and the English approach (referring to the procedural context as a way of defining the distinction).

The Court then related the two possible procedural situations to the purpose of the Convention – namely, jurisdiction and recognition of judgments. It concluded that a defence, being an integral part of the main action, does not, by its nature, require constitution of jurisdiction. Consequently, it is regulated by national law and not by the Convention.

This non-system-specific approach is consistent with, if not positively required by, the role assigned to the Court by the Convention, which is to ensure that the Convention is applied uniformly in all the contracting States. Only in this way can mutual recognition and enforcement of judgments become a matter of obligation rather than discretion. As the Court said in *Reichert*,

> "In order to ensure that the rights and obligations of the Convention for the Contracting States and for individuals concerned are as equal and as uniform as possible, an *indepen-*

> *dent definition* must be given *in Community law* to the phrase 'in proceedings which have as their object rights *in rem* in immovable property'"[6].

However, as the case of *Webb* shows[7], the terms of the Convention may themselves be system-specific. A father had conveyed immovable property in France to his son. They subsequently fell out and the father claimed in the Chancery Division that the son held the property as a trustee for him. The question put by the Court of Appeal was as cagey as could be:

> "Whether on the true interpretation of Article 16(1) of the Brussels Convention the proceedings in the Chancery Division ..., the short title and reference to the record of which is *Webb v. Webb* 1990 W. No 2827 are proceedings in respect of which the courts of France have exclusive jurisdiction?"

Ultimately, the question was whether the father's action for declaration of trust was "proceedings which have as their object rights *in rem* in immovable property". The reference in the Convention to "rights *in rem*" is, by its nature, system-specific in the sense that it presupposes a system where a meaningful distinction can be drawn between rights *in rem* and one or more other categories of rights (notably, rights *in personam*) and which provides us with criteria for making the distinction. The problem in *Webb* was that the civilian concept of rights *in rem* and the English concept of equitable rights belong to different category-systems.

In its judgment, the Court relied on the conventional conception of a right *in rem* as a right that can be vindicated against the whole world, and concluded:

> "The father does not claim that he already enjoys rights directly relating to the property which are enforceable against the whole world, but seeks only to assert rights against the son. Consequently, his action is not an action *in rem* within the meaning of Article 16(1) of the Convention but an action *in personam*"[8].

Perhaps it was only to be expected that an English commentator would dismiss this approach as an "airy certainty", asserting that:

> "A claim that, by reason of the conduct of the parties throughout the years, a plaintiff is entitled, one way or another, to be made, recognized or constituted as the legal owner of land appears to fall squarely with the wording of Article 16.1 of the Convention"[9].

A civil lawyer in his turn might be forgiven for regarding that proposition as the quintessence of airy certainty. Be that as it may, the episode demonstrates very clearly why the Court tries, where possible, to abstract from system-specific concepts.

---

6 [1990] E.C.R. I-27, at p. I-41, point 8, emphasis added.

7 Case C-292/92 *Webb* [1994] E.C.R. I-1717.

8 [1994] E.C.R. I-1717, at p. I-1738, point 15.

9 *Adrian Briggs*, Trusts of Land and the Brussels Convention, (1994) 110 L.Q.R. 526, at pp. 529 and 530.

A further example of the same type of problem is Article 5(3) of the Convention which provides that "a person domiciled in a Contracting State may ... be sued ... in matters relating to tort, delict or quasi-delict, in the courts for the place where the harmful event [*le fait dommageable/das schädigende Ereignis*] occurred". What, in that context, is "the harmful event"?

What, in particular, is the situation where an industry in State A pollutes a river causing injury to downstream users of the river water in State B[10]? Did the harmful event occur in State A or State B, or was there "a harmful event" in both? Where a magazine publisher in State A distributes his magazine containing a defamatory article both in that state and in a number of other states, do the courts of each of those states have jurisdiction and, if so, (a) only in relation to the damage to reputation sustained in that state or (b) in relation to all damage to reputation everywhere[11]? Where, due to a bank error, the plaintiff has been arrested and detained in State A on suspicion of money-laundering, do the courts of State B (where the plaintiff has his principal place of business) have jurisdiction in relation to the damage caused to that business in that state[12]?

It goes without saying that the private international law of each state will offer a solution to each of these problems. A civil lawyer's first reaction would probably be to define "the place where the harmful event occurred" as the place where, for the first time, there has been concurrence of *damnum* and *iniuria*. But that will not do as a uniform solution for states whose law is not derived from the *lex Aquilia*.

How does one solve the problem without using expressions that have become system-specific, such as 'initial loss', 'consequential loss', 'pure economic loss', 'direct and indirect loss' and so on? Even with a common final court of appeal, Scots law and English law are liable to move in different directions in this field.

The answers are not obvious but it is clear that the dictates of uniformity, in order to achieve effective mutual recognition of judgments, run counter to any contribution which the civil law, as such, might have to offer. The Court must try to abstract the problem from the national context in which it arises, decouple it from loaded terminology, and present the answer in a system-neutral way which, hopefully, all national courts can then apply in roughly the same way.

IV. The *Real* Civilian Influence

While the issues the Court has to resolve may be novel, and the Court must try to provide system-neutral answers, its jurisprudence did not evolve in a vacuum. The "new legal order"[13] did not arrive, God-given, on tablets of stone. Indeed, the

10 Case 21/76 *Bier v. Mines de Potasse d'Alsace* [1976] E.C.R. 1735.

11 Case C-68/93 *Shevill and others v. Presse Alliance SA* [1995] E.C.R. I-415.

12 Case C-364/93 *Marinari v. Lloyds Bank* [1995] E.C.R. I-2719.

complaint of the former Warden of All Souls (Sir *Patrick Neill, Q.C.*) in his much-publicized Case Study of Judicial Activism is that the Court of Justice has gone beyond the tablets on which the treaties were written and, in pursuance of a private judges' agenda, has invented doctrines designed to distort the intentions of the contracting states and usurp their powers.

This is not the place to rebut this attack, which has gained a good deal of currency in the press. Its relevance for present purposes is that it calls in question two essential features of the way in which the Court approaches its task. The first is its view that Community law is and ought to be systematic: that Community law is a *system* of law and not just an *ad hoc* collection of rules and diplomatic compromises written down in the treaties. The second, which may simply be an aspect of the first, is the view that obligations beget rights, and breaches of obligation beget remedies.

1. System and Coherence

In one of the first cases to come before the Court of the original Coal and Steel Community, Advocate General *Lagrange* had to deal with the argument that the principle of strict interpretation of the text must always prevail. He approached the problem in this way:

> "[There] is a commonly accepted principle ... that it is necessary to interpret and seek the presumed intention of the authors of a text only when the latter is obscure or ambiguous and that when the letter of the law is clear it must always prevail. ... I am in full agreement as to the method of interpretation.
>
> The essential question is, however, whether the text is clear and requires no interpretation. In that respect, the very existence of the present action and the ramifications to which it has given rise are sufficient to show that it is not. ...
>
> The text lays down a procedural requirement ... but it fails to state by whom [it is to be accomplished]. It is therefore necessary to interpret the text in order to fill that lacuna. Even though the Code Napoléon is not applicable here I cannot refrain from recalling Article 4:
>
> 'le juge qui refusera de juger, sous prétexte du silence, de l'obscurité ou de l'insuffisance de la loi, pourra être poursuivi comme coupable de déni de justice' "[14].

The reference to the *Code Napoléon* shows, of course, that the Advocate General was inspired by more than a purely historic civilian tradition. Nevertheless, the underlying assumption is that there exists a body of law – a *corpus iuris* – which the lawgiver is presumed to intend should be complete and coherent. ('Coherence' is a word often heard in the mouths of lawyers from civilian jurisdictions.) The

---

13 Case 26/92 *Van Gend en Loos* [1963] E.C.R. 1, at p. 12.

14 Case 8/55 *Fédération Charbonnière de Belgique v. High Authority* [1954 to 1956] E.C.R. 245 at p. 277.

task of the judge is to find the piece of the jigsaw whose shape and appearance is marked out by the existing pieces, but which for some reason is missing.

Thus, in the two landmark judgments of the early 1960s – *Van Gend en Loos*[15] and *Costa v. E.N.E.L.*[16] – the Court lays out the available pieces of the jigsaw (the aim of the treaty, its structure and its terms) as the premises from which the principles of direct effect and primacy can be deduced. Notably, in *Van Gend en Loos*, the fact that the treaty involves individuals in the working of the Community and imposes obligations on them implies that they may also derive rights directly from it. Similarly, in *Costa*, the primacy of Community obligations follows both from the institutional structure established by the treaty and from the member states' reciprocal obligation of performance.

Perhaps even more striking is the Court's development of the idea that the treaty creates "a complete system of legal remedies". Coming to the treaty for the first time, the common lawyer might feel himself at home. In very few cases does the Treaty state positively that there shall be a right of action in particular circumstances. Rather, it sets out, article by article, a series of forms of action – the action of annulment, the action for failure to act, and so on.

In *Les Verts*, the question was whether acts of the European Parliament could be challenged under Article 173 even though the Parliament was not mentioned in that article as a potential pursuer or defender. The Court recognized that, whatever might have been the position in the past, the Parliament was now empowered to adopt acts which could encroach upon the interests of individuals or groups, other institutions or the Member States:

> "The European Economic Community is a Community based on the rule of law, inasmuch as neither its Member States nor its institutions can avoid a review of the question whether the measures adopted by them are in conformity with the basic constitutional charter, the Treaty. In particular, in Articles 173 and 184, on the one hand, and in Article 177, on the other, the Treaty established *a complete system of legal remedies and procedures* designed to permit the Court of Justice to review the legality of measures adopted by the institutions"[17].

In the *Chernobyl* case the question was whether the Parliament had a privileged right of action under Article 173 to protect its institutional position. In holding that it did, the Court again reasoned from the system as a whole (the institutional balance) to conclude that "Parliament's prerogatives … cannot be breached without it

---

15 Case 26/62 *Van Gend en Loos* [1963] E.C.R. 1.

16 Case 6/64 *Costa v. E.N.E.L.* [1964] E.C.R. 585.

17 Case 294/83 *Parti Ecologiste 'Les Verts' v. Parliament* [1986] E.C.R. 1339, at p. 1365, point 23 (emphasis added). It is right to take this opportunity to record that the Judge Rapporteur in *Les Verts* and subsequent cases of the same family was Judge *René Joliet* who died on 15 July 1995. He had studied in America and was a most unlikely participant in any supposed judicial agenda to usurp the powers of the Member States.

having available a legal remedy ... which may be exercised in a certain and effective manner"[18].

Again, in *Foto-Frost*, the Court reasoned from the coherence of the system established by Articles 173, 177 and 184 to conclude that only the Court itself could definitively declare invalid acts of the Community institutions[19].

The Court's insistence on sympathetic coherence reflects a recurring theme of the Aberdeen conference: that the true civilian tradition consists in taking a rational overview of the law as a whole, relating one part to another so as to form a structure or 'system'.

2. *Obligations, Rights and Remedies*

One has only to read, on the one hand, the speeches in the House of Lords in *Garden Cottage Foods*[20] and in the Court of Appeal in *Bourgoin*[21] and, on the other, the judgment of the Court of Justice in *Francovich*[22] to perceive a fundamental difference of approach to the problem of obligations, rights and remedies.

Garden Cottage Foods raised the question whether English law provided a remedy as between private parties for damage caused by breach of Articles 85 and 86 (the competition rules) of the Treaty. The majority view in the House of Lords appears to have been that, as well as the possibility of injunction, there was a remedy of damages for "breach of statutory duty" – that being the best available procedural pigeon-hole into which the breach of the competition rules could be fitted. *Bourgoin* raised the question whether English (or perhaps United Kingdom) law provided a remedy for loss caused by ministerial action in breach of Community law. The Court of Appeal held that there was a remedy only if misfeasance was proved.

In *Francovich* the question was whether the Italian state was liable to make reparation to individuals who suffered loss through the state's failure to implement a directive for the protection of employees on the employer's insolvency. The Court said that "the issue must be considered in the light of the *general system* of the Treaty and its fundamental principles"[23].

In a sense, the Court had already answered the question 21 years before in *Humblet*:

---

18 Case 70/88 *Parliament v. Council (Chernobyl)* [1990] E.C.R. I-2041 at p. 2073, point 25.

19 Case 314/85 *Foto-Frost v. HZA Lübeck-Ost* [1987] E.C.R. 4199, at p. 4231, points 16-17.

20 *Garden Cottage Foods v. Milk Marketing Board*, [1984] AC 130; [1983] 3 CMLR 43.

21 *Bourgoin v. MAFF*, [1985] 3 All ER 585; [1986] 1 CMLR 267.

22 Joined Cases 6/90 and 9/90 *Francovich and others v. Italy* [1991] E.C.R. I-5357.

23 [1991] E.C.R. I-5357, at p. I-5413, point 30 (emphasis added).

> "If the Court rules in a judgment that a legislative or administrative measure adopted by the authorities of a Member State is contrary to Community law, that Member State is obliged ... to rescind the measure in question and to make reparation for any unlawful consequences which may have ensued. That obligation is evident from the Treaty ..."[24].

In *Francovich*, the Court went back, not only to *Humblet*, but to the logic of *Van Gend en Loos* and *Costa v. E.N.E.L.*:

> "The E.E.C. Treaty has created its own legal system, which is integrated into the legal systems of the Member States and which their courts are bound to apply. The subjects of that legal system are not only the Member States but also their nationals. Just as it imposes burdens on individuals, Community law is also intended to give rise to rights which become part of their legal patrimony. *Those rights arise not only where they are expressly granted by the Treaty but also by virtue of obligations which the Treaty imposes* in a clearly defined manner both on individuals and on the Member States and the Community institutions. ...
>
> It follows that the principle whereby a State must be liable for loss and damage caused to individuals as a result of breaches of Community law for which the State can be held responsible is *inherent in the system of the Treaty*"[25].

This reasoning has been criticized by certain British commentators as being inadequate if indeed, according to them, it can be characterised as reasoning at all. Certainly, there was no attempt by the Court to classify the obligation to repair according to the nature or seriousness of the breach, a point which was only decided six months after the conference[26]. One English commentary has suggested that there are four possible causes of action depending on the nature of the Community obligation breached[27]. In England, correct classification of the action at the outset will be important, and failure to pick the right one may lead to difficulties.

What seems interesting for present purposes is, first, that from a civilian point of view the notion that an obligation begets rights and that breach of that obligation, when it causes loss, begets a remedy is a proposition that hardly needs to be supported by reasoning. Second, while common law commentators say that *Franco-*

---

24 Case 6/60 *Humblet v. Belgium* [1960] E.C.R. 559, at p. 569.

25 [1991] E.C.R. I-5357, at pp. I-5413 sq., points 31 and 35 (emphasis added).

26 See Joined Cases C-46/93 and C-48/93 *Brasserie du Pêcheur* and *Factortame III*, [1996] E.C.R. I-1029. Note, in particular, at points 53 and 55, the Court's insistence on coherence between the rules governing the liability of the Community and those governing the liability of the Member States. Note also the Court's refusal, at points 76, 79 and 80, to use any national concept of "fault" as a criterion of liability since the national conceptions are different and exclusive reliance upon them would undermine the Community nature of the obligation. But the Court did accept, at point 78, that factors which would be relevant in national law are also relevant in Community law.

27 *Brealey and Hoskins*, Remedies in E.C. law – Law and Practice in the English and E.C. Courts, London, 1994, pp. 75 sqq. They suggest that the possible causes of action are: (1) misfeasance in public office; (2) breach of statutory duty; (3) innominate tort; and (4) negligence.

vich created 'a new cause of action' not provided for in the treaties, the civilian might ask why the treaties should need to create a cause of action.

In principle, the national courts are the Community courts of general jurisdiction (*tribunaux communautaires de droit commun*). Where there is no right of access to the Community courts in Luxembourg, it falls to the national courts to protect Community rights and obligations through their own procedures. *Ubi jus ibi remedium* – to complete a right there must be a remedy. Civilian logic therefore *presumes* that the national systems will provide appropriate remedies offering effective protection of Community rights.

V. Conclusion

The examples of possible civilian influence that I have considered in the last section are drawn from what might be called the "constitutional" elements of Community law. It is in these structural areas in particular that the Court defines the way it looks at law.

There is of course no proof that the Court has lighted on this way of thinking *because of* the civilian tradition. (It has, after all, dipped into the common law toolbox from time to time.) So perhaps it is just coincidence. Perhaps the Court has brought an apparently "civilian" approach to bear simply because it is a sensible way to think about law, which neither consciously nor unconsciously reflects the civilian upbringing of most of the judges.

Whether coincidence or not, there can be no doubt that in important respects the Community conception of law mirrors what, in modern Europe at least, can be identified as the civilian conception. It is also fair to say that, without this way of thinking, Community law would have been deprived of its effectiveness and content. It would not have become a system of law capable of being described as a second *ius commune*.

The Influence of the Civil Law, via Modern Legal Systems, on European Community Law

By John A. Usher

I. Introduction

In the context of a conference celebrating the Quincentenary of the University of Aberdeen, another 500th anniversary might be recalled. It would appear that in 1495, the German (or Holy Roman Empire's) 'Reichskammergericht' was established, with a requirement that half its judges should be *doctores juris*. To a common lawyer, this elevation of the academic lawyer, and the treatment of legal writing as a source of law, are very much a characteristic of civil law systems; it might be suggested that one of the institutional provisions of the E.C. Treaty which has had a profound effect on the development of Community Law is Art. 167, under which the judges and advocates general of the European Court of Justice are to be chosen from persons whose independence is beyond doubt and who possess the qualifications required for appointment to the highest judicial offices in their respective countries "or who are jurisconsults of recognised competence". This has enabled a number of eminent academic lawyers to be appointed to the European Court of Justice. By way of contrast, though it may in practice be a distinction without a difference, Art. 168a on the Court of First Instance, drafted when the Community included common-law jurisdictions, provides only that the members of that Court shall be chosen from persons whose independence is beyond doubt "and who possess the ability required for appointment to judicial office".

More generally, while it is not the purpose of this paper to enter into the definitional problems of what exactly is a civil law system[1], its aim is to examine (albeit on a selective basis) the extent to which features of civil law systems are reproduced in Community law, to look at how certain fundamental legal concepts are treated in Community law, to investigate the substantive influence of civil law systems on Community legislation, and to consider the input of civil law systems into the development of the Community judicial system.

---

1 See *Alan Watson*, The Making of the Civil Law, 1981, at p. 2. This paper is essentially concerned with the influence of those systems which fall within what *René David* terms the Romano-Germanic family (Les Grands Systèmes de Droit Contemporains, 1964, para 13).

II. A Law for Citizens?

Whatever the other definitional problems, it is at least generally accepted that the Roman *ius civile* originally referred to law that applied only to Roman citizens. In this respect there is a strong link with the modern E.C. law relating to movement of persons and provision of services. Under Art. 48 of the E.C. Treaty, free movement of workers applies to "workers of the Member States", under Art. 52 freedom of establishment is conferred on "nationals of a Member State", and under Art. 59 restrictions on freedom to provide services within the Community were to be abolished in respect of "nationals of Member States". Similarly the 1990 Directives on the right of residence in other Member States[2], on the right of residence in other Member States for employees and self-employed persons who have ceased their occupational activity[3], and on the right of residence in other Member States for students[4] apply only to nationals of the Member States.

The Maastricht Treaty has taken this a step further by introducing the concept of 'Citizenship of the Union'. Under Art. 8 of the E.C. Treaty as amended, every person holding the nationality of a Member State shall be a citizen of the Union, thus enjoying the rights conferred by the E.C. Treaty and being subject to the duties imposed thereby. Art. 8a(1) provides that every citizen of the Union shall have the right to move and reside freely within the territory of the Member States, subject to the limitations and conditions laid down in the Treaty and by the measures adopted to give it effect, and Art. 8b also gives certain political rights to every citizen of the Union residing in a Member State of which he is not a national: these are the right to vote and to stand as a candidate at municipal elections in the Member State in which he resides, under the same conditions as nationals of that State, and the right to vote and to stand as a candidate in elections to the European Parliament in the Member State in which he resides, under the same conditions as nationals of that State. Indeed Art. 8c creates a right to protection by the diplomatic or consular authorities of any Member State, on the same conditions as the nationals of that State, in the territory of a third country in which the Member State of which he is a national is not represented.

However, there is no Community or Union definition of a citizen of the Union other than the reference to persons holding the nationality of a Member State. Thus, in the case of the United Kingdom, only British citizens, British subjects with the right of abode in the United Kingdom, and British Dependent Territories citizens who acquire their citizenship from a connection with Gibraltar are treated as nationals of a Member State[5]. On the other hand, the German Declaration an-

---

[2] Directive 90/364 (O.J. 1990 L180/26).

[3] Directive 90/365 (O.J. 1990 L180/28).

[4] Directive 90/366 (O.J. 1990 L180/30), replaced by Directive 93/96 (O.J. 1993 L317/59).

[5] Note of 31st December 1982 amending the Declaration annexed to the 1972 Treaty of Accession.

nexed to the E.C. Treaty refers to Art. 116 of the German Basic Law, which contains a definition which was wide enough, in the period before German reunification, to cover most East German citizens. The problems of reliance on national definitions are however most clearly revealed in the context of artificial legal persons. By virtue of Art. 58 of the E.C. Treaty, for the purposes of freedom of establishment and freedom to provide services, companies or firms formed in accordance with the law of a Member State and having their registered office, central administration or principal place of business within the Community are to be treated in the same way as natural persons who are nationals of Member States.

For natural persons, the freedom of establishment comports both the right of primary establishment, i.e. the right to move yourself and your business to another Member State, and the right of secondary establishment, i.e. the right to set up a branch, agency or subsidiary in another Member State. In so far as a company or firm formed in one Member State may wish to move its business activities to another Member State without re-registering as a company or firm formed under the law of the host State, this had been thought by many commentators writing at an early stage of the Community's development to raise complex problems of the recognition of the artificial legal persons of another legal system[6]. These views were proved correct in Case 81/87 *R. v. H. M. Treasury, ex parte Daily Mail*[7] where it was pointed out that companies exist only by virtue of national legislation and that the Treaty rules on freedom of establishment did not overcome the national law problems as to retention of legal personality on the transfer of the registered office or real head office to another Member State, so that they did not confer a right to transfer central management and control to another Member State. Hence a company incorporated under a system, such as the French, which requires the 'siège réel' to remain in the state of incorporation, will not be able to take advantage of primary establishment. It was suggested that in the case of companies, the right of establishment would usually be exercised by the setting up of agencies, branches or subsidiaries. In the light of this, it is of some interest to observe that the recitals to the Second Banking Directive[8] state that Member States must ensure that the head office of a credit institution is situated in the same Member State as the registered office, and that authorization must be refused where it is clear that the credit institution has opted for the legal system of one Member State for the purpose of evading the stricter standards in force in another Member State in which it intends

6 It had been held in Belgium, before United Kingdom Accession, that an English company moving its primary establishment to Belgium became wholly subject to Belgian company law (Belgian Cour de Cassation, 12th November 1965, Pasicrisle Belge 1966 I 336), and it would appear that in French law a company would in principle be regarded as a nullity if its 'siège réel' was different from the country of incorporation (see e.g. *Renauld*, La reconnaissance mutuelle des sociétés dans le Marché Commun, in: Revue pratique des sociétés civiles et commerciales, 1968, 207, at p. 211.

7 [1988] E.C.R. 5483.

8 O.J. 1989 L386/1.

to carry on or carries on the greater part of its activities. Indeed Directive 95/26[9] amending E.C. financial services legislation with a view to reinforcing prudential supervision imposes an express obligation on each Member State to require that any credit institution which is a legal person and which, under its national law, has a registered office, shall have its head office in the same Member State as its registered office[10]. The clear import of this is that there is to be no Delaware in Europe.

A rather different problem arising from Art. 58 of the E.C. Treaty is that the formula "companies or firms formed in accordance with the law of a Member State and having their registered office, central administration or principal place of business within the Community" is apt to cover a company incorporated and operating in a Member State which is the wholly-owned subsidiary of an undertaking based in a third country, so that, for example, in the financial services sector, a credit institution which was such a subsidiary could take advantage of the E.C. banking 'passport' under the Second Banking Directive[11]. What eventually became Arts. 8 and 9 of the Second Banking Directive acquired a certain notoriety while they were under discussion for their insistence on reciprocity in the context of the acquisition of participations in credit undertakings and the establishment of European Community subsidiaries by third country undertakings. However, in their final form, they require notification to the Commission by the national authorities of their authorization of a subsidiary of a third country undertaking or of the acquisition of a holding in a Community credit institution by such an undertaking. They further provide a channel of information with regard to difficulties encountered by Community credit institutions in carrying out banking activities in third countries. In the latter circumstance, the Commission is given power to enter into negotiations to remedy the situation, and a mechanism is provided under which the Commission may issue decisions requiring Member States to limit or suspend authorizations, or approvals of acquisitions of holdings, sought by parent undertakings governed by the laws of the third country in question, initially for a period of three months. It may be submitted that this is hardly a requirement of reciprocity as such. The matter is likely nevertheless to be one of growing importance following the agreement reached in the Uruguay Round relating to the provision of services.

It must not however be thought that E.C. law is exclusively law for citizens of the Union. The nationality of the owner of goods is irrelevant in the context of the free movement of goods, provided the goods are in free circulation within the Community[12], and in the context of monetary movements, Art. 73b of the E.C. Treaty, introduced by the Maastricht amendments, provides that all restrictions on the movement of capital and on payments between Member States and between Member States and third countries shall be prohibited. By definition therefore it is

---

9 O.J. 1995 L168/7.

10 Art. 3(2).

11 Council Directive 89/646 (O.J. 1989 L386/1).

12 E.C. Treaty Arts. 9 and 10.

capable of affecting nationals of non-Member States. Even in the area of social policy, the benefits of Art. 119 of the E.C. Treaty on equal pay for equal work as between men and women are not on the face of it limited to nationals of the Member States. Last but by no means least, the rights of action before the European Court and the Court of First Instance under the E.C. Treaty are in no way limited to nationals of the Member States[13].

III. Style and Nature of E.C. Law

Since all the original Member States of the E.C. are in the Romano-Germanic family and, on any definition, have civil law systems, it is hardly surprising that the basic structures and style of Community law bear considerable traces of their influence. Thus the distinction between private law and public law and between civil law and commercial law is expressly recognized in the E.C. Treaty, notably in Art. 58 on legal personality discussed above, the second paragraph of which provides that the phrase 'companies or firms' means companies or firms constituted under *civil or commercial law*, including cooperative societies, and other legal persons governed by *public or private law*, save for those which are non-profitmaking.

On the other hand, while Community law is self-evidently a system of written law[14], codification, which is a characteristic of modern European civil law systems, if not a necessary condition for classification as such a system[15], is (regrettably) the exception[16] rather than the rule. However, while it may not always be clear, to adopt *Merryman*'s terminology[17], whether a piece of Community legislation is meant as a handbook for the citizen or as a tool for professionals, it is clear to an English common lawyer that it is not drafted in the style of United Kingdom legislation and in particular that it is not drafted as an exception to or restriction on pre-existing common law; rather the E.C. legislation is the basic source material on the particular topic, and interpretative techniques developed in civil law systems have been used in relation to it[18].

---

13 Although under Arts. 33 and 35 of the E.C.S.C. Treaty, the only litigants other than a Member State or a Community institution able to bring actions for annulment or failure to act are coal and steel undertakings and associations of coal and steel undertakings as defined in that Treaty.

14 Subject to the development of general principles of Community law, which will be discussed later in this paper. See *John A. Usher*, The Influence of National Concepts on Decisions of the European Court of Justice, E.L.R. 1976, 359; and *idem*, Principles Derived from Private Law and the European Court of Justice, E.R.P.L. 1 (1993), 109.

15 *Watson* (n. 1) 3.

16 See e.g. Council Regulation 2913/92 on the Community Customs Code (O.J. 1992 L302/1).

17 *John Henry Merryman*, The Civil Law Tradition, 2nd ed., 1985, at pp. 30 and 33.

Thus, there is a cautious willingness by the European Court to apply E.C. legislation by analogy, as in Case 6/78 *Union Française de Céréales v. H.Z.A. Hamburg-Jonas*[19]. In that case, the French applicants had exported a cargo of wheat from Germany intending it to be unloaded in the United Kingdom. However, the ship sank in the North Sea, and the German customs authorities refused to pay the accession compensatory amounts which would otherwise have been due on such a transaction, on the basis that the exporters had not fulfilled the requirement expressed in Art. 5(2) of Commission Regulation 269/73[20], laying down detailed rules for the application of the system of accession compensatory amounts, and that, in the circumstances, the compensatory amount should be paid only upon proof that "import formalities have been completed and duties and taxes of equivalent effect payable in the Member State of destination have been collected". Since the wheat had never arrived in the United Kingdom, such proof could not, of course, be produced. Nonetheless, it was suggested on behalf of the exporters that it would be possible to apply the legislation in the related field of export refunds by analogy. Under Art. 6(1) of Commission Regulation 192/75[21], laying down detailed rules for the application of export refunds in respect of agricultural products, payment of the refund was conditional not only on the product having left the geographical territory of the Community but also on its having been imported into a third country "save where it has perished in transit as a result of *force majeure*".

The exporters appealed to the Finanzgericht of Hamburg against the German customs authorities' refusal to pay the accession compensatory amounts, and the Finanzgericht referred the case to the European Court, asking specifically whether Art. 6(1) of Regulation 192/75 on export refunds could be applied by analogy to the payment of accession compensatory amounts, so as to exonerate the exporter from the need to prove that the goods had arrived in a third country when they had perished in transit as a result of *force majeure*.

In answering this question, the Court examined the system of accession compensatory amounts established under Art. 55 of the 1972 Act of Accession, and held that they were intended to replace the export refunds which had been payable in trade with the new Member States when they were still third countries, that is, to enable Community producers to sell in markets in which the level of prices was lower, and, in particular, that they were intended to encourage Community preference in trade between the original Member States and the new Member States. It was found that the insurance contracted on behalf of the purchaser would only cover the value of the goods in the country of destination, and that to require the ex-

---

18 Quite apart from the development of 'purposive' interpretation, in particular as a result of language problems. See *John A. Usher*, Language and the European Court of Justice, The International Contract Law and Finance Review 1981, 277.

19 [1978] E.C.R. 1675.

20 O.J. 1973 L30/77.

21 O.J. 1975 L25/1.

porter to bear the difference or insure it himself would place him in an unfavourable position in comparison with exporters in third countries and conflict with the principle of Community preference. The Court concluded that, in not allowing for *force majeure*, Regulation 269/73 contained an omission which, given the similarity between accession compensatory amounts and export refunds, could be remedied by applying Art. 6(1) of Regulation 192/75 by analogy, and that the principle of Community preference required that the exporter should receive 'accession' compensatory amounts at the rate at which he would have received them if the goods had reached their destination and the import formalities had been completed.

IV. Property Rights

1. Possession and Ownership

While questions of civil law in the narrow sense of private law do arise in the context of Community law, as in the 1968 Judgments Convention and the 1980 Convention on Contractual Obligations (although some commentators might object that these are agreements between the Member States rather than Community law as such), in relation to the product liability Directive, and in the series of Directives on Company Law harmonization, fundamental concepts of civil law have relatively rarely been at issue.

An exception is the question of property rights, which arose in the context of sea fish in Case 100/84 *Commission v. United Kingdom*[22]. According to Advocate General *Mancini* in his Opinion given in that case, it was the view expressed by writers on the civil law in all the Member States that "fish are considered to be caught and hence the property of the fisherman when, by entering the net, they lose their natural liberty"[23]. The Court reached the same conclusion, albeit without referring expressly to concepts of civil law. The background to the case was that a group of British trawlermen wished to obtain some cod, for which they were not allowed to fish in Community waters, but which did happen to be available in the area of the Baltic over which Poland claimed exclusive fishing rights, and where British trawlers had no right to fish[24]. At the same time Polish trawlermen were wanting herring and mackerel, which were not available in the Polish area of the Baltic, but which could be caught in Community waters – except that Polish boats had no right to fish there. A group of British trawlers therefore set off for the Baltic laden with herring and mackerel, and met the Polish trawlers off the Polish coast. The British trawlers cast their empty nets into the sea, and these nets were then

22 [1985] E.C.R. 1170.

23 [1985] E.C.R. 1170, at p. 1174.

24 Case 100/84 *Commission v. United Kingdom* [1985] E.C.R. 1170.

taken over by the Polish boats, which trawled them but did not take them on board. After the trawl was completed, the Polish trawlers passed the ends of the nets to the British trawlers, and the cod was landed onto the British trawlers; in return for this, the British boats transferred the herring and mackerel to the Polish boats.

When the British trawlers returned to the United Kingdom, the customs authorities identified the cod as being British, and therefore not liable to pay common customs tariff duties. The reason for this was that under the E.C. Regulation determining the origin of goods for customs purposes, fish are treated as wholly obtained in one country if they are "taken from the sea" by vessels registered in that country and flying its flag. The British view essentially was that since the nets were actually pulled from the sea by the British trawlers, the fish were "taken from the sea" by the British trawlers, whereas the Commission's argument was that fish were taken from the sea when the net closed round them, irrespective of when they were physically hauled out of the sea.

Faced with this dispute, the Court first looked at the texts of the Regulation, and noted that the French version used the phrase "extraits de la mer", which appeared to support the British argument, whereas, for example, the German version used the word "gefangen", meaning caught, which tended to support the Commission's argument. After referring also to the Greek, Italian and Dutch versions, but not, it would appear, the Danish(!), the Court concluded that a comparative examination of the various language versions did not enable a conclusion to be reached in favour of any of the arguments put forward, and so no legal consequences could be based on the terminology used. It therefore expressly turned to consider the purpose and general scheme of the Regulation determining the origin of goods for customs purposes, and came to the conclusion that in the context of a fishing operation carried out by a number of vessels registered in different countries, the origin should in principle depend on the flag flown by the vessel which performed the essential part of the operation of catching them. Faced with the fundamental question of legal philosophy as to when a free object becomes property, the Court took the view that the *essential part* of catching fish is locating the fish and separating them from the sea by netting them, and that simply hauling the nets out of the sea is not the essential part of the operation. Whatever may be thought of the Court's analysis, this judgment at least illustrates its general approach to such problems.

2. *Extent and Restrictions*

Questions as to the extent of property rights arose in Case 44/79 *Hauer v. Land Rheinland-Pfalz*[25], but in a modern public and constitutional law context. Mrs. Hauer, in 1975, applied to the *Land* authorities for permission to start growing vines on her property in Bad Durkheim, such permission having a few days earlier

25 [1979] E.C.R. 3727.

been granted to the owners of some neighbouring land. Under the relevant German legislation[26], vines could only be cultivated on land recognized as being suitable therefor, and the *Land* authorities turned down her application in January 1976 on the ground that her property was not suitable. Mrs. Hauer put in a formal complaint objecting to the decision in her case, later that same month, and her complaint was rejected in October, 1976, this time not only on the ground that her land was not suitable, but also on the ground that Council Regulation 1162/76 on measures designed to adjust vine-growing potential to market requirements[27], which had been enacted in the meantime, prohibited all new planting of vine varieties classed as wine grape varieties[28], and also prohibited the grant of authorization for such new plantings.

Mrs. Hauer thereupon commenced proceedings before her local administrative court. During the course of the proceedings, the *Land* indicated that it would after all be willing to grant the necessary authorization under the German legislation once the prohibition on planting new vines under Regulation 1162/76 had elapsed; it might, however, be noted that by the time the European Court delivered its judgement, the period of that prohibition had been extended until the end of December 1979.

Hence, the remaining obstacle facing Mrs. Hauer was the Regulation, and it was argued on her behalf that it did not apply to her situation, since her application had been lodged before its entry into force, and that in any event it was incompatible with various provisions of the German Basic Law. The specific questions referred to the European Court by the *Verwaltungsgericht* related, however, to the interpretation of the Regulation rather than to its validity. The first asked, reflecting Mrs. Hauer's argument, whether the prohibition on new plantings of vines applied where permission to grow vines had been requested before the entry into force of the Regulation, and the second asked whether it applied generally, i.e. irrespective of whether the land in question was regarded as suitable for cultivating vines, within the meaning of the German legislation.

Like Advocate General *Capotorti*, the Court was able to deal relatively briefly with these two questions, finding that the prohibitions in the Regulation did indeed apply where permission to plant vines had been sought before its entry into force, and that they applied irrespective of the nature of the land in question. This, however, brought the Court to the real crux of the matter. In its order for reference, the *Verwaltungsgericht* had indicated that if the Regulation was so interpreted, it might

---

26 Gesetz über Maßnahmen auf dem Gebiete der Weinwirtschaft, § 1(2).

27 O.J. 1976 L135/32.

28 It might be noted, however, that although the Regulation is dated 17th May 1976, the prohibition on planting only commenced on 1st December 1976. Nonetheless, Art. 2(1) second subparagraph provided that Member States should no longer grant *authorizations* for new planting as from the date of the Regulation, and its entry into force, which was the third day after its publication in the Official Journal.

not be applicable in Germany on the grounds that it was not compatible with Arts. 12 and 14 of the German Basic Law, concerning rights of property and the right to carry on a business activity. Hence the Court found itself faced once again with the problem of the relationship between Community law and principles of the German Basic Law which had been encountered in particular in the *Internationale Handelsgesellschaft*[29] and *Nold*[30] cases. In resolving it, the differing formulations, negative in the former and positive in the latter, which had been used in the two cases were repeated and brought together.

Paraphrasing its judgement in *Internationale Handelsgesellschaft*, the Court said that the question whether fundamental rights had been breached by a Community act could only be determined within the framework of Community law itself, and that to have recourse to criteria from the legislation or constitutional system of one particular Member state would have an adverse effect on the uniformity and efficiency of Community law. On the other hand, it refrained from repeating expressly that "the validity of a Community measure ... cannot be affected by allegations that it runs counter to ... fundamental rights as formulated by the constitution of [a member] State"[31], although the terms used were still negative. It could be suggested that this approach has unnecessarily given rise to the impression that fundamental rights in national law are not taken into account in assessing the validity of Community rules, whereas the true position can be stated in positive terms as being that fundamental principles of national law are taken into account as sources of general principles of Community law, but that the European Court has no power to apply them as rules of national law[32]. Indeed, what actually happened in *Internationale Handelsgesellschaft* was that the European Court applied the principle of proportionality, the fundamental principle at issue, but as a rule of Community law rather than of German law.

A more positive approach had in fact been used in *Nold*, and the Court quoted passages from its judgment in that case *verbatim*, repeating that fundamental rights form an integral part of the general principles of law of which it ensures the observance, and that in safeguarding these rights it is bound to draw inspiration from constitutional traditions common to the Member states, and that it cannot uphold measures which are incompatible with fundamental rights recognized and protected by the constitutions of these States. It also repeated that "international treaties for the protection of human rights on which the Member States have collaborated or of which they are signatories, can supply guidelines which should be followed within the framework of Community Law"[33], and noted that this approach had been approved in the Joint Declaration on fundamental rights made by the Eur-

29 [1970] E.C.R. 1125.

30 [1974] E.C.R. 491.

31 [1970] E.C.R. 1125, at p. 1134.

32 *Usher*, E.L.R. 1976, 359, at p. 373.

33 [1974] E.C.R. 491, at p. 507.

opean Parliament, the Council and the Commission on 5th April 1977[34], which referred expressly to the European Convention on Human Rights. This is now, of course, overtaken by the express terms of the Maastricht Treaty on European Union, Art. F(2) of which provides that "the *Union* shall respect fundamental rights, as guaranteed by the European Convention for the Protection of Human Rights and Fundamental Freedoms signed in Rome on 4 November 1950 and as they result from the constitutional traditions common to the Member States, as general principles of *Community* law" (emphasis added).

The Court in fact took the *Verwaltungsgericht*'s doubts as to the compatibility of the Regulation with provisions of the German Basic Law as an invitation for it to assess its validity in terms of principles of Community Law. So doing, it turned first to the question of rights of property in the Community system, taking as its starting point Art. 1 of the First Protocol to the Human Rights Convention, which it described as reflecting the concepts common to the constitutions of the Member States[35]. It noted that while this provision recognized that "every natural or legal person is entitled to the peaceful enjoyment of his possessions", it still preserved the "right of a State to enforce such laws as it deems necessary to control the use of property in accordance with the general interest". None the less, although it took the view that the Regulation amounted to a control on use of property, the Court felt that the rule in the Convention did not enable it to give a sufficiently precise answer to the problem and so it considered also the rules applied in the various Member states. This it did not merely in general terms, but by reference to specific provisions of, in this case, the German, Italian and Irish constitutions, which would appear to represent a reversion to a practice hardly encountered since the early days of the E.C.S.C. Treaty[36]. A possible explanation of this more open approach by the Court itself may be that it represented an attempt to reassure those national courts which feared that their fundamental principles were threatened by the primacy of Community law that in practice these principles were taken into account at the Community level. The conclusion the Court drew from its analysis was that property ownership is subject to inherent obligations, to social requirements, and the requirements of the common good. It further noted that all the wine-producing countries of the Community imposed restrictions on the planting of vines, selection of varieties and methods of cultivation, and that nowhere were these restrictions regarded as necessarily infringing property rights.

On the basis that Regulation 1162/76 was an example of this type of restriction, the Court then considered whether the prohibitions introduced were appropriate to the aims pursued by the Community viticultural legislation which were to establish

---

34 O.J. 1977 C103/1.

35 In Case 36/75 *Rutili* [1975] E.C.R. 1219 the Court had described the Community rules limiting the powers of Member States with regard to the movements of migrant workers as being a specific manifestation of the principle embodied in Arts. 8 to 11 of the Convention.

36 See Joined Cases 7/56 and 3-5/57 *Algera v. Assembly* [1957 and 1958] E.C.R. 39, at pp. 55-56.

a lasting balance in the wine market, and to improve the quality of wine put on the market. In this context Regulation 1162/76 was a temporary measure aimed at preventing any increase in the overproduction which already existed. It was thus held not to be an undue restriction on the exercise of property rights, being justified by the aims the Community was pursuing in the general interest. In this, the Court agreed both with the Opinion of Advocate General *Capotorti* and indeed with the observations put in by the German government.

The Court then turned to the question whether the Regulation constituted a breach of the right to the free pursuit of business activity. This was the selfsame principle that had been at issue in *Nold*, and the Court repeated its statement in that decision that far from constituting an unfettered prerogative, such a right "must be viewed in the light of the social function of the ... activities protected thereunder"[37]. In this context, it was pointed out that the Regulation did not prevent anyone from cultivating existing vineyards, and in so far as the prohibition on new planting affected the freedom to carry on the activity of viticulture it was the natural consequence of the limitations on property rights, and was justified for the same reasons.

Thus, in the Community, as in the Member States, rights of property and the freedom to carry out business activities, may be subjected to restrictive measures taken by the relevant authorities in the general interest, although it appears that in the Community context it must be shown that such restrictive measures are not only in the general interest, but also comply with the aims of Community policy and are not out of proportion to the end they seek to achieve; in more English terminology, they must not be unreasonable.

Advocate General *Capotorti* did discuss whether compensation should have been payable for such a limitation of property rights, but concluded that this would be the case where the measure amounted to expropriation, which he did not consider to be the case[38].

V. Contract and Delict

1. Contractual Liability

The E.C. and Euratom Treaties make a clear distinction between what they term the "non-contractual liability" of the respective Communities, with regard to which the European Court has express jurisdiction, and their contractual liability, with regard to which the European Court only has jurisdiction if it is expressly conferred upon it by a provision in the contract. The E.C.S.C. Treaty does not use the same terminology, but nevertheless distinguishes between express jurisdiction under Art.

37 [1974] E.C.R. 491, at p. 508.

38 [1979] E.C.R. 3727, at p. 3762.

40 in relation to reparation for harm caused by a wrongful act or omission of the Community or of its servants, and the possibility under Art. 42 that a contract entered into by or on behalf of the Community may confer jurisdiction upon it.

Under Art. 215(1) of the E.C. Treaty[39], the contractual liability of the Community is to be governed by the law applicable to the contract in question, but under Art. 181[40] the Court has jurisdiction to give judgement pursuant to any "arbitration clause" contained in a contract concluded by or on behalf of the Community, whether that contract be governed by public or private law. In the result the European Court or the Court of First Instance may find itself having to determine questions of national law.

Two chief problems have been encountered: the first relates to the determination of whether there is a clause conferring jurisdiction on the Court, and the second to the application of the proper law of the contract. The first problem was clearly encountered in Case 23/76 *Pellegrini v. Commission*[41]. Pellegrini had since 1960 had the contract for cleaning the Nuclear Research Centre at Ispra. In 1971 the Commission invited tenders for a three-year contract commencing in 1972 on the basis of a draft agreement it had drawn up. Pellegrini was an unsuccessful tenderer, but, following the withdrawal of the successful tenderer, the Commission asked Pellegrini to continue for two months, subject to the terms and conditions of the draft agreement. This arrangement was confirmed in writing and renewed for periods of one to three months at a time until December 1975, when, following a fresh invitation to tender, Pellegrini was informed that a tender from another firm had been accepted. One of the clauses of this draft agreement conferred jurisdiction in disputes relating to the agreement on the Court, and it was held that the exchange of letters between the Commission and Pellegrini read together with the draft agreement to which they referred had the effect of conferring jurisdiction on the Court – a conclusion on which both the parties were in fact agreed.

Under the terms of the draft agreement, it was expressed to be governed by Italian law, but the problems of the interpretation and application by the European Court of a national law governing the contract are perhaps more apparent in Case 109/81 *Pace (née Porta) v. Commission*[42]. The applicant here had been employed as a teacher at the technical school attached to the Ispra Centre from 1963 to 1980, for the first five years without a contract, then under a series of annual contract-letters, and from 1976 on a series of more formal contracts which contained an arbitration clause conferring jurisdiction on the European Court and which were expressed to be governed by Italian law; the Court held that, acting under the jurisdiction conferred by these last contracts, it could take account also of the earlier

39 Art. 188 of the Euratom Treaty is in identical terms.

40 Art. 153 of the Euratom Treaty is in identical terms as is also Art. 42 of the E.C.S.C. Treaty.

41 [1976] E.C.R. 1807.

42 [1982] E.C.R. 2469.

relationship between the parties. The substantive question raised was entirely a matter of Italian law; the applicant claimed that under that law she should be regarded as having been employed under an indeterminate contract of service, with all the consequences that entailed as to, e.g., payment during school holidays, and, most importantly, pension rights. The First Chamber thereupon followed Italian case law to hold that the applicant was an employee rather than an independent contractor, and applied Italian legislation on fixed-term contracts of employment, under which all contracts of employment are deemed to be indeterminate unless they fall within defined exceptions, which were not relevant in this case. It was therefore held that the applicant was entitled to the benefits of an indeterminate contract of service under Italian law, and that the Commission must pay her the equivalent of the Italian pension she would have been entitled to if it had not failed to pay any contributions on her behalf. It was perhaps fortunate that both the President of the First Chamber and the Advocate General in this case were Italian lawyers.

2. Non-Contractual (Delictual?) Liability

A direct action for damages is limited under Art. 40 of the E.C.S.C. Treaty to reparation for harm caused by a wrongful act or omission of the Community or of its servants, whereas Arts. 178 and 215 of the E.C. Treaty (as also Arts. 153 and 188 of the Euratom Treaty) refer to "non-contractual liability" relating to damage caused by the Community's institution or servants.

As to the scope of "non-contractual" liability, it was argued by the Commission in Case 46/75 *I.B.C. v. Commission*[43] that quasi-contractual liability was a branch of the law of contract and therefore did not fall within this concept, but Advocate General *Warner* was able to reject this argument in his Opinion by reference to the laws of the Member States[44]. However, it will be seen that in practice a claim based on quasi-contract is unlikely to be made against a Community institution, since the structure of the E.C. is such that sums due under Community legislation are generally collected by national authorities, and it is well established[45] that claims for restitution of such sums must be brought against the national authority which received the payment.

The E.C. and Euratom Treaties also refer to liability as being imposed "in accordance with the general principles common to the laws of the Member States", which is the only express mention of general principles derived from the laws of the Member States in the Treaties. The consequences of this phrase may be illustrated in relation to liability for harm caused by legislation.

---

43 [1976] E.C.R. 65

44 [1976] E.C.R. 65, at p. 86

45 See Case 96/71 *Haegeman v. Commission* [1972] E.C.R. 1005.

It was established in 1971 that in order to recover damages for harm caused by a legislative act of a Community institution, it was necessary to show that a "sufficiently serious violation of a superior rule of law for the protection of the individual ha[d] occurred"[46]. In his Opinion in that case, Advocate General *Roemer* made reference to a conference on the liability of the State for the wrongful conduct of its institutions held at the Max-Planck Institute in 1964[47], and suggested that the requirement to have regard to the general principles common to the laws of the Member States should not be taken too literally; rather, what was indicated was a process of assessment taking account of the particular objectives of the Treaty and the peculiarities of the Community structure, and he concluded that the guideline should be the "best-elaborated national rules".

However, in 1973, following the Accession of the United Kingdom, Denmark, and Ireland, it was argued very strongly on behalf of the Community institutions in Cases 63 to 69/72 *Werhahn and others v. Council and Commission*[48], that, in particular having regard to the legal systems of the new Member States, there was no general legal principle that the Community should be liable for legislative acts. As a matter of substantive law that was possibly true, but what this argument missed was the point made by Advocate General *Lagrange* in an extra-judicial capacity[49], cited by Advocate General *Gand* in 1969 in Case 9/69 *Sayag v. Leduc*[50], in which he observed that the only truly common legal principle was that which by then disapproved in all Member States of the doctrine of non-liability of the State, i.e. the principle underlying the Crown Proceedings Act. Applying a purposive interpretation, the argument may be developed that the structure of the Treaties is such as to create Communities whose institutions are answerable for their wrongful acts. Since the vast bulk of the acts of the Community institutions are legislative or quasi-legislative in nature, if the institutions were not answerable for their legislative acts, then they would virtually be above the law. To develop a point made by Advocate General *Roemer* in his Opinion in the *Werhahn* case, the idea in the United Kingdom that there could be no State liability for legislative acts was very closely correlated to the concept of the sovereignty of Parliament. This was a concept which had very little relevance in the case of legislation which emanated solely from appointed bodies, not from elected ones. Indeed Advocate General *Roemer* pointed out that this may make it necessary to put special stress on the concept of the strengthening by the Court of legal protection within the Community. Whether the same approach should be applied when certain Community legislation emanates jointly from an elected Parliament and an appointed Council by virtue of the Maastricht Treaty perhaps requires further debate.

---

46 Originally formulated in Case 5/71 *Zuckerfabrik Schöppenstedt v. Council* [1971] E.C.R. 975, at p. 984.

47 See [1971] E.C.R. 975, at p. 989.

48 [1973] E.C.R. 1229.

49 *Lagrange*, The Non-contractual Liability of the Community, C.M.L.R. 1965-66, 32.

50 [1969] E.C.R. 329, at 340.

In the result, the Court itself simply repeated the formula it had used in 1971, which would appear to imply that the nature of a "general principle common to the laws of the Member States" is a matter of Community law determined by the Court.

At a more basic level however, specific national legislation may impose obligations on Community institutions, breach of which gives rise to liability. In Case C-308/87 *Grifoni v. Euratom*[51], which involved a fall from a roof at the Joint Research Centre at Ispra in Italy, it was stated in general terms that "any Community institution which carries out work for the construction or maintenance of buildings is under an obligation to comply with the provisions concerning the prevention of industrial accidents applicable at the place where the work is carried out". In that case therefore, the Commission was required to comply with the relevant Italian legislation, under which those working on a roof should be supplied with a suitable safety harness and there should be a protective rail to prevent falls. Since the Commission did not meet either of these requirements, it was held that it had failed to show 'due diligence' and had acted unlawfully, thus giving rise to liability.

A further example of the Court's use of principles derived from national legal systems is its acceptance of the concept of contributory negligence giving rise to a reduction in the damages payable, but not necessarily their elimination. In the *Grifoni* case, it was found that the applicant himself had failed to take the necessary care for his own safety, given that he was a specialist in the field, and the Commission's liability was reduced to 50%. A similar situation arose in Case 145/83 *Adams v. Commission*[52], where a senior employee of Hoffman-La Roche in Switzerland had sent the Commission confidential documents relating to the way Hoffman-La Roche conducted their business with a view to instigating proceedings under the E.C. competition rules. It was there held that where the Commission's officials learnt that the informant had been identified by Hoffman-La Roche and that Hoffman-La Roche intended to have criminal proceedings brought against him in Switzerland, the Commission was under a duty to take every possible step to warn the informer, and the failure of its officials so to do gave rise to liability when the informer returned to Switzerland and was prosecuted and imprisoned for having passed the information to the Commission. However, the Commission's liability was reduced by half on the basis that the applicant had contributed to the harm he suffered by his own negligent conduct, particularly in returning to Switzerland.

3. Fault

There is a clear distinction between the drafting of the E.C.S.C. Treaty on the one hand and the E.C. and Euratom Treaties on the other with regard to the requirement of fault. Under Arts. 34 and 40 of the E.C.S.C. Treaty, liability is limited

---

51 [1990] E.C.R. I-1203 (interlocutory judgment).

52 [1985] E.C.R. 3539.

to reparation for harm caused by a wrongful act or omission of the Community or of its servants. The former provision requires the Commission to take the necessary steps to comply with the judgment if the Court declares a Commission decision or recommendation void, and adds that if the Commission fails to take within a reasonable time the necessary steps to comply with the judgment, proceedings for damages may be instituted before the Court.

Art. 40 provides that without prejudice to the first paragraph of Art. 34, the Court shall have jurisdiction to order pecuniary reparation from the Community, on application by the injured party, to make good any injury caused in carrying out the Treaty by a wrongful act or omission on the part of the Community in the performance of its functions; it also states that the Court shall have jurisdiction to order the Community to make good any injury caused by a personal wrong by a servant of the Community in the performance of his duties. There is therefore a clear requirement of fault under the E.C.S.C. provisions, and it has been held that this means something more than the mere illegality of the act alleged to have caused harm[53]. However, in analyzing its earlier case-law in Cases C-363/88 and C-364/88 *Finsider, Italsider and Falck v. Commission*[54], the Court noted that the Treaty provisions gave no details as to the nature of the fault required and that it itself had treated the matter on a case-by-case basis. It found that in each case it had taken into account the characteristics of the activities in question in order to determine what amounted to fault of such a nature as to render the Community liable, and it concluded that it was necessary to take into account in particular the complexity of the situations the institution must regulate, the difficulties of applying the legislation and the discretion available to the institution under that legislation. It also however emphasized that it must consider whether the facts at issue constituted "serious" faults of such a nature as to render the Community liable[55].

Articles 178 and 215 of the E.E.C. Treaty (as also Articles 153 and 188 of the Euratom Treaty) refer to "non-contractual liability" relating to damage caused by the Community's institution or servants, which would appear to recognize the possibility of liability without fault. While there would appear to be no decision so far in which the Court has imposed liability without at least the involvement of an unlawful act[56], the question of principle has been discussed and has not been rejected.

---

53 Cases C-363/88 and C-364/88 *Finsider, Italsider and. Falck v. Commission* [1992] E.C.R. (30th January) at 20.

54 [1992] E.C.R. (30th January) at 21-24.

55 Compare the use of phrases such as "inexcusable mistakes" in Cases 14 etc./60 and 1/61 *Meroni v. High Authority* [1961] E.C.R. 161, "gravely neglected the duties" in Cases 19 and 21/60, 2 and 3/61 *Fives Lille Cail v. High Authority* [1961] E.C.R. 281, and "lack of care" which was "increasingly obvious" in Cases 29 etc./63 *Usines de la Providence v. High Authority* [1965] E.C.R. 911, noted in 22 of the judgment.

56 Although as had been seen above, in Cases C-363/88 and C-364/88 *Finsider, Italsider and Falck v. Commission* [1992] E.C.R. (30th January) the Court held that fault under the E.C.S.C. Treaty required something more than a mere unlawful act.

Advocate General *Mayras* suggested in Cases 9 and 11/71 *Compagnie d'Approvisionnement v. Commission*[57] that Art. 215(2) was not limited to unlawful acts, and Advocate General *Trabucchi* suggested in Case 169/73 *Compagnie Continentale v. Commission* that the Court had implicitly accepted that such an action lay[58]. The matter was discussed in some detail in Case 59/83 *Biovilac*[59] where the applicants argued that even if the measures adopted by the Commission were not unlawful, it was still liable to make good any harm suffered by the applicants if they were affected in a different way and much more seriously than all other traders and producers. This argument was derived from the German concept of *Sonderopfer* (special sacrifice) and the French concept of *rupture de l'égalité devant les charges publiques* (unequal discharge of public burdens), and therefore a clear reference to the laws of the Member States as accepted in Art. 215(2). It may be observed that the Commission neither accepted nor argued for the outright rejection of this approach, and Advocate General *Slynn* suggested that such an action "if existing at all" must be within a narrow compass. The Court itself avoided having to decide the point by noting that it had consistently held that an action for damages under Art. 215(2) for unlawful legislative action could not succeed unless the damage alleged by the applicant exceeded the limits of the economic risks inherent in operating the sector concerned[60], and that that principle would have to be applied *a fortiori* if the concept of liability without fault were accepted in Community law. It went on to find that on the facts of the case those limits were not exceeded.

The question of no-fault liability therefore remains open, and it may be submitted that it remains a real possibility to the extent that it is recognized in the national legal systems of some of the Member States, given the express reference to the laws of the Member States in Art. 215(2).

VI. National Influence on E.C. Legislation

1. General

Much substantive E.C. legislation may be traced back to specific national legal systems. Hence the famous transfer of undertakings legislation, Council Directive 77/187[61] safeguarding employees' rights on transfers of undertakings, businesses or parts of businesses, may be seen as applying on the Community level a provision which has existed in French law since 1928[62]. This states that "s'il survient

57 [1972] E.C.R. 391 and 422.

58 [1975] E.C.R. 117 at p. 141, though this was doubted by Advocate General *Slynn* in his Opinion in Case 59/83 *Biovilac* [1984] E.C.R. 4057.

59 [1984] E.C.R. 4057.

60 See, e.g., Cases 83 & 94/76, 4, 15 & 40/77 *Bayerische H.N.L. v. Council and Commission* [1978] E.C.R. 1209.

61 O.J. 1977 L61/26.

une modification dans la situation juridique de l'employeur, notamment par succession, vente, fusion, transformation du fonds, mise en société, tous les contrats de travail en cours au jour de la modification subsistent entre le nouvel entrepreneur et le personnel de l'entreprise". On the other hand, this is clearly not classical civil law; indeed when the author was a student in France in the late 1960s it was taught in courses on the law of obligations as an exception to the basic rule in Art. 1134 of the code civil that contracts are binding on those who make them.

Other modern French transplants include the European Economic Interest Grouping introduced into E.C. law by Council Regulation 2137/85[63], clearly inspired by the French legislation on 'groupements d'intérêt économique' enacted in 1967[64], and the E.C. system of value-added tax[65] is modelled on the French *taxe sur la valeur ajoutée* introduced in 1954[66] rather than the German system of turnover taxes (*Umsatzsteuer* as governed by the law of 1st September 1951).

It should not however be thought that the only influences are from civil law systems: Council Directive 87/102[67] on consumer credit draws heavily on sections of the United Kingdom Consumer Credit Act 1974: its aim is to ensure that the consumer (defined as a natural person acting outside his trade or profession[68]) receives certain information about the credit agreements into which he enters. In particular, they require information to be given about the annual percentage rate of charge (A.P.R.), both in advertisements and offers relating to credit[69] and in the agreement itself, which must be in writing[70].

2. *Companies*

One area where the clash of legal cultures is particulary evident in E.C. law is that of company law harmonization, which to a large extent reflects German influence. Thus, for example, the United Kingdom has encountered considerable difficulties in finding a satisfactory method of implementing the provisions of the First Directive[71] on the validity of contracts entered into by the 'organs' of a company,

62 Law of 19th July 1928. Formerly Art. 23 al.8 of *livre* I of the *Code du Travail*, now Art. L.122-12 al.2 of the *Code du Travail*.

63 O.J. 1985 L199/1.

64 *Ordonnance* no. 67-821 of 23rd September 1967.

65 Originally introduced by Council Directives 67/227 and 67/228 (O.J. 1967 L71 pp. 1301 and 1303).

66 Law of 10th April 1954.

67 O.J. 1987 L42/48.

68 Art. 1(2)(a).

69 Art. 3.

70 Art. 4.

71 Council Directive 68/151 (O.J. 1968 L65/8).

because those provisions are drafted on the basis that the general law lays down the powers of those organs, and the problem is that of attempting to restrict those powers, whereas in the United Kingdom the reality is that the powers of the organs are largely laid down in the company's own memorandum and articles of association, and the problem is that of knowing whether the organ has the power in the first place[72].

The problems may particularly be illustrated by reference to the concept of groups of companies, where in the United Kingdom effect has been given to Community requirements, but traditional concepts are still applied in matters not subject to such requirements.

As indicated earlier in this paper, companies, and the specific relationship of parent and subsidiary, are mentioned in Arts. 52-58 of the E.C. Treaty in the context of freedom of establishment and freedom to provide services. While there is no Community law right to move the main business of a company into another Member State[73], the Treaty provisions give companies established in one Member State the right to set up subsidiaries, branches or agencies in other Member States. Under these rules, however, not only branches and agencies but also locally incorporated subsidiaries are in principle treated as emanations of the parent company, and it has been held that it is unlawful for Member States to discriminate between these different forms of secondary establishment. This appears clearly from Case 270/83 *Commission v. France*[74], where it was held that if the French authorities granted a particular form of tax relief to the French subsidiaries of foreign insurance companies, they must also grant the same relief to the French branches or agencies of foreign insurance companies. The underlying premise is that subsidiaries, branches and agencies are all forms of establishment of the parent company.

However, the logic of this has not always been followed in other Community legislation: a difference in treatment between branches and agencies on the one hand and subsidiaries on the other does appear to result from the Second Banking Directive[75], which establishes the principle that a credit institution which has been authorized in its home state may by virtue of that authorization supply its services or establish a branch in another Member State. Nevertheless, the establishment of a subsidiary still requires authorization by the host state. While this may be ex-

---

72 See *John A. Usher*, Harmonization of Legislation, in: D. Lasok, Les Communautés Européennes en Fonctionnement, Bruylant, 1981, at pp. 188-189. The current United Kingdom implementation is in s. 35A of the Companies Act 1985 (inserted by the Companies Act 1989).

73 Case 81/87 *R. v. H.M. Treasury ex parte Daily Mail* [1988] E.C.R. 5483. The reason for this is that under the company laws of some Member States, a company would be regarded as losing its legal personality or ceasing to exist if it carried on its main business or had its centre of management in a state other than that in which it was incorporated.

74 [1986] E.C.R. 273.

75 See n. 3 above.

plained by the fact that a subsidiary is a separate legal person governed by the law of the host state, it can hardly be reconciled with the earlier case-law.

In a rather different area of Community law, it may finally be observed that when the system of quotas for steel producers under the E.C.S.C. Treaty was in force, it was held to be legitimate for the Commission to allocate a quota to a group as a whole, rather than being obliged to allocate separate quotas to each producer within that group[76], again, therefore, showing a willingness to recognize the reality of a group.

There has been little willingness on the part of courts in the United Kingdom to recognize the existence of groups except where specific statutory provisions so require. The apparent exception is *D.H.N. Food Distributors v. Tower Hamlets London Borough*[77], which involved compensation for disturbance. There land was owned by one company, and business was carried on on that land by another company, and these two companies were in a relationship of parent and subsidiary; it was held that, for the purposes of compensation, the owner of the land could be treated as carrying on business on the land, i.e. the parent and subsidiary were treated as a single undertaking. However, that decision of the Court of Appeal was criticized by the House of Lords in the Scottish case of *Woolfson v. Strathclyde*[78]. While *Woolfson* can be distinguished on the basis that the land and the business were divided not between parent and subsidiary companies but between a trader and the company he controlled, the view was expressed in the House of Lords that it was doubtful whether the Court of Appeal had properly applied "the principle that it is appropriate to pierce the corporate veil only where special circumstances exist indicating that it is a mere façade concealing the true facts"[79].

The Court of Appeal itself has now suggested that *D.H.N.* should be regarded simply as a decision on the relevant statutory provisions for compensation, in *Adams v. Cape Industries p.l.c.*[80]. That case involved what in an E.C. context would be called establishment, the question being whether the operation of a subsidiary in a foreign country amounted to the presence of the parent company in that country. Since the foreign country was the United States, no question of E.C. law arose; instead, the Court of Appeal strongly reaffirmed the principle of separate legal personality, and expressly rejected the argument that a parent and subsidiary could be regarded as a single commercial or economic unit[81], holding that "save in cases which turn on the wording of particular statutes or contracts, the court is not free to disregard the principle of *Salomon v. Salomon and Co.*[82] merely because it

76 Case 103/83 *Usinor v. Commission* [1984] E.C.R. 3483.

77 [1976] 3 All E.R. 462.

78 1978 S.L.T. 159.

79 1978 S.L.T. 159, at p. 161.

80 [1991] 1 All E.R. 929, at p. 1019.

81 [1991] 1 All E.R. 929, at pp. 1020-1021.

82 [1897] A.C. 22.

considers that justice so requires"[83]. The case-law of the European Court on the competition rules of the E.C. Treaty was put to the Court of Appeal, and appears to have been categorized as "the wording of a particular statute"[84]. Whether this is an appropriate classification given the scope and status of E.C. law remains to be seen, but since the House of Lords refused leave to appeal, it would seem that developments in this area will be largely statutory.

A similar attitude underlies other aspects of company law involved in the relationship between parent and subsidiary companies. So, the directors of a parent company owe no duty to a subsidiary with an independent board[85], and a director of a subsidiary acting as such owes his fiduciary duties to the subsidiary, not the parent[86]. On the other hand, while it is not enough that directors, in considering for example whether one company in a group should guarantee the debts of another company in the group, should simply look to the benefit of the group as a whole[87], separate consideration of the benefit to the individual company would appear not to be required if "an intelligent and honest man in the position of the director concerned, could, in the whole of the existing circumstances, have reasonably believed that the transaction was for the benefit of the company".

Leaving aside tax legislation, express mention of subsidiaries in the United Kingdom companies legislation dates back to the accounting provisions of the Companies Act 1929, and the Companies Act 1948 introduced a general definition of a holding company, a subsidiary and a wholly-owned subsidiary, which was reproduced in s. 736 of the Companies Act 1985. Under that definition, a company was deemed to be a subsidiary of another if it was a member of it and controlled the composition of its board of directors, or if it held more than half in nominal value of its equity share capital, or if it was a subsidiary of a subsidiary so defined.

This definition ignored situations such as a minority shareholding which controlled a majority of the voting rights, and United Kingdom legislation on group accounts had to be changed to comply with the E.C. Seventh Company Law Harmonization Directive[88]. In the result, the Companies Act 1989 amended the 1985 Act so as to introduce a new definition of the parent/subsidiary relationship, and a different definition of that relationship for the purposes of the preparation of group accounts.

The general definition is given in the new s. 736 of the 1985 Act, which looks to control rather than the size of the shareholding. Under this provision, a company is a subsidiary of a holding company if the latter holds a majority of the voting rights

---

83 [1991] 1 All E.R. 929, at p. 1019.

84 [1991] 1 All E.R. 929, at p. 1019.

85 *Lindgren v. L. & P. Estates* [1968] 1 All E.R. 917, at p. 922.

86 *Pergamon Press v. Maxwell* [1970] 2 All E.R. 809.

87 *Charterbridge Corporation v. Lloyds Bank* [1969] 2 All E.R. 1185.

88 Council Directive 83/349 (O.J. 1983 L193/1).

in it, or is a member of it and has the right to appoint or remove a majority of its board of directors, or is a member of it and controls alone, pursuant to an agreement with other shareholders or members a majority of the voting rights in it, or is a subsidiary of a subsidiary so defined. A subsidiary is 'wholly-owned' if it has no members other than the holding company and its wholly-owned subsidiaries or persons acting on their behalf.

The specific definition relating to the obligation to prepare group accounts again is based on the idea of control, but is more complex and includes provisions derived from the E.C. Directive which may be said to reflect certain concepts of German company law, in which the concept of the group is highly developed. Section 258 in fact defines parent and subsidiary "undertakings", a concept which however includes companies. It defines the parent rather than the subsidiary, a parent being an undertaking which holds a majority of voting rights in the subsidiary, or is a member of it and has the right to appoint or remove a majority of its board of directors, or has the right to exercise a dominant influence over it by virtue of provisions contained in its memorandum or articles or by virtue of a 'control contract', or is a member of it and controls alone, pursuant to an agreement with other shareholders or members, a majority of the voting rights in the subsidiary undertaking. An undertaking is also a parent undertaking if it has a participating interest in the subsidiary undertaking and it actually exercises a dominant influence over it, or it and the subsidiary are managed on a unified basis. Under s. 260, a 'participating interest' is an interest in the subsidiary held on a long term basis for the purpose of securing a contribution to its activities by the exercise of control or influence arising from or related to that interest, and in principle a holding of 20% or more of the shares is deemed to be such an interest.

The concepts of dominant influence, the control contract, and a participating interest are derived from the Directive and not reflected in the general definition in s. 736. The control contract, under which the parent undertaking may exercise a dominant influence over the subsidary undertaking causes particular problems in the light of the long established view that directors of a subsidiary owe their duties to the subsidiary, not to the parent company[89]. However, the new Schedule 10A to the Companies Act makes it clear that the rights conferred by the contract must be authorized by the memorandum or articles of the undertaking in question, and must also be permitted by the law under which that undertaking is established.

While the scope of s. 258 as such is limited to the obligation to prepare consolidated accounts, it may be observed that the concepts it has taken from the Seventh Directive are also used in a draft Ninth Directive on groups of companies, which in particular contains provisions designed to protect creditors and minority shareholders.

---

89 *Pergamon Press v. Maxwell* [1970] 2 All E.R. 809.

VII. Judicial Process and Organization

1. Court Structures and Remedies

The Community judicial system may be regarded very much as modelled on French administrative law[90], the distinction in the European Court and the Court of First Instance between judges and Advocates General reflecting to a large extent the distinction in the French Conseil d'État between judges and the Commissaire du Gouvernement[91], and the four grounds for annulment under the Community Treaties (lack of competence, infringement of an essential procedural requirement, infringement of this Treaty or of any rule of law relating to its application, or misuse of powers[92]) may be regarded as reflecting those developed in French administrative law (*incompétence, vice de forme, violation de la loi* and *détournement de pouvoir*[93]).

This does not however mean that they are applied in the same way. To take a simple example, it would appear from the Opinion of Advocate General *Mayras* in Case 37/72 *Marcato v. Commission*[94] that in French law an applicant who can show an interest in the result of his or her action need not show an interest in each ground for annulment that is invoked. The Court however reached a different view, which was more clearly expressed in Case 90/74 *Deboeck v. Commission*[95], a staff case heard by the First Chamber. The action was for the annulment of an internal competition for the recruitment of secretarial assistants, and one submission of the applicant was that the notice of competition had not been preceded by a notice of vacancy as required by the Staff Regulations[96]. The Court held that she had no interest to raise the point, since she was not eligible for transfer or promotion (the procedures which may precede the holding of a competition) without taking part in the competition, and she had in fact taken part in the competition. This followed an Opinion delivered by Advocate General *Warner*[97] in which he briefly reviewed the situation in the Member states, contrasting the tradition in French law and French derived systems whereby a person having an interest in the result[98] may raise any ground for the annulment of the act in question, with the view, *inter alios*, of *Lord Wilberforce* in *Malloch v. Aberdeen Corporation*[99] that a "breach of proce-

90 Even if, in the context of the present paper, that has little to do with Roman law.

91 One distinction however being that while a French Commissaire du Gouvernement may participate in the judges' deliberations, the E.C. Advocates General are excluded.

92 E.C. Treaty Art. 173, E.C.S.C. Treaty Art. 33, Euratom Treaty Art. 146.

93 See, e.g., *Vedel* and *Delvolvé*, Droit Administratif, 12th ed., 1992, vol. 1, p. 299.

94 [1973] E.C.R. 361, at p. 374.

95 [1975] E.C.R. 1123.

96 Art. 4(2).

97 [1975] E.C.R. 1123, at p. 1141.

98 Conseil d'Etat, 17th January 1947, p. 668.

99 [1971] 1 W.L.R. at p. 1595.

dure, whether called a failure of natural justice, or an essential administrative fault, cannot give (the appellant) a remedy in the courts, unless behind it there is something of substance which has been lost by the failure" – and decisions by the Danish, Dutch and German courts that a plaintiff cannot complain of irregularities which have not caused him any harm.

To the English common lawyer, one distinguishing feature of modern civil-law court systems is the use of the technique of *cassation* at the level of supreme courts. Under this system, a case goes to the highest court in the relevant judicial hierarchy only on a point of law, and the highest court adjudicates not on the merits of the dispute but on the judgment rendered by the intermediate appeal court. If the highest court confirms the judgment of the intermediate appeal court, that judgment stands, but if it annuls that judgment, the case is sent back to another intermediate appeal court to give a final judgment on the merits. More particularly, in the French administrative court system, the *recours en cassation* before the Conseil d'État is used with regard to the decisions of specialist tribunals as well as intermediate appeal courts, and closely resembles an action for the annulment of an administrative act. The appeal (using that word in a broad sense) can be based on three of the four grounds which give rise to an action for annulment: *incompétence*, *vice de forme*, and *violation de la loi*[100]. *Détournement de pouvoir* is not available, and distinguished British commentators have suggested that this is presumably because the French cannot imagine persons charged with a judicial function offending in this respect[101].

Be that as it may, this French concept of *cassation* in administrative matters is reproduced in the relationship between the Court of First Instance of the E.C. and the European Court. The additional provisions of the Protocols on the Statutes of the Court under the three Community Treaties introduced by Council Decision 88/591 establishing the Court of First Instance[102] lay down that:

> "An appeal to the Court of Justice shall be limited to points of law. It shall lie on the grounds of lack of competence of the Court of First Instance, a breach of procedure before it which adversely affects the interests of the appellant as well as the infringement of Community law by the Court of First Instance".

In effect, this reproduces three of the four grounds for annulment under the Community Treaties (lack of competence, infringement of an essential procedural requirement, and infringement of the Treaty or of any rule of law relating to its application) while omitting misuse of powers. The parallelism with the French system seems so great as hardly to be coincidental. The more general concept of *cassation* also appears in the 1988 Decision. It provides that if the appeal is well

---

100 See e.g. *Vedel* and *Delvolvé* (n. 93) vol. 1, p. 229.

101 *Brown* and *Garner*, French Administrative Law, 1967, at p. 126; the comment does not appear to be reproduced in the current 4th ed. by *Brown* and *Bell*.

102 O.J. 1988 L319/1.

founded, the Court of Justice shall quash the decision of the Court of First Instance, but then provides the Court with a choice between reference back (in this case to the Court of First Instance itself) or delivery of the final judgment. In terms of the Decision, the Court "may itself give final judgment in the matter, where the state of the proceedings so permits, or refer the case back to the Court of First Instance for judgment". Where a case is referred back to the Court of First Instance, that Court is bound by the decision of the Court of Justice on points of law. The prevailing practice of the European Court so far would appear to be to dispose of the case itself.

2. *Precedent*

It may be suggested that in civil law systems precedent is not a binding source of law[103], although *Watson* has pointed out that in codified systems precedent becomes, ironically, of greater importance[104]. One interesting sidelight of Case C-70/88 *E.P.* v. *Council*[105] on the rights of the European Parliament to bring an action for annulment is the approach taken by the Court to distinguishing its previous decisions. The Court has for many years been quoting its previous decisions when it is following them; indeed, citation of a previous judgment appears frequently to be regarded as a sufficient reason not to have to give a detailed reasoning of the same point again in the Court's judgments. On the other hand, it has long been notorious that the European Court does not state directly when it is not following its earlier case law. What was novel about the judgment in this case was that the Court referred expressly to its earlier judgment in Case 302/87 *E.P. v. Council*[106] holding that the Parliament had no such right of action, referred in detail to the reasoning in that judgment, and then concluded that the remedies it had suggested that the Parliament should use in that judgment were not in fact sufficiently effective or certain. The Court then went on openly to reach a different conclusion.

This approach was repeated in a different area in Case C-10/89 *C.N.L.-S.U.C.A.L. v. H.A.G.*[107]. This case involved once again the famous H.A.G. trademark which had been at issue in Case 192/73 *van Zuylen v. H.A.G.*[108]. It will be remembered that in that case the European Court laid down the doctrine of common origin, holding that the holder of a trademark having the same origin as that used by a trader in another Member State could not invoke it to prevent imports under that mark from the other Member State. That doctrine had been heavily criti-

103 See *Merryman* (n. 17) 48.

104 *Watson* (n. 1) 175-6.

105 [1990] E.C.R. I-2041.

106 [1988] E.C.R. 5615.

107 17th October 1990.

108 [1974] E.C.R. 731.

cized, and in the 1990 judgment, the European Court expressly stated in as many words that it found it necessary to reconsider the interpretation given in the earlier judgment in the light of its later case law. After expressly reaffirming the approach derived from the *Centrafarm*[109] cases that where a product has been sold by the holder of the patent or trademark himself or with his consent in one Member State, then the owner of the right cannot prevent those goods being imported into another Member State where he holds the rights, the Court expressly reversed the common origin rule, at least where the right to the mark had at some stage been expropriated so that the marks were operated independently. Could it be suggested that these decisions indicate a subtle change in the Court's attitude to precedent; no longer are earlier cases merely something which save detailed reasoning in later cases, but they are of sufficient importance as sources of law for the Court to need to state expressly when it is no longer following them? In effect, the attitude of the Court to its previous decisions appears to be taking a distinctly English turn.

3. General Principles – Legal Professional Privilege

The general principles of E.C. law developed by the European Court may on occasion represent an amalgam of civil law and common law elements. This appears to be the case in relation to the question of legal professional privilege, where the Court took a doctrine of English law, and tempered it by concepts derived from civil law systems in Case 155/79 *A.M. & S. Europe v. Commission*[110]. In brief, following an on-the-spot investigation under Regulation 17/62, the Commission requested A.M. & S. to produce certain documents, and ultimately issued a formal Decision to that effect under Art. 14(3) of Regulation 17/62[111], whilst A.M. & S. claimed that the documents were "covered by the doctrine of legal privilege" and, after refusing to produce them, sought the annulment of the provision in the Commission's Decision requiring their production. The documents concerned fell into four main categories: solicitors' instructions to counsel; communications between an outside solicitor and A.M. & S. or one of its parent companies containing legal advice or requests for legal advice; documents containing legal advice or requests for legal advice from or to an 'in-house' lawyer employed by A.M. & S. or one of its parent companies; and communications between executives of A.M. & S. or one of its parent companies recording legal advice or requests for legal advice.

In effect A.M. & S. and the Commission were originally in dispute not so much as to the existence of a principle of legal professional privilege but rather as to the procedure whereby it should be determined whether or not a document was protected from disclosure, and it was the French government, intervening to support

109 Cases 15 and 16/74 *Centrafarm* [1974] E.C.R. 1147 and 1183.

110 [1982] E.C.R. 1575.

111 O.J. 204/62.

the Commission, which raised the fundamental issue of principle. Following an interim order in which it required the documents to be produced to it in sealed envelopes[112], it was the issue of principle which the European Court dealt with at greatest length in its final judgment. It was expressly stated that Community law derives not only from the economic but also the legal "interpenetration" of the Member States; hence, in this case, account had to be taken of the principles and concepts common to the laws of the Member States concerning the observance of confidentiality as regards communications between lawyer and client. It should be noted, however, that the Court took from the outset the view that the purpose of the protection of confidentiality is to enable any person, without constraint, "to consult a lawyer whose profession entails the giving of *independent* legal advice to all those in need of it" (emphasis added). After noting that in some States, protection against disclosure is regarded as being derived from the very nature of the legal profession, whereas in others it is based upon "the rights of the defence" (i.e. the protection of individual litigants, in particular their right to be heard) the Court concluded that what was common to the laws of the Member States was the protection of written communications between lawyer and client subject to two conditions: the communications must be made "for the purpose and in the interest of the client's rights of defence" and "they must emanate from independent lawyers, that is to say, lawyers who are not bound to the client by a relationship of employment".

In the context of competition proceedings before the Commission, the Court was willing to accept that the principle of 'confidentiality' must be recognized as covering all written communications exchanged after the initiation of the administrative procedure under Regulation No. 17 which may lead to a decision on the application of Arts. 85 and 86, which presumably means from notification or application from receipt of a complaint or from the commencement of proceedings on the Commission's own initiative[113]; the Court also accepted that it could apply to earlier written communications relating to the subject matter of such a procedure, and in this case it was found that the documents in question, which were apparently drawn up during the period immediately before and after the Accession of the United Kingdom to the Community and were principally concerned with avoiding conflicts between the applicant and the Community authorities with regard to the competition rules, were sufficiently connected with the procedure to be protected from disclosure. Though perhaps not wholly relevant, this protection of pre-dispute advice contrasts somewhat with the Court's views on costs, since it has long held that remuneration for legal advice given before the commencement of litigation is not recoverable[114].

The second condition itself gives rise to two problems: the definition of a lawyer, and the question of his independence. The emphasis on independence, quite

112 [1982] E.C.R. 1575, at p. 1616 (order of 4th February 1981).

113 See Arts. 2,3 and 4 of Reg. 17.

114 See Case 75/69 *Hake v. Commission* [1970] E.C.R. 901, at pp. 902 sq.

simply defined as not being bound to the client by a relationship of employment, appears to reflect the Court's view of the purpose of legal professional privilege, as has been noted, and may not be unconnected with the fact that in some Member States, lawyers may not enter into contracts of employment, although a salaried solicitor in an independent firm of solicitors would appear to be protected. More particularly, the Court states that the requirement of independence "is based on a conception of the lawyer's role as collaborating in the administration of justice by the courts, and as being required to provide, in full independence, and in the overriding interests of that case, such legal assistance as the client needs". This might almost seem to treat confidentiality as a protection of the independence of the lawyer, but such a view hardly squares with the fact that later in the judgement it was held to be open to the client to waive the privilege. Be that as it may, the practical consequences for many large undertakings employing 'in-house' lawyers is that their advice will not be protected.

With regard to the definition of a 'lawyer', the Court stated that the protection of written communications between lawyer and client must apply to "any lawyer entitled to practice his profession in one of the Member States, regardless of the Member State in which the client lives". Although the phrase "practise his profession" could be open to a wide interpretation and although English is the language of the case, it should be noted that the French version of the judgement refers to an "avocat inscrit au barreau" of a Member State, the phrase used in Art. 17 of the E.C. Statute of the Court, and the parallel provisions of the other Statutes, and there rendered into English as "a lawyer entitled to practise before a Court of a Member State". Moreover, the Court emphasized that the protection of confidentiality had as its counterpart "the rules of professional ethics and discipline which are laid down and enforced in the general interest by the institutions endowed with the requisite powers for that purpose" and referred expressly to Art. 17 of the Statute as demonstrating this conception. It may also be noted that the Court cited Council Directive 77/249/EC[115] on the provision of services by lawyers as determining the limits beyond which the protection of confidentiality may not be extended. The result of all this appears to be that for his communication to be protected, the independent lawyer must be qualified, and entitled to practise one of the professions listed in Directive 77/249, in a Member State, he must be subject to the professional discipline of that profession, and he must be acting within the scope of the Directive. Hence communications from an American lawyer, for example, not qualified in a Member State would not be protected; more contentiously, it may be doubted whether communications from a lawyer qualified in one Member State, but practising in another Member State not under the terms of the services Directive but by pursuing activities to which access is not restricted[116], would be protected.

---

115 O.J. 1977 L78/17.

116 See *John A. Usher*, Establishment, Services and Lawyers, 1979 S.L.T. (News) 65, at pp. 69-70.

Finally, the influence of the 'rights of the defence' may be seen in the fact, already alluded to, that in the view of the Court, the protection exists for the benefit of the client rather than the lawyer, despite the emphasis on the lawyer's independence. It was stated that "the principle of confidentiality does not prevent a lawyer's client from disclosing the written communications between them if he considers that it is in his interests to do so", which is exactly the same view as the Court has taken with regard to the confidentiality of medical information, which has been held to exist for the benefit of the patient, not the doctor.

VIII. Conclusions

It will be evident that modern civil-law systems have had a considerable influence on the development of Community legislation, Community structures and Community jurisprudence, even if the aspects which have had such an influence are not necessarily those which can be traced back directly to Roman law. However, even where the influence is fairly obvious, national concepts received into Community law have sometimes taken on a life of their own or become mixed with other national influences – and have caused particular problems when they have had to be applied in Member States with national (or local) legal systems which do not reflect the civil law tradition.

What is in any event of particular importance is that civil law in the narrow sense has provided a specific impetus to taking account of principles of national law at the Community level. If I might trespass into the area covered by the paper of Judge *Edward*, it was Art. 4 of the French *code civil*, providing that "le juge qui refusera de juger, sous prétexte du silence, de l'obscurité ou de l'insuffisance de la loi, pourra être poursuivi comme coupable de déni de justice", which led Advocate General *Lagrange* to point out in his opinion in Case 8/55 *Fédération Charbonnière de Belgique v. High Authority*[117] that the European Court could not be absolved from giving judgement because of a lacuna in Community law.

---

117 [1954 to 1956] E.C.R. 245, at pp. 277-8.

The Development of Civil Law Principles at the National and Community Level: Achieving a Balance

By Lord Mackenzie-Stuart

I. Introduction

In Continental academic writing, particularly in Germany, the use of the first person singular is discouraged. I have never fully understood the reasons for this embargo. It may be that the use of the third person adds an appearance of impartiality and objectivity but the appearance is misleading since everybody knows that what is being said is no more than an expression of the author's own point of view. I make no apology for not following the traditions of Mainland Europe in this paper. What I have to say is based on personal experience and my own subjective approach. Objective it is not. So please forgive the frequent intrusion of the personal pronoun.

The title of this paper is 'The Development of Civil Law Principles at the National and Community Level: Achieving a Balance'.

It is, accordingly, and in the first place, necessary to define one's terms. To what extent is it proper to speak of the 'civil' law at all in the context of Community law which, to the Continental jurist, is largely concerned with what he would regard as public law? In the second place, I would like to discuss the situation as I found it in Luxembourg in 1973. In this connection I have thought it useful to mention some of the difficulties which, at that time, the professional and academic world envisaged and to see whether, in fact, their fears had any substance. In the third place, and to anticipate matters, I am of the view that the most important area of difference between the six original Member States and the United Kingdom and Ireland lay in their respective approach to administrative law. This in turn requires a brief excursion into the question whether there can truly be said to be a 'civil law' content in the administrative law practised in the Europe of the Six. I would then like to consider whether membership of the European Community has affected the British approach to administrative law and, here, my answer is 'Yes'.

II. Civil Law and Public Law

Community law is largely concerned with the relationship between the citizen and the decision making Institutions of the Community, the Council and the Commission, or with the relations between those Institutions and the Member States – the domain of public law. Civil law – as the many civil codes bear witness – is primarily concerned with private rights, the relationshp between citizen and citizen. 'Civil Law' has also its secondary meaning of a body of law inspired by Roman legal philosophy. Here early Roman law, as such, provides little help. While *Ulpian* clearly distinguishes private law and public law he does not carry the discussion much further and the maxim *quod principi placuit legis habet vigorem* is a recipe for fascism. The only discussion of the problem of which I am aware is the chapter 'Public and Private Law' in Professor *Jolowicz*'s Roman Foundations of Modern Law[1] which he concludes by saying, after a reference to the passage from *Ulpian*, "[i]t is on this one text, probably of no importance to Roman lawyers themselves, that a great modern edifice has been built".

As legal thinking progressed during the Middle Ages there was always to be found some recognition that the will of the emperor, king or dictator is subject to some higher, perhaps divine, authority. Via *Thomas Aquinas* and, for the lawyers, *Bracton*, there is the hint of something supreme, a natural law against which the actings of the monarch can be judged. Let me, however, jump to Scotland in the 17th century when, the feudal law and the law of merchants apart, our legal system truly matured, and to *James Dalrymple*, *Viscount Stair*, a true civilian in the sense that he was concerned almost exclusively with private law and that his 'Institutions' are wholly Roman inspired, the author of it all.

For *Stair*, "[m]aterial Justice (the common law of the world) is, in the first place, orderly deduced from self-evident principles, through all the several private rights thence arising, and in the next place, the expedients of the most polite nations"[2]. On the other hand, *Stair*, while he recognizes the distinction between private law and public law, has little to say about the latter. Alas, his promised treatise on the Royal Prerogative never saw the light of day. There is, nonetheless, an important sentence in a rare pamphlet by him, published in 1690 entitled 'An Apology for Sir James Dalrymple of Stair, President of Session, by Himself'[3]. In it, writes *Stair*, "I have ever been persuaded", and this I regard as the key sentence, "that it is both against the interest and duty of kings to use arbitrary government; that both kings and subjects had their title and rights by law, and that an equal balance of prerogative and liberty was necessary for the happiness of the commonwealth". This I re-

1 Greenwood Press, Connecticut, 1978, p. 49.

2 Dedication to Charles II: *Viscount Stair*, Institutions of the Laws of Scotland, 6th ed., D.M. Walker, ed., 1981.

3 *Viscount Stair*, Institutions of the Laws of Scotland, 3rd ed., J. S. More, ed., Appendix to the Introduction.

gard as valuable expression of the civilian standpoint in what today we would class as the bailiwick of administrative law. Moreover what *Stair* has proposed bears an uncanny resemblance to what was said by Advocate General *Dutheillet de Lamothe* in 1970: "The fundamental principles of national legal systems ... contribute to forming that philosophical, political and legal substratum from which, through the case law, an unwritten Community law emerges"[4]. Of these unwritten rules I once said that, "[s]ome can be expressed in the Latin tags which are, or were, the common coin of lawyers in Western Europe, and which directly or indirectly derive from the texts of civil or canon law. Sometimes, indeed, these 'principles' are no more than expressions of elementary logic and common sense"[5]. For these reasons I consider that one can discern, without stretching the traditional definition of 'civil law' to an unreasonable extent, civilian roots in the development of Community law.

III. The Problems as Seen in 1973

1. Civilian and Common Law Systems

I joined the Court as the first judge to be nominated by the United Kingdom in January 1973. The appointment of a Scots lawyer inevitably caused some surprise, particularly in London, but the counter-weight was provided by the happy choice of Mr. Justice *Warner*, then a very distinguished member of the Chancery Bar, as Advocate General. Indeed it was not until the accession of Greece in 1980 and the appointment, as the judge of Greek nationality, of the late Judge *Chloros*, who had spent much of his professional career teaching comparative law in English universities, that the Temple was able to say: "Now at last we have an English common lawyer in Luxembourg".

Nevertheless Mr. Justice *Warner* and I, together with the Irish judge, were widely regarded as being in the opposite camp to the civilian tradition. Press and professional comment was not lacking. Much of it took the form of questioning whether the naive common lawyer could avoid being seduced by the wiles of the crafty continental civilian or, much the same, suggesting that there would be a head-on collision between the legal thinking of the original six Member States, on the one hand, and the United Kingdom and Ireland on the other. Equally, it was suggested across the Channel that the common lawyer with his notions of such imprecise concepts as reasonableness would undermine the purity of civilian thought. It gives me great pleasure to affirm that in sixteen years at Luxembourg I found that neither of these fears had a shadow of foundation.

---

4 *Internationale Handelsgesellschaft* [1970] E.C.R. 1125, at p. 1146.

5 Hamlyn Lectures, The European Communities and the Rule of Law, London, 1977, p. 32.

Nevertheless it was necessary to develop an effective reaction to the anxieties publicly expressed. I saw my job, the purely judicial aspects apart, as that of disarming suspicion both at home and abroad. To that end, in a series of talks, seminars, colloquia, conferences or whatever name might be invented, and which stretched out to the crack of doom, I sought to minimize the risk of conflict and to play down the differences between the two legal traditions.

This I tried to achieve by stressing three broad propositions. In the first place I argued that Community law was largely *sui generis* and did not give rise to problems of national law. The interpretation of a badly drafted Regulation on the fat content of skimmed milk powder, I used to say, did not present deep questions of legal philosophy. I could have said, but in those early days I did not because its significance had not then fully struck home, that at Luxembourg we were dealing almost exclusively with the field of public law, a category of law which, at that time, the courts of the United Kingdom had barely recognized. To this I return.

In the second place, I maintained that when a problem was stripped of its technicalities and the reality was perceived behind the cover of legal jargon and vocabulary, the answer was in most cases the same, irrespective of one's origins and legal training.

In the third place, I contended that there was, in truth, no such thing as a single civilian approach. On a given legal topic the Danish solution could easily be closer to Scots law than the Italian.

Twenty-two years on I consider that these basic propositions have stood the test of time.

What I did not say, since I deemed it tactless for a Scots lawyer in English company, was that the substance of English law is far more Roman than English lawyers care to admit. While it remains true that English law developed through its procedural rules – *F.W. Maitland*'s great sentence, "The forms of action we have buried but still they rule us from the grave"[6], still remains fundamentally correct – it must not be forgotten that during the 16th century the law of England was within an ace of being Romanized. To invoke *Maitland* again, in his neglected but brilliant lecture on 'English Law and the Renaissance'[7], he reminds us that Cardinal *Pole*, in the reign of *Henry VIII*, and Sir *Thomas Smith*, in the reign of *Elizabeth*, were ardent Romanists. After all, were, in those days, the clumsy English remedies for breach of contract, *assumpsit* or trespass on the case, more than poor relations of the Romanist and Canon maxim *pacta sunt servanda*? The only effect of the forms of action was that they gave rise to the totally illogical and unneccessary English doctrine that consideration was essential to found a binding obligation, a doctrine which bedevils the English lawyer to this day.

---

6 The Forms of Action at Common Law, 1948 reprint, at p. 2.

7 *F. W. Maitland*, English Law and the Renaissance, Cambridge, 1901.

To revert to my basic propositions, the first of which was that Community law is a legal system *sui generis*. In the fields covered by the Treaties the law which the Court has to apply is in great measure to be found in the regulations and directives of the Council and Commission of the Community. That is to say the Court is administering a unique body of law and the opportunity for any one national legal tradition to influence the substance of the Court's decisions is very limited indeed. Looking back, I can only recall one important case where the Court of Justice had to reconcile differing approaches derived from national traditions. That was the well-known case in 1982 of *A.M. & S. Europe Limited v. Commission*[8], concerning the protection of communications between lawyers and their clients. In the latest text-book on the Court of Justice the case is summarized as follows[9]:

> "The Court pointed out that the protection of written communications between lawyers and clients was generally recognized in the legal systems of the Member States, although under varying conditions. Apart from such differences however the Court found that the national laws of the Member States protected, in similar circumstances, the confidentiality of those communications provided, on the one hand, that they were made for the purposes and in the interest of the client's rights of defence and, on the other hand, that they emanated from independent lawyers, that is to say, lawyers who were not bound to the client by an employment relationship".

Behind that summary, however, lay considerable differences of opinion concerning the role and status of the legal adviser, differences which at their heart derived from national concepts of the state and its role in the administration of justice.

2. Dissenting Opinions

It is probably fair to say that, with the one major exception of administrative law, any encounter between common law traditions and civil law traditions has been rather in the field of procedure and legal technique. In this connection it is relevant to look at the views being expressed by academic writers at the time of Britain's accession to the Community. One such expression was an article which appeared in the American Journal of Comparative Law for 1973[10] entitled 'The United Kingdom and the European Court of Justice: An Encounter between Common and Civil Law Traditions'. The authors were, respectively, Italian and American. It is interesting to review some of the topics which seemed of importance to them in 1973 against more than twenty years' practical experience.

---

8 [1982] E.C.R. 1575; [1982] C.M.L.R. 264.

9 *L. Neville Brown* and *Tom Kennedy*, The Court of Justice of the European Communites, 4th ed., 1994, at p. 283.

10 *Valerio Gerementiere* and *Cornelius Joseph Golden Jnr.*, The United Kingdom and the European Court of Justice: An Encounter between the Common and Civil Law Traditions, (1973) 21 American Journal of Comparative Law 664.

For example, one of the major procedural differences between courts in the Anglo-Saxon tradition and the Court of Justice, and which the authors considered important, was the absence of any dissenting opinions. They said: "The common law judge may find it difficult to reconcile himself to this prohibition; consequently, this occasion may present a good opportunity to eliminate it as an impediment to the development of Community jurisprudence". This viewpoint presupposes that the publication of dissenting opinions is of itself a good thing. Even at the time I took leave to question that proposition. No doubt it is a fascinating exercise for academic lawyers to examine with care the independent judgments of a group of judges and to find that the reasoning adopted by A and B is to a large extent the same although their ultimate decision differs, while the reasoning of B and C, which is totally in conflict, reaches the same result. Nonetheless, I sometimes wonder whether these studies are not sometimes more of a barrier to the effective development of the law than a method of its advancement. As regards the Court of Justice, I feel this is particularly true when it is realised that in the last resort the Court does not recognize the doctrine of *stare decisis*, the doctrine that a court is bound by its own previous decisions. On a more practical level, anyone who has had to face the necessity of explaining to a client the self-evident fact that it only required one of three judges to change his mind for the family fortune to have reached a different destination will certainly have reservations about the virtues of dissenting opinions.

On the contrary, it seemed to me then and it still seems to me these many years later, that there are positive advantages in the retention of a single public decision by the Court. In the Community, then and even more now, divided voices are only too numerous and I believe that it is desirable that the ultimate arbiter of the law of the Communities should speak with a single and, I trust, authoritative voice. There is, however, in my opinion, a more fundamental reason for not publishing dissents.

As the authors of the article note: "The judges of the Court of Justice enjoy a relatively short tenure of appointment – six years. They are then eligible for reappointment upon nomination by their own government and approval by member states. This creates a potential for national political influences to penetrate judicial decisions more strongly than with longer terms or no reappointment". I can happily say, in retrospect, that I can recall no case where an individual judge has bowed to national political pressure although I have certainly seen misguided politicians in the Member States attempt to play party games when the appointment or reappointment of a judge or advocate general was in the air. The Member States concerned have certainly been disappointed by the total lack of pliability on the part of their nominee once appointed. The fact, however, that responsible people like the authors of the article believe in the possibility of judicial subservience to a national point of view, is to my mind a strong argument for retaining a single collegiate judgment where the secrecy of each individual's opinion is preserved and his protection thus assured. If the publication of dissenting opinions is to be permitted or required, there is much to be said for the method adopted in Germany in 1970 for its Constitutional Court where the introduction of dissenting opinions was coupled with the extension of the period of office to twelve years with no possiblity of re-appointment for a further term.

I recognize, of course, that this view is not shared by everyone. I note that in a recent pamphlet produced by the European Research Group[11], a body of European Parliamentarians of a right-wing persuasion, they consider that publication of dissenting opinions should become obligatory. This, I feel, perhaps paradoxically, strengthens my argument.

Linked to the question of the dissenting opinion is the particular nature of an English or Scottish judgment. A Swedish lawyer, writing in English in 1960[12], said that "the English judicial process is, in essence, a continuous discussion which in all but superficial or detailed respects resembles any discussion among educated, informed and reasonable men". This is as true of appellate jurisdictions as at first instance. Instead of one individual mind one finds a group of minds at work but each member of the group is responsible for his or her own view. It is an inherent part of the system that each judge should declare his own individual opinion. The judgments of the Court of Justice, on the other hand are, in theory and in practice, collegiate and the result of collective drafting. A judge frequently proposes constructive amendments to the text even if he is not in accord with the final decision. All this leads to a perceptible difference in style between a common law judgment and a judgment of the Court of Justice. This merits a separate comment.

First, may I take up one or two other matters raised in the 1973 article.

3. The Advocate General

One need not detain us long – the role of the advocate general. As you well know, his function, once the written and the oral procedure in the case is completed, is to deliver an opinion to the Court, very much in the style of an English judgment, in which he rehearses the facts and the relevant law and gives his opinion to the judges on how they should decide the case before them. I shall not detain you with any discussion concerning the origins of the office of advocate general. It is enough for me to say that after many years of experience I consider that the advocate general in very many cases fulfils a most useful function in the working of the Court of Justice. The Court of Justice is not only a court of first instance, it is also a court of last resort, and it is thus most desirable that there should be a member of the Court, as is the Advocate General, charged with the duty of presenting, in a considered manner, the substance of the case which the judges have to decide. The part played by the advocate general ensures that there are at least two

11 *The European Research Group*, A Europe of Nations, House of Commons, London, 1995.

12 *J. Gillis Wetter*, The Styles of Appellate Judicial Opinions, Leyden, 1960, p. 32.

independent stages in the decision making process and while for the common lawyer the office of advocate general was at first a novel one it became more than easy to accept. Indeed, my only surprise, then and now, is that someone might have suggested the contrary. My sole comment, in 1995, is that the interposition of the advocate general inevitably adds to the Court's delays and I do not now feel that the opinion of the advocate general is necessary in every case, especially in straightforward cases where the Court of Justice has already developed a substantial body of case law. This is the approach adopted by the relatively new Court of First Instance and it may be that we shall see changes in the Court of Justice itself, although this would require treaty amendment.

4. Rights of Audience

Another matter which caused the authors of the article concern was the distinction between advocates or barristers, on the one hand, and solicitors, on the other, and their respective rights of audience. I dismiss this by saying that there has here been not the slightest difficulty. The Court takes the view that the right of representation is a matter of domestic national law, so that over the years we have seen British solicitors appearing as well as members of the Scottish or English bars. Indeed, in an Art. 177 reference the Court hears anyone, whatever his qualifications or lack of them, who was entitled to appear before the national judge. The only problem that I recall concerned an Italian, let us call him Signor *Futuro*. When we knew him he was employed in Belgium by one of the large Italian trade unions to help the many Italian workers employed by Belgian firms. In Belgium he could appear before the local Social Security Tribunals and they in turn made many references to us. Signor *Futuro* knew more about Belgian and Community Social Security law than any man alive. He was a natural advocate and a pleasure to listen to; he talked sense, shortly, and put his points in an agreeably relaxed manner. He was not, however, a qualified lawyer. At the hearings we welcomed Signor Futuro and gained from his presence. On one occasion however the case did not come to us direct from the 'Tribunal de Travail' but had first been appealed in Belgium and it was the local appeal court which had made the reference to us and before which Signor *Futuro* was not entitled to appear. I saw from the papers that Signor *Futuro* was billed to appear in Luxembourg. I had, as President, to see that Signor *Futuro*, was tactfully reminded that we could not give him a right of audience and he dropped out of the case and a non-specialist but correctly qualified advocate was instructed in his place. I do not think that I was alone in wishing that it had still been Signor *Futuro* who had represented his client.

5. Precedent

The last point which I wish to mention, among those raised by the learned authors of the 1973 paper, is their concern that there might be a conflict between the English doctrine of *stare decisis* and, as the authors put it, "[t]he civil law principle that only decisions of the Court of last resort have any real influence on the national jurisprudence. One must speak of 'influence', of course, since it is theoretically contrary to civil law notions to speak of precedent as having any binding law-making effect beyond the case in hand". The authors contrasted this with the English concept that not only do the judgments of the House of Lords form a binding precedent for lower courts but so too do those of the Court of Appeal, and, indeed of the High Court itself. In practice, however, one must recognize that the rigidity of the rule is frequently tempered by judicial ingenuity. The classic English standpoint is of course that of the Master of the Rolls, Sir *George Jessel*, when he said: "It is no part of my duty to make new law simply because I think that the old law is unreasonable; that is the province of the legislature and not of the judge. Where I find a point decided, however I may lament the result, I think that I am bound to follow the decision, and to construe it fairly, and not to seek to evade it or fritter it away by introducing distinctions only invented for the purpose of pronouncing another decision, which in my opinion will be more in conformity with reason"[13]. The fact remains that judges both in England and in Scotland have found methods of mitigating the impact of a decision recognized as being incompatible with modern thinking. This can be, and is frequently, done without resort to the view of the cynic who suggested that any two cases, however similar their facts and however similar the point of law in issue, could be distinguished provided only that the parties did not have the same names.

The problem, of course, does not arise in the Court of Justice of the European Community since it is not bound by its own decisions. The Court has, in the second of two cases, where in fact the parties were identical[14], impliedly overruled the former and in *C.N. Sucal S.A. v. Hag G.F. A.G.*[15] expressly acknowledged that one of its former decisions was wrong.

At the same time the civil law is by no means as flexible as it may seem in theory. The notion of 'jurisprudence constante', that is to say a body of case law embodying the same proposition, has very much the same practical effect as the British doctrine of precedent. This is only common sense. Once a court has by a series of decisions developed a body of principle which, *ex hypothesi*, it considers correct, it is not lightly going to depart from the rules so established. Again I can affirm from my experience that *stare decisis* has never presented the Court of Justice with a problem.

---

13 *Bellairs v. Bellairs* (1874) L.R. 18 Eq. 510, at p. 513.

14 *European Parliament v. Council*, [1988] E.C.R. 5615; [1990] 1 E.C.R. 2041.

15 [1990] E.C.R. I-3711; [1990] 3 C.M.L.R. 571.

6. Judicial Style

The one procedural difficulty which I personally encountered lay in the style of the Court's judgments. These from the Court's inception followed the French style of syllogistic reasoning and grammatically consisted of a single sentence, preceded by endless repetitions of the words 'Attendu que …'. Of the French style of judgment it has been said, by the same Swedish author: "The judgments are concentrated and almost abrupt in their strict brevity. They speak more to law's men – in no respect are they addressed to laymen or the parties … suffice it to point out here that in a bureaucratically organised judiciary, or among all men trained in a rigorous, quasi scientific legal atmosphere, such as the French, judgments of the courts are never addressed to the parties or at least not to laymen". This I can confirm from personal knowledge. I once tackled a senior 'Conseiller d'État' with the obscurity of the 'Conseil's' pronouncements. His reply was that "[w]e do not write our judgments for the parties, their legal advisers or, still less for the general public. We write them for ourselves".

The style has its partisans. My much respected former colleague, Judge *Pescatore*, once referred to the style as one of "serene limpidity". The fact remains that once the judgment of the Court at Luxembourg is stripped of its introduction and the necessary deploying of any relevant Community legislation, the operative part is often very terse. Even although during my time at the Court we abandoned the single sentence formula, the model remained, and remains today, substantially the same. I missed the light and shade of the English or Scottish judgment, even the occasional hint of humour that is permitted to a British judge. One noticeable change was, however, made. The Court abandoned its French-inspired habit of repeating passages from another judgment without revealing their source. This had been left to the academic critics to discover for themselves. We began to say, and it is now the custom: "As the Court of Justice said in the case of…". This paper, however, contains the sub-title 'Achieving a Balance'. In the matter of writing our decisions I do not feel that a balance was achieved and I do not conceal that the art of writing a Community style judgment did not come easily to me.

IV. Administrative Law

1. Recent Developments in England

For me, however, the principal interplay between the civilian tradition and the common law tradition in the last quarter century has been in the field of administrative law. I cannot in a short paper, even if I were capable of it, attempt anything like a complete survey of the recent development by the English Courts of a coherent body of administrative law – the Scots have followed but their contribution is less obvious – and their increasing readiness to examine critically any 'act' (to use the wording of Art. 189 of the Treaty of Rome) of Government, including not only executive acts and subordinate legislation but on occasion the content of an Act of Parliament itself. For my purposes it is enough to refer to the well known observation of Lord *Reid* in *Ridge v. Baldwin* in 1964[16]: "We do not have a developed system of administrative law – perhaps because until fairly recently we did not need it", without going back to Lord *Hewart*, then Lord Chief Justice of England, who, in 1935, extrajudicially described administrative law as 'Continental Jargon'[17]. When one compares Lord *Reid*'s *dictum* with the masterly survey of the topic, only twenty years later, by the late Lord *Diplock*, in *C.C.S.U. v. The Minister for Civil Service*[18], the contrast is striking as Lord *Diplock* himself recognized. In that case he introduced his speech with these words: "The English law relating to judicial control of administrative action has been developed upon a case to case basis which has virtually transformed it over the last three decades". Again in that speech he recognizes, *passim*, the special qualities of public law, a category which, a generation before, had received no judicial acknowledgement. Perhaps the latest, but certainly not the last, expression of the current trend is to be found in the terse and pungent speech of Lord *Keith* in 1994 in *R. v. Employment Secretary, ex parte Equal Opportunities Commission*[19] where he examined the content and purpose of an Act of Parliament for its compatibility with Community law and held that the operation of the Act could be suspended by the Court in Luxembourg pending its final judgment.

None of this, I venture to think, would have taken place without the approach of the Court of Justice of the European Communities and the role which it has played in translating for the common lawyer the well-established attitudes of the civilian tradition to the relationship between the state and its citizen.

2. The European Sources of Administrative Law

Before attempting to show the influence of mainland European thinking on English law a short digression is necessary to answer the question, which I raised at the outset, of whether that thinking can properly be described as civilian. Modern European administrative law dates from the aftermath of the French Revolution and the establishment of the 'Conseil d'État' under Napoleon. In the origins of this new phenomenon it is, I confess, less easy to see the direct and immediate influence of the civil lawyer. Nonetheless, in the 18th century, as part of their writing on civil or international law, the nature of the State and its obligations and its rights were being examined by a number of distinguished civilians – such as *Christian*

16 [1964] A.C. 40, at p. 72.

17 Not Without Prejudice, at p. 96, cited by Professor *S. A. de Smith*, Judicial Review of Administrative Action, 2nd ed., 1968, at p. 5.

18 [1985] A.C. 374, per Lord *Diplock*, at pp. 410-411.

19 [1994] 2 W.L.R. 410.

Wolff at Halle and *Emile de Vattel* in Geneva. One might even mention the otherwise undistinguished *Barbeyrac* who translated *Grotius* and *Pufendorf* into French and thus enabled *Rousseau* to read them.

Here, I pray in aid Professor *René David* with his capacity, only equalled by *Maitland*, for the graphic generalization. After discussing the formation of what he calls the 'Romano-Germanic family', which includes the legal systems of the original Member States of the European Community, he continues:

> "The second factor which explains the existence of a Romano-Germanic family of laws, even outside the private law where it originated, is the common *formation* of jurists. In order to translate new philosophical and political ideas into legal terms and develop new branches of law, recourse was had to jurists educated in the civil law. Very naturally, the new rules were established by taking as a model, or at least as a point of departure, the concepts of the civil law. In the various legal orders, therefore, the civil law has played the role of a 'common law' which other branches of the law (such as administrative law) have emulated or attempted to perfect"[20].

This, I consider, is true of the law developed by the 'Conseil d'État' and its parallel institutions in other countries.

Even taking into account the emergence in Germany in the early 19th century of the concept of the 'Rechtsstaat', which embraced as an essential feature judicial control as a defence against the arbitary exercise of power, the 'Conseil d'État' was the first true administrative court in Europe and, in certain cases at least, became the precise model for other similar courts in other Member States of the Community. It is not excessive to regard the administrative courts of the original Member States as having civilian roots and the law which they apply as being in marked contrast to traditional common law thinking.

3. European Principles and the English Courts

It is against such a background that the Court of Justice of the European Community approaches its task of reviewing the decisions of the other Community Institutions and I consider that its approach has had a substantial influence on the English Courts.

I referred in passing to Lord *Diplock*'s speech in *C.C.S.U. v. The Minister for Civil Service*. Space does not allow me to discuss this case in detail nor to look at subsequent cases where various aspects of the *C.C.S.U.* decision have been considered. Nor by concentrating on Lord *Diplock* do I in any way seek to ignore the importance of the other speeches. My intention is only to indicate how much his speech was, in my view, influenced by European administrative law, both at na-

---

20 *Dalloz*, Les Grands Systèmès de Droit Contemporains, para. 65, trans. by *David* and *Brierly*, in: Stevens, ed., Major Legal Systems in the World Today, 2nd ed., 1978, at p. 81.

tional and Community level. It will be remembered that Lord *Diplock* separated the grounds upon which administrative action was subject to judicial control under three heads, – 'illegality', 'irrationality' and 'procedural impropriety'. He explained:

> "That is not to say that further developments on a case by case basis may not in the course of time add further grounds. I have in mind particularly the possible adoption in the future of the principle of 'proportionality' which is recognized in the administrative law of several of our fellow members of the European Economic Community"[21].

Lord *Diplock* might have added, "and also by the Court of Justice of the European Community". I am bound to say, however, that subsequent English cases have as yet shown an unwillingness to adopt the proportionality principle, e.g. *R. v. Secretary of State for the Home Department ex parte Brind*[22], in 1991. Professor *Gray* considers that the courts will eventually recognize the principle. So do I, even if they call it by a different name.

'Illegality', for Lord *Diplock*, meant a breach by the decision maker of his obligation to understand correctly the law regulating his decision and to give due effect to it. This is a comprehensive duty and very similar to the ground of action for annulment of a Community Act which one finds at the end of Art. 173 of the Treaty of Rome, viz. "infringement of [the] Treaty or of any rule of law relating to its application", itself a provision taken directly from French administrative law.

'Irrationality', for Lord *Diplock* meant what judicial short-hand, I do not use the word 'jargon', calls '*Wednesbury* unreasonableness'. It is one of the unfortunate quirks of case-law that the inoffensive Midland town of Wednesbury should be associated with unreasonableness of a very high order. Here, perhaps, the parallel is not so marked. The continental lawyer would probably tackle this ground by invoking the notion of a material error of fact which, in his eyes, is an error in law.

More important is Lord *Diplock*'s discussion of the third category, 'procedural impropriety', which for him was wider than a failure to observe basic rules of natural justice, although such a failure would certainly come under this heading. In this connection I would instance only two grounds, both derived from the administrative law of one or more of the six original Member States, which the Court of Justice has used to annul a Community Act. The first is that of 'proportionality' already mentioned in the quotation from Lord *Diplock*. My first President, *M. Robert Lecourt*, with characteristic logic, preferred the word 'disproportionality', and I think that he was correct because the concept requires that a decision-maker should not choose a solution to a problem which is disproportionate to the end sought to be achieved. I would only add that perhaps Lord *Diplock* was wrong in considering 'proportionality' as remedy to be invoked at some date in the future. Is it not a specific aspect of the wider duty to act reasonably? This notion was first

---

21 *C.C.S.U. v Minister for the Civil Service* [1985] A.C. 374, at 410.

22 [1991] 1 A.C. 696.

put forward by Professor *Neville Brown* in an important paper which he gave at Florence as long ago as 1977[23] and was the approach of the House of Lords in *Brind.*

The other doctrine or principle which has been imported from Europe into the law of, at least, England, is that legitimate expectations should be respected. This too, was recognized by Lord *Diplock* in the same speech where he classed, amidst other grounds for judicial review, the situation in which the decision-maker has deprived the subject of some "benefit or advantage which either (i) he had in the past been permitted by the decision-maker to enjoy and which he can legitimately expect to be permitted to continue to do until there has been communicated to him some rational grounds for withdrawing it on which he has been given an opportunity to comment; or (ii) he has received assurance from the decision-maker will not be withdrawn without giving him first an opportunity of advancing reasons for contending that they should not be withdrawn"[24]. It would be difficult to find a better definition of the doctrine as understood across the Channel.

V. Conclusion

Although I have stressed the importance of administrative law, civilian reminders are to be found in the case law of the Court of Justice in other fields. Others will no doubt deal with this aspect more fully and I have already referred to well-known Latin maxims, as familiar to the Scots lawyer as to the continental civilian. For example, and I could give many others, there are cases which turn on the application of *audi et alteram partem* or *ne bis in idem*. The principle that all transactions must be founded on good faith is frequently endorsed. Art. 215 of the Treaty of Rome which deals with liability for non-contractual damage is often referred to as an Aquilian remedy and, in any event, makes specific reference to liability being determined "in accordance with the general principles common to the laws of the Member States". Here I content myself with adopting a passage from the opinion of Advocate General *Trabucchi* in *Nold v. Commission*[25]:

> "It is always a question of those principles *quarum causa omne ius constitutum est*: we find them in the ancient laws, as the written basis of human society, we find them in the codes of the 19th century, which were conceived precisely for the purpose of setting out the validity of those declarations in the form of Articles; we now find them more formally proclaimed in modern Constitutions".

---

23 New Perspectives for a Common Law of Europe, M. Cappelletti, ed., Florence, 1978, at pp. 171 sqq. See also the author's Holdsworth Lecture, Control of Power within the European Communities, Birmingham, 1986.

24 *C.C.S.U. v. Minister for the Civil Service* [1985] A.C. 374, at 408.

25 [1974] E.C.R. 491, at pp. 513 sq.

On the other hand, trade was not all one way. Even in 1980 Judge *Pescatore* was able to write,

> "Arguments based on 'common sense' and references to what is 'reasonable' have become increasingly frequent. References to the Court's own precedents have multiplied and, as a result, making the role of case law more important. One has even observed the discreet appearance, in recent cases, of the idea of estoppel"[26].

I said at the beginning of this paper that it was a personal offering to the Commemoration of Aberdeen's Quincentenary of civil law teaching. If I were ever in danger of forgetting my own roots in the law of Rome, there existed in Luxembourg tangible reminders. From the desk in the Court of Justice which I used for my first ten years I could make out, across the intervening buildings, the edge of a forest of beech trees. Through that forest ran – and the traces are still clearly visible – the great Roman road leading eastward from Rheims and Paris. A mile or two further on, in the fertile valley of the Syr, the road joins another Imperial artery, the north bound road from Lyons (the first capital of Transalpine Gaul) and Rome itself. Their joint destination, only thirty miles away, is Trier – Trèves to the Francophone – where still stand the mighty *Basilica* of *Constantine* and the lowering *Porta Nigra* which guarded the northern marches of the Roman Empire. It did not require exceptional imagination to picture a dusty legionary marching through the beech woods of Luxembourg, sustained by the thought that only another dozen miles would bring him to the banks of the Moselle and a *stabulum* where the wine was as good in those days as it is today.

I end, or nearly so, with the only specific reference to the law of Rome to be found in the law reports of the Court of Justice. In *Klomp v. Inspektie der Belastingen*[27] a question arose concerning the jurisdiction of the Court, there having been a change in the relevant rules. The Court in its judgment observed: "In accordance with a principle common to the legal systems of the Member States, the origins of which may be traced back to Roman Law, when legislation is amended, unless the legislature expresses a contrary intention, continuity of the legal system must be ensured".

In an annotation to the headnote of the official Reports the observant reader will see two references to the Digest. The observant *and* well-informed reader will recognize them as quotations from the jurist *Paulus*. The works of *Paulus* were confirmed as part of the authoritative canon of Roman law by the Emperor *Constantine* in A.D. 327, that same Emperor whose *Basilica* lies at the end of the road through the beech trees. If it is not invariably true that all roads lead from Rome it is surprising how many do.

In short, despite the prognostications of the early seventies, the dividing line between the common-lawyer, if a Scot may for these purposes be so described, and

---

26 Revue Internationale de Droit Comparé 32 (1980), at p. 351.

27 [1969] E.C.R. 43.

the civilian has but rarely materialized. If it did, it was never in a context where, with goodwill and understanding, and there was much of that, it could not be deflected. For the Anglophone, a new vocabulary had to be learned, of course, particularly since the working language of the Court was and is French. The ideas which lie behind such phrases as 'droit subjectif' or 'pourvoi en cassation' soon became plain enough. For the rest, as I have tried to show, it was remarkably easy to achieve a balance. Only in the field of administrative law was there much to learn and much to admire. Here, as I hope I have demonstrated, it was not a matter of achieving a balance, since the United Kingdom and Ireland had little to offer, but rather one of submitting to a take-over bid. I also like to think that the common law has given something in return.

Table of Cases

Index

The index is arranged alphabetically in word by word order. Location references are to page numbers, with 'n' denoting a footnote (e.g. n339 is a footnote at the bottom of page 339). Persons named are those referred to in the text.

Index compiled by Christine M Gane, BA LLB, Accredited Indexer

List of Contributors

Peter B. H. Birks, Q.C., D.C.L., LL. D., Dr. iur. h.c., F.B.A., is Regius Professor of Civil Law in the University of Oxford.

John W. Cairns, LL.B., Ph.D., is a Reader in Private Law in the University of Edinburgh.

David L. Carey Miller, B.A., LL.B., LL.M., Ph.D., is a Professor of Law in the University of Aberdeen.

Jeroen M.J. Chorus, LL.D., formerly Professor of Roman Law and Legal History in the University of Leiden, is vice-president of the Amsterdam Court of Appeal.

David A. O. Edward, C.M.G., Q.C., M.A., LL.B., LL.D, formerly Salvesen Professor of European Institutions in the University of Edinburgh, is a Judge of the Court of Justice of the European Communities.

Robert Feenstra, Dr. iur., Dr. iur. h.c. mult., is Emeritus Professor of Roman Law in the University of Leiden.

William M. Gordon, M.A., LL.B., Ph.D., is Douglas Professor of Civil Law in the University of Glasgow.

David Johnston, B.A., Ph.D., is Regius Professor of Civil Law in the University of Cambridge.

Lord Mackenzie-Stuart, Q.C., LL.D., was formerly President of the Court of Justice of the European Communities.

Hector L. MacQueen, LL.B., Ph.D., is a Professor of Private Law in the University of Edinburgh.

J. J. Robertson, M.A., LL.B., is a Senior Lecturer in Law in the University of Dundee.

Lord Rodger of Earlsferry, Q.C., D.C.L., F.B.A., is Lord President of the Court of Session and Lord Justice-General of Scotland.

W. D. H. Sellar, M.A., LL.B., is a University Fellow in Private Law in the University of Edinburgh.

Peter G. Stein, Q.C., F.B.A., M.A., LL.B., Ph.D., Dr. iur. h.c., is Emeritus Professor of Civil Law in the University of Cambridge.

John A. Usher, LL.B., is Salvesen Professor of European Institutions in the University of Edinburgh.

Daniel Visser, B. Juris, LL.B., LL.D., Dr. iur., is Professor of Roman-Dutch and Private Law in the University of Cape Town.

Reinhard Zimmermann, Dr. iur., LL.D., is Professor of Private Law, Roman Law and Comparative Legal History in the University of Regensburg.

MIX
Papier aus verantwortungsvollen Quellen
Paper from responsible sources
FSC® C105338
FSC
www.fsc.org

Printed by Libri Plureos GmbH
in Hamburg, Germany